A WORLD OF WORDS

A WORLD OF WORDS

Ron Batchelor

Book Guild Publishing
Sussex, England

First published in Great Britain in 2012 by
The Book Guild Ltd
Pavilion View
19 New Road
Brighton, BN1 1UF

Typesetting in Garamond by
Keyboard Services, Luton, Bedfordshire

Printed in Great Britain by
CPI Group (UK) Ltd, Croydon, CR0 4YY

A catalogue record for this book is available from
The British Library

ISBN 978 1 84624 795 8

To my parents, who set things rolling with a bike, to Pat, my wife, who has kept them rolling for many a year, and to Philippe who has a joke for every spoke. Not forgetting six grandchildren, Jamie, Tom, Max, Toni, Grace and Sofia, who are continuing the cycle of life, and will one day happily pedal through these pages.

Contents

Introduction:

You've Got a Tongue in Your Head, Haven't You?

Well yes, I have. In fact, I've got four. One that Pancho Villa and Emiliano Zapata were landed with from the Iberian Peninsula and spoke in Mexico, a tongue stretching just one helluva way from the Río Grande down to Tierra del Fuego. Some distance, like hearing it all the way from London to Beijing. Some tongue. And don't forget the United States. Thirty million Spanish-speaking tongues there. A country in a country. No argument here. Another that General de Gaulle fortified the French nation with on June 18, 1940, all the way from London, and that most of West Africa still has as the glue that sticks them together. Not always keen on the French, are they? But they're stuck with French. Same as the English glue in India. A most enviable third gracing the operas of Verdi and Puccini. The fourth? You're reading it at this very moment. Four tongues. Am lapping it up. They all converge in a happy, exciting blend with adventure in mind. Make things clearer, leading to a window on world cultures. There's something neatly serendipitous about the whole thing, throwing up surprises. Endless strings of undreamt encounters, hoarded treasures stored and sifted, voyages of discovery in the fabric of the mind called up by threads and layers of memory. Relics of a life long-gone. Therapeutic, anti-Alzheimer.

Above all, a wealth of intensely felt, rich and warm languages makes you feel at ease and comfortable anywhere and with anyone. You feel at home.

1

Chasing after foreign languages is a great adventure. Don't listen to Masha in Chekhov's *The Three Sisters*. Three languages for her were useless, at least in her town. Super for me in more ways than one. The wonder of words, or, as they say over there, *la merveille des mots*. Marvellous! Alliteration works wonders there, too. Pretty rare, that. Words are everywhere. As much fun with them as with life itself. Enthusiasm and exhilaration as we speak them. Happy, personal contacts. Generosity and warmth of feeling. Accomplishment, enjoyment and even well-being. Spontaneous response, it's all part of the mix. Cultural appetites are whetted. Talk between native speakers and non-native speakers. Always creates a stir with *gazpacho* at the beginning, *paella* in the middle, *flan* at the end, and all washed down with *vino*. We're all in this together, amigo, and we're going to make the best of it. Had a good time this year, see you next year. How about a trip up north, to England? We could see how the Queen does things, changing of the guards, *le five o'clock*, as the aping French say. They're always monkeying around with our lingo. The *chicos* (lads) would love it.

But there's more. The odd thing is that speaking more than one language takes the speaker outside his original self. He sort of forgets who he is. Lost in translation? Not really. Doesn't do translation. Just dives into the next language. Psychologists who look for the trick of how things tick have probably written reams on divided personalities and schizophrenia, and other similar stuff. They'd say that a new, second language, and a third, could be a topsy-turvy world, an upside-down way of looking at things. They don't really see the fun and high spirits in it all. Don't bother about the language, all that Berlitz business, get on with the literary criticism. Promotion is the angle. Not so here. Let's play around with our personality, Harlequin-style, switching from one merry role to another, elation of language. Look at the motley colours of the *commedia dell'arte*. All good fun, so don't let that melancholy clown's motley fool you in *I Pagliacci*. It's clear for all to see, unless you're a bit colour-blind. Constant change and exciting diversity. The more languages the merrier, and Harlequin would agree. Adds all that colour. Even gets you out of scrapes.

Have fun in those risky foreign parts. Forget the dangers faced by a discourteous Cortés (anything but cortés = courteous) and a piratic Pizarro (I prefer Pissarro but there you are). Let's just enjoy the new fruits of a foreign language and what goes with it. Cortés tasted them, even got him in the marrying mode, the native La Malinche. The conquistadors' search for treasures, that's the goal, and probably the gold. Marvel we do at Aztec or Mayan pyramids. But we don't share their architectural skills or basic religious needs, which come as a sunny surprise to us, just as we English wonder how on earth Spaniards could do without kettles or the French without rectangular pillows. Come on, you Spaniards, it's about time you found a word for kettle, and *tetera* (teapot) just isn't good enough. Why should you square-pillowed French find it odd that we Anglo-Saxons dream on rectangular pillows? You're just a bunch of squares. We know you think tea is a sort of medicine for upset tummies. Tea and red wine just don't go together. Have you tried to find a teapot in a French wine cellar? Heresy, I hear our French *amis* cry. And all that public kissing on the cheeks. Play them at their own game. Meet them head to head. And daily, all-round handshaking. OK until you come up against hands the size of a discus and twice as heavy.

Two things about speaking: all those signs on a written page and the sounds they help us make. Get the knack of sounds and it's music to your ears. Earmark the sounds of Italian, French and Spanish. Romance languages they call them. They sound as alien as those odd-looking customers coming over at Dover. Romance sounds don't have much in common with ours; we like them somehow because they strike a different chord, and romance is a winner in itself. Ask Mimi and Rodolfo. Listen to their mellifluous tones in *La Bohème*, and you'll see what I mean. No sound in English plucks the heart strings like Mimi's soulful: 'il primo sole è mio ... il primo bacio dell'aprile è mio' (the first sun greets me ... April's/Spring's first awakening kiss is mine). No wonder

Mimi's songs are as sweet as honey, the *melli* bit of *mellifluous* comes from the Italian for 'honey' = *miele*, and the second bit from *fluire* = to flow. To flow with honey, the joys of Italian opera.

Hitch on to those odd ways of speaking, even when you're hitching a lift, and burrow around down below all those funny sounds; it's really quite a bundle of fun, a jolly encounter for both speaker and hearer. Having fun together has got to be the target for all language learners: go on, don't be frightened, keep talking and talking, even if at the beginning it's tosh. They'll love listening, especially if it's with someone with a different gender. The Gallic *le* and *la* say it all. *Il* and *la* for Mimi and Rodolfo. After all, they are singing in Italian even if they are French. You're carried over the Paris mansard rooftops as their voices drift through the skylight. The romance of Romance sets you singing from the rooftops. Let's dance to it. You sure feel on a high.

An appetizing menu of tongues, so flavoursome, so succulent, straight off the palate. Talking French, Spanish, Italian, always like a good, square meal. All very mouth-watering. Pity I can't change the *water* bit here into *wine*. Like that Jesus fellow. Even so, all those tongues swirling around are a miracle in themselves, each one in a magical, cosy, watertight compartment.

But what's it like wandering from one set of funny words to another set, and another? Well, it's like jumping from the metaphoric to the literal, and back again, and back again. We do all this jumping through the book. It's a sort of metaphor in motion, like speaking on a bike, while you're moving. Keeps the grey matter oiled. Soiled we don't want it. *So, get ready for all these jumps. Lots of 'em.*

You, reader, are the guest in the quest for adventure – go for it. The Grail, but not very holy. Put those new-fangled words into travel: that's the formula and the theory bit done with. Now for the practical part. As my mother would say insistently to me: 'You have a tongue in your head, now use it.'

1

Two Wheels

And I certainly did!

1946. That's when it all began for a twelve-year boy on the rubble-strewn streets of downtown Southampton. He had learnt very quickly to use his legs. Underground shelter? Helter-skelter, here I come, and if he couldn't get there in time, it was a surface shelter, topped with a foot of reinforced concrete, teacher reading stories to comfort children in hell's alley. Mother courage spread-eagled over her children in the passageway, below. Above, Nazi eagle. *Mamma mia!* Shelter's a bridge too far. Hitler's Valkyries cavalcading across the coastal skies. Heinkels, Dorniers, Junker 88s, or a Stuka direct hit with that terror-generating scream. Night after night, the nocturnal demolition squad. Tracers punctuate the air like dots on this page... Midday. Now round-the-clock. *Chez le dentiste.* Sirens. All three under the table. Blast! Windows shattered. Nearby school deleted. All and sundry stitched to the ground. Touch and go whether you would be reading these pages. Not convinced? Well, read these pages. The *Daily Telegraph*, Monday, December 2, 1940: 'Although Southampton had been the target of former bombings, it has never experienced anything like this. Convents, churches, theatres, cinemas, hotels, schools, private dwellings in all parts of the town were on fire.'

But what about that lad's tongue? Tied down by Nazi cannons? Like the canons of ordinary living? Things were different then. Three inescapable reasons. First, the slack, wartime social restrictions let town children roam with impunity on bombed buildings, climb up stairs, hanging perilously in space, from one floor to another. Ripping up floorboards. Cost nothing so no rip-off. Setting fire to anything combustible. Tramps' straw for sleeping rough was most receptive to a single match. Football in graveyards? Easy. Stick all the stones, not bones, up around the surrounding wall, and play over those millennium-old bones down there somewhere. Death above complemented by death below. Far from one foot in the grave, we had both feet above it, and kicking that ball to death. A real bonus to play on these bones. No bones of contention here. This was education, the true marrow of learning. Funny this, but however grave the blitz appeared, it played into the hands of those graveyard children. Cowboys and Indians, just like in Tombstone City, Arizona.

Rode roughshod over religion. Danish Søren Kierkegaard's *Fear and Trembling* gave theologians something to tremble about, and back at the graveyard at that. The place to read him, in fact. He must have been born with graveyard in his soul, if his name is anything to go by, the *Kierk* bit being *church* and the second bit *yard.* Predestination, they call it. No goals would they have scored in my graveyard.

Our tombstone goals were pretty well the same goals as for everyone. All good, reckless fun, then. No police, social workers, or even parents around. No gaols, either, only cemetery goals. School attendance officers? What, or who are they? And certainly no Rousseau's social contract. Dad could have been with Montgomery in North Africa, for all we knew. Uncle was. Staying alive was the number one priority. Rules and regulations, what were they? Health and safety edicts, never heard of them, and what did 'edict' mean anyway? Young people were left hanging in space, to do their own thing, and the future would sort itself out, if there were one. The more intense the bombing, the lesser the social controls.

Second, comfort, what was that? No tyranny of convenience, mod cons, agreeable sleeping arrangements, abundant hot water, constant changes of clothes, in short, cleanliness. Obsessive hygiene? Six strife-laden years cleaned you right out of that. 'Now wash your hands', a washbasin joke in the 1950s. A sanitized community meant nothing. The word 'sanitized' didn't mean too much, either. Had it been invented then? A touch sceptical about antiseptic.

Third, mass travel *à la* Cook had not taken off. Holiday migration still in its infancy. And car(e)free cycling, well that was paradise, but steer clear of those treacherous tramlines. Building houses, not cars, was the order of the day. Hitler's Luftwaffe had seen to that.

It all started when father offered his young son a small, black-framed New Hudson bicycle, a BSA model. Could this have been generous compensation from an impecunious father for his son's failing his eleven-plus examination, not that his failure caused much dismay for his parents? Top priority was down under in a shelter, staying alive during the Southampton blitz. How could years of underground shelter on a camp bed prepare for the eleven-plus? Grammar schools were for bomb-free areas.

But, adventure was now on the scene. Newly acquired independence by freewheeling through the debris of demolition was the next step up from the playground of the graveyard.

I loved my bike just as I loved the larger red Raleigh Rudge, equipped with sturdy Sturmey Archer gears this time, later bought to accommodate a growing frame, itself accompanied by an increasingly determined frame of mind. Raleigh Rudge, the name in the frame projected for years to come. For the ensuing five years, the world seen from a bicycle saddle: the shape of things to come. Rigged out with a number of bespoke extras, waterproof saddlebag, and toughened panniers, I cleaned, oiled and nurtured it with all the affection I could muster. Even had a hub dynamo, lighting up the way to the brightest of futures heading towards me via the dynamics of language. Trouble is you have to pedal harder even when it's switched off. Hub dynamo. Ay, there's the nub, to misquote Hamlet. Put in 'rub' and runs more smoothly. At least the quote does.

And nothing bought on line. Always cycled to the shop. Hardly footfall economics.

No spokes in my wheels as I youth-hostelled in Hampshire. Radius of interest was widening all the time. Hampshire was nowhere near enough. French, just a hop across the Channel, set the legs whizzing round. A felicitous and fruitful combination of physical and cerebral activity, rather like those Tour de France intellectuals T. E. Lawrence and Jean-Paul Sartre wheeling their way, either visiting crusader castles in southern France for an Oxford thesis or, in the latter's case, making tracks for tracts in the *zone libre. Résistance* against the Nazi invaders. This heady mix of high literary endeavour and purpose, and the drive of physical enterprise had a fetching kind of Nietzschean intoxication. Cycling turned into revolutionary change. The raw materials of a bike were being subtly converted into an ideological step forward.

Want another shot at an exam? OK, if it's there. Sort of examination: the thirteen-plus. Had never heard of it. Just happened once. Sped straight into the raptures of foreign languages. Mind started to go round and round, reached the dizzy heights of two side pockets neatly filled with two solid little Harrap French and Spanish dictionaries. Not John Wayne carrying holstered six-shooters in the 1938 epic of *Stage Coach* but the next best thing. Let's give it a really good shot. These two dictionaries were to be cherished sidekicks as I set off in the summer of 1952, funny, foreign words already bouncing around inside me and my pockets. Thus, at the age of barely seventeen, I mounted my bike and pedalled off with two school friends who saddled me with the task of finding them food and shelter. Lost in translation they were. Me? French irregular verbs and the *les* and *las* of gender? No deterrent. The bike would see to that. Life in the saddle sat comfortably with academic ambition. Cheap way of hearing the lingo. And no gall in Gaul, for all de Gaulle's tantrums. The French were an adorable lot. Especially their early sexy, fire in the blood films played out at the Classic cinema brazenly opposite the fire and brimstone of an Evangelical Free Church.

A challenge and no trouble over the gauntlet. Unfazed by Mum's natural worries. Make sure you come back all in one piece as quickly as possible. Following a cycle of five summers, and during the school and university breaks, I covered, twice alone and thrice accompanied, some eight thousand miles, twelve thousand kilometres – sounds more impressive (we stressed the *i* in those days, not the *o*). Twelve thousand ks and no foot prints! Environmentalists, are you happy?

No holds barred, but always holding on to the handlebars, pedalled daily distances, of anything from fifty to a hundred and forty miles. Easy? Try it, weighed down by heavy panniers and a saddlebag stuffed to bursting, but buoyed up by the prospect of the Grand Tour, the European adventure. Romping over derelict bombed buildings replaced by eating up countless Continental miles. A doddle. *C'est du gâteau,* as the French say, which is just about what we say, with the 'piece' stuck on at the beginning, before 'cake'. But I never had cash for cake, so couldn't eat it, whatever Marie Antoinette said.

The adventure of uncertainty, the unknown and the unforeseeable. Don't worry about jinking along in that foreign jabber, just keep jabbing away. Get round to all the vocab for a bike, and then in later years, the ups and downs of windsurfing'll get you nicely balanced. *Sacoche* (pannier), or *vitesses* (gears), would roll on to their Spanish equivalents: *alforja; velocidades.* No challenge this; no bumpy ride in these two languages, a frolic of a challenge. Soon the long tail of Italy made it a tale of three languages.

Running along with a jumble of languages, it really was becoming cerebral. Ask neurosurgeons digging into our brain processes. Chopping and changing from one language to another, and then another, and even a fourth... They talk about patterns of brain imagery. Jumping about like that up top left me wondering how things didn't get muddled up. The clever chaps seem to say that we start off on the right hemisphere with one native language, which, with age, goes mainly to the left hemisphere. Where second and subsequent languages are concerned, both hemispheres are more in action than with monolingual folks, and then the fun starts. We mix thoughts and words up, racing from right to left, left to right, a bit giddy this, drawing on former bits of native information buried somewhere deep down from a long way back, and these bits keep pushing up, elbowing their way to the surface to try to get in between what we say in more recently acquired ways of saying things. Get it? Adventure propped up with all this cerebral activity was a good bet for the future.

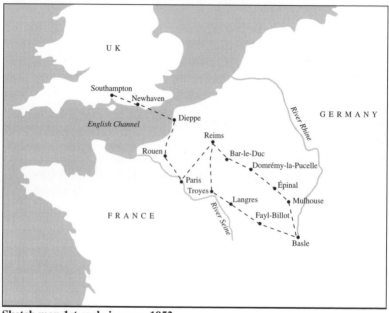

Sketch map 1st cycle journey 1952

No internships for young people in those days. Not even the Conservative chairman's injunction 'On yer bike!' It came naturally. With two school friends, John 1 and John 2, the **first crossing** of the English Channel took place in a pre-World War II boat, *Hantonia, a royal saucepan,* pronounced *à la française:* rwayal sospann. Wouldn't land a seaworthy certificate these days. On we got, bike, panniers and all. The *Hantonia* had no panniers, but baskets it did have, human ones, and lots of them, not the sit-up-and-beg type those Oxbridge females had. Basket after basket patrolled to the stern, and dumped basket after basket of rubbish into the sea. Cycling, yes, recycling, no.

The summer of 1952 found us with a foothold, or pedal-hold, in France. Hooray for our first foray into foreign parts. Keep your feet on the ground, lads, even when they're off.

Cycling into the world of adventure was forming our main hub of interest. Criss-crossing the Seine. First stop: youth hostel at Rouen. Rouen in ruins. Razed but not raised. Few left sane on the Seine. What about the cathedral, then? Curiously in immaculate condition. Stands to reason. Virgin Mary watched over it. And she was immaculate. Pope and co. decided that in the nineteenth century. Jesus couldn't have been immaculate if his mum hadn't been, could he now? God's immaculate logic. Sign of the divine or a bucket of luck with an American buck from the Marshall Plan?

Followed the Seine and flowed on to Flaubert country and Emma Bovary. Emma didn't go with the flow, though. Poor Emma, bored by her medical man of a husband. Bored, or should we say gored? Much more by three young country bucks. Bucked the trend, did Emma. An arch way of saying things, arching up high as she must have done.

Rouen. We're in Joan of Arc territory, aren't we? She wouldn't have done any arching, would she? Was a virgin, had it checked out by the ecclesiastical authorities. Even so, difficult to get through all that armour sitting on a horse. Safe as a chastity belt. While they were at it, vetted her sex. Hardly any time to squeeze all this in. Born in 1412 and died in 1431. Two years from voices at seventeen to martyrdom at nineteen. Life lit up in 1429. Lit up even more in 1431. What was the burning issue? Was she a witch? But, hey, she did raise the siege of Orléans, was present at Charles VII's coronation at Reims, set the English on the run. Of course, the Burgundians were in cahoots with the English. Cauchon was her chief prosecutor. He was bound to condemn her, wasn't he? With a name like that. Pronounce *Cauchon* as it should be pronounced: *cochon* = pig, swine. Automatic flame for the charismatic dame. We know all about you, Joan of Arc. Archivists have got you taped.

Poor Joan wasn't around Rouen for long. We weren't there for long either. Stakes were high, as with Joan. Decision time. Had to keep moving. Luxury living awaiting in Mulhouse. And before that, Eiffel Tower, Sacré-Cœur and so on.

The Rouen youth hostel provided bed and food. The portly female warden: Need any *blanquettes*? Covered in confusion, if not in *blanquettes*, for a moment, I understood that this was the *mèreaubergiste*'s (female warden's) youth hostel speak for 'blankets', with the nasalization of the 'a'. She must have learnt this word from previous English youths passing through, although she could not bring herself to denasalize the 'a'. After all, you have a nasal sound with *blanc*. So she stuck to the blanket statement 'Avez-vous des blanquettes?' Bland or should we say blank? Answer: 'Oui'. Had our own sheets, as well. Starting to get things neat and straight. I sure was ironing out bits of French.

Day 2 on French roads. Already a number of lessons. 1. Traffic, following Napoleon's command, must travel on the right side of the road, i.e. not the left side. (Try to explain to a foreign speaker of English that the left side can be the right side, though it must be easier than explaining cricket's third man. Nothing to do with Carol Reed's *The Third Man*). 2. Traffic, such as it was, announced its arrival from half a mile behind you. Continued with a blaring, harassing horn while passing you. Fortunately, in the countryside, the small number of vehicles caused little disturbance. Lunatic practice, finally banned in the sixties. 3. Configuration of French roads out of towns was *bombé*. What on earth's that? And we are talking about earth. Cambered. A *route bombée* sloped gently from the centre of the road to the sides, presumably to help excess rainwater run off the road into ditches. Like cycling on an indoor race track. Oddly at an angle. Couldn't even see straight. They soon ditched that idea.

Bombé's gone but his down-to-earth friend, the *pavé*, is still around. Although you no longer slant on your bike at a ten-degree angle, you may still have to tough it out with cobblestones on some French roads. Tough they are, and they still look up from below at the traffic in some towns. They once played havoc with cyclists who could spend hours swaying, rattling and jolting. The handlebar bell would sing all day. Wheels jumped and jumped. Of inner tubes you had a plentiful supply, but buckled wheels... You soon buckled down to say *buckled wheel* in French: *une roue voilée*. They're still buckling down this very day in the Paris–Roubaix race: *pavés* lot of the way.

Youth hostel handbook. Bursting with a promising range of accommodation across the whole of France. Yet, no availability for sleeping everywhere. Nocturnal gaps to face. Make do the motto. Paris or anywhere. With no apparent sanctuary for the night, and shielded by only meagre financial reserves, always the case in those days, we headed for a farm. Met with overwhelming generosity. No, this farmer was not out on the roads demonstrating with his tractor. At home, ready for an early bed. Request for hay in a barn to sleep. Early risers, farmer and wife left us trustingly in charge of the kitchen, victuals in plentiful supply. Funny word to pronounce that, or even spell. Why not *vittels*, or even *vittles*? You learn quickly. Fortunately. What I thought was salt (*sel*) on a shelf turned out to be of the *purgatif* type. A running recipe. Back to the barn. Dying to hit the hay. A sort of hay fever? Thought: with all that *sel purgatif*, things could have gone haywire. But, so tired we could have slept anywhere. In the heyday of vigour and health.

Headed east to start with. What for? John 1: Let's witness the scene of the disastrous crash near Beauvais of a British-built balloon-type airship. My encyclopaedic ignorance showed up. General knowledge and air-raid shelters don't go together. Education thwarted by Thor, god of war. World War I obese air ace Goering saw to that. How he got into a two-seater fighter defeats any understanding of volume. The date of the airship crash, 1930, remains fixed. Alternative French term: *dirigeable*, new to me, showed John's cultural class. Plaque on the roadside stood out most conspicuously to commemorate the deaths of 48 passengers.

Zeppelin had started the whole thing off in Germany in 1900.
Built hundreds. Ultimate in luxury air transport. Until Lakehurst,
New Jersey, in 1937. Repeat of the Beauvais performance. The
Hindenburg went up, and down, in flames. Hundreds lived the
bubble bursting once and for all. Not before forty Zeppelins had
been shot down over London in World War I.

Drop in for a visit to the railway carriage at Compiègne? Hitler,
naturally and foreseeably, reversed the roles of conqueror and
conquered of World War I. Appointed it as the venue for the
Allies' surrender. This visit would have to wait for three weeks
on our return journey.

Managed to reach the youth hostel in Paris before darkness,
which is when the capital comes to light. Paris by night. *Ville
des lumières*, that's its posh name. Onset of night > onset of plight
> race for cover. The hostel lay on the southern side of the capital,
in a grubby, inauspicious area called Malakoff, a forbidding and
alien sort of name conjuring up images of Russian revolutionaries.
Was it preparing us for the police station (*Commissariat*) at Bar-
le-Duc, a few days later? No more than a base for three days, a
sort of French pied-à-terre, Malakoff saw us make off for the
Gallic centres of artistic excellence, museums, the Louvre, together
with the usual tourist attractions like the Eiffel Tower and the
Sacré-Cœur. Eschatological expedition, it was, too, stringing out
a series of visits to the establishments of eternal repose. First in
line: Napoleon's tomb in Les Invalides, followed by the denizens
of the Panthéon, and these included a magnificent constellation
of *enfants de la Patrie* – Braille who saw the future better than
most, despite not seeing; Marie Curie (née Skłodowska, double
Polish Nobel Prize winner ending up in France at twenty-four
and first in all she did) and her equally brilliant husband Pierre
Curie, head in the clouds and head under a bus; Lagrange a
mathematical genius still testing the brightest of Cambridge
luminaries; Malraux (splendid adventurer/novelist in the mould
of, and inspired by, T.E. Lawrence, and on whom yours truly
eventually penned a whole series of articles); Rousseau (who spent

a spot of time in England and didn't learn a spot of English); Victor Hugo (who did learn a spot of English, exiled to a quiet spot on the Channel Islands) and Émile Zola (egregious novelist with parents hailing from Italy who spent time in England. Life threatened by rabid French anti-Semites. Intrepid defender of the cruelly maligned Jewish Captain Dreyfus, publicly stripped of sword and rank, ending up on dank Devil's Island, finally and grudgingly reinstated).

On we marched in further search of those who had shuffled off their mortal coil. Not difficult to unearth the Père Lachaise cemetery. Almost in the dead centre of Paris. Resting places of Bizet of *Carmen* fame; Maria Callas who sang the eponymous role; Chopin, a Pole who spent nearly all his adult life in France and deprived the poet Musset of the favours of George Sand; Paul Dukas whose *L'Apprenti sorcier* found a charming, bouncing interpreter in Mickey Mouse; Édith Piaf (*la môme* = the kid) who claimed never to have regretted anything; Proust whose memory certainly keeps the present author out of every one else's memory, and that most iconoclastic of Irish authors, Oscar Wilde, who died beyond his means in a wretched Paris hotel of little repute.

A note of history here. The cemetery provided the arena for the most violent of battles in May 1871. Here the final remnants of the Communards uprising held their last stand. Survivors? Hardly. Over one hundred, executed there. Convenient really, dying by ready-made graves, although, on reflection, the sod was too hallowed for the s——, well you can guess the next word, same as the other word with an *s* on the end. Odd about *sod*. The earthy sort you walk on is very posh. The earthy sort who walks on you is anything but.

Learning a bit of language. *Cimetière* is masculine (*le*); looks feminine, doesn't it? Tricky that. You don't pronounce that first *e*. So, you lads out there, don't always be lured by the siren calls of the *e*, even if you desperately want *charme* to be feminine, because it isn't. Not even e-mails will change it. Suppose e-females would. No mistakes over gender, now, even if the female of the species exudes all the charm in the world. And even if *cimetière* has three *e*s in it, you still can't bet on its being female. No sex in the cemetery.

Very cold it had been at Malakoff. A cough he had. It nearly carried him off. Who's that? A fair-head, blue-eyed Austrian lad, panting in his short leather pants, *Lederhosen* and not much else. No money for a bed, and that floored him. Literally.

Left eschatological disquisitions up in the air. That's where they've all gone to, I suppose. Deadlines had to be met. Made a beeline eastwards, to Reims, champs country. Free visit to the champagne cellars but that was as far as we could get. Real confusion over champagne there was. All that *e* business again, but no computers yet. The province Champagne where the stuff is grown is feminine but the drink is masculine. How about that? The gender business can really get your knickers in a twist. Still, *Vive la différence!* I say, so let's drink to it. Nearly all Europe'll drink to it, so there. They all bend the rules of gender, from Russia to Portugal, sticking in neuter genders as well (don't like the neutering bit), and it's only the No Sex, Please, We're British, with countries on the edges of things, like Finland and Hungary that see no fun in spicing up nouns with a bit of sex. It all started with those randy Greeks and Romans. Tradition and the other thing have been kept up ever since. Good to hear it first-hand, and handed down from generation to generation.

Another lesson: don't let the French deceive you with their spelling. They could spell like us English, but that's the cunning bit. *Reims* in French and *Rheims* in English. Was until recently. Could write reams on it. Marseille we had with an *s*, and Lyon was once Lyons. Lost the *h* now in English Rheims. The letter *aitch* it is and always was. But the *h* of *aitch* seems to be giving us *haitch*. But *aitch* is itching for a comeback, in a big way. *H*igh definition, we hear. That's clear enough.

Reims' claim to fame? Apart from providing the champagne libations for *gaudeamus igitur* celebrations at Eton *et alibi*, the first king crowned at Reims was Clovis. What's funny about that?

Clovis wasn't really French at all, but from over the Rhine. Don't tell the French. Don't whine, you French, even with the wine of Champagne.

Bar-le-Duc, to the south-east of Reims, and straight through the region of Champagne. Drink? Only from the heavens, free and lots of it. Lovely weather for the ducks at Bar-le-Duc. So don't bar the ducks from Bar-le-Duc.

On a dry run or not on a dry run? That is the question. And to make matters worse, we were in close contact with French military manoeuvres, tanks and all. But still no tankards. To be frank, no francs. OK, no champagne, but we were soon bubbling up with excitement.

The real fun began in Bar-le-Duc. Learnt some military strategy. No youth hostel, so from the depths of a drizzly day, a thin, red cycle line straight to the local *commissariat* (police station). After all, we figured out, they couldn't leave stranded on the streets three boys from a country who had been the saviour of the French nation. Even so, de Gaulle had no time for us, didn't hit it off with Winston.

Commissariat? Lost. Twice over. In translation and in time warp. *Commissaire's* office, then. Sounds a bit like *commissar*. Fancy a flight to Revolutionary Russia? Youthful dreams. Whom do I, Yuri Jivago, have before me? Strelnikov, husband of Lara, and budding communist interrogator. Transported am I to Pasternak's *Dr Jivago*. Would even have learnt the lingo if Lara were the prize. Could have avoided her Gulag grief. Not the romance of Romance. Here the romance of Slav.

Maybe I am dreaming, and Julie Christie is not for me. Surely it must then be Inspector Porfiry grilling me, Raskolnikov. Honest, guv, I only put a hatchet through that old woman moneylender's head. Author's aside: a little ahead of Stalin-driven, Trotsky's head-splitting business in Mexico City. Touch more than a headache. Just fifty years or so further on after Dostoievsky's *Crime and Punishment*. That's what it's all about, crime and punishment, if you believe Dostoievsky. Failing Lara or Julie, I would have settled for Sonia, Raskolnikov's Siberian redeeming love.

Back to banal Bar-le-Duc and *commissariat*. We ducked no questions bar the one on cash flow. Not in the red, but close to it. Strelnikov would have appreciated that. Still, we went with the flow. The conversation, in French, not in Russian, but still pining for Lara, and pinning hopes on her. With the policeman in charge (PC, personal computers not invented, nor politically correct for that matter) and the three boys (RB = me, JR, JP), the encounter went something like this:

PC:	Bonsoir, jeunes hommes.
RB/JR/JP:	Bonsoir, Monsieur.
PC:	Vat do you vant?
RB:	We have little money. Any ideas on sleeping?
PC:	Are you Eengleesh?
RB:	All three. Oui, Monsieur.
PC:	Where do you leeve?
RB:	We come from Southampton.
PC:	Ver is zat?
RB:	Near Londres.
PC:	Ow do you write eet?

I try to spell the name. This prompts:

PC: Zat ees Sutamton. [*The* a *and the* o *are nasalized.*]

RB: Non, Monsieur, Southampton, and you pronounce the *h* twice, like Northampton.

PC: Zat eez eelogeek. In French, ve are very logeek. I ave an idea. I call some peopul. Are you Catoleek?

Not on our bikes, but we spun things out for a while. Confab with John 1 and 2. No, we were not wheeler-dealers. Not hot on religious niceties, either. Sects, dunno, but sex, keen on that. All that divine stuff, knew a thing or two from that Catholic graveyard. 'Ve are Catoleek and ve love zee pope.' Policeman dials (it was *dials* in those days) a number and then directs us up a hill. Looms up a monastery, surrounded by high, ancient and ominous-looking walls. God has to be up there somewhere. They say he's high up, on high and so on. Ding, ding, bell at the end of a long wire at the side of an enormous metal-lined door. Lo and behold! Ave Maria! or two Ave Marias! Could have been Schubert style, none other than two nuns – nuns if you please! – come, whimpering and framed in their wimple, peek round the door, scuttle away and soon appears a priest/monk. Shows us in. An entry into a dark, unfamiliar world of cassocks, crosses and virgins. Bikes find a place of safety. The cassock leads the way up to a dormitory capable of sleeping some sixty or seventy boarders (we hit it right, it was holiday time in late July). All clothes dried in a spacious drying room, plentiful food provided. Back up to the dormitory to feast eyes on fairyland: a magic moment, Bar-le-Duc below with twinkling lights in by now a clear, starry night. Dreams of Lara and Sonia all over again.

Bar-le-Duc was not Revolutionary Russia. *Zut alors!* On the Damascus road. Pauline (would have settled for *Pauline*, I suppose, whoever she might have been) conversion at a drop of a hat. Beat that! RI teacher showed us how Paul had done it on that Syrian path. Sacred fire was the answer. In fine spirits, if not spirit. Breakfast, coffee and croissants. Épinal next at the foot of the Vosges, still in a south-easterly direction.

Fast-forward forty years. In a *logis* (family-run hotel) in southern France, at table with my more than indulgent wife. She has had to suffer the slings and arrows of her husband's outrageously unabashed overtures to foreigners. We find our terraced dining table on a balmy evening next to an ebullient French group. And *voilà!* We are privy to a conversation the topic of which is, you've guessed it, Bar-le-Duc. Sudden Proustian throwback. It all comes flooding to the fore, bar youth itself. Freewheeling on my bike again across Europe, and always with one eye for the main chance. I suppose I was a sort of Cyclops. I ask the waiter if he would be kind enough to enquire of the group if, at the end of the meal, they would find it agreeable to listen to an Eengleeshmann entertain them with an anecdote of their town. *Mais oui, Monsieur, avec plaisir* (with pleasure). Like Clamence in Camus's *La Chute (The Fall),* I settle my drink at their table and launch into Bar-le-Duc mode. Information is forthcoming on the Catholic boarding school: it has been converted into a young offenders' institution. In true Pauline fashion. Has been recreated as a *maison de redressement,* and now called *un établissement pénitentiaire de mineurs.* Did all the Catholic boarders became converts the other way and end up as young delinquents overnight? Not clear. Converts to perverts?

Resumed journey south-eastward, to the foot of the Vosges Mountains. Ahead lay Épinal, a town that pops up, but nothing like champagne, in the popular imagination of the French, a traditional picture of peaceful contentment, a charitable, gentle way of living coming under the name of *image d'Épinal.* Now at eternal peace with the world after Bar-le-Duc. Direction > Épinal. Had decided to repeat the wheeze of seeking police help in another youth hostel-less town. Straight to the *commissaire* at the police station. Got it off to a *T,* even at *T* junctions. Easy with all those *T*s. Ligh*t* a*t t*he end of *t*he *t*unnel. Ultimate achievement playing with all these *T*s. Flames of sacred fire were burning brightly.

Caught in interrogation mode again. Is this the examining magistrate Ivanov I have before me? You know, of Koestler's *Darkness at Noon* fame. But, me, Rubashov, I've done nothing wrong. Innocent like that Dmitry Karamazov fellow in Dostoievsky's *The Brothers Karamazov.* Four of them, all brothers. Why pick on me, Dmitry? Smerdyakov, my epileptic half-brother did my dad in. He deserved it anyway. And which one do I answer to? Examining magistrate, public prosecutor or police inspector? Siberia for me? But comfort with Katerina. Even if I'd been rushed off my feet by Grushenka. All very red and Russian, even before the Revolution. Things had started to look black for us. After all, *Kara* in Turkish means 'black'. Same for the Black Sea. But it all brightened up after a while. Finding lodgings, I mean.

20

So back to Épinal, but no longer pining for Lara. Lost for a moment. Flushing, cutting through all that red tape. *Monsieur le Commissaire* launches forth. Same questions, Strelnikov style at Bar-le-Duc:

'Are you Eengleesh?' 'Oui, Monsieur.' 'Ve love Vinston Shurshill. E elped us a lot in zee var. Vat do you vant?' 'We have little money etc.'

Without further ado, policeman picks up phone. Not a minute later: 'Protestant?' Nasal *a* and *t* falling off the end. Tempted are the lads once again by a fervent attachment to Protestant verities. Cycling back from gilded Catholic mass to dull Protestant dross: an unseating experience. But, Jees! Enjoying free ride two days running.

Never in the field of religious zeal have so many conversions been submitted to in so short a time. Cycled from Anglicanism to Catholicism to Anglicanism in two days. Even if Billy Graham, peddling his wares throughout Europe at that time, had done a deal with his contemporary papal foes, Pope Pius X11 or John XXIII, the alacrity and spontaneity of this astonishing double conversion from impiety of indifference to Catholicism, and then to Protestantism, could not have been matched. Yes, indeed, we fumed a most virtuous, zealous passion for Calvin's *Église réformée*, for all the burning business of Michael Servetus who staked all at the stake on his anti-Trinitarian views. Three into one wouldn't go for him. Repeat performance in 1553 of Joan. Eked out a few more years, though.

Within conversion distance of Geneva. Even heard of that Czech fellow John Huss, and Luther's 95 Theses nailed to the door of the castle church at Wittenberg. Staggered by such youthful knowledge, piety and allegiance to the Protestant ethic, the examining magistrate – or was it Lara's Strelnikov? – sent us on our way. Directions to the private house of a Protestant *pasteur*. No pope this time. And Épinal was no penal colony.

Unlike crime, faith seemed to pay in most wondrous ways. Three comfortable single beds allotted, in a large well-appointed room. Generously fed, both evening and the following morning, we set off again and wondered if the next conversion would be to Judaism in a rabbi's house, or even to Islam in an imam's mosque. Islam was never beyond us in our search for shelter. A night *chez* an imam? Not that desperate. Anyway, not many around in the 1950s. Charles Martel had halted the Moors' progress at Poitiers in 732 in central France. Gave them a real hammering. Charles had more claim to the 'Hammer of the Moors' than Edward I's self-styled name of Hammer of the Scots. Charlie's *Hammer* (*Martel*) was actually his name. *Martel* creeps into English with *mallet*. Nailed a bit of etymology here. Let's drive it home with Edward's tombstone inscription in Latin: *Eduardus Primus Scotorum Malleus hic est* (Here lies Edward I, Hammer of the Scots).

With two conversions under our belt, or above our belt, I'm not sure where conversions lie, and filled with aspirations to sanctity, the Pentecost stuff, we climbed the Vosges. You go up with conversion, don't you? Feel on a high.

Things were looking up, as we started to go down. Had reached the summit of the Col du Bussang. Fifty miles now on a downhill gradient towards Mulhouse, our final destination. Cycling had been getting tougher, up to nearly 3,000 feet, and heavy panniers. But the spurt of conversion does a lot for you, and a double one… One for each pannier. Still, our overriding aim was to reach the town before dark.

Why Mulhouse? John R1 had an aunt married to a wealthy owner of a silk factory in the 1930s. Stripped of much of his estate under the Nazi occupation, yet able to retain an easy lifestyle, he saw wine flowing, and the table was always abundant. They still lived in a luxurious, splendidly regal, detached house that one would call a *pavillon*, or even a *hôtel particulier*, if you lived in the Paris area. Fine, but how to find it? A plan of Mulhouse was not ours to consult. Tourists' plans were not available. No tourists in 1952, and we were after all only seven years after the end of the war. Strelnikov always seemed to do the trick, but no *commissariat* nearby. Not, please, another conversion. Again, fine! But how does a seventeen-year-old English boy understand the Germanized French of the locals in Alsace? In fact, they spoke *alsacien*, a dialect, a sort of impenetrable cross between the two languages. Somehow, I managed to gain some knowledge of direction and distance. John's aunt and uncle, here we come! Cycling in front, I pressed on, and progress had seemed favourable all the way from *Sutampton*, in our homeland. Ahead of the two others, I turned a corner too hastily for comfort. Complete the journey and press home for the fruits of our labour as soon as possible.

Feel like striking back at those irate, striking French farmers blocking your road again? Easy. Ride roughshod over the whole lot, not once, but twice. How twice?

Once roughshod, the real thing, with tar-laden shoes from a freshly laid macadam road. Have you ever tried to cycle through a long, freshly laid, still hot, treacly mess of macadam? Continue or retreat, the former fell my way, driving deep furrows into the macadam, and, needless to add, into everyone's brow. All a knee-jerk reaction for me. But no real choice. Had I not seen the notice 'TRAVAUX' (road works)? I stuck to the task, struggled to the very end.

Second roughshod, totally ignore their vituperation upon vituperation. They shot out: 'Ce con d'étranger!' (That bloody idiot of a foreigner!). 'Hey, Mac, damn you!' Black as pitch, or should we say, macadam, *Madame*? Gave me a really rough ride.

You never know what's round the corner, in more ways than one. I had turned a corner, on the road and in language mode. Tried afterwards, in vain, to smooth the path to reconciliation. Seemed soothing apologies. Unequal match. Definitely not tarred with the same language brush as the tarmen. No way out of the hot seat. Anything to say, boy? Slow-motion response. What do you expect with O level French and wheels glued to the road? How on earth do you create the right impression by making the wrong impression? Hesitant, jolting, my French sat awkwardly in the saddle as I ploughed through the tar. Not a chance of the colloquial stuff. Tongue about as sluggish as the wheels in the glue. *Excusez-moi, Messieurs.* Not even a cliché-ridden response. Not yet in the French groove. Only in the tar groove. Slowly it slipped off the tyres. But no scar with the tar. Went on spinning like all those Parliament politicos. Watch Cameron spinning. The irony can't be lost on the whiz kid, the king of spin, whirring in and out of the House of S(p)inners.

Trio had been blithely freewheeling through life. No furrowed forehead. Soul free of ruts. Yet, irony of ironies, the one in front had suddenly been mired in a rut, rolling in zigzags. Would he be hauled off to the coppers' station? Could plans for a week's luxury living be mucked up by tar? Managed an escape from the scrape.

Getting a bit loco trying to locate the address. Ah, I'll try this fellow. Damn it again! He's only into the German Alsatian dialect. He could be barking for all I knew. What about this guy? Another German-speaking *Mensch* (man). Anything but an *Übermensch* like that American comic-strip hero with a big chesty *S*. You know, Superman. Drunk, zigzagging like me on tar. Thick with liquor, and Alsatian to boot. Bootlegging, that's the spirit. No French for the *Mensch*. I'll die if I hear that Alsatian dialect again.

No computer-driven, SATNAV, driving directions. But, saved! human resources in the Post Office. Round the corner. Soon, right track for the three Macs. Felt like the three Marx Brothers. All the same, a toast for the post. *Pavillon* was soon in sight. After the usual *embrassade* (kisses all round), we were blessed with Riley's life for a week.

All fine, save for the wine. John's uncle spent more time with the bottle than without. So what? Bottle in left hand and short sabre in the right, all whirling like a Turkish dervish. Never sober was the man with the sabre. Caught on the cutting edge of existence, we were, all three. We went stiff before the hard stuff. In some ways, a visit to the Swiss would not be amiss. Just up the road. We banked on the banker to avoid the wanker.

One concession to slothfulness during the week's stay at Mulhouse. Train to Basle, Bâle for the French keen on their *chapeau chinois* (Chinese hat) riding high over the *a*, and Basilea for the Italians, just like the Spaniards. Easy the Spanish following suit like that. One item less to digest. Phew! Then there's Basel for the Germans. Sure would be confusing for Basil. Bet his Basel would be pretty fawlty. Not much help from Manuel with Basilea. But don't mention any of this to the Germans.

Towns, all sorts of names. English cosies up to the French, and on a par with Paris. Touch of *entente cordiale* here. *París* in Spanish, don't forget that accent, and the most congenial and sweet-sounding of them all, the Italian *Parigi*.

Basle, rattling trams, and wobbly, too. But punctuality's the game. Must keep a watch on the Swiss. Last train to Mulhouse, with a return to Blighty in sight.

To be fair, generous fare it had been in Mulhouse, and all the way. Westwards we went, slightly to the north. Halted in a small village, Fayl Billot, unmanned by a local *agent de police*, so no Strelnikov. How to say where we were? Couldn't even pronounce the name. *Fel, Fail, Fal,* how do you pronounce it, Monsieur Strelnikov, if we can find you? We spent the night, in most uncomfortable conditions and surroundings, in army billet style (with a name like Billot, it had to be) at a wayside café. Three not only in a room, but three in a three-quarter-size bed. Three boys in a bed, almost *Three Men in a Boat*, Chesterton-style. John 1 yielded to hard logic. Slept on the floor, while John R2 and his mate kipped down on a lumpy mattress. Like it or lump it. No sleep at all that night. Paid for it the following day. Kept our spirits up by singing the first three notes of the scale for Domrémy, next town on our list, with no accompaniment from John 1's violin. Travelled north for the birthplace of the saviour of mediaeval France: Jeanne d'Arc, *Pucelle d'Orléans*, where she lifted the siege of that town. The village in question was, in all likelihood, originally called Domrémy but *la Pucelle* was appended, after she was upended. *Pucelle* (damsel) > Domrémy-la-Pucelle. Saddled with the divine mission of saving her *patrie*, kept her virginity by staying in the saddle. Unsaddled by no one. Saw that in Rouen. Two-thirds of the Jeanne d'Arc arc done, Rouen and Domrémy, but the other third, Orléans, would have to wait, and another two years, 1954, at that.

That other self-styled saviour of France, Charles de Gaulle, spent his moments of peace for writing his *Mémoires* just to the north, at Colombey-les-Deux-Églises. Not before spending moments of *résistance* (to the UK, of course), in South Kensington, avoiding even a spot of English. *Honneur oblige*. After all, he was the incarnation of France. Only ever interrogated himself, didn't need Strelnikov: 'Quand je veux savoir ce que pense la France, je m'interroge' (When I wish to know what France thinks, I examine myself). He may have conquered a few words on the Emerald Isle for continuing his *Mémoires*, but had to order a giant-size bed for his six-foot-seven frame. Shaking hands with Oriental dignitaries would see him inclining like a giraffe. No wonder the slogan rang out in the fifties when he returned for the nth time to rescue his *patrie*. *La girafe au zoo!* The dénouement of *The Day of the Jackal* does it nicely, and Charles would be even more on cloud nine up there to see *dénouement* in English print.

On and northwards we pedalled, spending a night in a workmen's hut at Troyes. Sounds like *Troie* (Troy) but no Paris or Helen. Then, the scene of the signing of the two armistices at Compiègne, with all the memorabilia the railway carriage could muster.

Forest of Compiègne. Second armistice, June 22, 1940. They're en route for the carriage after routing the West. Hitler, Ribbentrop, Goering, *et compagnie* at Compiègne. Haughty Hitler in same chair as Maréchal Foch of World War I. Didn't stay for all the signings. Subalterns for that. Left before game was over. In no mood for musical chairs. But he did turn the tables. Should already be learning to look under the tables, though. Nearly got stuffed with Stauffenberg, four years later.

Evening was drawing in. Wandered around the exhibition. The past cast a lasting shadow over the rest of the stay. All the while,

John 2 had been channelling his thoughts to crossing the, well, you can guess. Girlfriend in mind.

Dieppe to Dieppe on two wheels. Journey had come full circle. Now a dip at Dieppe before the ship. The crossing of the Channel back to Newhaven. And no punctures! Sounds like 'And no passes'.

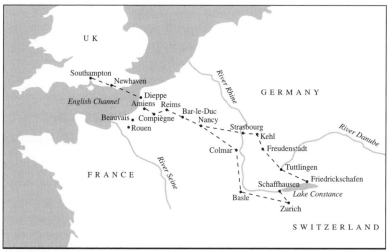

Sketch map 2nd cycle journey 1953

The **second journey**, the following year (1953). Equally eventful, and longer, with one thing learnt. Carrying too much weight over long distances was making for a lean time. The scales had by now fallen from my eyes. Lean on the lean side. Lighter equipment and less in the panniers, not quite Tour de France style, but there you are. This time, no two Johns unavailable. Another friend offered accompaniment. Let's cross France and enter Germany via Strasbourg. Parry away any thoughts on Paree.

Mike combined French with German. My German was reduced to *Bitte* (please) and *Danke* (thank you). Ignorance is bliss: imagine a French speaker in Germany. Stuck with *dick* or *prick* for *Bitte*. You'd feel a bit of a prick.

Results of A levels were in the air: high grades all round needed. Circling east and south round Paris, did an arc, like Joan. After lifting the siege of Orléans, she tackled Paris, at that time the biggest city on Europe. In the hands of the Eengleesh. Strategy? thought Joan. We could plaster Paris with fireballs. Could encircle them. Won't work. I'm only an Arc. Let me chew it over a bit. It's September and winter's on its way. Could starve them out. Don't want to make a meal of it, though. Take too long. But here goes. *Entrée* to the east and south. Pepper them with assault and battery. That way, you could get your just desserts, I told her. She sure did, with a bolt in her leg. Continued on horseback. Mount a second attack on Paris? Forced to rein in her ambition. Withdrew to porcelain-famous Gien further south. Its main church was dedicated to her. Would have loved to signal her triumph with an *Arc de Triomphe*. But, vision driven. Knew Napoleon would complete the arc, only four hundred years later, to transform it into a circle, *place de l'Étoile*. He sure was the star of the *Étoile*. Had to be, if *Étoile* means anything at all. His Arc stands right in the middle of the *Étoile*. Naughty Eengleesh tried to steal a march on them all with a Marble Arch. Empire ending up overarching the whole world.

Followed an itinerary slightly south-eastwards similar to that of the first trip. Reims, then Bar-le-Duc, and here – no surprise! – a night at the Catholic *collège*. Oh, you backsliders, you'll slip in anywhere. Not down the Protestant route. Bypassed the *commissariat* conversion. No entanglement of the two *h*s in Southampton and Northampton. Welcomed like distant family members, devoted to the pope, but armed with neither rosary nor cross, I resumed acquaintance with the dormitory. After breakfast, off to Nancy, of Polish king Stanislas Leszczynški fame who received the duchy of Lorraine from his father-in-law, Louis XV. Compensation for the loss of the Polish crown in 1738. The place Stanislas, of opulent, ornate appearance, must be number one in France, still embellishes the centre of Nancy.

A night at the youth hostel in Strasbourg. The low mountains of the *Schwarzwald* (Black Forest), after crossing the Rhine at Kehl. Darkness and rain, a moment's hesitation. But we rode it out, as well as our luck. Uncertainty overcome, we reached Freudenstadt. No youth hostel. Mike's job now. Hotel, about basic sleeping arrangements. Sure enough, German kindness was forthcoming, forget all that Stuka stuff. A straw-strewn barn and sleep in relative comfort. Following morning, our first ride in a Volkswagon beetle around Freudenstadt. A most moving experience to be beetling along in a car driven by a couple only a few years before our most fearsome enemies. Hitler, had he ever existed? That same day, Tuttlingen was in our sights.

Disaster. Never so close have I come to the science and study of scatology (don't mix it up with *eschatology*; see Chapter 5 for your convenience), as at the hostel at Tuttlingen on the *Donau* (Danube). I almost got on top of scatology. Oddly enough, total immersion was not far away. But the narrative here would be stealing the thunder – or could it be wind? – from the bodily functions in the later chapter. So wait for the scatology bit. It's not far behind. Suffice it to add that the zest and recklessness of youth discharged their duty in large dollops.

Result of Hitlerian promotion of endeavour in the rising generation. German youth hostels (*Jugendherbergen*, heard sixty years ago; memory still working, no German Dr Alzheimer here) were still the pride of the nation, and not even the wreckage of World War II seemed to have damaged their resources. Even in the smallest habitable spots one would come across these establishments. Such as the case at Horb, which barely figures on the even more detailed maps of Germany. The residue of Prussian martial discipline was all too apparent. Groups of youngsters ordered around in harsh, strident tones by leaders dressed in their *Lederhosen*. No red thighs from *VAT* (*w*ear *a*nd *t*ear). N*o W* in German. Could have been tears at the beginning, though, with all that chafing. At least no strafing.

Commands thrown across the room in German. Different from the singing sweetness of Italian. La Scala, Milan opera house, after Wagner's *Der Ring des Nibelungen* (The Nibelungen Cycle), a crowd of Italians chorused: 'Verdi! Verdi! Verdi!' A touch of national feeling here. *Verdi* equals the king of Italy: **V**ittorio **E**manuele **Re d'I**talia. A regal acronym.

Peeled off the miles to Friedrichshafen on the *Bodensee* (Lake Constance), spent one night in the hostel which we could count on being there (give the Germans their due, organized they certainly are), and headed along the northern side of the lake for Austria. Alas, 1953. Ruskies still in occupation. Banned was this yodelling land. No visa, you see. Exemplary ignorance once again. No experience either. 'Si jeunesse savait, si vieillesse pouvait' (No true equivalent but here goes: If the young man did but know and the old man were but able). I was all right on the 'pouvait' bit, the muscle part, but left floundering on the 'savait', the savvy bit. Other way round now.

Retracing steps, or should we say 'wheels', back into Switzerland at Schaffhausen, on the northern side of the lake. Hostel invaded non-stop by the roar of the impressive *Rheinfalls* (Rhine Falls), not quite the spectacular *Cataratas do Iguaçú* wedged between Argentina, Uruguay and Brazil but still impressive. Cleanliness and order in Switzerland there certainly was, and they impressed us mightily. You could have had breakfast in their loos with no ill effect. They had, after all, avoided the traumas of world conflict. Keeping up the good work as bankers. They have always been pretty clever at looking after every one's cash, including Hitler's. Best kept that way. They still spoke German in Zurich. OK for Mike but not for me. Baden, Bern and Basel followed. In quick succession of *B*s. Something like Lancashire Blackburn, Bolton and Burnley. Beat them with 4: Blackpool.

Be careful over the whole business of *faux amis* (false friends, words with deceptive meanings), or you could put your foot right in the dish (as they say over the Channel = *dans le plat*), and that's what I did, and in style. High living and luxury were, strange to say, the topic of conversation in the backroom of a grocer's shop west of Nancy. I plunged straight in, with *luxure*. *Luxure*, the mark, I said, of the ordinary English home. Pocket dictionary, still standing out on my hip *à la* John Wayne, brought me blushing to the roots: most English homes had a passionate affair with *lust*! Learning ever faster on the job. Spaniards playing the same trick = *lujuria*. And Verdi's company gleefully followed suit in their lustful deception: *lussuria*. Lust and a bike – surely not on a bike! – are caught up in the mists of time. Case of young and rising sap. Try everything in the book. Lust or bust, or lust on the bust.

Moving back through to northern France, and on to Dieppe saw us unmoved by the frenetic activities around us. Frenetic activities, certainly, without our knowing. Dieppe, deep in the widespread social unrest in France in the summer of 1953. The French had unleashed one of their periodic jaunty *grèves générales* (general strikes), not that I knew beforehand what a *grève* was, let alone a *grève générale*. Maybe it was their way of celebrating a holiday. After all, August was, and still is, the traditional month for downing tools, abandoning the large Citroën, Renault, Peugeot and Simca automobile factories and swarming to the sun-kissed beaches to ape Brigitte Bardot at St-Tropez (*St-Trop* for the snobbishly initiated) on the *Côte d'Azur* (Riviera). Pedal power of a bicycle, together with food easily acquired in the agricultural landscape of the French countryside, left cyclists unmindful of the demands of a community appealing against the usual indignities, whatever they were at that point. Pedalling away, no problems with the food chain, or the bicycle chain to come to think of it. The two chains were linked. Food did end up though in short supply in the towns. Same for fuel. The only time not to envy motorists.

Operation muscle-flexing. Done maths? What about the theory of inverse proportions? Yes? Then give this a balanced assessment: increase in speed of calf = decrease in cost by half. Brakes off and brakes on, as it were.

On the return boat. Hot debate on the right of the workers versus the might of the employers. Just a load of bilge for those two cyclists. Hot food on the plate was their only debate. At the same time, only back in England, at the port of Newhaven, was justice meted out to appetites. Importunate the strike might have been, but we arrived safely back at port. A copious breakfast, misnomer if ever there was one, for it was evening time, but eggs, bacon and fried bread twice over were needed for gastronomic satisfaction. Much better than café and croissants, but not good for cholesterol. Not yet come under the public microscope.

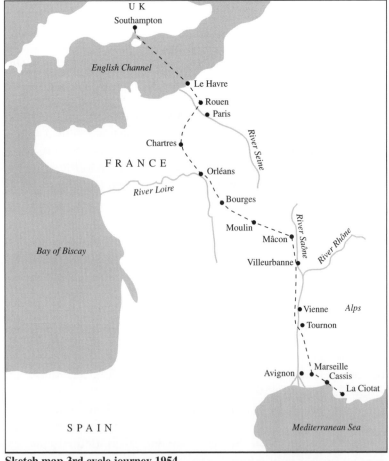

Sketch map 3rd cycle journey 1954

Third journey, summer of 1954. Loneliness of the long-distance cyclist. French, Spanish, Latin spinning around up top, with sunny Italian trailing but not left out in the cold. Felt less and less hairy with passing time, although well blessed with a shock of blond hair. Still very little *vino*. Alone but not lonely. Got the difference, you non-native speakers of English? Solitude was a close companion for some six weeks. Solitude could be enjoyed. But no budding Buddhist was I.

Boat from Southampton to Le Havre, straight over the *Sleeve* again (funny: *Manche* = sleeve). Only the English Channel in my way. No Paris this time. Straight to the south, the *Midi*, as the French prefer to call it. Summertime and friendly weather. Further south, warmer, then hotter.

Chartres leads to one abiding memory. Recalling Lincoln cathedral, it stands in the middle of the extremely fertile wheat-growing area, La Beauce, boasting a majestic, sublime cathedral, rising up on a knoll, high out of the very flat plain. You could pick out the spire twenty miles away. Spire inspires you to get there.

All architectural pundits concur on the unique beauty, blend and striking colour of the *rosace* (rose window). Now comes the confession, not for the confessional box, however close to priestland. Author has been ill-treated by his genes. A very slight colour-blindness impairs appreciation of colour, and therefore painting. However, you make a virtue out of weakness. It was soon learnt that colour-blindness in French, and in Spanish and Italian for that matter but with a nuance of modification, is *daltonisme* from the mid-nineteenth-century English physicist Dalton, similarly afflicted. Afflicted to such an extent that he wrote a treatise on the subject. Now, few speakers of the Romance languages I was becoming familiar with knew this fact. And they still don't.

On sped cheerfully the red Raleigh Rudge, this time to Orléans, the third part of the Jeanne d'Arc arc. Reims, Domrémy, Orléans. *Madame, où est l'auberge de jeunesse?* (Where's the youth hostel?). A long 100-metre wall. Stood flummoxed before 220, avenue de la Course. No youth hostel, no nothing. *Mais. Monsieur, eet ees*

33

220 bis. What's the *bis?* Like you say in eengleesh, 220a. Ah, *bis* is the extra bit. Like biscuit, done twice, bisexual, done twice. Working out this *bis* business is as complicated as all the double entendres on the pages before you. Have to address the issue.

Odd this. Something odder coming up, and something to do with the dog days. Not real dogs, but when it gets real hot, hotter than hotdogs, in the summer. And hot it was.

Is the ant extant? Colonies and colonies and colonies there are marching up and down. Numbers? The whole of the ant race. Encyclopaedia says 'One quadrillion'. What's that? 1 x 10 to the power of 5. What's that? A helluva lot and they're all in the youth hostel. Want to talk to the warden? Host'll fix it. Monsieur, can't you call in the anti-ant brigade? *Non, je m'en occupe* (I'll deal with it). Up and down ladders, shots of insecticide onto walls, windows, ceilings, beds. An infinite infestation. Warden pants and pants, rants and rants. Has he ants in pants? No answer to the ants? Sure thing. Honey. Lots of it. In pots. But no pans.

The ants dive in, gorge themselves by the million in this gooey mess. Upshot of all this ant stuff? *Fourmi* in French, *formica* in Italian. Ended up wondering why the building material Formica comes exactly from the Italian word for 'ant'. Still don't know. Finally, bitten by the ant bug, was comforting to know that the French *fourmi*, the Italian *formica* and the Spanish *hormiga* are all feminine. Why the Spanish starts off with an *h* is another story. Confusion somewhere, in the Middle Ages. El Cid and Co. mistook *f* for an *h*, like *horno* (oven) for French *four.* The two letters melted into each other, like in the, well, oven.

Bike, and legs, went south-eastwards. Passed through Moulins. Funny, thought I'd see windmills. Was this a time warp? Am I in Don Quixote's La Mancha country? You know, south-east of Madrid. You're talking nonsense. Not so, if Moulins has any meaning at all. But no windmills to be seen. Mad tilting at these giant monsters would have to wait. Quixotic madness was infectious.

After two dogged days through the wine country of Burgundy, Mâcon. Also famed for its celebration of Bacchus, not that I could have joined in. Money for youth hostels, bread, fruit and *Vache qui rit* cheese would not lead to any bibulous state, but a franc or two lurked in my pocket to take in the poet Lamartine's museum. Cycling there, poetry in motion. And what do you know? Youth got in free. Poetic licence, surely.

Lamartine, the French Romantic equivalent of Wordsworth who often popped off to revolutionary France, and very much Lamartine's contemporary, was one of the few poets on the A level list. Not too much cerebral activity. Politician he might have been, but it was his soul emerging in the museum. 'Le Lac', the one poem still threading its way through memory to this very day, and reminiscent of Wordsworth's lacustrine contemplation, brings to mind the transient nature of experience. Especially that of the forlorn lover: 'Ne pourrons-nous jamais sur l'océan des âges / Jeter l'ancre un seul jour?' (Can we never cast off the anchor for a single day on the ocean of time?)... 'O temps, suspends ton vol!' (O time, delay thy flight!).

Attractions of Burgundian wine were soon replaced by the traditional gastronomic goodies of Lyon. Would have swallowed up an entire six-week budget in one fell swoop. Is that why Lyon was avoided? No. The youth hostel lay to the north, at Villeurbanne, just on the outskirts of Lyon, currently gobbled up in the suburban spread. Torrents of rain fell on those days. No surprise, for the joining rivers Saône and Rhône swelled the water contents of the area to precipitate continuing cascades. Like Rouen, Lyon was a *pot de chambre* (chamber pot) for the area. Glad to strike south to warmer, drier and more congenial climes. Mercurial changes in the weather don't get drivers overheated, but just ask a person on two wheels.

Vienne next. You're kidding. All the way to Austria? No silly, just to the south of Lyon. Catch some Frenchies out, too. Don't mean condoms.

Heat now. As the rhythmic saying goes: 'À Valence, le Midi commence' (At Valence, the Midi begins). No hostel here, so keep going! And you end up in Montélimar which was, and still is, famous for its nougat. Whole town thrives on it. Cycling through Montélimar resembled one long journey through a protracted candy shop. As far as I could see, with eyes set firmly on the road, every single establishment, from dentist to garage to cobbler, sang the praises of nougat, as hard as nuggets of gold. Heavens knows how the dentist coped with the ensuing holes. Must have had shares in holes. Or even holes in shares if the holes weren't big enough.

Why nougat in Montélimar? Simple. The town lies in the middle of thousands of almond trees. Add that to gallons of honey, and look no further, Honey, for ingredients. Life is sweetness itself, especially for the dentist.

Pont-St-Esprit soon came my way. What's the name of someone who lives in Pont-St-Esprit? Back-to-front answer: Spiripontain. Got it? If you haven't, just talk to Latin teacher Mr Kay, genned up on Latin origins. He crops up time and again. Mr Kay's the key to opening so many doors. All very well, but countless continental names almost end up back to front. Over the Pond to Mexico. Name of an inhabitant of Monterrey? *Regiomontano.* Just before you get everything back-to-front, try the Spanish *abulense* (Ávila), or *onubense* (Huelva)? Not back-to-front, but still muddled up.

Tournon in the morning, Marseille at night. That was really pushing it. Look it up on the map! It makes you shudder now. North of Valence, Tournon stretched a distance of some 250 kilometres from Marseille. Tough, even on the professional. A slight downward gradient, from the high Alps to the sea, was helpful, but by nine o'clock in the evening, with fading light, Marseille remained a distant, forlorn objective. A knight in a shiny lorry came by, observed the lad's plight, lifted bike and panniers onto the back of his vehicle, and swept him all the way to the outskirts of the Mediterranean port. Gee whiz! I whizzed along. Bike hiking.

A few hours' sleep in a field, just inland from the sea. Up early in the morning, not with the lark. Didn't see any. Birdsong all the same. Felt like singing: 'Alouette, alouette, gentille alouette'. That's what they are: larks. Attracted by the never-before experienced rumbling rollers of the Med, close by, with its own peculiar liquid, full-throttled dawn chorus, accompanied by the full-throated concert of cormorants and wagtails.

A quick walk in semi-light for light relief. Choice: along the coast or inland. The field was still open. Off again, this time, circling the city, climbing along a coast road to Cassis, the first small fishing port to the east. Amiability, with an increasing dose of the natives' lingo, is the name of the game. A farmer, overflowing with human kindness and surplus produce, offered an abundance of tomatoes, pears and cherries. Fortified by this cheritable gesture, I soon entered the youth hostel, at ten o'clock in the morning! Five o'clock in the evening was the appointed time for arrival, but here I was, numbed by Morpheus, the ancient god of sleep and dreams.

Morpheus. Ecstasy for the ladies. Imagine all young ladies every night in the arms of Morpheus. That's what all our Latin neighbours say (Fr. *dans les bras de Morphée* / Sp. *en los brazos de Morfeo* /It. *in braccio a Morfeo*). Tough luck on the lads. Any chance of a caressing goddess? Aphrodite, cracker of all crackers in the ancient world, would suit quite nicely, thank you. Much better than a dose of morphine for a euphoric sleep. We lads ought to spend more time incubating a succubus. You know, a spirit having it off with you while you're in slumberland.

Remained on the mattress till the following morning. Nearly twenty-four hours' sleep in as many hours! Out for the count. Ready to sing like Orpheus after that. From Morpheus to Orpheus. Alphabetical order. I like that. From to lie to a lyre. Suited Offenbach with his horizontally inclined pleasures. He would always have stuck to a goddess, although same-sex pairs were common enough in gay Paree. Often par for the course.

The MEDITERRANEAN. Down below the pines. To pine for. Alone. First view of the deep blue sea. Sense of achievement and relief reaching *la Grande Bleue*, a blueprint for all subsequent wanderings. First experiences cling to most people. First impact of the world of the sublime retains indelible imprint of perfection. First impressions can be vivid, and their power loaded with an irrecoverable intensity, freshness and suddenness. Try a sudden, evening entry into Verona's open, circular opera arena in northern Italy. Illuminated buzz of expectation. *Carmen* under a dark, velvety, moonlit sky. All you could wish for. *Carmen* in Verona? Inflamed Don José with an all-conquering passion under the same moon in Seville. Ignited him like all those cigarettes she made in the tobacco factory. Missed *Carmen*? Wait in the warmth of a still evening till the next night for a sparkling array of stars under the stars, and feel your heart strings tugged by: 'Di quell'amor ch'e' palpito dell'universo intero' (Love that beats in the heart of the universe) swelling up from *La Traviata*, Verdi's masterpiece of romantic opera. Not rendered speechless? Try the Perito Moreno, that frozen cataract of a glacier in southern Argentina; the staggering Iguaçú Falls, miles wide; the Copper Canyon in northern Mexico as deeply impressive as the Grand Canyon, and as ignored as is celebrated her northern neighbour; the soft, welcoming dunes and oases of the Sahara, especially at Taghit; driving solitary along the Top of the World Highway in wilderness Alaska; Prague Spring Festival kicking off with Smetana's nostalgic *Má Vlast* (My Homeland) – they all give a sense of elation with a 'first time' encounter.

Fifty miles' round trip to La Ciotat to collect mail from the *poste restante*. Easily covered. Two days via express delivery from the UK to a pretty well unknown village in southern France seemed good going. On a tight schedule. Often down to the wire. Had to be. *Poste restante* was usually at the Telephone Exchange. Could never stamp out Mum's anxieties. Mail at Lyon, Mâcon, Le Havre. Always kept posted for exam results. University promises were well and truly delivered. Ever felt faint-hearted opening letters? Pedal power keeps you firmly in the saddle.

Clarity of sky and brightness of sun. Miffed with that mistral, the wind that had suddenly, and surprisingly, sprung up from the icy tops of the Alps and raced down the Rhône corridor to make sea-bathing unpalatable. And that's before the salt. Worse to come. Cycling south, easy-peasy. Leaving Cassis for the long drag of a return journey north, the reverse kept me almost in reverse. The slight gradient upward joined punitive forces with a cold headwind, head to head it was. Arles, Nîmes and Avignon took twice as long, and twice as cold. Deprived of drive, with no warm denims from Nîmes, no compensation from Bizet's *L'Arlésienne*, Avignon's *Palais des Papes* offered no solace either. Papal interest had faded for renegade Ron.

The wind slackened, but it didn't when, bikeless but not feckless, with a backpack, I found myself again in Nîmes, three years later, and this time, a *ticket global* which doesn't take you round the globe, but visits to five Roman monuments. One of these monuments, the Maison carrée, was set in a large, thickly populated pine park, and here the last ticket was ticked. Lying lazily in the shade, a sudden rush of flames close by, a crackling of tinder-dry twigs, shrubs and undergrowth. Next, plumes of smoke. A sudden and alarming fire had burst out, fanned by gusts of wind. Full-blown conflagration, result of spontaneous natural combustion. It couldn't have been the overheated, multi-layered screen from my Kindle? Surely not. Fifty years too early. God can accomplish miracles though. Read that on your Kindle Bible. Chapter 111, Exodus. Could I be Moses, on my Kindle hotline to god, fired up in his pious delirium against that infernal firebrand Pharaoh? All those minute pixels on my screen glowing with digital massaging. No sex, please, it's god-fearing stuff here. Elohim sending me flames of encouragement with the burning bush? It all flashed out. No fire raiser around. But someone had to be raised. Didn't beat about the bush. Alerted park authorities straight away. They did beat about the bush. Fire soon doused. Good I was roused. In all this, Moses' Elohim not to be seen, or heard, either. No surprise. I had a burning conviction he'd never be on call.

Heat rash replaced by a rash of showers. Mâcon, again through Lamartine's *patrie*. Traversing the misty and mysterious Sologne, a vast wooded, low-lying, swamp-like area swarming with fauna and birdlife, game for hunters, setting for *Le Grand Meaulnes*, nostalgic cross between dream and reality, from the juvenile pen of Alain Fournier. Literary gift to the nation. Found grandest of successes on the screen. One novel alone, that's it folks. Just managed to pull it off in 1913 before falling on the Western Front in 1914. Literary canons silenced by cannons. Life's creativity snuffed out in the stripling of a young man. English War Poets all over again. Fournier winding down before he'd hardly started. The winds of fortune: just like Margaret Mitchell and only *Gone with the Wind*. Went with the wind in 1949. Automobile crash.

On to Bourges, a sleepy town awakening from its slumber in 1982. Bourges it was that housed the Exocet (XO7) missile factory. Falklands War. Exeter and Sheffield were on the end of it. Boats as burnt as the burning bush.

A few, uneventful remaining days in strategically placed youth hostels, ever moving northwards. Le Havre, a fitting name (haven). Six weeks plus of front-seat strenuous pedalling now called for a back seat. Still no punctures (Hallelujah!), and no weight lost.

Those were the days, my friends. You had to fend for yourself. No tutor talk on where, when and how to go, how to behave, what course to follow, where to live; cope on your own, language or no language. Back at your alma mater, no Strelnikov, but polite and indifferent, he asks of you, in true gentlemanly, slightly condescending, university style of those far-off days, if everything was 'all right'. Darwin's *survie des plus aptes* (survival of the fittest) had played its part. And continued to do so. Off you go, my lad, anywhere. You choose. Settled on Poitiers.

The **fourth journey** of the summer of '55, a dream come true. Seam after seam of dreams, deeper and deeper, from far-away places. Where d'you dream that up? Poitiers, of course. French with Vietnamese, Cambodians, Algerians, all French West Africa. Just talk to them. And Guadeloupe and Martinique? What about New Caledonia? Law, physics, biology, the whole caboodle. Rowing on the river, the French just flowed. Guy, law-oriented postman's

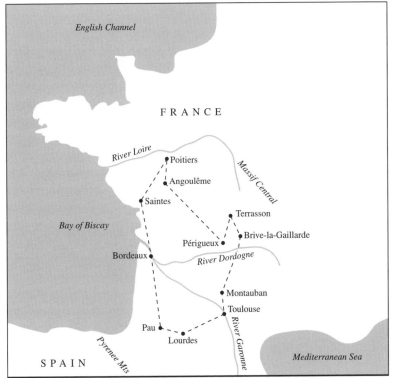

Sketch map 4th cycle journey 1955

son, ruled on the Code Napoléon. What's that? How we should behave, *mon ami.* Made sure right is right on the road, he did. Thought about *perfide Albion,* too. Cross over to Dover? Then he'd right things on the right. The Brits still left it to the left. The Corsican lad couldn't cope with his own code. Napoleon's dream? No more than a nap. Drowned in the water of Waterloo.

But back to the summer of '55. Pedalled round Poitiers in Poitou (the province) to get into shape, regularly whizzing off to Lusignan, and Châtain, tiniest of villages with host family farmhouse. Personal *Tour du Sud-ouest,* a less strenuous version of the Tour de France, now defunct. Direction? Bordeaux. That's on the edge of the water, isn't it? Why Bordeaux? Host dad at Poitiers inspected agricultural frauds. *Inspecteur de fraudes en agriculture.* You could have guessed that. *Lait frelaté* (adulterated milk) with lumps in it gave him a bumpy ride. Needed the cream of French lawyers, the *procureur général de Bordeaux* (attorney general). Poitiers and Bordeaux were only a few hundred kilometres apart. Fleeting invitation, and plans were already underway. Mid-June, towards the end of the university year, bike on the road. All on my tod. No chain of command.

Except in the legal system. Bordeaux's legal system. *Bordeaux* and *law* go together. All self-respecting French people know that. Started with Montesquieu and Montaigne. Of high importance, they were. As high as the Mont Blanc. Mauriac, novelist, kept it going. Had to with all those capital Ms.

The *jeune homme* still had to get there. Confidence was there. He had thousands of miles under his belt, literally. Steady, fluent pedalling was translating into fluency in French. All to do with rhythm.

First stop. Halfway. Saintes. Well behind in the tourist stakes, when it came to Roman remains, was Saintes. The site of a massive amphitheatre and a *musée archéologique* displaying a unique collection of Roman artefacts as fine as anywhere in France. *Ville romaine* (Roman city), that's what the signs said, but with no female saints around as far as he could see, although *Sainte* Bernadette was further down the road, at Lourdes, at the foot of the Pyrenees. No help here though. Along the tree-lined, cambered roads. Rider alone. Ready for action? A few kilometres beyond a village, mother and child are standing distressed on the other side of the road. 'Qu'est-ce qui se passe?' (What's the matter?). Answer: 'une crevaison' (puncture), never to be his Continental fate. *Mobylette's* rear tyre as flat as a pancake. All hands to the pump. Off jumps the lad from his bike, out comes the puncture kit, off comes the tyre. Barb extracted, no longer a thorny issue, but a sticky one. The solution is found and sets fast in his mind. Couldn't leave mother and child stuck on the side of the road, could he? Not on his patch, anyway. On go glue and puncture patch, and after ten minutes for things to set, all put together again. Evening drawing on. Under pressure to finish the job, and put pressure in the tyre. Tired of toiling with the tyre? Or, as our American friends would say: Tired of the tire? Nope. An easy path to tread.

The *prochain village* (next village) is only a short time away. Four *bisous* (kisses), fairly distributed to mother and daughter, but not the eight, common fare amongst the fairest in intimate Parisian communities, and Hi-Ho Silver, away! Feel a bit like the Lone Ranger, without Tonto. Good job, too. Indian friend is called 'Stupid'. All change in Spanish to *Lobo* (Wolf). Mother's last words: ''Ave you enuff patches?' 'Oui, Madame, I have batches of patches.'

Straight off to Saintes. Not one for hot air. No standing on pomp and ceremony. But pumped full of adrenalin he is for the rest of the day.

Next day. Finds the Bordeaux address, a fine, stately home adorned with a most spacious, inspirational spiral staircase, gold-plated fittings for the bath, and sleeping quarters that could never be dreamt of. Week with the son, Philippe, at least when he's free. *Baccalauréat* bound. At that time, pass rate: thirty per cent. Eighty per cent now, soon predicted up to ninety, things getting easier? Philippe sailed through with flying colours, not that his Brit friend would have fully recognized them. Colour blindness doesn't fade. Philippe landed a *mention très bien* (distinction), following in the tracks of a twenty-seven-year old brother. And he made plenty. Qualified engineer. *Ingénieur* carries much more weight in France than *engineer* in England. Deals with heavier things. Some gravitas about him. You could be a heating engineer in England, offering plumbing services, and still be plum dumb. An *ingénieur's* reputation? Built on weighty construction: bridges, roads, railways etc. Care with translations, please. Weigh up the differences. Especially for the heavy stuff.

Luxury living left behind. At the foot of the Pyrenees lies Pau, pronounced like *pot*, as in *pot de chambre*, and a fair amount of natural peeing done here. Rain-blessed, fertile mountains on the French side, and dry and even barren on the southern Spanish side. Fellow up there didn't get water favours evenly distributed. But before that, a unique moment of wheeling glory: pleasure and pride approaching a small village, still a mile or so off. What's that? Blaring sounds of horns, not up to vuvuzela decibel level yet. Louder and louder vocal excitement.

Now seen from the other side, the village side. There's the yellow fellow. You know, the leader with the *maillot jaune*. The overall leader, but not in overalls. In overalls, he would have been overhauled.

Back to the solitary cyclist. Village now a short distance away. Sounds subside. Under a hot, dazzling June sun, loud acclaim from the crowd. Buzzing fans, but not the circular, whirring sort, set him off suddenly pedalling afresh, quickened by the twice winner of the Tour de France and five-times winner of the Giro d'Italia, even conqueror of the Paris–Roubaix *pavé*-covered classic, the legendary Italian Fausto Coppi. Perhaps would love to copy Fausto's photographed antics riding in the saddle with Sofia Loren. One imagines this as the first step towards the celebrities' sandals slipping off. Could lead to the scandal of the sandals. Wouldn't stop there. The temptation of Faust. He went on to Giulia Occhini, if you see what I mean, the Argentinian beauty. Damned by the Church, with a child out of wedlock. Must have been aware of his fate built into his name, prescribed by the gods, and doubtless proscribed by papal bull. All bull to me. Marlowe, on a path to self-destruction, was the first to see the damnation of Faust. Damned again by Goethe, Berlioz and Gounod. Slow down, Ron. You really are getting ahead of yourself. Back to the innocence of village life.

Then a cloud of disappointment, for them and him. Hero to zero, triumph to defeat in a nanosecond. Who – should I be saying *whom* here? – the villagers are acclaiming is the mistaken leader of the *peloton* (pack). *Route de France*, it is, amateur version, now defunct, of the Tour de France. *Motards* (motor cycle police) roar up with a disdainful 'Dégagez!' (Out of the way!). Send me packing before the pack, they do. What's that? *Peloton* mass flashes indistinguishably by. Could be an emulation of the giants of the saddle, Fausto Coppi, French Louison Bobet, Belgian Eddie Mercx, the forerunners, or should it be the forecyclists, of the Spaniard Miguel Indurain, and the two Americans Greg LeMonde and Lance Armstrong. National excitement reaches fever pitch. Road races in France close half the country in summer for the French revolution. Revolution, twice over. Wheels whiz round on *Quatorze juillet* (Fourteenth of July), Bastille Day.

Memories of two years before, 1952. Half an hour of wheels into the roads of France. All three of us stood by as whoosh! They buzzed by. 'Vas-y Michel'. Bent over the bars, angled on the *route bombée*, eyes behind rose-tinted glasses, with rose-tinted future, no security-conscious helmet, the whiz kid raced through avenues of back-slapping admirers. Me on the way to Pau? Hopes well and truly punctured.

The remaining journey: age-old adage, no gain without pain. Look up the distance Bordeaux–Pau on the map. Add the intense summer heat of the dry, flat, sandy, pine-clad Landes. Toll-taking. Not that sort of toll, didn't exist then, anyway it was a bike. Not so sure about that other sort of toll, either. Not yet exhausted. Not far from Robert Jordan's bridge in line for a blow-up in *For Whom the Bell Tolls*. Just over the Pyrenean border, that one. But still a bridge too far at the moment.

The long, long, dusty plain, under a torrid metallic sky. Punishing pedalling to the foothills. Water, water, water, gallons of it, went down. Madame, is this water *potable*? Hold on, *potable* is not the cue for billiards or snooker. Not here, anywhere. Bottle this stuff, you can, even if you don't have bottle for snooker. You can pocket it free, and along you go, as smoothly as making a 100 break, in tip-top condition. But you couldn't have bet on me as a hot tip to reach the Pau youth hostel before dusk. Still 100 kilometres to go. Tipping point of dehydration never far away.

Don't get confused over Condom, either. Just to the east, on the way down to Pau, a very small town in need of condoms? Condoms in Condom? Heavens preserve us from French *préservatifs*, their condoms. In any case, you could get a blowout. You talking of inner tubes? No. Let's stick to blow jobs. No next generation if you do, though.

Host welcoming at the hostel in Pau. Body chastened by a flagrant disregard for its call for rest, no sleep that night.

First full day in Pau. Not Pau, rather Lourdes. But legs too heavy for Lourdes on a bike. Weighed down by two heavies in the same sentence. *Heavy* and Lourdes = same thing. Lightened by a lift from a French couple. Went to see the centre for heavy hearts. Front seat to back seat. But front seat again *chez* Sainte Bernadette, a latter-day Joan of Arc. Girl of celestial visions, in a grotto. Now a taudry, grotty lotto. Stricken assembly aided by Catholic clergy and wimpled nuns. Pious hope. Bernadette, I'll owe you a debt, if cure me you can. Water, trinkets, charms, crosses, icons, jumble of hotels, chanting of biblical verse. Source of hope? It's the source of water from that rock. Still feel a bit heavy about all this. Ought to scale down my interest.

Pau saw the birth of Henri of Navarre, finally to become *Henri quatre* (IV) of France. But not before he had cottoned on to the wheeze that conversion to Catholicism from Protestantism would open the doors of kingship in Paris. Perhaps I was to master the same art, but the other way round and back again, in 1952 at Bar-le-Duc. And we did both end up in a sort of castle.

Henri was born in the most majestic of castles in Pau. He enjoyed the fruits of his small kingdom of Navarre, indulging endlessly in the fruits of all maidens in the region. Not for nothing is he still called *Le Vert Galant* or, in more colloquial parlance, *un chaud lapin* (a randy guy). Reproduced like rabbits. And it did not stop in Navarre. Marriage to Marguerite de Valois raised no barrier to his inflated, erectional behaviour, legendary even in his lifetime. How his partners appreciated Henri's advances is difficult to understand. Alleged to have exuded sweat at all times, especially between the toes. No amount of perfume would have overpowered his odour at the height of passion, and hygiene was not a priority. Parliamentary-punished Profumo of the film *The Scandal* fame might have helped. *Profumo*: Italian name for 'perfume'. In bad odour was Profumo. In such bad odour, we can smell him in the next chapter. In the footsteps of all great cheese eaters. For cheese and wine, he never dragged his feet.

Never knowingly under-loved, often caught with his pants down, in flagrante delicto (red-handed), wrongly yet appositely translated as 'in fragrant delight', Henri was as fickle in religion as in love. 'Paris vaut bien une messe' (Paris is certainly worth a mass), he ejaculated. Eye to the main chance, or thousands. Switch from Protestantism to Catholicism, Henri, and the French throne is yours. Have all the lovers you want. Religion and sex, sends you sky high. Good combination. Best with the combinations off. High esteem in France, Casanova he was. Amorous escapades, Berlusconi style. *Le bon roi* (the good king). Certainly not bad in bed. And even better on a horse. Often preferred horse to bed. You know what I mean. He would have loved his equestrian statue at the Pont Neuf, overlooking the Seine. A bit like the Italian again, *il cavaliere* (cavalier/knight).

City of Pau, with its sumptuous view of the Pyrenees from the boulevard des Pyrénées, Napoleon's creation. The realm of the kings of England stretched right down there. William the Conqueror carted off half France to England. Sort of Yankee Route 66, Route 1 if you play football, all the way to Touraine, Poitou and Aquitaine. Result: Hundred Years' War. Thanks very much, Will. Pau lay at the end of this English line. Up to the nineteenth century, and our compatriots had got there before my bike. Fifteen per cent of the Pau population went English. Nice, soft, agreeable climate at all times of the year. Emulating English elegance led to horsemanship and polo. And lots of horseplay, saddle skills, like Henri.

North again. Fed up with life? Off colour? Want those rosy cheeks again? You could tune into Édith Piaff's poignant rendering of 'La Vie en rose'. If the shop's out of CDs (and we're not talking about *Corps diplomatique* on the backs of United Nations cars), then Toulouse is the place for you. Not *la vie en rose*, but *la ville de rose* = the pink town. Large parts of the town's buildings sport pink-coloured bricks, a kind of faded red material from nearby quarries. Not just the old quarter, but elsewhere as well. What about the roofs? Pink tiles as well. It's flat round here, so I can't see them. Easy, take a plane from the local airfield. All fits. Toulouse is the centre of aviation research: Aérospatiale's the company. *Concorde* could have given you the flight of your life. Until it gave the doomed passengers the fright of their life over the Atlantic. Not another Concorde flight. No concord here. Similar plight for the doomed pilot Antoine de St-Exupéry, source of inspiration for the hundred-year local aircraft industry.

Not sure you're happy up there in all that blue, looking down on all that pinky red? Check it out with a litmus test. We are in the world of science, aren't we? Blue or red is that paper, depends.

Still not hit the high spots? Come back down to earth and listen to those Toulouse people chatting away. Their accent? Like in Marseille. Fun all the way for northerners. Parisians can't stop laughing. It's the sunny, southern way of saying things. If you don't laugh your socks off, you'll *rire comme une baleine* (laugh like a whale). Parisians sure do open as wide as for the dentist when they hear:

Paris engineering company takes on a top-class aviation man from Toulouse. Progress in turmoil with the workforce. Email to Toulouse: 'Il est très bien, votre ingénieur. Mais il fait rire tout le monde toute la journée' (He's fine, your engineer, but we spend all day laughing). Hilarity all the way. Forget those blues. You must be in the pink now.

Toulouse was well blessed with youth hostels, as was Montauban. Linger there to admire the paintings of Ingres. Born there. Hostel at Brive-la-Gaillarde lists as the lusty spirit of youth (*gaillard* = energetic, lively, strapping). Took a leaf out of any Midi town, it spreads out with a central, tree-lined avenue. Keeps out that summer sun.

Then westwards to Terrasson, on the river Vézère, just for one night, Saturday. Sunday. Still there. What's up? The warden (*père aubergiste*): Tomorrow a spanking-new hostel inaugurated here. Mass not on the agenda, would make a mess of things, especially in French (*messe*), for all my regular conversions. Presence at the inauguration a *must*. Keep pinching our words, do the French. And I am sure glad I understand *must*. Monsieur le Maire, with his fine array of assistants, as well as other town dignitaries like *notaires*, even dentists, all dressed in splendid apparel, grace the proceedings of which *Monsieur l'Anglais* is an integral and most willing participant. A buffet lunch, interspersed with the polish of French speeches, leads on to the *vin d'honneur* (toast), champagne in these circumstances, and congratulations all round. We all go pop with pride.

Mayor's spokeswoman puts her spoke in. Presses the need to look after sore-seated cyclists at the end of the day. Break the cycle of local indifference. Put young people firmly in the saddle. Spoke volumes about our democratic future in the hands of these young cyclists. We want no more than the revolution of wheels, not 1789 all over again. They're out for a good, long spin, that's all. Politicians understand that, good they are at the spinning art.

Hey, what's all this bicycle lingo? Spinning it out a bit, aren't you? Well. It's a sort of extended metaphor, that's what the arty types call it. Runs right through the book. Killing two birds with one stone. A stone certainty to keep you, reader, at the ready. A bold move in language. All the way back up to Poitiers, incident free, but the language keeps rolling on like bike wheels.

Journey five. Summer of '56. Last, longest and most challenging on a bike. John R1, back on the scene from Take 1 in '52, with bike pointing southwards. 'Le Havre to Barcelona, pumped up again for it, John?' No sooner said than astride the saddle.

At the outset, progress over countryside covered two years before. Rouen, then Chartres. New pastures after that. Not new for the Charolais cattle, but new for us. Route south-westwards, taking in the Loire *châteaux*, Blois, Chenonceaux, Azay-le-Rideau, giving

Sketch map 5th cycle journey 1956

Tours a miss. No castles in the air here, or *châteaux en Espagne*.
Will be when we get there, though, Spain, I mean.

Why not do a tour around Tours? Stands to reason. Balzac,
the French Dickens, was born there. So? Was already getting

ballsache, saddle sore and all that. More ballsache would be too much. So no Balzac. There's more. Some of his novels are as long as they are tedious, a dickens to read.

Directly south to Poitiers, on to Beaulieu in the Dordogne valley. Which one? Twenty-four more Beaulieux spread all over France. Pride in their countryside have the French. *Beaulieu* = lovely spot. The beauty of it is they couldn't resist carrying one over to England, too. Hampshire, with all its Montague exhibition cars.

On southwards, first to Toulouse. Had a good time there once before. Remember we were in the pink? Next, to Carcassonne. Fortified part good protection for the youth hostel. Fortifications look mightily impressive. Built back in Middle Ages. Decay set in after the town's destruction during the seventeenth-century war with Spain. Spaniards were a bit miffed, maybe. Too much like Ávila. The *cité* or old part was rebuilt on the orders of Prosper Mérimée, author of the short story 'Carmen'. Bizet's *Carmen* in Carcassonne? Would be just the job. Fits nicely. Two carcasses at the end, Carmen's and Don José's, what more do you want at Carcassonne?

Swept along by the music. Really intoxicating. Same for John, but more so. Heat and thirst > John drunk on plonk. Out for the count for a couple of hours. Quite a turn. Food? Companion's turn to shop. Look for a cook. Reluctant me. As steaming as the spaghetti. John lies low. Keeps his head well below the parapet. Can't do anything else. Keep a cool head, Ron.

Sights set squarely on Barcelona, still some four hundred miles away, take in Narbonne, and Perpignan, cycling between the bare, eroded landscape on the right and the Mediterranean, had to be on the left. No geography needed here. Catalan-speaking country, foretaste of the Catalan of Catalonia. All to do with palate and tongue, isn't it? A new language disk, please.

Crossing the frontier at Portbou. Sleep on a hill. Passing lorries allow no sleep. Up at dawn, whizzing down the other side of the Pyrenees. Figueras. Town centre, a small plaza. Met by a lad, unused to seeing biking foreigners in 1956. Job it is to feed customers into the local restaurant, and then feed them. The *comida* (meal), he calls out, is 'muy económica', not that we could afford it at any price. Figueras deserted. Destined for tourism on a grand scale much later on in the century. No *comidas económicas* left. Salvador Dalí's museum saw to that.

Only *comidas económicas* would do. Available in Barcelona's *barrio gótico* (Gothic quarter)? But where are the *pensiones*? Alighting on a *pensión* (the Spaniards like their accent in here, please, but not in the plural! – *Pensiones* – whole lesson for that) in El Gótico, typically narrow street named Calle Paja. Discuss terms in Straw Street. There eat and sleep for a fortnight. Bed a bit rough. Straw Street seemed to fit.

So, venture forth into the Rambla, a Barcelona main and nearby thoroughfare. The *rambla*, you amble through there. Dried-up river-bed, really, not that you would have got much shut-eye. No English speakers are wandering around, either. Has always been the ideal spot for a *paseo*, the lazy evening walk. Nothing ventured, nothing gained. Large numbers of *barceloneses* congregate in (or on?) the Rambla, reaping the benefits of the fresher time of day.

Plaza de Cataluña. Assailed by Spaniards from all walks of life, including conscripted soldiers. In a dictatorship, with some residual odour of the Axis, and we all know that Franco actually met Hitler in Hendaye, just over the border in France, knowledge of the outside world was at a premium. Communication from modern technology, even the radio, leaves everything to be desired, with the inevitable consequence that there crop up questions about the *calidad de vida* (quality of life) beyond that barrier of mountains to the north, whether food, wine, hygiene, health, transport, newspapers, clothing is OK. (Did they use OK then? They certainly do now.) Reserved they are on *preservativos*, condoms. What are they, anyway? Free speech, yes, free speech, well it is a democracy in all Western Europe, save in Spain, and Portugal. Salazar has a sort of window on the West, but it doesn't make him any more open to democracy.

Split-second cycling glory the previous year. Now, holding court in the Plaza de Cataluña, covered in a bit more glory. Stood in a circle in the square, squaring the circling as it were. In more ways than one. Rely on religion to set things in motion. Blasphemy of Protestantism and deicidal Jews. All comes together with the Spanish Ballsache: Pérez Galdós. Less genital trouble here. *Gloria*, where the tragedy-bound, eponymous heroine dies, together with her shipwrecked English lover, Daniel Morton, rescued on the Galician coast. Not a Protestant at all. Horror of horrors, he was a Jew! With a name like Daniel he had to be. A real lion's den he was in.

Of the most striking features in architectural Barcelona stand out Gaudí's (with the accent) odd, now finished church, La Sagrada Familia (Sacred Family), his Parc Güell (an awkward accent here), overflowing with the wildest and most unique creative fantasies, and buildings along some of the main thoroughfares, again of the same architect's ambitious, eccentric spirit. Creations as freakish as his dishevelled dress. Bedraggled in Barcelona, painted the most peculiar of pictures. A legendary tramp in his own lifetime.

Finance? Could afford only a quicky to Tarragona. By rail. The amphitheatre, the gladiatorial circus, the fortifications, all of Roman times, were taken in a swift stride, as well as the Arco de Bará. Aqueduct offering less impressive competition to the one at Nîmes in France than the massive structure at Segovia running right through the middle of the city. Segovia aqueduct provides a traditionally attractive edifice for suicidals. Death is definite, given the height and concrete below, as well as the obliging passing cars.

Spain still assumed in the 1950s the appearance of a forbidding country, unfriendly and ominous. Needed a visa for entry, and one for exit. Waited for ever for our university Spanish instructor. Señorita Iglesias was her name. Praying didn't seem to make any difference. Her name 'Church' should have done. Didn't seem to convince Franco. She didn't convince us, either, with Tirso de Molina's *El burlador de Sevilla* (The Seville Joker), the first Don

Juan who joked his way through countless women, in both senses. Spent all his time jumping in and out of maidens' windows, leaving behind an '¡Ay de mí!' (Woe is me!), a thousand times repeated. Didn't bother about *preservativos*, the lad. Hadn't he heard of *Condom*? In any case, would have needed an awful lot. Where's the chaperon? How did he get up there? How did it get up there? Learnt a trick from Romeo, a few years before? Charged everywhere on chargers. Saddle sore would have slowed him down, I bet. Or even reading Balzac. Things didn't improve with Mozart. Wrapped in, sorry, raped by, Don Giovanni (same dastardly fellow, although name seems different), 2065 lovers left in distress. Don's book of con(quest)s reveals all. Murder to boot.

Raffish Don Juan would have been in heaven with the topless bikini chic chicks. Would be first to cross the border into France, to Perpignan and Narbonne. Long way from Seville and Lisbon, though. Undeterred. What's on? The erotic rage of the age, the film *Emmanuelle*. And even *Emmanuelle 11*. Crystal clear with Sylvia Kristel. Our Don would have had rape on tape, a thousand times, like all those 1970s busloads of Spanish prurient parents pouring over the border, wondering what it was all about and how to do it. Serge Gainsbourg would have added thrust with 'Elle l'a appris dans les manuels' (She learnt it in the manuals). Never a dirge for Serge. Let's hear Emmanuelle again. 'Elle l'a appris dans les manuels, Emmanuelle'. Twice over, for Emmanuelle. A thousand over for our Don. All this to dismay the mitre-donned, archest of archbishops, he of Toledo.

The youth hostels of Perpignan and Narbonne were welcoming enough. No time for cinema. Besides, *Emmanuelle* not on the scene, or on the screen, yet.

Then youth hostel-less Albi. *Monsieur le commissaire*, in the cathedral-dominated main square, to the rescue. No conversion lark here. Could have worked with proximity of the Catholic top brass. No need for straightforward dishonesty. Same questions, different answers: cells available. Two cells with bedding, and after heating up food and drink with Primus stove, we settled down for the night. *Mon Dieu*! Vat ees zat? Uproar. A police station, OK, and that's what you'd expect. Eruption of shouting ran through the station in the early hours. Following morning: a woman had made the likely claim that her husband had not returned home, that he was most assuredly in an inebriated state, that the police should 'faire quelque chose' (do something). Culprit finally hauled in. Fracas more and more strident. Commotion slowly subsided, and peace was restored, and sleep. Hours later, Primus on its stand, vocab on methylated spirits, paraffin, etc., filled out another little language niche. That small cerebral pocket book was growing. Left the *commissariat*, walked round the cathedral. The heavens opened, not for blessing, although we were next to the cathedral. Amicable market stallholder calls out: 'Voilà, la jeunesse!' (difficult to translate: 'Come on, you young people!'). Out spreads an enormous parasol (or should we say a pararain?).

Good fun that. Next episode, no fun at all

In the right-hand corner is the white god (always had to be right and white), alias the almighty, the eternal one, prince of peace, Elohim. In the left-hand corner (got to be left, sinister and all that), we have the black champion, the devil, alias Satan, the evil one, prince of darkness, Lucifer. Darkness and Light slugging it out in the same ring. Hey, but Lucifer means bright, morning star. Confusion here, and that's just for starters.

Where's the ref? He's that mitred chap, Pope Innocent III, twelfth-century impartial arbiter of the whole world. No boxing tips from the pope. But he's already tipping things in favour of the prince of peace. Even so, no knockout punch. The devil still hanging in there. Would be much better if an even-handed ref were in the ring. Someone like those people from Albi, the Albigenses we sometimes call the Cathari. They saw god and the devil evenly matched. No knockout blow ever to come their way? They weighed things up and decided good and evil were about the same size, cancelled each other out. Nice and neutral.

Pope Innocent XII gave the knockout his blessing. Sent in Simon de Montfort for a thirteenth-century crusade against the heretics. Heathen lot out for the count. Count Simon saw to that. Countless massacres, call it genocide these days. Cities of Béziers and Carcassonne paid a heavy price. Knockout right on the nose. All that monolithic deist stuff had to get rid of the Manichaeism heresy. Duality of good and evil, something to do with Mani, of noble Persian descent. Nice dose of simony for Simon. Never held to account was the count.

But the Cathari, all they craved for was to be pure and clean? That's where the word comes from: *katharoi* in Greek. What's wrong with that? On to a good thing, surely? Catharsis, something to do with laxative, having a therapeutic clean out, is the next best thing to godliness. OK? Have a purge, and we're all tidy again. Squeeze them all into purgatory. Thousands of them. Hope they'll be laundered and hygienic enough to pay respects to the almighty. A sort of sanitary slaughter in the name of truth. Torquemada's Inquisition, we're on our way. 'Slay them all. God knows his own' rang out. All in a good c(l)ause. Or should it be *claws*? Funny that the route to paradise is lit up with the fires of hell.

But while you're at it, thou shalt not spill blood. Too sacred to be shed. Never decapitation, Henry VIII style. Burning's OK. Ask the Italian Giulio Vanini. His sin? No belief at all. And a bit of a lad for the ladies and even men, too. Blasphemy was on his tongue, until they gouged it out, before his fry-up, just up the road in Toulouse. 1619's the date. Had worked it all out. A life is worth nothing but nothing is worth a life. Pity he didn't hang on to the second part of this adage. Should have done a conversion job, like Henry of Navarre.

Architectural heritage to commemorate this corrective, cleansing slaughter of the Albigenses? The Sainte-Cécile cathedral, massive, extraordinary, overshadowing the whole square and surrounding streets. Severity of the exterior compensated for by the overwhelming, exuberant colours of the interior, a legacy of the Renaissance period. Preferable to build a monument to music? After all, Saint Cecilia is the patroness of musicians. They could have played for time to prevent the slaughter. Did it at Auschwitz? At least saved the musicians. Arthur Miller plays on the theme in his play *Playing for Time*.

The cathedral, one of the most enormous in Europe, as gigantic as Milan's, has a strikingly strange appearance. In fact, reminiscent of Toulouse-Lautrec born in mid-nineteenth-century Albi, laughing stock of aristocratic stock. Its arresting outer shell jolts the onlooker as much as the dwarf-like, grotesque, contorted shape of the post-impressionist painter. So colossal it dwarfs all the surrounding centuries-old buildings. But the goodies are inside, for cathedral and painter. The cathedral's wealth of pictorial artistry matches the painter's poster and graphic skills.

Return journey north went through the Massif Central, less exacting than the Alps or the Pyrenees, but exact to say it offered the stiffest of bicycle challenges. Toil it was, and took its toll. Progress slowed. Pressed hard, even off the saddle. Progress could have been at a standstill at times.

Insult often added to injury. John's pep was punctured. You'd expect a puncture, wouldn't you? But a damaged tyre, to deflate us even more. Inner tube? Went down as smoothly as a piece of chocolate cake. Ah, but the tyre? A sewing kit! No patch was I on John. Beat me hands down, with all his manual skills. DIY expert that he was. Tyre into shape, sewed it neatly with very strong thread, inserted a resistant material on the inside of the tyre, against the repaired patch. No rough thread rubbing against the inner tube (ay, there's not the rub any more) and hey presto! as they say in Italian, *mission accomplie*, as they say in French! John's pride inflated once again.

The final port of call before leaving the Massif Central was the little known town of Bourganeuf, where the youth hostel afforded the most bizarre, and – may one hazard it? – the most exotic of experiences. Where's the beds and the kitchen? Top floor, *Monsieur*. That's all we got from the bar at end of the road. Oh, yes, he passed us the key. Fifth floor of *la Tour du Prince Zizim*, so start climbing. What's this, *la tour*? I thought it was *le tour*.

That's where you're wrong, Ron. That high thing in front of you, like the Eiffel Tower, is feminine. Bit like *torre* in Spanish. You know *Torres*, that footballer, and the *vino* from Catalonia. The Itis do us a favour. Torre with them too, you know the *Torre di Pisa*, the Galileo trick. All feminine. Easy.

The prince would have liked some feminine company. What's the masculine bit, then? Well, 'trip' or 'going round something'. See, you can play around with the *tours*: 'Le Prince Zizim fait *le* tour de *la* tour' (goes round the tower), which would have taken just a touch less time than around *la Tour Eiffel*. All very tortuous. Prefer to wrestle with sex than genders.

The tower is unusual, so let's dwell on it for a moment. This most eccentric of edifices, three metres thick, complete with a machicolation (projecting gallery), and loopholes (not built by Poles by the way) or arrow slits, not that arrows were ever shot from them, is least 20 metres high, which means that it surveys not just the town but also the whole surrounding area. Why on earth, or on deep foundations, build a tower of these proportions in a backwater like Bourganeuf that no one, not even today, has heard of? 1483 to 1486, those are the dates. Fratricidal war of 1481. Two Middle Eastern brothers couldn't get on with each other. Ottoman prince Djem found himself defeated and homeless. Guy de Blanchefort, chivalrous sort, had the tower built to shelter the prince. A gem of a place for prince Djem. Three years, and then Italy. Got the name about right. Arabic DjemDjem.

Ever been in a spooky tower? If not, try Mr Zizim's place. Mount numerous flights of steps, pass musty old prisoners' cells, then up to the main area of the hostel. Going up and down, all alone. Not alone these days, and no youth hostel either. Guide'll take you up, and down. Don't expect a lift. You don't need a lift, not tomorrow anyway. On yer bike.

Still pedalling north, skirted the vast, low-lying, watery area of the Sologne. Had visited it two years before. Set in the Sologne lies the *château* of Nohant. Almost yielding to a romantic urge to visit it. George Sand spent some of her turbulent time there, with or without her stream of lovers, Alexandre Dumas, Musset and Chopin, among others, we finally chose to go on north. A touch worrying, this. *Château* and the village La Châtre seemed too castratingly close for comfort. *Châtrer* (to castrate) *un chat*, you sure could, but all a close shave, this. Thoughts came to mind of the twelfth-century theologian Pierre Abélard who had put his student Héloïse in the family way. More than chastised he was. Off with his goolies. Poor Pierre Abélard no longer able to get a hard on. His name ended up as a sort of misnomer: *Abel Hard*.

Castration didn't seem to cut any ice with Edith Wharton. *A Motor Flight through France* (1910) is there to prove it. Mrs Edith, one imagines, feared no danger of genital mutilation, although her companion Henry James could have, or her chauffeur, to come to that. Maybe their collective French was no longer concerned with reproduction. Mrs Edith was now beyond it, born as she was in 1862. Our Henry seemed to be sexless, and the chauffeur, well, he could have got quite heated. That's the role of a chauffeur. He really stokes things up to get them moving. That's what he is, a stoker.

Covering the ground felt easier and smoother across the western end of the North European Plain. No peaks now to scale. So didn't feel peaky any more. Back to the flat Jeanne d'Arc country of Orléans and Rouen, Le Havre soon in reach. Back over *The Sleeve* to Sutamton, so port to port, and finally *porte* to *porte*. Not with the *rwayal sospanne* (can't get that right), now out of commission and probably doomed to the knacker's yard. New crop of ferries.

Pocket just survived five continental capers. Had always held a tight ship. Never felt too much of a draught.

Eight thousand miles over the years, done on a bike with many gears. Passage as smooth as the rhythm of this last sentence. Cycling fitted in to the pattern of learning, and language was starting to oil the wheels of adventure. The engine of progress was to be no longer the bike, or even the car, but the languages of those foreign friends.

The cycle of five long, arduous wheely trips had come to an end. Moments of triumph sealed by the long awaited letter containing university success. No smartphones those days.

Everything's seen in double. Two wheels, two pedals, two inner tubes, two tyres. Even spelling tyres in two if you're from over the Pond: tires. A brace of brakes. All very bracing for the mind. Lift these twos into the higher realms. Health/illness, fertile/barren, life/death, order/chaos. That Manichaean duality everywhere. Albigenses from Albi got it right. Two, two, two, all going round on a *double chaîne*, a double-chain wheel. Two sides of the same coin. Scientists see it as a matter of matter/antimatter. Right and wrong. Left and right. Our Continental philosopher friends sway between thesis and antithesis and end up with a complete synthesis. Greeks set us on that grand dual path two thousand five hundred years ago. **Clues to the twos throughout the book**.

Metaphor and literal. That's the key, said Mr Kay. And he'll be back, time and again. Jees. He's back straight away. Latin already here to help. On what? Czech declensions. Long way off, but still… What's that, declensions? Well, it's like a word with endings changing all the time. Teacher asks us to decline, so we go down and down, and up and up. Keep turning the tables. Just depends where you put *mensa* (table) in the sentence. *Mensa, mensam, mensae, mensae, mensā*. And that's just the singular. Mr Kay, master of Latin, had put the cards firmly on the table. Play your cards right and you'll be at the top of the table. Never declined to decline *mensa*. Always OK with Mr Kay. Liked the fellow. One of those J. P. Priestley good companions.

Now comes the break in the bike saga. Bike or car? It was make or brake, could be break, but I doubt it.

2

Thumbing It

Sketch map 1st hitch-hiking trip

Faced with a new phase. Yet unfazed. Two legs and pedals, fine, but new challenges were on offer. Two wheels no longer fitted the bill, although it had given me a clean bill of health. How to square wheels with lack of cash? Had to square the circle, somehow. No cache of cash stashed away. We're not a couple of swells, Don't stay at the best hotels. Twenty-one-year-old, how to get around, and further afield at that? New jaunts and japes anew. Had to be. Bike became a thing of the past. All to do with changing gear: twice. Walking boots instead of cycling shoes, and petrol engine for pedals. Walking and talking, the new path to tread. A major change. A new challenge afoot. Ahead lay open, unexplored country. Beauty of it all, we're rolling back the years. Put your feet up and join in the adventure.

Young. Just press on. No stress. The future is riding on it. Hitchhiker's guide to globetrotting, there you are. A big step forward. Change two-wheel years to four-wheel years. Not my four, though. Charitable nature of drivers, appealingly looked at, keeps the show rolling on the road. No hitches in hitch hiking, so no bad press. Stopping or not stopping, you choose, guv. I just keep walking. Show willing. Drivers in an awkward or even enigmatic circumstance. Here am I, they say, awash with dosh, and there's a lad lean but not mean. Broadmindedness and roadside altruism. Never heard of that before? The fellow's four wheels slow. Hopes rise in the mendicant's heart.

No button-pressing those days to lower the window, unless they have a Rolls-Royce. You've already learnt the art of flagging them down. Unflagging you are in this. He shows a benevolent touch so winds down the window. You relax, winding down straightaway. You stop, and show your hand, not just your thumb. Where're you going? 'Où allez-vous, Monsieur'/ 'Á dónde va Ud, Señor?'/ 'Dove va lei, Signore?' Got the first? Did French to age fourteen, didn't you? Second with that funny question mark upside down. Topsy-turvy they are in Spain, most bullfighters end up that way. Sing a bit, and you're on your way. Ask Giuseppe di Stefano.

Drift with the wind, you do. Got my drift? Go anywhere. No

hands tied. Keep those fingers crossed, even when you're thumbing it. A challenge. Start winning hands down. Win better hands up. Thumbing it, just keep walking, although never an easy feat. Thumbing it, yes. Bumbing it, no. And, one step at a time. Thumbs up! And don't drag your feet.

Things a bit blurred in 3D: **d**irection, **d**istance, **d**uration. Doubly blurred, in fact. Depended on the decision of the driver. Definitely no driving seat for me. Wheels of fortune were still turning in all directions. Brakes were still on ambition. Further snag. The passenger seat in French? Wait for it: *la place du mort.* Expression slowly dying out. Maybe the *place du mort* (dead person's seat) has been doing its job too well.

Travel light. Rucksack (not *backpack* those days), tent and sleeping bag. Anything for reading? A few paperbacks. Weight of hardbacks made for a hard back. Primus for lighting up the evening. Make sure for meths and paraffin. They have to match for the matches to work

Cars on European roads? All at an angle, like in the Indianapolis 500. Just as fast, too. Feed your speed. Fuel the duel. Overtaking and soon you're undertaking. Thousands yearly slaughtered. Police have no policy. Keener they are on fags and cycling mags. Driving licence was a licence to kill. Where were the cars? Wrapped round trees, avenues of them. Ask the Nobel Prize fellow, Albert Camus. Not time to say 'Merde!' in his publisher son's Merc. Loved the ladies, he did. All passion spent. In car and caress. So, keep going straight, mate. I'm in the *place du mort,* you know. Too timid to bark out orders. And those trees are leaning right towards me. See 'em now, 'Arbres inclinés'. Inclined I am to stay calm.

No acid test. Can't tell if it's an insane invitation or a gentle glad-eye. Roll on a Rolls, and I'm on a roll. He'd stop with toothache, sure he would. Quid pro quo. You manage the motor and I'll dig out a dentist. Allah be praised! services fancy free. Facilitator and fun.

On offer, gratis translations, hospitals, police stations, garages, at the pharmacist's, doctor's, lawyer's, all soon par for the course.

Roll up, roll up, stroke or a heart attack?, sanguine is Ron. And no blood money. 'Où est Ron?' Blood pressure for everyone? See that in Chapter 7. Clear run to Antonio, the trainee doctor. Lined them all up, and did them all one by one. Photos to prove it. Apartment's AGM? Windsurfer's sail torn? Easy. Our *amigo* will even try to get twenty per cent off your parking fine. Never worked, though. Lift broken down? *¡Hola Madrid!* Engineer there in a jiffy. Lord of the Rolls no different, as long as he drove on the right. Stay on the left, he wanted. Can't imagine why Lord and left don't go together.

Carefree with their car. That's me. A to B took me all the way to Z. Correct kit. Rucksack converted to backpack, German to American, part of the Marshall Plan. Metal frame it had, strong beige cloth, several compartments. Sleeping bag strapped to the top. Companion to the tent. Bought in Marseille, on the Canebière.

Lesson one for fun, with thumb. Don't just stand there, boy! Start walking. Show them you mean business, whether they pick you up or not. God helps those who help themselves. Walk on the right side of the road, not ideal or recommended. Traffic coming up from behind. Can't eye them behind. Practise Houdini contortion?

Lesson 2: They drive, you skive. BUT, stay alive. Keep the chat turning. On with the charm and accent. Chirpy as a bird. Taught by Miss Hibberd. 'Non, vous n'êtes pas Anglais' / 'No me lo creo, no es Ud inglés'/ 'No, è impossibile che Lei sia inglese'. All three: *You can't be English.* Sure am, and I am serious, whatever McEnroe thinks.

Lesson 3: Don't stick out like a sore thumb. Elegance of stance, intelligent, literary look. Ladies will stop for likeable, not likely, lad. Glasses, blond hair, healthy brown legs, peace-loving demeanour. Prospect of a lift. An entrance back into youth. Entranced she feels. Funny the stress goes here from the 'e' to the 'a' here.

Quid pro quos of letters of thanks, telephone numbers, penpals for progeny later on, and exchanges. All from a thumb. And don't act dumb.

Lesson 4: Car care here. For the overtaker. Attention! Next stop: undertaker. Don't undertake to overtake. Moral: undertaker takes over from the overtaker.

From where did it come, the art of the thumb? Saint-Jorioz youth camp, Lake Annecy, in the French Alps. Eight hundred boys and *moniteurs*, including me, for a period of two months. In actual fact, the art of thumbing had a helping hand by a German couple (all right for *German* here), surviving owners of that famous beetle car. Hitler's stinging challenge to Ford, Henry. 'Beetle' for a car? Nowhere near as winning as French *coccinelle* (ladybird), but we can't win them all. The Germans are off to the French Riviera. *La Côte d'Azur*, for the initiated, or even *La Côte*, for the snobs in the know. WE know what we mean by *La Côte*, don't we?

The glorious, quite breath-taking *Route Napoléon* snaked and twisted down the Alps, pretty well from Annecy, to Gap, on to Digne, and the coast. Never a chance of taking a nap, maybe at Gap. Glorious for two reasons: first, must offer one of the longest, most continuously stupendous mountain routes in Europe, starting up from Cannes, on to Sisteron and Gap, then to Grenoble, birthplace of Stendhal. Who's that? A novelist with a tricky analysis of man/woman relationships, among the finest with *Le Rouge et le noir* (The Scarlet and Black) and *La Chartreuse de Parme* (The Charterhouse of Parma).

Second, panic stations for Napoleon. Things into reverse. *Nap* and *pan*, OK? That little Corsican fellow's playing with us once more, going backwards and forwards. Got rid of him once. Pan-European army gave him a right panning near Paris in 1814. We sent him to Elba. But now, he's booted from Waterloo to St Helena, surrounded by water, no chance of another *Hundred Days*. Hundred days it had taken him escaping from Elba to Waterloo, that watering place. Plenty of water for the loos. Napoleon even got bogged down in it. Poured down it did the day before. No plan B. Got mired in the mud. He ought to have gone for Wellington('s) boots. Might have beaten the Duke then.

Digne. You're on your own. Wait a mo in Digne. Two pressing memories. The first, personal, the second national. No hole in my memory of Digne, but a hole in the floor, *oui, Monsieur*. Ever done dollops, squatter-style? Try Digne for the exquisite art of evacuating bowels. But we're streaming ahead. Pick up the dramatic flow of events in *Scatological Interludes*. A dramatic introduction to the art of defecation it certainly was.

Memory 2. Saw the Drummond Affair in the French press, recently drummed up again on BBC television. In 1952 Sir Jack Drummond, a British Boots scientist of international repute, was murdered, together with his family, while camping in a lonely spot in the Digne area. A peasant farmer of Italian stock, one Gaston Dominici, finally convicted on unsafe evidence, sentenced to the guillotine. Two scions, sons, didn't stick their necks out. All they got was a sharp rebuke. Gaston? Pardoned. Released. Recent investigative journalism reveals international skulduggery. Shades of Dr David Kelly, and the Iraq nuclear weapons issue.

Left Digne for Grasse.

On my own, still unflagging in flagging down motorists. Nothing slipping through my fingers. A town standing supreme as the world's scent industry, and you can see, or smell, why. The whole surrounding area is redolent of the sweetest-smelling perfume imaginable, a delicious, all-invasive mixture over the entire countryside of lavender, mint, roses and orange flower. Do I sense a foretaste of the luscious scents of the Corsican *maquis* (dense bush country)? Or of the *Forêt de l'Hospedale* on the same island? Recent light rain was to shower down a smell of scent-soaked pine resin. Walking there was indeed an unexpected pleasure of perfume. Not unexpected for John Profumo, though. Back to Grasse.

Mass at Grasse? No, silly. Mass of grass, lavender grass. But Pope pops in to sense incense. Could be useful for our John P. Yes, perhaps mass at Grasse, after all. The pope could do him an absolution job. Just right for John. Hold on, who's this John Profumo fellow? Could smell him a mile off. Stinks, and that's not the perfume. Foreign Secretary for Macmillan's government in the early sixties, wasn't he?

Remember *Profumo* = Italian for 'perfume'? Whiff of scandal here. His very name attracted him to the Mandy Rice Davies / Christine Keeler caper, two perfumed horizontal sexperts. Just the job for John again, not an absolution job this time, but a blow job. On an even keel with Keeler was Profumo. Loved it, he did. And he wasn't the only one.

Imagine FRIDAY AFTERNOON. Weekend stretches out pleasurably for yours truly. Knock on department door. 'Salut, Claude. See you on Monday.' Funny, he has a French way for replying *Monday*. Sounds like *Man*. So 'See you on M*a*ndy.' She'd love *Man*, all of them, wouldn't she? And all of them loved her, including the Ruskies. Immersed in fragrant delight they all were. Just like Henry IV. John was so intoxicated by his own perfume, he lied and brought the Macmillan house down. Remember?

> What on earth have you done? cried Christine
> You have wrecked the whole party machine
> To lie in the nude is in no way rude
> But to lie in the house is obscene.
> *Guardian*, 1963

Riding Mandy and Christine was one thing. Riding regional buses was another. Combined them with lifts from local drivers > Marseille > Martigues: *Quelle horreur!* (How awful!). Want it in Italian? *Che orrore!* What about Spanish? *¡Qué horror!* A romantic night on a camping sight in the delta area of the Camargue? Forget it! No banging here, bang in the Camargue's mosquito-infested, swampy wetlands. Amorous passion yielded to insect swotting. No risk of passion spent here. Forget Mandy and Christine.

Mosquitoes buzzing away, they did. An Italian *zanzara* sure buzzes more busily than a *mosquito*. Just look at the word, *zzing* from beginning to end. Toxic enough for most people. Zap! Zap! Zoom in all night long. End up zombie-like.

A real sting in the tail. Campsites and mosquitoes go together. Learnt that years later. Where? Almuñecar, southern Spain. They loved Pat and gave me the cold shoulder. They really got it off p(P)at. Mind you, I kept the shoulder well inside the sleeping bag. Shouldered no responsibility for poor Pat. *Zanzare* (nice plural there, well, there were clouds of them) were lying in wait in Sardinia, two weeks later. Five days spent at a beach hut occupied by a coast guard in Cagliari. Sleep? Zero! Zilch! Can hearing them *zzing* now.

Medical progress. Buzzing creatures didn't bug anyone. That's what our Italian friends thought. Malaria, where's it from? In the air, isn't it? 'Bad air' (*mala aria*), maybe from the sewers. Influenza from the sewers too? Thought it was just flowing round in the air. In + flew = influenza. Wrong! Both times. Mosquitoes in warm climes, then? Wrong again, *amico*. Take a quick nip up to the lakes of Finland or Alaska, quite chilly there. Stagnant water a real joy for those little monsters. All very confusing. Mosquitoes versus medical minds. Battlefield: malaria.

Quick lift to the Canebière in Marseille. Boat for Corsica with a calm crossing to the capital, Ajaccio. Just out of Marseille. Look! There's the island of Château d'If, of *The Count of Monte Cristo* fame, and visited by Mark Twain. Claims to have seen the iron mask. But don't believe anything he says, even earmarked with 'Mark my word'. All apocryphal stuff, this. The man in the iron mask was not incarcerated here. Given to exaggeration, was Mark, but exaggeration went the other way, too. His death was exaggerated, after all. That's what he said.

Down there, in Davy Jones' locker, just off the Château d'If, *if* you can believe me, lie remains of aviator/novelist St-Exupéry. Shot down in hostilities in the Second World War. Mind you, if you can believe the fantasy *Le Petit Prince*, you'll believe anything.

Ajaccio. Purr of expectancy and excitement, as you draw close. Splendid view of the citadel overlooking and guarding the port. Ajaccio was waiting for the steamer in late afternoon. Not to be carried away. All the woes of nineteenth-century Europe in embryonic form here. Small beginnings had Napoleon, small as he was, and born in an out-of-the-way spot like Ajaccio. Inspired by the mighty Ajax? Cleaned out Europe, he did, like that scourer in our kitchen.

Cleaned out Ajaccio, too. Just statues of Napoleon, here, there and everywhere. Had to make room for him. Not enough room even as far as Moscow. The French make sure he's remembered. Equestrian statues, in three squares, the places Foch, d'Austerlitz, Général de Gaulle. Not enough? Museum and relics.

South from Ajaccio, the road winds, through eroded countryside towards Olmeto, scene of the vendetta-driven story 'Colomba'. Created by Prosper Mérimée. Vendetta-driven was 'Carmen'. Same author. Why no *Colomba* opera? Horses, rustic scenery, *Cavalleria Rusticana* all over again. Knifings in all three. You live by the knife.

Walking to southern tip of Corsica, Bonifacio. South-facing fortress over the sea. Afterwards, *tours génoises*, Genoan lookouts, dotted everywhere. They wouldn't have stopped Barbarossa. Or Hitler, for that matter. Hitler always watching for his friend Barbarossa. Had a soft spot for him. Invasion of the Soviet Union – Operation Barbarossa.

Number of nights of *camping sauvage*. Nothing savage, just no campsites. Met Charlie from Marseille, motoring up the long plain that runs up the whole of the eastern side of the island. Days at his *épicerie* (grocer's shop). Porto Vecchio. Chat zigzagged between French, Italian and the Italian dialect, *corse*. Guessing meanings is the name of the game. More than could be said later. Try French-speaking Algerians, switching from one language to the other. Cut off in the middle of understanding.

East of Corsica at Easter. A twofold joy. Wafting my way around for days on end in a rowing boat. Perfume in the air, everywhere. Garden of wild perfumed delights flooded the sea. Wind from the west carrying towards us that balmy fragrance of the *maquis*. *Maquis*'s not just the French for Corsican bush country. Perfect for Fernando's hidaway. So ideal ticket for the Résistance.

Where's the other joy? Fishing in a dead-calm sea. No European quotas then? Up into the boat they come: sea bass, tuna, mackerel, squid, prawns, silver-coated sardines, all in the interests of that rich and varied fish-based dish, *bouillabaisse*. A reel taste of success. But a smelly mismatch with the *maquis*, all the same.

North to Aleria, then inland to a most virgin, untamed region. Motorway? What's that? Makes walking easy, though. Just keep walking. Spirits high up top, pounding feet below. Spot for pitching a tent? Anywhere. There's Corte, the ancient capital, up there *à gauche*. A little higher up, the highest point of the island, Monte Cinto, of some nine thousand feet (2,800 metres). On through to Evisa, taking in the Scala di Santa Regina, breath-taking gorge cut through granite. Take a deep breath. More than three thousand feet down, most celebrated natural beauty spot in Corsica. Sublime. Not for nothing is Corsica called *l'Île de beauté*. The gorge plunged on down to a warm, sparkling sea. How do you entertain yourself? You roll off the tongue Italian names. Nothing to beat them: *forêt de l'Ospedale, forêt de Vizzavona, col de Bavella, Piana, Propriano, la Spelunca* (Latin but Italian is close by: *spelonca* = cave, grotto), *défilé de l'Inzecca* and so on. Why stop in Corsica? Languid, elongated vowels. Lovely they all are. No consonants at the end of words > no abruptness of sound. Lucca, birthplace of Puccini; Roncole saw Verdi's light of day; Limone (lemons must have started here), Verona, Venezia. Just listen to the waiter: *Parma è bella*. Same with happy Italian *signore* on a bus saying unendingly: *Allora... Allora... Allora*. And then there's Garibaldi. Bold in adventure, but not bald. Took everything on the chin, even a beard. Even when talking about biscuits is a source of bliss. Don't know any Italian? Start eating the biscuits and you'll soon learn.

Where's the coast? No English? *Dov'è la costa?* Never get there without a *pollice*. What's that? Not the police of Bar-le-Duc, to be sure. A thumb, of course. Rule of thumb, talk in the local lingo and *Roberto è suo zio* (Bob's your uncle). Do they say that? No, just testing. A restful night on Porto ferns, beside the sea.

A wave of contentment. South, with, on the left, the *calanche*. Hey, you French, don't call *calanche calanques*. Italian *calanche*. High, impressive, fiercely jagged shapes leaping at you when you turn on a bend. Feline forms. That's what you'd expect with those *calanche*. French *calanques*? Confined to the south of France, near Cassis. Creeks, fine for Barbarossa. Fine for Greeks, too.

You said 'those *calanche*'. We have *s* for more than one, like the French and the Spaniards. So why not Italian *calanches*? They just don't have *s* for the plural, so there. A bit like other European languages. Take a straw poll on the languages of Europe. Poles to start with. Nope. Check Czech. Checkmate here, too. No *s*s. Ruskies? No Sir.

Cargèse next on the finest of menus. Blindingly white church. Greek origin. Built by Hellenic refugees. Turkish Ottomans made things too hot for them in 1675. Crafty were the Ottomans, like Barbarossa, lord of the seas, a century before. They had craft, didn't they? The Greeks sought comfort, solace and a new homeland.

Still thumbing it. Yet far from slumming it. Made a meal of the meal. And the chat. Nice, long and languorous. But not from Nice. French mother with her daughter from Paris. Cash? Mum owned a spacious apartment near the Champs-Élysées. Bulging wads in her wallet. French francs overflowed like the *vino*. Discussion polarized between left and right. Me on the left and Madame on the right. Felt a bit of a heel treading on the toes of *une Française* so well-heeled. A moment's awkwardness but both of us were soon let off the hook.

Homed in on splendidly succulent *homards*. Turned out to be the least Mum could do. Stony-broke student, prosperous Parisian. There he had rowed, one of the restaurant waiters out to a *vivier* (breeding ground for fish). Landed *homards* in a jiffy. And that's what we landed. But, what is *homard*? Couldn't you have guessed – lobster? Sardines would have been too easy. Hooked on *homards* ever since.

Sardinia in front. Soon left behind is Bonifacio, a white bluff, truly colossal, no bluffing. Lawrence's *Sea and Sardinia* whets the reader's appetite. Across Straits of Bonifacio, turbulent waters and vague seasickness. Feel in straight street for a while. Straits of Messina later. Just the same. Waters rush constantly and uncontrollably between two islands. Longer spell would spell *mal de mer*. Or should it now be Italian *mal di mare*? Wobbly language, wobbly stomach, not much difference here.

Italian has become the order of the day. Hand is forced. Have to knuckle under. D.H. Lawrence, how'd he get on? Not as well as Alvina, I bet. Who's that? A bit lost, she was, in *The Lost Girl*, not so much as her author, though. Sure he was all at sea in Italy, or in Sardinia, or anywhere else, for that matter. Not very pliable in stiff English society, he plied the seas, even to the Americas and Australia. German spy with Frieda, wasn't he?

Me? Make the most of my Sardinian hosts. They've been ghosts, from afar, but now the real thing. Humblest of the humble, gentlest of the gentle. Not Lawrence's tormented sex mode, this. Two aging people, the husband a fisherman, are living out the remainder of their peaceful existence on the Isola Maddalena. Shades here of Hemingway's *The Old Man and the Sea*. Calm and serenity. The last thing you'd do is to row. The first thing to do is to row, all the way out to the Isola Caprera, treat if ever there is one. Pay homage to Garibaldi at the mausoleum on Caprera, that's one boat I wasn't going to miss. From 1860 Garibaldi lived there, first name Giuseppe. Everyone's called Giuseppe over there. Giuseppe Verdi's another. (No translation please. Jo Green!) All these Giuseppes, like Muhammads in England. He lived for his Brazilian wife, Anita, but loved her for not long enough. He saw her fall to enemy fire. So Garibaldi had to take second best. The love of the whole Italian nation. Lived out, on and off, final twenty years on Caprera. Goats on the island? Could be. I'm not acting the goat, though. Male is *capro*, and the female, *capra*. Like that film director, Frank. *It's a Wonderful Life*. A wonderful life for Giuseppe, sure was. Pity it didn't last longer. Gracie Fields made it last longer with her Italian friend on Capri.

Garibaldi. Fondly cherished by a grateful nation. You're telling me a thing or two here. Restless man he was. Couldn't settle. No flies on him. Got rid of the Austrians, like William Tell. Bill saved his lad, straight as an arrow, it went. The Swiss lapped up their own apples after that. And Gari? Hero of the *Spedizione dei Mille* (Expedition of the Thousand), from Messina to Rome, and the Risorgimento. Unified Italy, at last. Hero, not of one world, but of two. Travelled the world over, North Africa, United States and Peru. Even had a quick shot at England in 1864.

Not now on two wheels, nor four, but three. Whizzed through Sardinia by a travelling salesman, Anthony Quinn style, Fellini's *La strada*. Harrowing for actress/wife, Giuletta. I could have done an Anthony for Fellini. Only just missed it by a couple of years. Not to be, for me. Over a hundred and fifty miles of Sardinia, from Olbia to Nuoro, on to Cagliari, and all this on a rickety vehicle made up of a front wheel, two rear wheels and a sort of open-air cabin, two travellers cramped side by side. No time for English niceties in these parts. Private parts painfully jammed for hours on end, if you see what I mean. A fear of Lawrence's 'We are crucified in sex'? No, but loss of something, says he, back to La Châtre, removal of...?

Five days in Cagliari. Couldn't take the plane, only possible when the ship comes in. No use relying on Ryan Air. How to fill in these five days? Time on my hands, with no forms to fill in, either, for the once/twice-weekly boat for Palermo. Not daily occurrence in those days. Back again, those squalid *zanzare*, buzzing again. Cover yourself up. Not a scratch of good. Beach, more beach and more, more beach. And mountains of fruit, watching young, bronzed *ragazzi* (boys) diving deep down into the rich blue sea just for the fun of it. Had the deepest respect for their diving prowess. He dives real low does Giancarlo. Thrives on dives. Me swim like that? Out of my depth. One dive, then skive. Threw in the towel from the word *tuffarsi* (to dive). Towel not needed. Very hot. Thirty-five degrees. Ducked the dip. No joy. But was a joy to say *ragazzi*. Preferred *ragazze* (girls) all the same.

Marseille–Ajaccio, eight hours. Cagliari–Palermo, twelve hours. Half as long again by boat. Punishing for a pauper's pocket, a rapidly emptying pocket feeling the weight of increasing weightlessness. Moving into choppy financial waters. Keeping one's head above them was a trial. Buoyancy in water, easy enough, buoyancy in cash, we're going under. Diet of bread, cheese, fruit, and water.

Cagliari to Palermo. Real *Cosa Nostra* country, you know Mafia stuff. Obesity around then. The fattest person I've ever seen. Obese among the obese. Woman of global proportions. Clearly too fat for purpose. Haven't been to the States yet. There she is, sitting on an invisible chair, working a pulley sending food up to the tenth floor. Down with the rubbish. Has to know how to pull strings. Punch and Judy started there in Palermo. Puppet country. Fits really. Al Capone pulls the strings and you dance to his tune.

She sure pulls strings. Needs hoisting on the chair. Has a heightened sense of her own importance. Would not have got off the ground without the Town Hall. Pleased as Punch with the *Municipio*. Puppet on a string she is not. Good job, too. She leaves them to deal with the waste, or could it be waist? A weighty problem. Lean time for the town councillors. Absolutely fatuous to expect her to cut the calories.

Pickies of all this for old times' sake? Snap out of it. Never had a camera to take me in a picture of health. No reel recording of life's wheel of fortune. OK. No reel progress but still movement in progress, even without a still. No footage to show for all that walking. Focus on adventure, not on recording.

Not a single pic to pick. Even so, real square I was. Case of black and white. Never flush with cash, nor flash with it either. And no flesh photography. Left that to Brigitte Bardot. BB, you know. Not Boys' Brigade, or Bed and Breakfast. You needed more than that to be on the Beeb. Liked BB on the Beeb? Would have preferred to be on BB. Persuasive reason to speak French. Sex education hadn't taken off, but dreamt of that learning curve. Learnt so much, I would burst.

A bit of a dotty name, Bardot. Even the French don't get it. Asked lots. It's a sterile cross between a male horse and a female donkey. *Hinny, ninny*, in English. Any the wiser? So Brigitte's offspring don't have much spring? She had plenty. Had a babe, did BB. Knew all about Shakespeare's two-backed beast. All this is a bit fruitless. Like the lift with the gay guy, coming up. He sure was coming up.

Next on the lust list. Not mine. His. Fiddle he does. Fiddlesticks! Not mine, *Signore!* He's turned into a leafy lane. Turned on, he is. Doesn't turn me on. Doesn't turn me out, either. I do. Life's full of turns. This one sure gives me one. A page turner, this?

Explain. 'Le piacciono le donne?' (Do you like women?), he enquires. What's the answer supposed to be? A moment's hesitation, then: 'Non so' (I don't know). A cue for his cue. I sure miscue. A Miss would have been different, and not amiss.

On to the coastal town of Cefalù, and then Messina. An agreeable week with a family related to Charlie in Porto Vecchio saw me flying round the city on the back of a motor bike. Almost relived Vittorio de Sica's *Ladri di biciclette* (Bicycle Thieves). An unending cycle had to end.

No sterile cross for me. Straits of Messina > boot of Italy. No heel, just the toes and shin, and up to the knee. Rome, that is. Felt a bit pugnacious about it all. Puglia? No time. Puglia had *trulli*. Conical dwellings or storehouses. Lax over tax. Come off it. Everyone pays tax from heel to groin. Not here, *Signore*. Rules set in stone, or at least in cement or mortar. No cement or mortar so no tax. Relax, Max. Clever lot, these Italians, still at it. Berlusconi admired for it. Don't mix tax and sex. Pay no tax. Cash for more sex.

Walking up the boot of Italy in walking boots. Who's hard on his heels? Peasant farmers. Taken pity on a foreigner, lone lad. Hands him a box of *fichi d'India* (prickly pears). Pricks his interest for some days. Peel can be used for culinary purposes, but covered in tiny, almost invisible prickles. Three days spent extracting tiny spines, if you can see them. All energy lost. Zest without zest, as it were. Certainly takes the shine off things, for all the brilliant sunshine. I feel prickly for days over the whole business. How stupid can those peasants get?

Limone is just as sharp. Manage to squeeze this little town in just before Naples. At last, a cut in cutaneous troubles. Has been hard to kick against the pricks. That's what the crossman said to his apostles, anyway. Try *Acts* in the *Bible*. Mind you, I'd axed the *Acts* a long time ago.

Mafia den coming up. Just before, can you espy a spy in a small mountain village, Eboli? Dumped in there, he was. Who? Jew. Carlo Levi. Banished there. World War II. Wrote an autobiography *Cristo si è fermato a Eboli* (Christ Stopped at Eboli). No Christian and no spy. Ended up on the silver screen, with just a touch of silver lining. Carlo Levi not like Primo Levi then? Oh no! Primo, Ph.D. chemist he was. Very useful in Auschwitz. Survived playing with the chemicals. Put him in prime position. Got him in the end, though. Couldn't stand the guilt. Suicide down a stairwell.

It all started with the *legge raziale* (racial laws) of 1938. Mussolini hit the Hitler trail. A trial for all the Jews from about mid-1943. Had been left unmolested in gentle, charitable, Captain Corelli's Italy. Nazis noted a poor Italian job, not the Michael Caine one. That was poor, too. Hopeless in Greece, the Italians were. Signal for a Nazi attack on Albania and Greece, and then on Italy, not from the boot, but from the groin. Consequence? Half the Italian army ended up not knowing whose side they were on. Like Hašek's *The Good Soldier Švejk*. Little soldier captured on both sides by all and sundry. Fought against all sides. All he aspired to was a batman looking after his captain's riding crop. Crops up again in Chapter 10.

Pompei demanded a visit. Feel a bit bashful here. Sexual complexities of Roman Pompei life? This way, *Signore*. All together now, not chorus style. No. Defecation style. Confusing, if you realize that *signore* means one male or more than one female.

76

Doesn't really matter if they didn't know the difference, does it? 'Buona sera, Signore.' I've got the right sex, have I?

Need a brothel? Easy. Set in a flagstone, and most predictably, was, and still is, a hard, horizontal penis of Priapic proportions pointing to it. The phallus serves no rigid purpose now, in the absence of the brothel. But it's much clearer than a written notice, especially if your Latin's a bit modest.

Priapus' stood out a mile. A representation of a penis of, well, Priapic dimensions. There it protrudes, a robust picture of a phallus ready for active performance. Needed more than a fig leaf to cover up his bashfulness. Take a lot more leaves to palm it away. This is so long a tale it could be stretched out indefinitely. But there is more. Outstanding information to come.

A phallus, longer than a laundry list, over a metre, ages to launder it, and belonging to that dick of a god, cocky Priapus, rests in all its glory on a vast weighing machine. An organ the weight of an organ. Kilos and kilos. The scales fall from your eyes, as you contemplate Vesuvius, the penis king of the Apennines, those snowy peaks running down the peninsular leg of Italy.

That priapic thing is held up by, not clear what. Hands up, Vesuvius, you're to blame. A cocktail of ash covers a few things up. But, no balls-up, and we're not talking about Australia's defeat in The Ashes. No phallus-up, either. A touch limp, but still ready with a straight bat. Clearly, this lad Priapus has an inflated sense of his own importance. Turns our view of the male member on its head. Can you do that? A rising star in the ancient world. Trouble is, fails to give a balanced view of things, his thing. But he certainly projects enough for all to measure. He clearly needs to emphasize size. Size matters, say the ladies. Hold on. You need to see life with a sense of measure. You ladies first get a measuring tape. Interested? Even then, you need a reception area the size of a drain pipe to accommodate it. Length and width. Especially when it's turgid with blood in full gargantuan flood. Want to view it? An invitation not to be turned down, no siree! But a case for small is beautiful here?

Vesuvius, indignant and scandalized he was two thousand years ago. Couldn't put up with all that barefaced immodesty. Mind you, showed Priapus the way. Hot on ejaculation. Swollen with pride, Priapus was hard put to rival Vesuvius, vulva bound. But Vesuvius was pumped up for his Pompei and Her-culaneum. I'd love to play with *cul* here. Means 'arse' in French.

Rome speaks. Hang around for a visit. Don't be impatient. I've been here for nearly 3,000 years. Romulus and Remus, suckled by a she-wolf, set me going. That's all a bit of a myth. So is Aeneas, after Troy, with a passionate quickie in Carthage. Dido ended up as dead as a dodo. Knifed herself on a pyre. Can't really believe Virgil's *Aeneid* either.

Puccini called for a visit to his place, to Lucca, to the north. After all, he was born there, and the summer opera season was in full swing. Leaving Lucca in the early morning, bumped into Lady Luck. She smiled and waved down a van for me. Containing British lads. Not called *Brits* then. Seven British lads and a linguist drove a bargain all the way up Italy and half France. They take me north and I'd find them accommodation. When they said they'd be going via Dijon, the mustard place, I really warmed to their company. And when I realized it was just down the road to Besançon, that really gave me a lift.

Could we do a quick visit to Milan? came the request. Too far north and east, came the reply. Any Frenchman around wouldn't have been all that bothered, anyway. Milan, pronounced *à la française*, gave it only a thousand years (*mille ans*). No big deal for him. Not hot on their history, the French? Livy, Roman historian was already referring to it and that's two thousand years ago. So one over on the French. Not only that, visiting *La Scala* (ladder) would be a bit of a climb up towards the Alps. What about Turin, then? A bit of a rush too, and I personally would steer clear of the place. Especially if you work out, worrying this, what the Italian for Turin is = *Torino* = Little Bull. Mind you, I have a childlike affection for all those thousands of Italian diminutives, just like in Spanish. If they'd called it *Topolino*, I'd be the first one there. Why so? Well, that's the name they have for *Mickey Mouse. Mickey* alone good enough in French, though.

What about Verona? You know, Romeo and Juliet's *patria*. Spot on for the opera. Could be too many spots. Rainy ones. You're out in the open, exposed to the sky. Spots can even steal the show. Giuseppe di Stefano would have knocked spots off everyone. Not if it rained, though. All the same, he was the rising star, finest among all rising stars at eleven in the evening.

No Milan, no Turin. Over the border into France, and a night at the youth hostel in Nice, Garibaldi's birthplace. Now playground of France and Europe, once in foreign hands, until the middle of the nineteenth century. The deal cut with the English lads turned out to be simple enough: they did the donkey work. I did next to nothing. Opened my mouth. That's all. Pump stations, pharmacies, grocer's (grocers'?) shops, restaurants and hotels, breezed through them all. The Bermondsey boys bent on evening classes for the oncoming September. Dropped me off close to Besançon calling for another round of university work. Return to Besançon, with a statuesque welcome from France's greatest poet, Victor Hugo, author of *Les Misérables* and *The Hunchback of Notre Dame*. Born in Besançon in 1802. By chance. Yes, it was doubtless planned. Don't get it? Dad was a Napoleon military man. Travelled around, wife in tow, and in bed. Could have seen Moscow straight from the womb, couldn't he? Only that would have been ten years later. Did well to miss Tchaikovsky's 1812. Glad he got out before Moscow. 'Got out', you know what I mean. Saluting his statue on the promenade Granvelle every morning en route for students at the university was executed with military precision. First words of the inscription, still fondly remembered:

Ce siècle avait deux ans! Rome remplaçait Sparte,
Déjà Napoléon perçait sous Bonaparte...
[This century was two years old! Rome was replacing Sparta.
Already Napoleon was piercing through Bonaparte...]

Sketch map 2nd hitch-hiking trip

Thumbing episode 2. Summer of 1959. Thumb turned up. Besançon to the Massif Central. Trains and buses to the high hill country, then into the low mountains of the Auvergne. Surrounding the spa town of La Bourboule, favourite among the French health addicts. Doc's prescription and the 'Princess pays'. State really pays. But that's what they say, south of the Channel. On, right across westwards to Les Éyzies. What's that? *La capitale de la préhistoire* (have a guess at that, saves me in my dinosaur old age). Punctured with *grottes* (caves) galore. Heard of Lascaux? Equalled only by the Altamira caves, near Santander in northern Spain. They're there, but not on view. All that contaminating human puffing.

A generous lift went as far as *la ville rose* (Toulouse), to be

80

revisited, if only for the youth hostel. Driving a risky activity in those days. Especially when the driver uses the *route nationale* as a Formula One race track. Witness him speeding past an elderly compatriot, stopped and questioned at a police checkpoint at the entrance to a village. Drew up with a jerk. The jerk got out. Retorted in a non-compliant manner: 'Elle roulait comme une tortue' (She was driving like a tortoise). Severe admonishment, but no *PV* (fine). Off he went, overtaking more tortoises. Should have put a foot down. Mine, not his. In a Renault Dauphine. So light in handling, it frequently showed too much affection for the passing trees. French roads have become much, much safer. Statistics of the 1950s revealed over ten thousand fatalities per year, now reduced to four thousand, and with infinitely more cars on the road. Liberal distribution of *PVs* and totting up of points to the fatal number of 12 must have helped. I always thought 13 the fatal number. See Chapter 7 for that.

Before Toulouse, Agen, plum and prune country. Keeps half France regular, viscerally attached as they are to Agen. Farmhouse between Toulouse and the Spanish border. Blessing and coincidence. Driver drove me home. To farmer driver's home. No wonder we all fare well in France. Home full of agricultural produce. Splendid for human consumption, and for the rats. Caught sight of a rat the size of a beaver in the cellar storerooms. No wonder felt yucky seeing umpteen rats ferreting away in *Ratatouille* foraging for food.

Get over that border as fast as possible. Give as wide a berth as you can to Cerbère. Should be easy enough, it overlooks the Med. More than half the French nation don't seem to realize it, their passion for classical studies disappearing a long time ago. Don't follow? That monstrous, three-headed mastiff guarding the Hades of mythological Greece is, well, Cerbère. Go into Cerbère, and hell is just over the Styx. If there's no other reason for reinstating Greek on the curriculum, this must be it. Greek'll keep you geeks out of hell just that bit longer.

Frontier behind, nowhere to stay, next dropping-off point? Rosas. Still no Catalan road signs. Would only emerge with Franco's demise in 1975. Where's the flower of democracy? Not in full bloom yet. Not even seeds. Just the seething seeds of continuing discontent. Car noses into Ros*as*. *¡Dios mío!* No Catalan, Ros*es*. Would have preferred Roses to Rosas. *Noses* and *Roses* fit twice over, you see. Sound and smell. Thrown into confusion? Not half as much as Spain's foreign visitors, post 1975. Looking for Lérida? Try Lleida. Iruña? Try Pamplona. Iruña = Pamplona. Easy. Sure? Iruña is not Irún. You'll soon be running in the wrong direction. Borders on lunacy. That's where Irún is. Next to France. Iruña, fifty miles away.

Roses. Can put up with the Catalan name. People are welcoming, whoever they are, give or take a fascist or two. Catalan grocer, with shop commanding a view of the bay of the same name (Bahía de Roses) made a space in his *trastienda* (backroom). Bed offered, but time did not coincide with generosity. Girona was beckoning. Getting used to Girona instead of Gerona now. Walking through downtown Girona, looking for a night's lodgings, the lad addresses a policeman on point duty, and *¡Ya está!,* or *Voilà!,* if you prefer. Wait a short while, *amigo.* Solution to all sleeping arrangements lay before him. Evening meal, to boot. Come this way, *Señor.* A little distance, to his modest abode with wife and child. Shower in a most confined area, but more than adequate. Sufficient food on the table, enlightening conversation ranging from politics to religion to education, night's refreshing sleep, breakfast, and the door is opened, not before an unsolicited modest payment for a most rewarding few hours is made.

One-night stay in the Barcelona youth hostel and out on the road again. Sitges. Walk on secluded part of the beach. Quiet, odd, what's going on? Keep your eyes peeled. All their clothes are peeled off. As nude as a newt. A peccadillo, this? A bit of one. We are in Spain, after all. Archbishop of Toledo wouldn't like it. He doesn't have to do it, does he? You know what I mean. An attractive, sandy beach it is. Take advantage of the sand. No cost, so glee in the lee of a large, broken-down rowing boat, itself stretched out in the lee of the parish church looking out on the beach from the northern side. Built as a comfort for the fishermen of the area. Performs, to be sure, the same sort of protection for me. Stay turns out to be incident free. The President of the Immortals, in Hardy's cold words, must be doing something right, if not for forlorn Tess. Groceries? Just off the beach. Most reliable Primus stove. Melons flow with juice, with the sweetness of life.

Next down the line comes Tarragona. Tarry there for some time. 'Down the line', two lines of thinking here, like always. Beach runs parallel to the railway line crossing over the way down to the beach. As happy as a sandboy. Nowhere to sleep, at first, or to wash, but hey, you have a tongue in your head, and Spanish is finding a most comfortable bed up top. Want a shower, *chico*? Likeable café owner befriends me, allows ablutions in his patio, encourages use of an improvised *ducha* (shower). Warmer than the sea. Heated up all day by that yellow disc up there. All my belongings kept under lock and key, especially for sleep outside on the adjacent grass. Am finally converted into the forerunner of Manuel. Conversion? Not Bar-le-Duc and Épinal all over again. Easy as pie. Manuel's Barcelona just up the road. Serving the local clients. No Manuel's pointlessly inept '¿Qué?, ¿Qué?' (What? What?). Case for pride and pleasure for Pepe. Translator? He's got someone like Manuel, but this *amigo* actually knows a plate from a fork, and doesn't have a *mostacho*. And things buzz along in Spanish, French and English. Can turn his hand to Italian, too. Turns in a star performance. Really feels like Manuel, but with layers of language as well as with layers of lasagna. The girls can't resist, buy extra *vino*. They pour out the questions as well as the *vino*. What's life like beyond the Pyrenees? Have you seen *Emmanuelle*? *Topless*, what's that? They all know now, use it every day on the Continent. Waiter's imminent departure viewed with pained regret, and surely loss of income. Language has become a gold mine for him as his aid moves seamlessly from one lingo to another. No seams in his clothes either. Just a pair of bathers. Right on the beach he is. Pity he can't sing 'Sole mio', however much he adores the sun.

Sleeping bag all that's needed outside at night. Long period of stable weather. Dew the only drawback. Don't draw back under the gaze of the *guardias civiles* out on their midnight rounds. Just checking.

Open road again, *à la* Jack Kerouac. Little traffic in those far-off days, but chance goes through the coastal town of Peñíscola, scene of the final battle in the film *El Cid*. Multitude of extras were sought after. Subsequently came to know one of them from Benicarló, just up the road. Film was shot by the sea some years after my first visit there. Descriptions of the battle, which really took place on the plains of Valencia, ebbed and flowed like the sea. Gigantic piece of history, the size of Charlton Heston. Suddenly back to the Middle Ages, and all in Spanish. What else can be asked for? A rerun of this scene? No. An expanded road has cut right through the beach. Progress. A ripple of contentment all the same.

Córdoba, to the south-west, stood as the final destination. Sagunto, north of Valencia, didn't stand as a final destination. Just the opposite. It fell, a long way. An enormous citadel, high up on a hill, it surveys all the land and sea around, and can be seen most impressively from the A7 motorway. Sagunto, like Palestine Masada. Both carved in history for their mass suicides. A real carve-up. Sagunto resisting Hannibal in 218 BC, and Masada the Romans in AD 72. Carthaginians and Romans clearly had more horrors in store for the besieged than mere suicide. All dead with one difference. No Dead Sea Scrolls in Sagunto. Scroll down Sagunto, and you'll see what I mean. Long way down, mind you.

The interior was reached with one long lift, not the vertical aeroplane sort. Wine-growing area of Jumilla. Jaén, next. Near an expansive marshy area, a *nava*, of enormous historical significance. Here, at the *Navas de Tolosa*, in 1212, a sort of Spanish 1066 learnt by all schoolchildren. Castile, Aragón and Navarra ganged up on those heathen Moors. Believers but still miscreants. Can you be that? Decision time. Defeat and *Reconquista* job done. Had started in 718 in no more than a skirmish in Covadonga,

Asturias. King Juan Carlos's son, Felipe, now *Príncipe de Asturias* for this very reason. Emblem, he is, incarnation of the values of Christian Spain. Push off, you Moors, no mooring left for you. Started mooring again, have the Moors. All along that celebrity coast. Down Málaga way. Yachts galore. All the more for the Moor. Oil and soft-soaping. Keeps things turning.

1492. You should've heard of that. Nope. Fall of Granada. The Moor's on the floor. For five hundred years. But there is more, much more. 1492, forward go the Spanish Christians in the all-conquering, imperial western thrust. Best Western, this. Tarik may have stepped onto Spanish mainland in 711. But anything you can do I can do better. So spoke Columbus in 1492 on the island of San Salvador. Tarik on the Spanish mainland. Me, on the Spanish Main. Check all this in Chapter 9.

And more again on 1492. Sefardí Jew, in pain, expelled from Spain. Wandered Middle East and North Africa. Some in Central Europe, like the Russian Ashkenazi lot.

And more on Granada. Let's stay there for a couple of days. See the Alhambra fountains? Washington Irving's the man. Read his *Chronicle of Granada* and *Tales from the Alhambra*? They'll keep our feet firmly on the ground. Earthquake or no earthquake. And that's breaking new ground. A few paragraphs just below.

Tales are to do with canaries. Two tales. Or tails, if you wish. And canaries are not from the Canaries. No old wives' tale, this. Let **Narrative 1** run like this. Recorded in local newspaper. Scene seen by a bank clerk in Granada.

'What's that fellow up to? Coming in with four, covered-up boxes? Looks chipper, all smiles. Squeaking coming from his boxes. Odd, this. What's he got in his pocket? Hey, mate, what are you chucking all over the place? Coming over here, too. Looks like birdseed, to me. And you stay that side of the window. Hell! he's got four cages. Canaries inside. There's a catch here somewhere. He's undoing the cage catch. Bloody hell! What's going on? They're everywhere! At least *veinte* [20] *canarios*. Flapping about, clawing away, screeching, dollopping. We're flapping about, too. *¡Manos* *arriba!* [Hands up!]. Mustn't get in a flap. He's flying off with the till takings. Can't phone the *policía*. On tables, chairs, picture rails, typewriters. Can't cope.' 'Did they catch him?' 'A couple of days later. Clawed back most of the pesetas.' 'But surely the workers could have been a bit more cagey?' 'Dunno. He certainly wasn't a bird brain.'

Probably had it in for the *Banco de Santander*. Founder and boss with an odd name. What's he called? Won't believe this. Emilio Botín. So what? *Botín* = booty! The Barbarossa banker. Our canary man, ended up sick as a parrot when caught. Even so, must have learnt a trick or two from Long John Silver.

Narrative 2: A few days later. Canaries are touchy. Try an earthquake or two on them, or under them. Up and down on their perches, squawking, shrilling, they catch that tremor before their owners. Not a pause in their paws. *Granadinos*, all of a twitch, all of a shudder even, make a beeline for the canary man. The man from the Canaries? No silly. The man who sells canaries. But what for? To buy a canary.

Fly in the ointment. None left. All been snatched up by the bank fellow. A seismic shift in buying habits. Who's at fault? The fault line, I suppose. But he could never have got away with it. Flies in the face of the facts. Runs counter to any common sense. Even at the counter.

Jaén to Córdoba. An oven. No surprise. This whole Guadalquivir basin is called *la sartén de España* (the frying pan of Spain). *Spaniards* and not *Spanish speakers*. Genders between the Iberian Peninsula and Spanish America are always bending. Why Spaniards say *la sartén* and Pan-Spanish America changes the gender to *el* baffles us all. Surely Columbus, Cortés and Pizarro had nothing to do with this reversal of genders. They were straight?

The journey through the province of Córdoba cut into the mathematically precise layout of olive groves, distinguished by interminable rows of olive trees. Keeps the nation's heart beating in a healthy, rhythmic way. Serve it up in that frying pan, and a hearty meal is had by all. Winding around hills, the car came across Cabra, suddenly appearing from nowhere. Read Laurie Lee's *As I Walked out One Summer's Morning* and *A Rose in Winter* as you turn that bend, and you'll see what I mean.

Cabra, a lost little town hidden away in the Sierra Morena. Religious festivals there are aplenty. Poor old Virgin left out in the winter cold up on a hill in that sanctuary. Cries a bit, so bring her down for the annual September feast. Down she comes, carried on a portable platform by six stalwarts. Rough, stony path. See them a mile off. Clouds of dust. *Egabrenses*, the locals from Cabra, follow her, lachrymose. What's that word? Don't lose tears if you can't work it out. Deep in emotional and religious fervour. Deep in dust, too. Go up and meet them. No knee-jerk reaction, please. Even for those kneeing their way down. Or barefoot. Want some footage? Try Mascagni's *Cavalleria Rusticana*. Jesus carried too. Bound to get carried away, you are, with that tear-jerking *Easter Hymn*.

Intending to stay a couple of nights in Córdoba, applied at a bar for a room. Ten o'clock at night, early for *cordobeses*. Barman led along a long corridor. At the end, knock on door. Reply from the other side: 'Un momento', followed by bright gap in door. A few pleasantries. Then: Can this *señor* sleep in here? Extra body for the sleeper for the night in the same room. A single occupant sitting exams for the *magisterio* (teaching profession). Next morning's lowdown while still in bed. From Pedroches, up north, he hailed.

Stayed longer than anticipated, so thumbing it plan derailed. Rail travel back on track. Go back up north? *¿Hoy?* (Today?). Sorry, *Señor*, end of August, *días punta* (days of intense traffic). Valencia had to wait for three days. Rail plans derailed, too. New train of thought. Shared room, still there? Same bar. Same room, *Señor*? Bed occupied. 'No se preocupe' (Don't worry). Fears allayed. Another room, exiguous. Tough nut to crack is *exiguous*. You can guess it means 'small'. Same low price. Same incident but in reverse. Two o'clock in the morning, knock on the door. 'Señor, ¿se puede entrar?' ('Can I come in?'). Asleep, but quick off the pillow: 'Claro que sí' (Of course). Not really a bitter pill to swallow on the pillow. But wallet now under pillow. New occupant, a fellow, I suppose. Could only suppose in the dark. He lay, somewhere, got up at about five and left, presumably had marked out his day for the market. From the depths of slumber, to the sale of cucumber, that was his number.

The day for Córdoba station. Things had not moved since the *Renacimiento* (Renaissance). 'No me lo creo, No me lo creo...' (I don't believe it...), I kept on repeating. Can't be true. Should have guessed. Sign of the times. A timetable, unchanged and seemingly unchangeable, engraved in large letters, and in **STONE**, as if on a grave. A gravestone? Did this say something about their rail system, RENFE (Red Nacional de Ferrocarriles Españoles)? Córdoba > Madrid, Córdoba > Sevilla, Córdoba > Valencia, and the opposite, all times stood out for eternity. Had the Romans already assumed responsibility for the railways? Gravitas at work? Eternity the Romans aimed for in all their grand architectural designs. The railway line from Córdoba to Madrid led back to Roman aspirations to immortality. Ran along the same lines as the aqueducts in Segovia, Nîmes, or the monuments in the Roman Forum. Maybe the railway builders had in mind the Roman city of Mérida, north of Sevilla, close to Portugal. After all, they must have known the Roman origins of the name Mérida = *urbs emerita*, or even those of Zaragoza = *Caesarea Augusta*.

Spain's post-war (World War II) economy had been more than sluggish. Had suffered enormously, both from her civil war, and the economic blockade imposed upon her until 1954 by the victorious Allies. A consequence of her tacit support for the Axis. Any plans for investment on the rail network simply ran into the buffers.

How do you board a train with a valid ticket for a valid seat? Climb in, find the compartment, and sit down. But climb in you can't. Jam-packed, compartments, corridors, toilets, anywhere for space. So you climb in. Like in the Alps. Force yourself through the window! But, no seat for you. You'd guessed that. Guessed no rucksack room either. Forget it, *amigo*! Crammed in the corridor.

88

Try judicious reasoning. Threaten *Ferrocarriles Españoles* (Spanish Railways). Lost for all eternity. Keen to pee? Peevish, you stick it out, not that, silly. Urgency becomes more urgent. Peeing perils in foreign lands. Squash a way to the end of the train. Arc it over the rail, in a favourable direction. Train it away from the train, again and again. Heavens knows how the fair sex coped. Spanish railways are up there somewhere. Built for eternity and left us to it. Toilets for the ladies, then? Any chance of a peaceful pee? Three or four passengers respond in despair. No sign of movement, except yours. Diarrhoea doesn't bear thinking about. As devastating as trying to spell diarrhoea. (Look away now and have a go, the spelling, of course.)

Thus end, on a lavatorial note, thumbs up travels. Sounds like a travel agent. The train, with bloated bladders, trots on to Valencia. Get there undefiled? With the trots, you won't. Up to Barcelona, then back to France, home of private peeing and polite society.

3

Signs of the Times

What luck! Graduation on two fronts. A degree, and from two to three pedals, unless you're already up to an automatic. Still, clutch, brake and accelerator were good enough, and they found a way all over Europe, North Africa and the Americas (back to two pedals here), from Alaska to Mexico and Argentina. And that goes for languages, too. Really in the driving seat, twice over. A new, more powerful engine of development. Signing up to a revolution in travel. Wheels turning faster.

Bikes have run their cycle. Now, languages and cars. Changing gears and changing languages, same thing really. Have to be quicker on both. Language is the very texture of travel, you don't know if you're speaking English, French, Spanish or even Italian. End up speaking the wrong language to the new arrival. The brain, running on Moscatel, just keeps on in the same mode. 'Don't understand,' she says, at the fiesta. 'Zut alors! Thought you were Martine I was speaking to.' 'No, *Señor*, I'm Adriana. Spanish for me, please. We've changed places, Martine and me.' 'Don't understand. I'm John. Just flown in from London. No Italian for me.' *Zut, zut, zut!* A cerebral merry-go-round.

Three pedals and four wheels took my wife and me, with children, to the nooks and crannies of the world inaccessible to two pedals. And it wasn't any old car. No, the Ingmar Bergman classic, the trustworthy old warhorse of a Volvo Estate, the timeless vehicle you saw in the sixties and seventies, in *Wild Strawberries*, carrying the professor from Stockholm to Lund. Honorary degree for a lifetime's achievement. Reappears in, among others, *Scenes from a Marriage*. Something solid, reliable and congenial about the Volvo. The Bergman comparison ends there. No dreamlike, vaguely disturbing, dark flashbacks. No haunting by tenuous ghosts of the professor's memory. Youthful optimism in our Volvo. No Bergman morbid, tormented psychology here. Could see why his next-door neighbour, the Norwegian Ibsen, hived off to Italy for shades of bright blue. The Mediterranean did the same for our Volvo.

Steady on, Ron. Getting ahead of ourselves. Still, with the Mediterranean in mind, the temptation is always lurking. Back up to the cloudier Channel skies and disembarking at Cherbourg. First sign: 'Tenez la droite' (Keep to the Right), and they've got it in other languages, too. English signs, back in UK, must have put all these foreigners on the wrong track. No problem, really, for you just follow everyone else. Hold on, beware in the open countryside. Never used to see all those roundabouts. Circle after circle nowadays. Ought to be used to them by now. All to do with going round, wheels, that is.

Watch out for that stupid injunction at a junction. *Priorité à droite* looms up. Here you are, tootling along quite blithely and safely on a main road, lulled into a sense of security by those restful, wide-open spaces. Not followed or preceded by a *single* Citroën Deux Chevaux, when *Grands dieux!* (Ye Gods!), out pops from your right that cheeky Deux Chevaux of Pierre and his *petite amie*. Bothered by what is coming from their left on the main road? *Non, Madame!* 'Be prepared,' says Baden Powell's crew. You'd better be. He's right. Pierre's coming from your right. All right for a horse and cart, but... You're OK if the notice does not say 'Priorité', but 'Passage protégé' which means that you are protected from lunatic and unlooked-for lurches from your right. But don't bet on it. And keep the insurance handy. The bewildering, and even frustrating, feature of all this: not a single member of the French nation seems to accord a blessing to 'Priorité à droite'. Thirty kilometres into the French landscape and thirty *priorité à droites*. But you ain't seen nothing yet; just wait and see what the Spaniards are storing up for you below, not to mention Berlusconi's Italians.

One reassuring road sign, not just in France, Spain and Italy, but in all Western Europe is 'STOP!' Stop and admire it. You can really take it in. It means: you stop. Slow and crawl forward to that white line. But you say, can't always see from where I'm sitting, if the car stops at the white line. Got to go beyond. I'm sitting in the wrong place on the right. Nothing's right. But everything's right for *Monsieur*. Watch out for that gendarme behind the bush. He's not invisible, you know. With his blue *képi* sticking up over the hedge.

STOP. A splendidly all-purpose European notice preventing unwary drivers from careering into traffic that really does have priority. But funny, this. Our Spanish friends can't say STOP. They can't say an *s* without putting an *e* in front of it. Takes longer to say STOP and probably longer to stop. Accident rate higher over there. Congenital failure in saying STOP anything to do with it? They can only say *España* and *estop*.

Brits can't pronounce the Spanish *jota* and struggle with a sort of *h*. Keeps cropping up these days in Arabic names, like Bahrein. So, nothing for the Spanish nation to be ashamed about, you might say, for they do have sterling qualities, despite their inability to say pound sterling = *libra esterlina*.

Can forgive our trans-Pyrenean friends these tiny lapses but they flaunt their notice 'FC' everywhere. Baffles not just us Brits but all their other European neighbours. Anyone this side of the Pyrenees takes FC as 'Football Club'. After all, don't we say 'Chelsea FC'? And don't the French say 'Nantes FC'? When a non-Spaniard comes across 'FC' they imagine Messi, not Fessi (FC), scoring the winning goal for Barcelona in the European Cup Final. But, look as hard as Messi kicks that ball, and you will never find a football stadium by a railway track. Yet, throughout the country, whenever a road crosses a railway line, or vice versa, there are signs telling you that it is an 'FC'. Why so? The 'FC' sign in Spain means **Ferrocarril** = Railway. But, let us not be carried away and delude ourselves, for the Spaniards, to our great consternation, actually use 'FC' for Football Club as well. One hundred thousand Barcelona soccer-mad supporters are there to prove it. Barcelona *FC* is their crowning glory. Football supporters travelling to a match on the railway do cherish one goal, don't they? They go from one FC to another. All very handy for footie.

Almost uniquely, and no puzzlement for the Italians here. Probably the only European nation to call the game of football *calcio*, give or take a letter or two. And they're not calcium white by a long chalk. Always getting yellow cards. Even red ones. Never white.

Not all road signs are reassuring. You are a Frenchman behind the wheel. You strike up against the English 'Soft verges'. Care here. Alarm horns sound. And watch that horn. This has to be pressed home. 'Soft' (*molles*) stuck next to French *verge(s)*, you'll see why and you'll go limp with laughter. What sticks out in all this is *verges*; nothing to do with *virgin*. Not so sure though.

French doc checks on wee Willie's 'willie', his *verge* = his penis. Reread the sign *à la française*: *Verges molles* = *Soft willies*. No erection here on English motorways, please. English seem to be taking a hard line. Keep that willie weak. No thrust of lust, whatever the potent muscle of the car. Don't want a cock-up, and bang into someone, do we? However swollen you are with Gallic pride. We know *le coq sportif* is their pride and joy. So just play it down. Hard luck if you're feeling randy, and on the verge of... Think again!

Spare a thought for the same driver as he leaves the English main road. Stylish area of mansions, this. Desirable and Residential, of the millionaire sort. Erection embarrassment avoided, he needs to stiffen his resolve. What's up? Bangs into the occasional 'Most Dirty' signs. No sense here, he'd say. Highly desirable residential area side by side with 'For Sale'? Our Gallic friend, in driving mode, would see and read here 'Fort sale'. Even our schoolboy

French cottons on to *sale* as 'dirty'. And if he's got his GCSEs off to a T, he'd know that *fort* is a posher way of saying *très*.

Glee all round with the notice Art Sale. Nothing to do with pornographic nudity, at least this side of the Channel.

Spare a thought for their opposite number, the English driver. The 'verge' business but in reverse. You cross the Channel. Long, happy strips of road stretch out before you in the countryside. Crops are blooming, sky nice and clear. Very fertile, at least the soil is. But you may not be for long. All had been well with the world. Then BANG. You strike up against the startling notice: BALL-TRAP. Is this the latest form of castration, custom-prepared at La Châtre, not far away, or at Castres, praise be, further away, in the south? Panic-stricken, a touch of relief from the acceleration pedal. *Zut, alors!* There it is again, 50 kilometres down the road. BALL-TRAP leaps out at you. Almost catches you by the short and curlies. This time, you play ball, but hide both of them well away. You proceed warily. On the balls of your toes, you look over the fence. Not castration. White plates shooting skyward, targets for rifles. Cracked it, you have. Male relief. *Clay pigeon shooting*. Off you go. But the balls thing hangs around in your mind. What a low-down trick. Generates fun for them. Balls to that.

Just as well I kept well down, didn't get hit in the... Imagine medical exam. Check in for a check-up. While you're at it, doc, check my balls for irregular lumps to stamp out male cancer. Ouch! You must be nuts.

Road signs can be disorienting, if you get things wrong. When you come across the French *unique*, or the Spanish *único*, or even the Italian *unico* when they are talking about direction, don't fall for it. You'll almost certainly not be heading towards something unique, a spectacular view, a fabulous, undreamt-of, Shangri-La experience. Caught out again. Just the opposite = *one-way*, narrow thoroughfare, fraught with peril. Anything but attractive. Their idea of *unique*, cunning device to put English speakers off the track.

And don't speed away with the idea that the motorways A1 or A7 (*autoroute/ autopista/ autostrada*) in Europe are just like our A1, a mere trunk road, so free. Get your euros ready for the toll. Mind you, plan things well ahead and beat them at their own game. Toll won't take its toll on long lengths of motorway. France and Spain alike. Go round Madrid as many times as you like without lightening your pocket. See why the Catalans are always grousing. Need all their euros up front. Game of aim: coins, darts style, into baskets to keep going around Barcelona. Don't miss and have the right cash. Or else, hooting queues behind. Baskets there are aplenty. Go south, young man, it's cheaper, but keep away from that wild race on the Mediterranean A7.

Get ready for the hooters. Traffic lights. Charge of the light brigade. You leading it, in front of the queue? Amber to green, move before amber or those *madrileños*'ll put you on red alert. Hoot, hoot, hoot, they shoot. So common is the horn that even in pole position, the driver hoots. A bit of a hoot.

Should have given the cold shoulder to Valencia thirty years ago. High season and hot. Why? Whole of Europe in state of frenetic mobilization, steaming down in invasion mode. Driven by some hellish heliotropic passion along the coastal A7 motorway. Only delight, not Turkish, but Arabic. Costa de Azahar sign (Orange Blossom Coast). Solar stampede converging on traffic lights. Where? North of the urban sprawl of Valencia. Sudden, prolonged halt. Imagine thousands and thousands of vehicles streaming back for miles at a final A7 toll gate, at the height of summer. Welcome to the *semáforo de Europa* (traffic lights of Europe). Fun and games for the *valencianos*.

The Italians are in on the joke. *Semáforo*? Same word for traffic lights. That's all, in their appreciation list. Wait, Signore Berlusconi, like everyone else. Sweltering. Air conditioning, please. Take the heat out of frustration. Joke's on just about everyone. Lord of the Rolls and the big black Merc are the only ones to keep their cool. They alone could afford air conditioning thirty years ago. Not cool at all, this. Who's this young whippersnapper? *Cruz*

Roja (Red Cross), hordes of medical students in attendance intent on trying out, for free, newly found skills. Blood pressure? Certainly *Señora*. Bit of auscultating? They auscultate here, you know. What's that? No English medic on hand? Listening in on your ticker, ask any Continental Joe Bloggs. Swooning, dehydration, heart attacks, we deal with the lot. Spanish evening television loved it. Warning signs were there. See the semaphore boy in 'The boy stood on the burning deck'? He would have been just over there to the left on the sea. And 'burning', that's the word. Temperatures rising. Everyone jumping up and down, getting a bit mercurial. No chance of a time- or life-saving diversion. Orange, road-less groves over to the right as far as the horizon, and to the left, well, there could have been that semaphore boy. He's not needed now, though, for the A7 goes round Valencia. Never worked out what happened to him. Mark Twain's Tom Sawyer knew, though. Check it out in Chapter 12 of Mark's Tom.

Road signs are one thing. Signs on the sides of lorries are another. That's the case of 'TIR', and that's where European Transport comes in, in France = *Transport international routier*. All is revealed in the following. All very transparent. No glass-darkly, this.

Never heard two stained-glass windows talking to each other? It's a bit like Cervantes' two dogs having a chat outside a hospital in *El coloquio de los perros* (The Dogs' Colloquy). It went like this:

Scene is chez *Ron. LAL (Lady Light), LOL (Lord Light)*
LAL: Who's that?
LOL: It's Ron's Breton friends, Philippe et Martine. They're French. Seen them lots of times. You know the fellow, that's the Astérix nutter who's got more memorabilia of that little Breton than he has furniture. His wife Martine's going crazy for he just buys more and more.
LAL: What're they saying?

LOL: Ron said we were for the dump. Philippe et Martine went ballistic. They're a bit cracked about old things you can reuse. They call it *faire de la récup*, short for *récuperation*. Looks as though we're soon off to Nantes. That's in France. Long journey. We'll need recuperation.

Two weeks later. Still chez *Ron.*
LAL: Our replacements up there, in bedrooms and living room, look nice. Still, Philippe et Martine'll look after us in our new surroundings, won't they?
LOL: Plenty of room in this car. Enough for two piles of us. Frames 'n all. Pretty heavy, though. After all, we're fourteen, but it is an estate. Didn't we ought to have 'TIR' on the side of the car?
LAL: What's that?
LOL: All French lorries sign up to it if they go abroad. Without it, you'd be treading a dangerous path. Transport international routier. Neat, that. TIR also means 'aim' or getting your direction right. A bit like that clever 'AVE' for the new fast train in Spain.
LAL: What's clever about that?
LOL: AVE means Alta Velocidad Española (Spanish High Speed). But the real trick is that in Spanish ave means 'bird'. Now, that really is flying. The Spanish are just as smart. Three Ave Marias and you're there.

Following day.
LAL: Windows on the world, that's us. Lead lights led all round Europe. The crossing's easy. Feel quite posh in this tunnel. We should be going towards Paris. Hey, we're going south, not west. No sense, this. I heard the first stop is Bergères-les-Vertus. Odd name, even for the French, I suppose. Nothing virtuous there, is there? It won't be if it's anything like the Folies Bergères.

Next day.
LOL: Gee, we're off to Grenoble! What's going on here? Still, can admire the scenery, *vino* country, you know, Burgundy, and then there's the Alps, and that lovely peak, the Belle Donne and La Grande Chartreuse. Ron's going to unload us *chez des amis* in Grenoble and hear that heavenly Puccini and Verdi music at Verona.

Four days later. Back to Grenoble from Verona.
LAL: They're back again. Next stop, *amigos* in Barcelona. I heard the lady in Grenoble call us vitraux. I thought 'stained-glass window' in French was *vitrail.*
LOL: Yes, but *vitraux* is plural. Ron could explain it. He's pretty hot at that sort of thing.

One day later. Barcelona.
LAL: Same again. They're unloading us. PatRon (neat that, Pat + Ron, sort of fits together) are off to Calpe to see all their friends and do a spot of windsurfing and paella. Notice they're calling us *vidrieras* here? That's an easy plural. Just stick an *s* on the end.

Four weeks later. Barcelona again
LOL: PatRon are back again. Had a super time, what with all their friends speaking those weird lingos.
LAL: Nantes, here we come. And with a bit of French, too. At least we know the plural for *vitrail.* Once put in our proper place, we'll be preening ourselves like those coloured pheasants, as important as Chartres and Notre Dame, and it'll be so pleasant looking down on those Nantes people enjoying themselves with their friends. Everything rose-tinted for them. Even more for the visitors looking up at us. What could be better than admiring us up here and tucking into a *repas gastronomique* down there, washed down with a *bourgueil.* All we get is rain. Still, Ron loves talking French

with a bite to eat. And he can go on looking up to us every time they come, even from the toilet seat. One of us is even in the bathroom. Usually dry in there.

LOL: Hey, wait a mo. Didn't PatRon do some furniture shifting for Philippe and Martine, a few years back?

LAL: That's where the Nantais got the idea from. You remember Philippe was living in Littlehampton, decided Martine was the girl for him, so he ups sticks, leaves his job and off he goes back to Nantes. It looks like his *petite amie* outpaced his passion for us English. You know she was a cracker. I reckon you could have fallen for her yourself.

LOL: You bet. Still, that's all gone now. Anyway, Philippe had a ton of knick-knacks, and one of those tiddlers of a car, not much bigger than a Deux Chevaux. That's where Ron came in. Meeting at the dockside at Portsmouth, loading the kitchen sink into Ron's Volvo, and Bisto! It all ends up in Nantes.

LAL: That's not the end of the story, you know that. Following summer, Ron turns up again on their doorstep, and what do you know! Kitted out in chauffeur's attire – chauffeur's a French word, isn't it? someone heating things up – and cap n'all, polishes up his brand-new silver Bergman Volvo, lays on the usual trimmings. Church-bound are all three. Drives them there in style and then to the *mairie*. Town hall.

LOL: French wedding with an English chauffeur, Jees, that's hot stuff! Not James but Firmin, in one easy French lesson. Church and Mairie bit done, with Ron saluting every metre of the way. All three finally set off for the grandest of receptions, guests hooting behind along the way. That was all really swell.

LAL: Ron's free European transport service didn't end there. You know he had a French friend from Grenoble, really Algerian. She could lay it on in French and Arabic, pretty bright, really. Done more than a couple of books with Ron.

Had a phenomenal memory, recited whole chunks of lovely French poetry to Ron over the phone. Would listen to it all in sheer admiration and disbelief. Couldn't get over it. I know; I watched him from my high-up window before we were Volvoed off to Nantes

LOL: Malliga, smart girl, she. Switch from French to Arabic and then to English. On secondment (that's a clever word for a stained-glass window to come up with), stayed a couple of years at the university in Bristol, decided to return to skiing country, and what d'you know, Ron collects all her stuff from Bristol, and all three do that TIR trick again, Grenoble this time.

LAL: Ron must have been getting fed up with all this toing and froing.

LOL: Not a bit of it. He loved it. He loved it as much as Malliga's couscous. Should have advertised his transport skills to the rest of Europe, gratis, you know. And he could have learnt more Czech and Polish.

But back to signs, animal signs. In Spain, and all to do with sheep, although the signs are always of cows. I thought they were pulling the wool over my eyes until I really looked into it. So let's read the sheep's *Notes from a Spanish Dairy Diary*.

I produce cheese up in the north, Basque country. Nice, fairly sedentary way of life. Macario, the shepherd fellow who looks after me, got me interested in Internet. I tried my paw at it, and soon became a dab paw. I get male and female emails. Especially from an *oveja* (a ewe) who does a lot of wandering. I follow her trail by email. Here is one day in her life. She writes:

'You may be surprised I speak and write in English. You should be. Spanish is my first language. As with my feathered friend you'll come across in La Mamola in the next chapter, I learnt English a bit later. Started off with a pen in a pen.

Graduated to computers but never reached as high up the educational tree as that chirpy chap. Even so, did get more than a BA degree in BAA Languages. But, I reckon my leafy pal hit the heights with a doctorate. He's a real star turn. Brilliant. Doctorate, yes, but doctored no. Like some of my undoctored canine buddies. Ruttish, so still has plenty of (pro)creative energies. Not in a rut. No writer's block.

'My story is a bit wild and woolly, not properly thought out. What do you expect from a wandering sheep? If you have any questions at the end of this tail (I'm a bit dyslexic but can spell "dyslexic", so can't be that bad. However, was tempted by *dislexyc*. My maa taught me *i* comes before *y* in the alphabet), I'll be ready to field them. The event you are about to read forms part of the warp and woof of Madrid's tradition and folklore. You must believe this. It may seem a shaggy dog story in places, but it's more than just a yarn.

'Don't often visit the Spanish capital, but today's the BIG DAY. Mid-April. We first set off, a thousand of us, a week ago, from Ciudad Real, further south. Too hot there in summertime, but OK in winter. So other way round in October. They call it *trashumancia*. English readers don't need me to carry over a translation for that. Padded our way through Toledo, no time for a dekko at El Greco, but saw lots of geckos. We're a long way from road signs, aren't we? That's where you're wrong. Journey's pretty easy, really, but main roads are a bit tricky. Occasionally, I look up at the crossing, and see the picture of a bovine creature. A cow, for the agriculturally ignorant. There she is on a big board with, underneath, "CAÑADA". Humans often add "REAL", so we end up with CAÑADA REAL = ROYAL CATTLE TRACK or DROVER'S ROAD. We cross over here, sovereign of all we survey. Don't *beep-beep* for us sheep. Everything shipshape for the sheep. Motorists, wait, *por favor*.

'Wait even in Madrid. Checked out the history of this on Internet. Alfonso the Wise gave us this prize in 1273, but not for free. Just have to foot, or paw, a twice-yearly bill of 50 coins at the *Ayuntamiento* (Town Hall) for a sort of rite of passage. Don't ask me how much the coin *maravedí* is. Ask Don Quixote, he should help. *Maravedís* you pay fifty, but you have to be nifty. You pay for a day, that's all I can say. Nothing like it. Rumour has it that the *Ayuntamiento* is still fleecing us, at least our shepherd fellow. He gets his own back by fleecing our back. Sells the offcuts.

'In April we peak, that's really unique. Plenty of room for us, too. 70 metres wide is the path, how about that? No cars, buses, just the underground. Super day is the Fiesta de la Transhumancia. I just adore all those *madrileños* gawking at us. They've just arrived in droves. Bleating away they are. I've got a gut feeling they're *viscerally attached to the cleanliness of Madrid's main arteries. It's because of all those little round dollops. Dollops all the way from the Casa de Campo to the Plaza Cibeles, and that's before we get to the *Ayuntamiento*. Mind you, we have every right to drop in at Plaza Cibeles with our droppings. Cibeles was the Greek earth goddess, like the South American Pachamama. Those teeny round balls keep her nice and fertile. A trail of offloading, good job it's not offal, may be a trial for the locals, but we're in the ecology business, and we do a good job, a big job, in fact. This is not tripe I'm relating. It's tripe-releasing dollops.

'Done this trip a few times. Know the route but can't read the street signs. They're too high up for a tiny chap like me. And on my way up north I can't see for all the wool in Spain. Of course, when I'm up there, things get sheared and cleared. Goes without saying I can read "CAÑADA REAL" in both directions. I do know that after Cibeles we go off left to the Puerta del Sol (Sunny Gate), then down

---

*I challenge any of those Madrid onlookers to spell *viscerally*, let alone pronounce it. You can see my lexical dexterity takes some b(l)eating. It's as easy as eating. And that's in a foreign language, too. How about you, Mister and Mrs Reader?

to the Calle Mayor (High Street), and there you have the Town Hall. Drinks all around before the Calle Mayor again, and then north along the Paseo de la Castellana. I appreciate your attention which is why I'm translating as much as possible. I struggle with the Paseo de la Castellana, however. Macario told me it can mean two things: a lady who lives in Castile, and a *chatelaine*. Posh, elegant French word that: mistress of a castle. Sir Walter Scott uses it in *The Abbott*. A lovely, rich, romantic, aristocratic sound. So, that's why I like going that way.

'The locals like the colour and the music, all those horsemen and politely trained doggies rounding us up all the time. Sometimes, some of our number run off to the left and the right, even escape for a moment. Fortunately, no one's looking at me for a scapegoat. I'm supposed to be a responsible leader, you know.

'The children, a bit sheepish to start with, never seen so much wild life around, sidle up to their parents. They love the tinkling of our bells and the thousand-year-old sounds of the *arrieros* who chivvy us along to the northern side of the capital. Straight out of the Middle Ages, bang into the middle of Madrid. A fascinating marriage of the old and the new. All led by *Macario*, the Spanish shepherd *por excelencia*. Makes you think of *Sebastián*, Spanish chauffeur of the lord's car. Driving sheep and driving cars, not much difference really. Drive on, James. On the right, if you have to.

'One of my caprine friends asked me what I do up north. She butted in straight away, asking me what "caprine" meant. All to do with goats. *Capra* in Latin, I explained. I went on to say that in La Rioja it's not so hot as in the south, but I make up for it 'cos that's when I'm on heat. I occasionally enjoy a good ram. Rammed by a ram, can't go wrong. Especially when he feels horny. Mind you, he's nearly always horny. Seen any pictures of him? I love to get tangled up in those curly horns. Never on the horns of a dilemma when

I lock horns with him. Screw a ewe. Ram that dic(tum) home. Zoophilia's not a dirty word, whatever those prurient humans think. Debauched sign of the times when they zoom in on it, too.

'That male b(l)eating sends me into ecstasy. It's music to my ears, not that we bother about the rhythm method. My French's not so hot, so I would prefer a Spanish horn to the French horn, if you can buy one. Especially when played by RAM, you know the Royal Academy of Music. I bet you can hear me bleating from my mail. By the way, you've probably noticed *b(l)eating* twice. Quite a feat, don't you think?

'Tomorrow, we're off to Guadalajara, Soria, and on to La Rioja, furthest point north. Up there, a good clean-up. Posh hair cut for those humans' warm winter clothes, merino pullovers, merino's Spanish you know, and plenty of cheese. Got to get the best out of us, haven't they? I'm pretty public-spirited. Then, October sees us crossing back over those *cañadas* again. Five hundred kilometres for the round trip. You motorists watch out for us once more at the *cañada*, and don't hare past. Jug is for you if you race at the chase.

'Not only do I write and speak English, I read it too. Saw that with Sir Walter above. Very keen on sheep crossing roads, I am. No surprise to you readers, surely. Particularly when it rams two people together in amorous circumstances as the bus suddenly stops in Winifred Holtby's *South Riding*. Or when Richard Hannay of *Thirty-nine Steps* fame escapes from the clutches of his detective pursuers, blocked as they are by, you've guessed it, a flock of sheep. Hardy's Gabriel Oak beats them all in my affection stakes. Keeps us alive, he does, swollen as we are with wind. Punctures us on the side, as well as Bathsheba's pride. Deflation all the way round. *Far from the Madding Crowd.* I'm crazy about that novel.'

So ends the email from my woolly cousin. I'd better get

back to what I do best, have to chew like a ewe, must get ready for the squirting lark. I can't just go on milking my cousin's email for ever.

Want more animal signs? Over the Atlantic to Mexico. Horses bred not just for John Ford Westerns but for farm work, too. And *bred* is the point, or is it? Out in the Mexican countryside, ambiguity reigns without rain. What do you make of: *Cruce de caballos?* OK, *cruce* is crucial, and *caballos*, that's easy enough. Seen any saddled-up John Wayne films? What about *cruce*, then? *Cruce.* Two meanings. One nice and clear = crossroads. *Cruce de caballos* = a crossing point for Pancho with his horses. So far so good. So, where's the catch? Well, there is one. *Cruce*'s used for cross-breeding, as well as crossing of a road. Mare and ass. Is the sign a signal for mule-breeding, or 'Drivers, beware of horses crossing the road?' Or be even more wary of cross-breeding at the crossroads? Rein in your imagination, Ron. Never saw Pancho for an explanation, in the middle of the Sonora Desert. Always sitting under a tree, arms folded around knees, buried beneath his sombrero, deep in sleep. Nice and stable, even at the stable. Let mare and ass, tethered close by, get on with the two-backed beast business by themselves. As a rule, not stubborn as a mule is Pancho, just lazy. He just ties up loose ends after mare and ass have done their business. Tether and leather, keep them together. Don't want to be hide-bound, do we?

Speaking of deserts, ever been to the Algerian Sahara? Or more precisely, to the sand dunes between Taghit and Timimoun? Let's assume you have. You will have come across a bewildering sign. You can't miss it. Or maybe the Bedouins, the Berbers or the Touaregs have dug it up. They'd have shown a bit of common sense if they had. Incontrovertible absurdity. It reads: ROUTE BARRÉE = NO THOROUGHFARE. Reasoning powers disappear in the sand, and on two grounds. a) there was no possible road leading off into the vast expanse (thousands of square kilometres) of shifting sand dunes: *Le Grand Erg Occidental,* and b) our ethnic friends, French shy, would not have understood the funny acute accent over the E > É. Shaky foundation of an argument, that. Come off it. Sign never existed. That's where you're wrong. A snap judgement has immortalized an absurdity. Photographed is Hadj caressing the notice. Have to trust him, even if not fresh from the Hadj, you know, the yearly Mecca pilgrimage. There for all to see. Could have been a bit of a leg pull. Any other proof? All other thoughts put on ice. Just as well. They wouldn't have lasted. No deep freezes.

More zany signs of the times? Watch that lad coming towards you, Sheriff. It's that Mexican actor, Cantinflas. Can't stop talking but says nothing, means nothing, wants nothing, does nothing. Takes an hour to explain he says nothing, means nothing, wants nothing, does nothing. Went round the world with David Niven in *Round the World in Eighty Days*. Sees the notice, even in Spanish: PROHIBIDO ENTRAR. Make sure he takes the noticeboard on board. Don't know where he'd take it to, mind you. We're slap bang in the Arizona desert. Nothing for miles around, gate, hut and horse. Not even a one-horse town. And then there's those howling prairie dogs. Howl and howl, and how they howl. No trees. Just cactus.

Where you going, pardner? Through that gate, Sheriff. No, *Señor!* And where d'ya think you're going? Tombstone. Tombstone City. Not through this gate, you ain't. Says *Tombstone*, don't it? You go round thisa way or thata way, but not through 'ere. I'd get lost, Sheriff. Don't want to go round the world again. One film's enough. Don't want to be led up the garden path, do I? And no Boothill Cemetery for me. OK for the OK Corral this way? Tell ya, pardner, not through here. Nitwit nit-picking. On and on. No Tombstone. So no OK Corral. A gate too far. No gate-crashing, either.

Any better with African road signs? You're in British-dictated Ghana. French-dictated Ivory Coast bound. On the left, you are in a 4x4. Steady now. Border somewhere round here. Soon know with the customs post. Wanna bet? You know you're still on the left. Still in Ghana? Dunno. Where's Ivory Coast? Dunno. Bloody hell! He's on our side of the road! No he's not, we're in Ivory Coast. We're on his side. Right in Ivory Coast, I mean on the right in Ivory Coast, left in Ghana. Bet garage repairs do a smashing trade. More signs, please.

Thousands more. And don't be left behind. Sweden wasn't. Left the left, Swedes veered to the right. 1980s. For good. Enlightened lot, with their Saabs and Bergman Volvos all lit up. 4x4 for 24 hours. Gone down a new route. Drive on the right, please, Bergman *et alii*. But, Mr Strindberg, you needn't bother. It's all a play, this world. Just an act.

Swedes blazed the trail. Easy for them with that 24-hour lighting. Did the Brits follow suit? No need. The *entente cordiale* did it for us. Like this.

National French radio. *France Inter. 13 heures. Décret gouverne-mental*, straight from the horse's mouth at the Élysée Palace: 'In the interests of international cooperation and harmony, driving on the left in France will be *obligatoire* from July 1.'

Panic and pandemonium. All French signs, vehicles, insurance etc. would need to be adapted to *conduite à gauche* (driving on the left). French thoughts run like this: Forget Henry V's Azincourt 1415. And, *zut alors*! Crécy with all those longbow arrows, *les rosbifs* deserve something better, if all they have for lunch is roast beef, Yorkshire pud and two veg. We know they gloat once off the Calais boat. But we'll let them off their gloating and boating. Hopeless at spelling, they are. Jees! Can't even spell Azincourt. *G* instead of *z*.

Panic stations throughout France, all on the morning of April 1, 1974. Gasping like fish out of water. The penny, or the franc, finally dropped. Fish out of water? Well, it was a *poisson d'avril*, wasn't it? An April fool prank. Impact in France? *Pas possible, Monsieur le Président Général de Gaulle.* Convincing it was, though. Whole French nation staggered, bowled over by such signal generosity. Gesture reaching global proportions. Fish were pleased, in their globe. Overseas territories, thousands of them, all change, please.

That was the trick. Orson Welles' radio adaptation of H. G. Wells' *War of the Worlds*. Funny, *Welles* and *Wells*. Hell of a difference with that extra *e*. Genuine Martian invasion? '*Monsieur le garagiste*, ow soon you change my steering wheel from left to right?' 'No sweat. Overnight.' But *Relax, Max!* All righted the same evening. Includes that English radio listener. He swallowed the bait, or fish, too. Hope it was *bouillabaisse*.

The sign of all signs to come. There they are, more than one large picture, hanging above you as you drive south on the dual carriageway out of Cherbourg. He's hanging in space, indelible memory of World War II. A Yank yanking at his parachute cord. Stuck on a village steeple. May we visit you, Sainte-Mère-Église, please? Funny name that, Holy-Mother-Church. Not so sure I need to go to church, did the conversion job on those signs from miles to kilometres back at Cherbourg. Here goes, all the same, for the mother of all battles in *next chapter*. Won't keep you hanging around.

Sketch map for a Motorised Odyssey

4

A Motorized Odyssey

Signs neatly consigned to the department of memory? Driving on the right all right? All set, then. Let's take one of our motorflights, among the fifty or so, from the cooler of temperate Cherbourg to the oven of Andalusian Spain, and see what we come up with on a trip into the nostalgia of remembrance lane. Step on board for a six weeks' odyssey and four thousand miles, route all planned! Even so, we're cranking up the exploration of the nooks and crannies of Western Europe. A spanking good time lies ahead.

On your left, *Mesdames, Messieurs,* going down the dual carriageway to Caen, invitations in English, if you please, to visit five beaches with English names. The English is actually on French maps. But peaches of beaches they are not. Gold Beach, Sword Beach and Utah Beach. Goes a bit strange with Omaha Beach, sounds a bit like Obama, or even that Osama Bin Liner fellow recently departed. Strange as well with Juno Beach. A Roman goddess and protectress of women, but didn't seem to bother about the men. Homophobic? Her hubby Jupiter didn't bother either. Still, beaches are there all the way. Private Ryan must have ended up on one of them on June 6, 1944.

Brakes now off ambition. Decidedly in the driver's seat. No more wheels of fortune. Wheels of power turning another page in the adventure of language. Really making inroads into French and France. Maybe avenues now. After all, not bike fifteen but car fifty miles an hour. The choice is ours. Cauldron Spain bound, driving worries all melting away. Fifty kilometres inland, you come

111

across, not Private Ryan, but a lion of a man. Maybe accidental hero, Dustin Hoffman mode.

Road? N13. Pull up here for it happened to me, John Steele, June 6, 1944. Went like this. Real kosher story. I sure was under the cosh.

John Steele. 82nd Airborne Division. Reporting for duty, Sir. With a name like John, I stand and fall like all those GIs. All for one and one for all. We are in, or above, Three Musketeers country, aren't we? Had been stationed near port, South of England. Can't tell which one. Spies around. All hush-hush before rush-rush. Now ready to go. Up there, standing, waiting for the command. 'Go! Go! Go!' Fifty 'Gos!' shot out by the officer in the Dakota plane. Officer could have been French. They scream 'Go!' too. Quicker than 'Allez-y!' or 'Vas-y!' Clip unhooked from the rail. We shoot out, one by one. Flash comes to mind before I'm shot out, or shot at: that ten-year-old boy serving up hot drinks and food, to all of us. Even for Leclerc's French guys. On their tanks, he climbed. Memento of de Gaulle, with Croix de Lorraine. Ron showed it to me.

Now past Cherbourg, over Sainte-Mère-Église. Down I jump, only one way. Mother-fucking four in the morning. Speckled bright mass. Blinded by light. Anti-aircraft fire. AKA = ack-ack. Pull that cord, John. Steel yourself, John Steele. Hurtling down. 'Fuck! Fuck! Fucking bad luck!' Struck unlucky. Leg hit by shrapnel. Direction doubtful. 'Chute caught on church steeple. Now hanging in space. 'Can't shoot. Hell's bells, Heller. This your Doc's doings, catch–22? Get on top of things, John. Start praying. You're in the right place. Three bloody Hail Marys.' 'Hey, you Yanks, don't say *Bloody*.' 'No, but we do say *Bloody Mary*. Could do with one right now.' As good as morphine it is, with a shot of vodka. Is this Hemingway's Robert Jordan straight out of *For Whom the Bell Tolls*? His lot for me ringing in my ears?

No peals of laughter, I can assure you. Striking a plangent chord. Life hanging by a thread. Is that a square down there? Or Dante's first circle of hell? Maybe it's safer up here, away from the bullets of battle. But I've got to bite the bullet. Gee I can't stand this, even with all this Government Issue.

Who's that? A son of a bitch of a Fritz, he of the blitz. Bless my soul. German field hospital. Steep(le) learning curve. Not all Fritzes are sons of bitches. Not Rudolf May, anyway. Up here, on the steeple, a real tower of strength, was he. But mayhem, despite Herr May. Eventually got on my tits did the boys from the blitz. Escape to GI lines. Saw stars, now hope to see the Stripes. Took French leave. Gerries should have been smarter. They take French leave in German too (*sich auf französisch empfehlen*). The ding-dong of battle slowly fading. Would make a perfect film with the ding-dong of the bells chiming in.

Had been a para in Sicily. Now here. Rehab. in England. More jumping later in Holland. Not for joy. Ups and downs aplenty, more downs than ups. End of war. Died in 1969. All those buckshee cigarettes. Throat cancer. Thank you *Lucky Strike*. Prefer the Sainte-Mère-Église strike.

Hung on for twenty-odd yearly visits to Sainte-Mère-Église. Here I am, on a tourist flyer, pictured below the church steeple. ¡A la Madonna! (Did Argentinian Spanish in the States, you know.) A flyer on a flyer! Hand raised, pointing up to my effigy, suspended in space, for all eternity. Pilgrimage in place, *sur la place* (in the square). Top of the tourist industry. Saved the village twice over. Saved them in life and death. Dollars keep pouring in from Americans by the busload. 'On vous salue [We salute you], John Steele.'

John Steele's feat. Landed on his feet did the film producer. Our John found immortality on the screen. Silver for Steele, nothing less. 1966 box-office rage, as wild as the rage below. Parodied rage became all the rage with the film *La Grande*

Vadrouille (The Big Stroll). It excited them all, from Paris to Perpignan. To Nice, as well. Nice to be in Nice. See it there. Number three in all-time ratings of French cinema. Director, Gérard Oudry, could not have dreamt up a more zany main lead than gap-in-teeth Terry Thomas. Clearly saw a gap in the market. Had to plug it somehow. Toffee-nosed accent of Terry. But nothing toffee-nosed about our American John. Couldn't speak like that for toffee. Even so, Terry gave him a really high profile, strung up there. Swept the board, the clipboard.

Often wondered why our Terry was chosen just this once for a leading role in a French film. Gérard Oudry must have hunted around in vain. Suppose TT filled in a gap while keeping it. Raced around France like at the Isle of Man's TT. In a car, not on a train. No need to mind the gap.

But the N13 dual carriageway calls again. Next stop: another battle scene, seventy metres long and fifty centimetres wide, a sort of forerunner of Goscinny and Uderzo's Astérix series. *Bande dessinée* or comic strip. Found a merry, seductive niche *chez* Gallic people. Not paper or film this time. Stitchwork of motley woollen colours. William our Conqueror's invasion of England. Hastings. His French won, and his lot stuck around for four hundred years. They ran half France from the courts of England. Keep France for the French/English kings of France, they said. Give France back to the French? They kept passing the buck, almost till Buck House. Couldn't raise between them a single syllable of the Anglo-Saxon language.

What're you talking about? It's all in the Bayeux Tapestry. Kind of *débarquement* in reverse, as it were. William: English crown all stitched up in my favour. Mine, Harold's promises to me. But Harold had done the stitching, claiming the crown for himself. Duplicitous he was. But he got one in the eye from Bill. Bill and crew may well have outwitted the devious English Harold, but he needed an English Saxon School of Embroidery to tap into the tapestry art. All the same, he bequeathed it as an heirloom to the as yet incomplete French nation.

If you want to see the tapestry, get there early. Otherwise, instead of admiring the work of the weavers, you'll spend all your time weaving your way in and out of the tourists. Especially at the point where they're eyeing the eye, Harold's eye. Harold's arrow'll keep you transfixed. It really is eye-catching. But where is it? Just follow the arrow. Harrowing all this is. Even so, exquisitely designed and preserved is the tapestry. A sight for sore eyes.

Harold got his own back, posthumously as it were. William's son Rufus died mysteriously from an arrow allegedly bouncing back off a tree in the New Forest. Death marks the spot. The Rufus Stone is there to remind us of it. So we don't miss it, the event, not the arrow, there is a second commemorative plaque in Bell Street, Romsey, showing the route his body took from the New Forest to Winchester Cathedral. Straight as a bullet from a Winchester 73 through Bell Street. Bell tolling again, echoes of our John Steele. He's becoming a staple reference. Or should it be steeple reference?

Beyond Bayeux? Where to stay? *Chambre d'hôte* (Bed and Breakfast) or *logis*, sort of leisurely, intimate, family-run hotel rarely aspiring to the higher reaches of three stars or above. But *chambre d'hôte* it was. Squeamish? Look the other way now, and jump a few paragraphs. How to skin a dead sheep? Just call in the local expert. Skinner, surely not Denis of parliamentary fame? Hangs up dripping carcass on a hook, slowly strips away the outer covering from top to bottom, conserves it as a complete unit, and *voilà*, lamb chop ready for the table.

How about the gentle, most civilized art of enveloping your body with this rugged skin oozing with blood? Coveted skill, covering your bloody body. Lumps of flesh and eyes still staring at you. All human. Have a heart and explain yourself. Well, it goes like this. Over the Atlantic, Cortés and acolytes, what do they see? Aztecs doing just that, into the coronary surgery business. And on top of pyramids, for all the world to see, for heaven's sake! No good, says Cortés. Collar the lot. Our fellow stuck up on a cross is a better bet. Eating his flesh and drinking his blood, OK. Up there on that conical thing, not OK.

Want a dose of heart extract? Try this heroic Olmec. Not big-hearted enough? What about this Toltec soldier fellow? Do quite nicely. Hale and hearty, he is, the gen bellicose type. Bend him over that stone. Pull down the arms and legs, please. That'll do nicely. Got that black obsidian blade? Sharp as glass, neat incision. There it is, disheartening, but can't help that. Out it comes, held high for all to see. Gods up there need a bit of satisfaction. Maybe appeasement's the right word. Keep it raining for chocolate and maize. Messianic mission. Helps the world to go on ticking, like this guy's ticker. Well, not any more.

Thirsty? Spurting blood, not different from the pope's chalice stuff. What's Cortés and co. got to beef about? It's carnival time, so a bit of flesh, Jesus' white, round slim stuff's on the menu. All canned up, OK. No problem. Cannibalism? Not OK. What was all that about dressing up? Priesty carves out the lion's share. Dons skin for three days and three nights. A trifle unreasonable? I'd prefer trifle, but there you are. But trifle and pious ecstasy don't mix. That dessert dish doesn't do the job. What job? Walking round stuck in someone else's clothing. Sheep in wolf's clothing? Warrior skin seems to suit their tribal god Huitzilopochtli (donning the skin must be easier than spelling *Huitzilopochtli*, even for a whiz kid). A truly compassionate art unshared by our expert French sheep flayer who never seemed inclined to appease any deity, apart from offering up sacrificial lamb as a gastronomic delight. Careful about that cross chap, and his hangers on. He's a lamb, too. Lamb of god.

Hey, Señor Cortés. A touch of respect for a high priest. I'm not stepping down from my lofty pyramid position. Have I made the point? Appointed by Huitzilopochtli. He's your Zeus fellow. I'm a top-rate cardio-thoracic expert. Go straight for the jugular. Have a 100 per cent record for transplants. Don't you need an anaesthetic? Certainly not. A drop of tequila does the trick. And like all warriors, he's off to a nice place. Sort of Valhalla.

Running ahead of ourselves. Want more gore than here in Chapter 4? Go west for the rest to flesh things out. It'll be fine in 9.

116

South, keep to the east of the palindromic Laval at all costs. Oh, yes, our Continental friends play around with the back to front palindrome poser. At their wits' end with all those ends and beginnings in 1991. Exhausted by 2002. Quiz candidates with the next front-to-back back-to-front date, please. 2112. Bingo! Remember it just in case you're still around. From north to south, from south to north, always end up in the same place in Laval. Plain confused? Probably the same from west to east and east to west. And it's all set at the end of the great North European Plain, at an intersection of roads.

Laval. Same name for the Prime Minister in wartime Vichy? Sure thing. In President Pétain's government. France certainly got it the wrong way round at the time. Pétain was born in Châteldon, central France. Laval, at life's crossroads, jumped the wrong way, went backwards and forwards, even skipped off to Spain for a while. No fun in bed with the Nazis. Plenty of beds around though. Thousands of them in the hotel glut in Vichy, mind you. Easy enough to choose it for a spot of Jew baiting. Fish them out very easily here. Vichy: the most hygienic of spa towns. Laval should have come clean here. Saw things come to a grisly end. Couldn't shake off de Gaulle. All that shaking, there you are, backwards and forwards. Coming and going built into the name of the man Laval. Executed for collaboration in 1945 by a firing squad, not before writing his memoirs: *Laval parle* (Laval Speaks). Laval in Laval in a palindrome year, doesn't bear thinking about. You'd get suicidal.

Leave palindromic confusion behind. Go for some compensation to make up for lost time. Shoot straight south-eastwards, down the D21 to La Flèche. It's as unswerving and true for kilometres on end. Straight and unerring as the Harold arrow. Can't miss the target. *Flèche* stands for 'arrow', so there.

Palindromic confusion now behind? Not so sure about this confusion? You will be when you realize there's another Laval near Grenoble. It's at the opposite end of France. It would be, wouldn't it? On safe physics ground here. Opposite poles attract each other.

But it doesn't end there. There are about twenty more Lavals cavalcading across the whole of France. Admittedly, they have appendages like Laval-en-Brie and Laval-du-Tarn. We're getting even more confused here. At least, make sure you get the post code right.

Autoroute. Summer. Several rules apply. One: choose middle of the week. End of the month, *non, Madame!* No painful *semáforo de Europa* complex again. Two: toll booths coming up in an area spreading out as wide as an airfield. Which booth? Thousands but choice limited. There are as many options for passing through the tolls as there are corn flake packets in an American supermarket, if Bill Bryson is anyone to go by in his *Made in America.* Sail through on several booths. Need some special electronic device. Cock a snook at the interminably queueing laggards. Pay attendant with a credit card at others, and no *code personnel* or signature at that (room for fraud here?), meet your debt with straight cash if you can work it out, throw coins in a basket, or end up in the wrong line, unable to back up with others tight in behind you. Can't back, Mac. And for heaven's sake, don't put yourself behind greenhorn foreigners who either fail to understand instructions or cannot provide the correct sum. You'll never get there in time. Three: make sure you see blue for *autoroutes* in France or *autopistas* in Spain, and green on the Italian *autostrade.* For confusion's sake, main trunk roads in France display green, so don't think you have to pay there when you leave an Italian *autostrada.* And don't think you don't have to pay the other way round. Four: don't walk on motorways. That is, unless its construction's just been completed, and the whole city of two hundred thousand is invited to walk for miles on it. Back up twenty years. San Sebastián to Bilbao. All north of Spain came out on fiesta day. Frolic on at least one free trip, or walk. Freebee? Nothing for nothing.

Down the A20. Paris, Orléans and Bourges to the east. Turn off just before Limoges, porcelain country. No visit to the Limousin capital, or Peyrat-le-Château to the east for a spot of windsurfing on the Lac de Vassivière. No fun, this. Oradour-sur-Glane. Butchery of the most barbarous kind took place in a mindless massacre. Like Lidice to the west of Prague in Czechoslovakia? Why several hundreds of inhabitants, that is the entire village, save for a few escapees, were slaughtered in a church that was torched has never been clarified. Closest and most likely explanation: Nazis' desire to keep the more southerly population in a state of fear. Kill them all and they'll be unwilling to threaten or weaken the enemy's rearguard after the invasion of June 6. A monstrosity on June 10. Catch up with Lidice, and Auschwitz one day. See end of book for the end of things.

On a lighter and brighter note, sunny Sète, on the Mediterranean coast. Lingering visit. Homage to one of France's outstanding poets, Paul Valéry, now at rest in *le cimetière marin*, a cemetery overlooking the, what? The sea. You could have worked that out. Wait for evening in August. Jostle among the crowd. *Joutes.* Confused? Knock the *e* out and put the *s* before the *t*, and there you. are: Jousts Canal, neatly cutting the small town in two. But I thought Arthur's Gawain did jousting. On horseback? Not here. Propelled forward by rowers below, two vigorous-looking men approach each other, each at the high prow of a barge, and armed with a long wooden pole, the end of which is softened by a bulky, padded piece of cloth or sponge. Objective? Knock your opponent off his lofty perch into the water below. One contender cleaned them all out. Put them in the shade. And no trees. And not bog standard, either. All pristine white. A sumptuous treat on a balmy evening.

Another long hop > foothills of the Pyrenees. Time on your hands? Wait around for some rain. Crests of mountains, snow-covered, under the bluest of skies. Even bluer on the other side. Always is. Purity itself. Maybe that's what the Pyrenean Lourdes contingent are looking for.

Countless *logis* run all along the foothills of the Pyrenees. Not surprising. Over three thousand of them dotted around the wonderfully varied regions of France. Try Pau and Lourdes for size. Warmest of welcomes, and traditional regional cuisine embellished by *le goût du terroir* (appreciation of local produce).

Often in the most alluring of spots, by lakes, overlooking deep, open spaces, surrounded by vineyards, nestling in small villages, away from the bustle of traffic, they offer a feel-good sensation gilded by a table that only the French know how to prepare. And when they offer accommodation next to your favourite wine, you're in clover. Pau is just a stone's throw away from that sweetest of white dessert wines, Jurançon (don't forget to fill in the cedilla), blessed with a sort of light-gold hue and freshness of palate. Temptation is always to cart away whole crates. Very mellifluous sound of *Jurançon* enough to sell it by the dozen.

Let's do a bit of walking up into the mountains, right bang in the middle of the Pyrenees. We do need to check that the tiny, unpublicised lake named Oô actually has water in it. Well, of course it does, with a name like that. Name speaks for itself. Just pronounce it, lengthen the *o* a bit and you have Eureka! Eaueau! It's as clear as, well, well water.

Back down. *Logis* all gone. *Paradors* now on parade. Southern side of the Pyrenees. Useful were the Pyrenees. Comforting, protective barrier for Catholic Spain against those subversive, truculent, rationalist French. *Le siècle des lumières* (the Enlightenment) had to lighten up Europe. Informal, unceremonious *logis*, small by nature and warm in tone, stand in vivid distinction to the grand Parador, lofty and historic in appearance and aspiration, for it carries the visitor back into the grandeur of castles of former times. Imagine the magnanimous gestures of El Cid sidling up to his beloved Jimena. Or Sánchez II, king of Castile, but not all well in his castle. More later, on the Paradors over the border. No deep pockets? Equally inviting is the *casa rural* attached to more modest prices, and to your knowledge of a touch of Spanish, at least.

Does the adventure of romance triumph in your soul? Do echoes of the heroic resonate in your being? Does the monumental selfless abandon to the forces of treachery fill you with a sense of the epic? Yes? Then Roncesvalles in the Pyrenees is the very place for you.

You snake westwards to take in Roncesvalles, the most famous of valleys that witnessed, in the early Middle Ages, an ambush by Basques as the legions of Charlemagne's army moved northwards. Sly as serpents, those Basques. Vengeance seekers, these still untamed Spanish northerners, on the rearguard of an army retreating from Saragossa. Cunning Basques replaced by heathen Moors in the story. Not on heather moors, but on deep-sided slopes. Reality twisted for religious purposes, no doubt.

Not clear what Charlemagne had been up to further south. But now, *Roncesvalles*, the Spanish ringing out like the French *Roncevaux*. Rang out across that doomed valley. *Chanson de geste* (epic poem of derring-do) in the form of *La Chanson de Roland*. Exalting epic familiar to all students of French literature, of *El Cid* proportions. Self-denial and stoical courage of the eponymous hero dying in battle, at the side of his valiant paladin companion Oliver. Both fall at the hands of the perfidious Ganelon. Gained by jealousy, he inveigles the Moorish infidel into attacking the lifelong friends cut off from Charlemagne's main army. Oliver repeatedly entreats Roland to sound his horn ('Sonne ton cor!, Sonne ton cor!'). Roland resists, deep in his pride. Too late does he alert his father/emperor further up the valley. The horn Olifant rings out mournfully up and down the valley of Roncesvalles, reaching the straining ears of Charlemagne. In vain. Treason has done his worst. Quartering is now to do its worst. Ganelon is judged and condemned at Aix-la-Chapelle, Charlemagne's capital, now Germanized Aachen, on the Belgian/Dutch border. Sounds much more painful does Aachen than charming, idyllic Aix-la-Chapelle.

Get your *x*s right. Not Aix-en-Provence in the sunny south. Whether Ganelon would have enjoyed a ride in the meridional sun rather than in the gloomy north is anyone's guess. A wrenching experience, whichever way you look at it: a foursome outing, a cavalcade of four horses, all seeking different pastures, simultaneously! Elementary maths here. Quartering = 4. No splitting sides with laughter.

Epic of rare quality and beauty played out on a grand monumental scale. Exalts the higher and self-sacrificing strivings of men. But don't go looking for the spot. Monument there is, but check out the words. French *ronces* = brambles + *vaux* = valleys. Entangled you would be. And French, or Spanish, won't help. Prod your interest, it could, in the valley bottom, but in yours as well.

Westwards towards San Sebastián on the Bay of Biscay, but before that, looms up, or rather, looms down, the Foz de Lumbier, a deep, deep gorge cut out by a river, along the side of which runs a lengthy tunnel. Sure you don't know what *foz* means. Don't lose any sleep over it. Hardly anyone in the whole of Spain would know, so you're in good company. And these days, you won't see *foz* anyway, but *hoz*, a deep gorge. Remember the fuss over *f* and *h*? Spectacle is mighty impressive. Even more impressive if you look up. Countless vultures swirling around above. Circling, menacing, sinister snatches of shadow right down here.

What's eating them? Carrion. Carry on moving, swallow hard, risky staying dead motionless. Don't get in a flap. Don't want to fall foul of them. On those crags up there, quiet they are, almost eerie in their eyries. Find them all over central Spain. More than one eye in the sky. The Maestrazgo, further south, swarms with them. You don't warm to them, sitting under a tree, absorbed in a novel. You cast your eyes upwards, and *¡Madre mía!* see those dark stains circling. No need for an eagle eye, just a vulture eye. You feel edgy. Sort of unseats you. Just as well they weren't eagles, the rapacious sort swooping down from the Roman imperial standard, and kept flying on to Napoleon and Hitler.

You are pitched into a long, long tunnel, black as pitch. Darkness itself as you enter. Stays that way until you reach the bend halfway. Light at the (b)end of the tunnel, '*¡Al fin!*' (At last!) we all shout, stumbling forward, not forgetting that upside down exclamation mark. On reflection, forget it. You might fall over with that stick of an exclamation mark in the way. Especially if it's upside down.

More to come. Grope your way to the end of the tunnel. Darkness yields to the timely brilliance of the sun. Funnel your thoughts back two hundred years. Shadow of the Napoleonic eagle standard fades sharply against democratic enlightenment. Don't cotton on? Let me explain. On the right, just outside the tunnel, there stands low down the proudest of plaques. Plaque marks the spot. We're not talking dentistry. In a sudden burst of dazzling daylight, it reflects the defeat of French revolutionary tyranny. Could hardly believe our eyes. Effect of tunnel vision?

Light at the end of the Napoleonic tunnel. Would warm the heart of any true Englishman, or Englishwoman these days. Sends us back to the Peninsular War of 1812–13. Commemorates the passing of Wellington's troops with his Portuguese allies, Britain's oldest in Europe, as they mop up the remnants of Napoleon's vanquished army. Sean Bean's Sharpe would have known all about that. Would have known about Salamanca too, still two weeks down our line.

Still no San Sebastián. Pamplona next. Run with Hemingway in front of a ton of pot roast. Where the hell are they going? Bullring, *chico*. We call this running bit the *encierro*. Releasing these maddened animals into the streets and sending them crazily towards the arena. Wild excitement and the occasional fatal *cornada* (goring). Recipient ends up under another goring, the surgeon's knife. Week of sheer hell, wild drinking, unrestrained behaviour enjoyed by the young unbuckled bucks. Play off their bravura against the inflamed creature. Ernest Hemingway's *The Sun Also Rises* says it all.

Gone the parched, scrawny, badly eroded landscape of the plains away from the Pyrenees. We descend towards the coastal city of San Sebastián. You knew this by the number plates whizzing past you all carrying *SS*. Alarm, we feel. Then relief. Nothing to do with the murderous gang from Central Europe. Numbers on car plates have changed recently, which is a two-edged sword. On the minus side, Hell, where am I, you're anywhere in Spain without that simple, Ah!, we're now in Valencia (V) or Valladolid (Va). On the plus side, you don't have a sneaking feeling: am I being pursued by those monsters of moral degradation? Franco, like *Il Duce*, wielded the axe of the Axis. But didn't want a cosy time with Hitler's henchmen.

SS is the capital of Guipúzcoa, one of four Basques provinces, and by far the most verdant, most comely and fetching. The uniqueness of the architecture of its solidly built country houses, its massive *caseríos* sheltering cattle, covered with ivy and a riotous colour of flowers, is only equalled by the impenetrability of its language, Euskera. Not 'Basque' these days. Doesn't suit everyone's taste. Out of local political f(l)avour. Catalan done the same to Castilian. Had a go at spelling Euskera? Get them on to your wavelength. But they don't always wave you goodbye.

Careful when you approach San Sebastián for you may only see Donostia, its Euskera equivalent. Root of much confusion are the routes paraded often only in Basque. You may get even more confused at the Guipuzcoan table which, washed down with the richest of ciders and drawn from gigantic barrels fifteen feet high, rivals any in the whole of Spain. Fish is idyllic, especially tasted by the sea under an awning. *Besugo asado a la parrilla* (grilled bream) taken on the pavements of Orio, to the west of San Sebastián, direct from the sea fifty yards away. Out and in, as it were. Add your Spanish, however shaky and slender, and you are transported straight onto paradisiacal taste buds. We leave San Sebastián for another coastal town, Guernika, and this only for a temporary break, for we are to indulge ourselves in the intimate bliss of *en famille* in *SS*, and beyond, the rapturous chapter *Gaudeamus Igitur*.

Picasso's *Guernika*, or in Castilian *Guernica*, reminds the world of military madness. Serves no purpose to dwell on the monstrous devastation caused by Nazi planes. As an act of protection against artistic spoliation, it was once carted off to New York and now occupies a whole wall in El Prado. Only positive comment on this gigantic canvas, apart from its astounding pictorial expression: more than any other portrayal of pain, it has brought to the attention of a worldwide audience the power of the paintbrush to convey an artist's vision of humanity's chronic suffering. Guernika was both razed to the ground and raised by a creator's sense of horror. Remains, as doubtless it always has been, a model of democratic rule. Shade of the still-standing and most famous tree, surrounded by a protective rail, it casts a shadow over the history of mankind. All to do with genealogy. Trees grow, are chopped away. Branches reform. We turn over new leaves. Storms arise. Sweep them away. Mind-blowing.

Inland we go. Watch that time-honoured tradition. Which one? All that *besugo* shipped off to those *madrileños*. Shoals of *madrileños* waiting for it. Fresh as eaten on the coast, on that Orio pavement. First Parador in sight. Santillana del Mar. Plenty of fish there. Don't mar the occasion. Neat that, if you know that Spanish *mar* means sea. Eat the right stuff. And brush up your arty talents. Close to the cave paintings at Altamira, we are. Long queues. No chance. Chance twenty years ago, but time was the enemy. No visit these days, either, unless you can hang around for a few days. Had a hang-up for years over tickets. Never any on the day. No point in crying over spilt milk, if there is any. Which brings us to the parador.

Cold milk for breakfast in the Parador at Santillana del Mar? Forget it. No chance with the waitress from Poland. It went something like this (R = Ron, I = Irena, P = Pat, M = Manuel):

R: *Señorita.* Cold milk, *por favor.*
I: *(In her worst Spanish)* Ve do not jave cold meelk. Eet ess not possibol.

Two minutes later.
R: *Señorita.* Cold milk, *por favor.*
I: Ve do not jave cold meelk. Eet ess not possibol.

Third request. Same answer.
R: I'll try *kalt.* She should know that's 'cold' in German.
P: A bit close to *caldo* in Italian. That's the opposite.
R: What about our English 'ice'? That should do it.
P: You're joking. It's too close to *heiss* and that's the opposite in German. She's milking it for all she can. Must have some

125

in that churn. She keeps churning out the same old answer. Let's try a fresh start with Manuel.

R: Manuel, *por favor*. Why no cold milk?

M: Not beefor eelevn. Ve meelk zee cows at seex. Zee meelk ees too jot. Ve must – jow you say? – pastereeze it.

R: Got it! No stable to table without a label.

Oh yes, if they ask you what your name is, don't reply 'Ron' first thing in the morning. They'll bring you rum, a rum way of starting off the day. 'Ronald' should work, however, but they could confuse you with that Ronaldo footballer fellow from Portugal, or even Brazil. So no sure way of winning, however many goals they score.

Never any cold milk at the Santillana del Mar Parador. Ought to have it, what with improvements in supply chain. We're supposed to be in one of the flagships of Spanish tourism. Paradors are the cream of Iberian hospitality. Cream's all right. So why no cold milk?

Arranged are these Paradors in the most majestic of surroundings, often castles on the tops of hills. They range over miles around. Could see those heathen Saracens. Try and make friends with them, like El Cid. It figures. They gave us the *zero*. Brought it all the way from India. Not too heavy a job, carting zeros around. You can bank on that. Shakespeare's Venetian Moor set those zeros really rolling in Europe. Venice, that's where banking started, isn't it? Thinking about it, rolling those zeros like a kid playing with a hoop.

The castle Parador at Sigüenza on the Meseta. Everything sumptuous, from enormous, ten-foot high, fluffily comfortable bath towels submerging the user to commodious four posters. 'Ave a go at Ávila. Ante rooms for entertaining a sizeable party. Fit for a king. We know. Juan Carlos stayed there. Signed portrait to prove it.

Sample a walk down the corridors of power? Lined with the king of Aragón's armour. Dream of Ferdinand and Isabel's imperial Spain. Gloat at the moat separating England from the Continent.

Muse over Philip II's invincible conquistadors, and there you are, ready to set off with the Armada in 1588. Couple of cannons around. Just like those at Shieldaig. After the Channel caning, up they went, those galleons, round the top of windswept Scotland. Rescued from the wreck. Shield us from northern foes, now. Pointing seawards. Scuppered any chances of Nazi U-boats sinking our lot at Scapa Flow. A bit further north, that, but what's a few hundred miles among enemies? Scapegoat? The Royal Oak, again at Scapa Flow. Finally buried the hatchet.

Hatchet comes up again, financial this time. Down it comes at the Paradors. They do one right through the table. A real hole in your pocket. Basque *besugo* versus Parador fare? Better pay the fare for a *casa rural*. Escalona, Pyrenees. Cuisine on offer? No palace but perfect for the palate. Paradors tasteless. All show, a lot of dough, but no chow. *Casa rural,* no show, friendly fare and no hatchet.

Paradors and conquistadors go together. Epic sense of Spanish history with its religious and imperial drive. Rough, unsanitized view of the past. Like the untamed Spain's feral crusade into the Americas, the so-called noble campaigns of Cortés, Pizarro and Francisco Vásquez, Cabeza de Vaca ('Cow's Head'). Turned all natural laws on their head. Amerindians should have had more stringent immigration laws, and we would all be better off. Can't stop the curse of Christianity, though.

Which brings us to Santo Domingo de la Calzada, directly south. And its Parador. Almost homespun, helping hand, at the desk. Parador. No food paranoia here. But keep enough fare back from the one at the table. Back in time. H.G. Wells, can you hear me? Vacancies in your Time Machine? Paris, please, to Santiago de Compostela. Stopover at Santo Domingo de la Calzada. Staging post for pilgrims. Book me in for a few days. Sort of Canterbury Tales, for old times' sake. Take me a year, maybe even two. One way ticket. Return? Waste of cash. Dead before I get back. Could get scrofula, plague, highway robbery. Heat stroke. Tough on fanless fans. How much? That's daylight robbery. What're

you going there for? Make sure I don't get scrofula, plague…
Why not cough up for a few papal indulgences? Wouldn't be
coughing then. Need any insurance cover? No. Just cover for the
night. Very little fun in all this wandering. Feel like the Wandering
Jew. Got any maps? Sure. Just follow *la vía láctea* (the Milky
Way). Point your staff west. Haven't got any staff to help. Stick
staff, silly. Like the distaff. You're not pulling the wool over my
eyes, are you? No. Just follow all those sheep and you'll end up
in the *Field of the Star*. Compostela, see what I mean? Nope. I'm
having a field day with all this etymology: Campo de la Estrella
> Compostela.

Why Santiago? Believers, the devout sort, for a bit of relief,
relied on relics from the Holy Land. Saint James, on an obscure
zigzag route, so zigzag it could have been zagzig, set out from
the Holy Land, a high-stepping mission, followed a star, like those
three wise men. Starry-eyed they all were in those days. Erected
a sanctuary to Saint James at Santiago de Compostela. Dead
certain they all were all deep into Jimmy's tomb. Long way from
Palestine for a burial. Maybe already covered by insurance? Lesson
for those *señores* in the last para. Yes, but how do we get to the
name *Santiago* who is our *James*? Simple. *James* to *Iago*. Put *saint*
in the front. Everything up front for saints. Saint Iago. They had
it in for the Moor, though, like the other Iago, Shakespeare's
treacherous fellow who wanted it off with Othello's Desdemona.

Santiago, Patron Saint of Christian Spain. Religion and war, same
thing. Those miscreant Saracens needed chastisement. In the right
corner, has to be right, we have Santiago and Co. Intone *¡Santiago
y España!* In the left corner, they're all wrong so has to be left, we
have Muhammad. Allah be praised! And his heathen hordes led by
Califs, and in the middle the noblest of the noble, El Cid, born
just up the road in Vivar del Cid, village near Burgos. Everything
to do with keeping the world in some sort of order, your order.

Bellicose spirit, just the job for a bit of peace and quiet. Keeps
him happy up there above the clouds, too. Spoiling for a fight?
We're ready, got all those fortress churches. Feel fidgety without

a good fight. Fight it with all your might, they say. Pious stronghold always a safe haven. Creed on cloud nine, kill on cloud zero.

Modern spin-offs are the thing. Stronghold of a church, Ujué is good for a ride, and you won't be taken for a ride, cash wise. Navarra, to the east of Santo Domingo. Have your cake and eat it here. Cook up pictures of battle, and lamb chops cooked on a rustic, open-wood fire. *Migas*, or breadcrumbs, a dish of crumbs, fat-fried, from the chops. Keep your sanctity up with a snack.

Just round the corner, and sure enough, the *ermita*, you've been dying to live there. Don't delude yourself. Maybe the hermits, like hermit crabs, got fed up with the crabbed existence. Anyone inside? No? Try that one a couple of miles away. Might see painting of Saint Jerome in a cave. Model for moodiness, a hermitage. Mind you, I'd go for a hermitage any day. Keep a low profile there. Not like at the top of a pillar for sixteen years, Simon the Stylite, in the Nubian Desert. Needed a pulley for food up, and waste down. Help from that Palermo pulley lady from Chapter 2? But, no sewers for waste. Perhaps no waste and no waist. Ribs too thin for purpose. Not even a lamb chop. Serve that sort up as the sacrificial lamb, though.

Unwise to confuse the Spanish name for the recluse, Jerome = *Jerónimo*, with the most famous of all Amerindian Apache warriors, Geronimo. On second thoughts, Jerónimo's faith in the good of the Almighty and Geronimo's faith in the right of might balance rather well. Choose your weapons, head of the Church and head of the Indians: head to head. Don't think David'll win.

Moving further into Castilla la Vieja. What's all those castles dotted around? Lots of *castillos* in Castilla. They're fortresses to keep those Arabs out. Can't trust them. Gave 'em a chance to believe and behave. Call them *mudéjares*. Did a sort of quid pro quo. The Moors let us live on their patch. Call them *mozárabes*. Bit of an illusion, all this being nice to each other. Castles in the air, I call it. Pinched that from the Spaniards. *Castillos en el aire*. Not much faith in their castles.

What's that place just up the road? All pretty flat, can see it from the road miles away. You know what? Present Deputy Prime Minister, that Liberal Democratic character, could give you the lowdown. Knows all about low blows. Clegg, Nick Clegg's the name. Don't get it. Soon will. Place is Olmedo. Wife knows the place. Born there. Dad was a politician. Miriam's her name. Goes there on a summer spree to avoid Parliament patter. Not very important then? Don't be so sure. All this needs some unravelling. Lots of strands. So let's tie up the loose ends.

Clegg must be clued up on one of Spain's most celebrated dramatists, Lope de Vega. I've heard of Cervantes, but that's about it. The play's the thing. Lope staged *El caballero de Olmedo.* Wrote it as well. Olmedo, doom-laden for hero Don Alonso. Walks his way to Medina del Campo, time after time. Trysts with Inés. So what? An awful lot. Suitor there is, another, just as keen on her. Another *caballero.* Aroused in jealousy, consumed like Othello's Iago. Less saintly than Santiago, who does at least have *Sa(i)nt* in his name, villainous Don Rodrigo puts the knife into Don Alonso. Don Alonso ends up in real bad nick. Don Rodrigo as well when the boys in blue – or what colour was it? – failed to arrive in the nick of time. Body of evidence against Don Rod. Verona star-crossed lovers all over again. Baneful sense of the tragic from beginning to end, from Olmedo to Medina. Not much fun here, not even for Nick himself, racked by heat. In the fate-laden steps of Alonso, to Medina and back, and no horse, had to leg it, did hat-donned Don Clegg, poll ratings in free fall, AV r*av*aged, anxiously watches the self-same lowering skies of doom (written in September 2011). Not even a castle to save him in Olmedo. Maybe that's why he seeks safety in Medina's *castillo.* Cast in stone, a real protection.

Nick Clegg not genned up on Don Alonso? Dunno. Sure is though on the high Meseta summer. Infernally hot, and winter arctically cold. Learnt to chant: 'Nueve meses de in*v*ierno, tres de in*f*ierno' (Nine months of winter, three of hell). Summertime, cooling shade in those endless lines of poplar and cypress trees. Mark out the river courses for miles and miles. Breeze in the leaves as you breeze along. But how to keep warm on the Meseta, perhaps the winter before Mr Clegg's arrival? Sit at a round table, legs underneath. Below, and in the middle of the table, a brazier (*brasero*) would emit onto the legs heat kept in by a communal blanket. Each morning could be seen outside quantities of braziers cooling down before the ash was removed. A warming sight taking us back into bygone centuries.

Back to the summer period and the motor flight. Car stops for the *merienda* (picnic) by one of these long, long lines of interminable trees. If you can find a gap leading off the road. And keep swatting away at those *moscas* (flies). You think of one of the species of these trees, the *álamo* (poplar), Davy Crocket, alias John Wayne, comes to mind. Hey, Santana, they're killing your men in the Álamo. We'll have the last laugh, Santana. Back over the Río Grande you go. Taxes are for Texas.

Pronounce Valladolid? Good to know, for that's where we're heading. The *V* sounds exactly like a *b*, the double *ll* like a *y*, and those two *ds* like a lisping *th*. That's the difficult bit out of the way. Oh yes, and the *i* at the end sounds *ee*. So we end up with something like Bayatholeeth. No easier with *vallisoletanos*. You can guess, they're the people who live there.

Information on the city. Staggering under the weight of history. Passion for the past, intoxicated by this historical onslaught. You forget the *vinos finos* of the river Duero close by. Valladolid found house room, or palace room, for Castile's Queen *Isabel la Católica*. Did some alliancing for Castile, so married King Fernando of Aragón in 1469. Got to tighten up and crack the whip for those Saracens. Spliced they were in the then capital of most of Spain. Irresistible dynamic. Late fifteenth century, and the world became different and smaller. 1492. Columbus again. *Va*, used to be like this on number plates, welcomed him into her arms for his last days.

The Spanish call him Cristóbal Colón, and please ensure you keep the stress on the second *o* of the surname, or you finish up with a part of the anal anatomy. The original Italian offers no such dilemma, Cristofero Colombo. Valladolid resounds from a colossal hymn to Columbus. As ubiquitous in Valladolid as he is in the world. Motor round the roads. A street? Sure. Calle Colón. Museum? Sure. Casa Museo Colón. Five-hundredth anniversary of his death in 2006. Whatever the car's ccs, you'll always find CC.

Driving over the high, bare, rainless plains of Castile, the car carries on through the epic journey back into the black majesty of history. It never dries up. Pad your way round the walls of Zamora. What's this gate here? Sancho 11, king of Castile and León, made his final exit here. Who's the guilty party then? Bellido Dolfos, in 1072. Alas, our Sid arrived too late on the scene. He should have known better, and got there sooner. With a name like that, Bellido had to be double-dealing. Bizarre, incongruous-sounding was Bellido Dolfos. Mum didn't like him from the bell? A dark, shady villain doing the dirty. French shades of Bellido we see in four-hundred-years later Ravaillac. Henri IV, felled, fell as well, on the stairs, joins Sancho II in this litany of treachery.

First visit to Zamora saw women regularly washing clothes in the Duero. Gloriously communal scenes long since gone. To the relief of the working women? Scrubbing business has dried up. Interest drained away, so have the women. Folks at the *Ayuntamiento* have washed their hands of the upkeep. Eyewash. Ubiquitous, solidly built *lavaderos* (communal washhouses) have some use. Always a lot cleaner after that Bellido guy went down the plug hole.

Better not to dwell on the murkiness of treachery. Let's look at the gem of gems of all Castile, Salamanca, home of one of the oldest universities in Europe, ranking with Oxford, Cambridge, Paris's Sorbonne and the Italian Bologna. Set by the river Tormes, enshrined in the anonymous tale of *El Lazarillo de Tormes*, Salamanca, endowed with that series of sonorous *a*s, glows with the yellow hues of sandstone constructions inevitably opening out onto one of the glories of Spanish architecture, its *casa de las conchas* = house of shells (severally encrusted in the walls of a baronial, sumptuous building), and onto its Plaza Mayor. Stroll round the shop- and café-lined arcades. More spacious and enchanting than its sister *plaza* in Madrid, it ranks as one of the monuments of man's highest artistic open-air endeavours. Sitting there outside a café to savour its balmy evening beauty is a must. Recalls Nancy's place Stanislas.

Salamanca is more than appearance. Within its soul are concealed intellectual achievements. Who? Literary giants. Fray Luis de León, perhaps Spain's finest poet. Join the fray in the main university square, opposite the *rector*'s (Vice-Chancellor's) house. Impressive, elegant, independent, a statue surveying all humanity from on high, hand held out as if offering a warming handshake. A strikingly powerful effigy. Makes you think of someone else? Sure. The Roman epics man, Virgil, bard of Mantua. Fray Luis's lot was that of all freethinkers in the Renaissance. Drank gallons of vitriol dispensed by Torquemada's Inquisition. Imprisonment, and house arrest for heresy. 'As I was saying yesterday...', said he on release. Galileo fifty years later drank just as much vitriol. Not apocryphal this. 'Eppur si muove' (And still we go round ourselves and round the sun). Titan of the more contemporary scene, Unamuno, did just as much drinking. Finished his days, again under house arrest, on the last day of 1936. Free speech, please. Where did he get his final exit pass? Opposite the statue of Fray Luis, in the Casa Rectoral.

Miguel de Cervantes. One of the elite bunch. Never went to Salamanca. All curious, this. Salamanca. Can be split into two bits. *Sala* = room, *manco/manca* = one-handed, or with useless hand. Very strange that a room should be designated as having the use of only one hand, but there you are, the crazy vagaries of language. Explain yourself. Cervantes is known in all Spanish-speaking countries, in an alliterative way, as *el manco de Lepanto*, the one-handed man from the Battle of Lepanto, result of an incident in this affray. As far as is known, Cervantes never visited Salamanca but he showed familiarity with it by sporting his *manco* arm. Disarming really. Let's hope this was his left arm, and that he wrote with his right hand. The other way round and he would have felt the heavy, mighty hand of the Inquisition: write with your left hand at your peril, Miguel. Right is right, and left, well... Make sure it's left well behind. You've been a playwright. Keep playing that way.

A little-known fact about Cervantes, closer to the waves of tourists than these sun-seekers might suspect, centres on Denia, south of Valencia. You've heard of Don Quixote, haven't you? Well. If Cervantes hadn't set foot on Spanish soil at Denia, you probably wouldn't have heard of the knight with the doleful countenance. No Denia, no Quixote. Five years' captivity. Caught by pirates on returning from the Lepanto episode, he spent that time in a dump of a prison in Algiers. Ransom paid finally got him out. All touch and go. Barbarossa's crew in there somewhere.

Ávila, inhabited by those *abulenses*, is a few miles further south. We all want to see how Frank Sinatra, Cary Grant and Sofia Loren dragged that massive gun around its ancient walls. C.S. Forester's *The Gun* ignited our interest to start with. Sparked the film, *The Pride and the Passion*. Real, pukka walls, these are. What's pukka about them? Well, those around green-with-envy Carcassonne are anything but. Down from the Middle Ages, and up again in the nineteenth century. A solid detail, that. Something more weighty, more crucial to follow. St John of the Cross, in cahoots with St Teresa, gave mysticism a lift. From the bottom, as it were. Order of the *Carmelitas Descalzos* (Carmelites Unshod). Did a lot of climbing, spiritual sort, without boots, barefoot. 'You can walk around with nothing on your tootsies, but leave us to sort the rest out, you know, the up there beyond the clouds.' So said the Inquisition. Poor old John ended up, like Cervantes, in clink. John in jug.

No prison prize for Teresa, however. She went all ecstatic, even erotic. Her spiritual passion reached such dizzy heights, or carnal depths, according to how you look at it, that physical union with her Friend was always stabbing away at her. So pure and undefiled was she, tormented for not being tormented. Modesty-driven in her pride. Is that possible? What all the other nuns did below Mother Superior is far from clear. Teresa finally went off to the next village, Alba de Tormes, and that's where she still is. More details just to be sure? Rely on her relics to nail things down just a bit more. Hair and finger nails, or is it toe nails? Museum pieces, closely guarded under lock and key.

Straight south to Mérida, the seventh most important city in the Roman world, with a gigantic amphitheatre right in the centre, summer scene of plays, and that includes our Stratford bard. The road to Mérida plunged back into the history of ancient times. 'Plunged' on the stock market, too. Triple-named Camino de la Plata, or Vía de la Plata, or even the Ruta de la Plata no longer geared up to speedy commerce. N630, these days. A once-famous 'Silver Road', now a bit tarnished with all that wear. Silverware ran parallel to modern Portugal, right down from Astorga in the north to Seville in the south. Lost out on trade and no silver bullet to revive it, if bullets do that sort of thing. Perhaps a misnomer, Camino de la Plata. Saw no conveyance of silver. Maybe silver conjured up ease of profit, barrels of merchandise. Certain is the permanent robustness of the road surface, as resistant as when it was originally laid. Modern road builders, ¡Atención! adoquines (cobble stones) are your durable, maintenance-free answer, but don't expect cyclists to race over them. Saw that in the Paris–Roubaix competition. Anyway, only mad dogs and Englishmen would cycle there in the summer furnace. The stuff of legends. Not very different from the epic-strewn Route 66. Long gap, Oklahoma to California. No silver for them, though.

Urbs Emerita. Where's that? It's Mérida, from the Latin again. People got lazy, so shortened things. Happens all the time. In actual fact, a thumbnail mention in Chapter 11. Boasts a colossal *puente romano* (Roman bridge) astride the river Guadiana erected in the first century BC. Measures about 800 metres long, 5 metres wide, supported by sixty arches of solid granite. The Romans built for eternity. No arguing about that. Need water? The solution's on its way. The Acueducto de los Milagros, *a* stunning engineering feat feeding the city from the Proserpina Dam, just three miles away. It's bound to be stunning with a name like that: *Milagros* = Miracles. Its two-millennia durability's a damming indictment of modern building methods.

Want more? What about the Arco de Trajano (Trajan's Arch), or the Templo de Diana (Diana's Temple). Come a bit more this way down the centuries and seek out the Alcazaba. Got to be Arabic, starting with *al.* Allah sees to that. They're built al(l) over the place. Try Almería, Albarracín. Not unique. *Alcazabas* and *alcázares* (fortresses) abound in southern Spain. After all, the Moors needed all-out protection from those heathen *¡Santiago y España!* Christians screaming down from the north. Don't be alarmed. Just be alert. The Moors needed lerts.

A very thirsty province is Badajoz. That's where Mérida stands. A bit back to the north, will have passed through a painfully barren area, Las Hurdes, abandoned and isolated, afflicted by a high degree of infant mortality and degenerative diseases. Desolation of desolation, Luis Buñuel must have thought. Filmed a documentary on abandoned, unaided, suffering humanity. Slice of grinding poverty, and no bread.

A quick nip down to an unpretentious, even humble pension at a tiny coastal village of La Mamola. Ran by the simplest of hosts. We had a quick dip, but no nip. Sounds a bit obscure all this. Not so. An appetizing meal is set before you. Wine en route. The host pours forth that lovely, full-bodied, red wine. 'Bodied''s the word. Horror of horrors, reek of reeks, no chance of watering this down. A full body fell out straight from the stone jug, literally, into the glass, a large, inky-black cockroach. Bible-black, would say our Dylan, bottle-given that he was. Genuine. Pure, unadulterated truth. All whisked away in a flash. 'What's this *cucaracha* doing in my glass?' 'Breaststroke, sir.' 'Can't. It's dead drunk' was our response. Pour scorn on our host? Laughed it off, like a drain, gushing with compliments on the splendid fare.

How on earth could a *cucaracha* find itself in such vinous circumstances? Had obviously dived in for both dip and nip. As for the taste, look no further than the other end of Europe. Chekhov's captain Vershinin in *The Three Sisters* must hear the last word: 'This liqueur is delicious. What's the flavour?' 'Cockroaches' comes the answer from Solyony, his subaltern. No invitation to a dance here, or singing *La Cucaracha* either, all the way from Mexico.

Mexico. That's where those creepy-crawlies come from. Crawling all over those ill-kept lousy luggers on their way to Europe. 'Where's the word *cucaracha* come from?' 'From *cuco*. Means "insect".' 'Not gonna swallow that one.' 'It's true. My language coach says so. And "cockroach" comes from *cucaracha*. We poached it from the Spaniards. Both ugly words. All those guttural *k*s down in the throat, making their way up to the *ch*s. Makes you want to throw up. A bitter pill to swallow. It really does stick in your craw.'

Stone the crows! Spare the sparrows! A cautionary tail, this. But not a tall tale, even up here. Not even a fairy tale. Here I am, one evening, a wee little sparrow of a chap, your feathered friend, happy as a lark, safely perched on a branch, having a nice snooze and crack! What's that? Soon cracked it. A lump of lead flashes by. Game on (a branch), and it's not darts. He won't bull's eye me, even if it's only a game. No foul language, please. Trembling like a leaf, I am. Look down into the nocturnal gloom. Somewhat in the dark. I take a dim view of what's going on. There's that black, gallows bird fellow again. Garbled warbling he tries as a sort of bait. Popping us off, he is, one by one. No bird of prey, this. Bird of pray, he's supposed to be. Maybe he can't see the difference. He ought to. Got enough light, with that torch on the barrel of his shotgun. Not arrows for sparrows for priesty. To come to think of it, no bullets for pullets either, they're for us, although pullets must be tastier than we(e) spindly little sparrows.

Lines us up in his sight. Beams it up. And here we are, the target, waiting for a pot shot. That's where we end up. In a pot. Cooking pot. I get in a real stew over this. Sparrow soup, anybody? Not Cross and Blackwell's, but I feel cross and, well, black as thunder. All he's doing is feathering his nest. Cheap at twice the price. I'm gonna branch out somewhere else. Missed the bullet. Fine, but watch that dog on his collar. Wouldn't trust god, even if spelt in reverse. Search your soul, father confessor. Help me shed light on your religious rites. Here you are, trying to illuminate our darkness and there you are, carrying out the darkest of deeds. Too much illumination with that torch, that's the trouble. It's blinding you to your real aim in life. You may be a *cura* (priest) but you're not going to cure anyone like that. Not even dolly birds. I bet they're fair game for you too, pope or no pope.

Thank you, St Francis, that he's not that hot at the pot shot. Priesty failed to kill one bird with one stone, let alone two. Keen on St Francis, I am. Always imagining myself on that windowsill watching him in Giotto's panel painting at Alviano feeding the sparrows, my kith and kin ancestors, as well as preaching to them. Bit difficult swallowing the St Francis story, not very religious, but it makes me feel nice and balanced on this branch.

Amazed at my English up here on the top of my tree? You should be, I'm Spanish, bilingual you know. Not trilingual like Ron, but there you are. My woolly *trashumancia* friend in the previous chapter did highlight my skills. It's in my nature. Never needed any lessons. Fortunately, 'cos they don't come cheep (sorry *cheap*, this dyslexia business is contagious, must have got it from my Madrid pal). Let's say I'm a natural. Speaking a couple of languages is quite common in Spain. Take those Gibraltarians. They slip in and out of English and Spanish, just like slipping across the frontier at La Línea. Pretty much like their Barbary apes, and they're no more a bunch of barbarians than I am a bird brain.

You may not have noticed it, but a bird needs a bit of panache when he calls to his feathered friends, all in the service of the self-preservation society. I originally aspired to Shakespearian heights. I do reach for the highest standards. So don't put me down. I then took a leaf out of a few other English writers, although Cervantes would have served me well. Finally got keen on an Irish writer, settled on that smooth Shavian style, close to my dad's more general avian approach. He did at least teach me to stand on my own two pins. Which is why, for two pins, I'd give that priesty guy a shot or two of his own medicine, or should I say, a shit of his own medicine? Of course, my dad started off years ago chirping with a quill and inkwell. Trouble was, he would overfill and spill. So costly, so much ink, he could never really meet the bill. Me? I went straight to a typewriter.

I can't help preening myself on my own personal style. I've reached the top of my trade and am really peaking with my beak now. Pity I couldn't alert the Society for the Protection of Birds. I've already reached out for the long arm of the law. They agree this is nothing short of fowl play. But they just seem to chicken out. Sure enough, police inaction triggered me into action. Bird safety's not high on their agenda. Nor are bulls, for that matter. They're usually low on the police's list of priorities, especially when they are dragged off to the butcher's after a dose of butchery. The whole business makes me feel a bit peaky.

Too early in those early days to think about tweeting on Twitter. I was pretty good at whistle-blowing, though. Still, I've just recently started tapping on my smartphone. Easiest of the lot. I'd been jumping up and down for months avoiding that priesty fellow's shots, so tapping on the branch came naturally. Tap dancing really. Good job he never hit me. I'm gonna get my own back, if my shit fails. His Málaga police station website's in for a few (s)hits. Hightail there if I have to. Málaga's not too far as the crow flies. If priesty thinks he can get away with this, he's in cloud cuckoo land. I don't care if I am jumping the gun and ruffling a few feathers. Above all, I don't want to be pigeon-holed as a troublemaker. Blow that for a lark.

Learnt the whistle-blowing in Orwell's *Animal Farm*. Gentle old overblown Snowball, the piglets, they had a go. Did them a fat lot of good though. Porkies went on and on. Orwell's style, clear, candid and unaffected, it sure affected me. Brought me down to earth. Debased me and all my fellow creatures. What worried me was the meaning. Too demeaning.

Stop Press. Latest Release. Avian dollops on preying priesty. Real t(r)ail-blazing stuff.

Amble inland to Seville. Easter's gone. But let's bounce back to spring. Would then have marvelled at the unending carpets of blue, yellow and purple flowers stretching luxuriously beyond the horizon in much of Andalucía. Oven of scorching heat next on the seasonal menu. Fiesta-type processions, like in unpronounceable Valladolid, would have filled us secular-oriented onlookers with a sense of cross solemnity. Slow, rhythmic beat accompanying the soldier-like steps of the faithful, some carrying crosses, the heavier the better. More painful, love that. Closest thing in the closet to hair shirts. Oh, the joys of masochism. Sinister Klu-Klux-Klan headgear, upside-down ice-cream cornets, others walking barefoot, no shoes to order here. Good saving, economical trip to paradise. This is a shoe-in. To cap it all, the *andas*, the portable platforms giving a free ride to Mary and her retinue.

Epic-sense gripped, we see in Seville the departure point for the conquistadors and their voyages of *descubrimiento* (discovery). Even Cervantes was down there later as a quartermaster. Just as well his mad Don wasn't on hand yet, or on his mind. 1588 was on his mind. Fed the Armada. They needed wind. Sailors' obsession, rather like Quixote having a tilt at the windmills. But, you exclaim, Seville is about thirty-odd miles from the sea. That's true, and it's also true it's not really a port any more. River Guadalquivir is now all clogged up with silt, not salt. Keep that for the trip. Topsy-turvy with scurvy.

How come all those Spanish Americans speak like Spanish southerners? Easy answer here. Back to Spanish evening classes. Start from where the class is. That's what the experts say. 1. American English's not like British English. Seems to resonate here a twang of the Irish, one of the main groups of nineteenth-century settlers. 2. Same with Spanish American. It's at odds with much of the northern Iberian stuff. Conquistadors and colonizers came largely from southern Spain. 3. Columbus? Caught me there. Was Genoese. Saw that earlier.

Henry Newbolt's Drake would not have bothered too much about that nicety of language. At least, he showed little respect for the local Spaniards speaking like it. Sailed straight into Cádiz harbour, firing on all cylinders, set about, in 1557, burning Philip II's fleet. Sizzle them for Liz was his motto. Grill Phil, that fits the bill.

Uplifting feeling of the epic. Empire building. Stop those Spaniards grabbing all the colonial goodies. Momentous deeds of the English buccaneer-hero. How to spark all English kiddies' imagination? Play ducks and drakes with Drake, skating over the water. We all sing about singeing the King of Spain's beard. There we were, on the Parador balcony overlooking the Bahía de Cádiz (Bay of Cadiz). Generous lot, the Spaniards. Waived the extra fee for the grandstand view. Glowing with pride we could have been. Especially with that admirable admiral just round the corner at Cape Trafalgar. All that sort of patriotic stuff went up in smoke a long time ago.

So, the Holy Roman Emperor, Charles V, like William the Conqueror in England, then? Spoke pretty well no language of the country he was supposed to be running. Charles obviously got fed up with managing the affairs of half of Europe, passed the job to his son. Cleared off for an extended holiday. Retired early. Pension secured, so went for abdication. Lived out the remainder of his gaga days playing with clocks – trying to adjust them backwards? – in a Yuste monastery near Cáceres, tormented by his place in eternity. Unrestrained passion for clocks, well documented. Explanation, *por favor*. Either measuring the time available to him in eternity or purgatory. Or was bequeathed a touch of madness by his insane mother Juana la Loca (Joan the Mad). Poor lady. Failed to keep a steady hand on the reins of the state and found herself interned in Tordesillas. Attempts to get her released failed. Deadlock for Loca locked up in a castle. And that's where she died.

Back inland, and a quick nip to Ronda. Better hurry up, if you wish to see a corrida. Best place for a gander? I'm talking about bulls. Hemingway, Orson Welles, Tyrone Power, all attracted to the gore, as well as to the lore, of the place. Learn to swagger in a *traje de luces* (matador's brightly coloured suit), sway arrogantly before your final bull, and you're up with the greats, Joselito and Paquirri, even if praying on your knees before those snorts. But, as I say, hurry on down to my place, Honey, to Ronda. Animal Rights' Committee will have decided for you. They have already in Catalonia. Bullring strikes you, full of colour, both inside and out. Excellent backdrop for the final act in the Rossi 1986 film. Domingo, as Don José. Opera? *Carmen.* Real beauty of it, location of the short story by the French writer Prosper Mérimée and its operatic adaptation by Bizet takes place in the Serranía de Ronda, the mountains just round the corner. Death in the afternoon. Death at five o'clock. Ronda paso doble yes. Rondo sonata no.

Let's strike out north-east. Toledo in a day? September. Glowing fields of yellow and white? What's that? *Azafrán.* Saffron. Back-breaking stuff that. Intense days of work of, at the most, two weeks' picking off the stigmas. Usual casual labour drafted in for the job. The natural autumnal hues of saffron resonate back to the abundant floral, yet fleeting rush of the Andalusian spring. I'd never seen all this bending and stretching. Was breaking news to me. I'd just fold up.

Longest, toughest journeys, across country, how do you cope? Two, like everything else in the book. Two drivers, switch from one to the other. Fits the metaphor/literal scheme of things. Jees, that's good. The best there is.

In Toledo now. Home of El Greco. Don't want his full Greek name, please, just give me Domenikos. You'll never know if I don't, so here goes. Theotokopuli. Sounds like copulating with God. Teresa'll be hot on this. Should know. It's *not* all Greek to her. Greek to us but Chinese to our Continental friends. That's what they say: 'It's all Chinese to me.'

Ever been to Toledo? No? Call in an army of guides. Jumble of a town, squashed and squashed again. Christian, Arabic and

Jewish all rolled into one. Exercise in multiculturalism? Streets as labyrinthine as Daedalus' labyrinth. Is that why you'd call it a *dédalo*? I'm lost, already. Who's who? Where's where? Jammed inside the Río Tajo (Tagus). Deep *cut*, and this cut runs right round it. The river goes on running right through Portugal and out at Lisbon, a long way, not that Byron would have balked at it. Just as well he wasn't there during the earthquake of 1755. The tsunami would have dampened his spirits. As it was, he cut a flamboyant figure across the Tagus.

Inside the Tagus, at Toledo, and you're saved. Impregnable was Toledo. Republicans tried to take it. Assault after assault. Reduced it to ruins. Alcázar, as well. What's that? Bigger type of Arab fortress than the Alcazaba we came across in Mérida. All those *a*s. Bit surprised? The Moors loved them, just like the *al*s. Spaniards are mad on them. Salamanca, Granada, Guadalajara, Zaragoza... Infection somewhere? Three of them in *damasquinado* (damascene work), too. Toledo's famed for it all over Spain. Any the wiser? No? Here goes. From the Syrian capital, Damascus. Fine metal work set in steel. El Cid's sword, Tizona, sure had some. Muslim cross-party buddy, Yusuf al-Mu'taman, saw to that.

Back to the Alcázar. The one viewed now is a total reconstruction. Why 'reconstruction'? Forced labour of Franco's prisoners. Anyone left from that started on the colossal monument to religion and military vengeance in the Valle de los Caídos (Valley of the Fallen), to the north of Madrid. Massive, and more than impressive sanctuary set within the Sierra de Guadarrama (there we are again with the *a*s), topped with a gigantic cross. Just right for a bit of gargantuan piety, next chapter.

Toledo, sure enough, owes its tourist celebrity status to El Greco. His *Entierro del Conde de Orgaz* (Burial of the Count of Orgaz) dominates all enquiry. There seems no point in dwelling lengthily on this masterpiece. Gallons of ink have been spilled on it already. Not on the *Conde*. Would have blackened his reputation.

There is a point, however, in recounting a particular experience of twenty-five years' standing. Imagine you arrive at the Toledo

Parador on a winter's afternoon. Toledo visit at all costs. Down you drive, over the medieval Alcántara bridge, edge along the Tagus and nonchalantly leave your car, well, somewhere nearby. You walk and walk, taking in El Greco's house, now converted into, guess what, a museum, whiz round all the synagogues, and find that winter darkness has fallen. Wound up by all the windings, Theseus himself would have been of no avail. Surrounded by overhanging houses in tiny streets, no way of locating a position. A plus: no Minotaur to contend with, although the country was alive with bulls. Like them, I did at least have a tongue in my head. Not on the hotel menu, though. Two *albañiles* (workmen cum brickies), at the end of their shift, heard our SOS (yes, they do use SOS as well). Briefest of explanations. 'Señor, estamos perdidos' (We're lost). Response: 'Descríbame el lugar...' (Describe the place to me...). Near a small supermarket, they sure did rescue us. Jump in, a bit of a squeeze, all four of us on the front seat, no health and safety rules here. In a jiffy, back at our car. Grateful comments all round. The *albañiles* more than happy to oblige an *inglés*. Covered in dust, but all done and dusted, off they went. Anything easier than that? Parador, you're in our sights again. Settle for paradise once in a while.

East the car goes to Cuenca. What's that dark, sinister-looking water in those pools? *Torcas*, they call them. Notice up: *Prohibido nadar* (No swimming). Must be Nessie down there somewhere. Monsters too, north of Cuenca. Another quirk of nature: *La ciudad encantada* (Enchanted City). Gets curioser and curioser. Alice in Wonderland land. Rocks, big ones, look like cats, dogs, elephants, ready to pounce but don't. Back in Cuenca. Half the population are hanging over cliffs. Everything wonky in *conque*. Well, almost. Inhabitants called *conquenses*. Craziest and architecturally defying houses, neatly painted white. Called *casas colgadas*, bit like the Hanging Gardens of Babylon. Yawning out over the abyss of a steep valley. How on earth do you paint them? If you're on the earth. Call in Michael Caine. He must have worked it out by now in *The Italian Job*: 'Hang on, lads, I've got an idea.'

Now well north of Don Quixote country. Heresy not to pay homage at his home. University don visits Don, as it were. Choice: El Greco or Cervantes. Fell for the former. But let's draw upon a previous journey. Don Nick, you visited the windmill country? Plains of La Mancha, scene of the wacky hero driven by chivalrous ideals. *El Quijote,* that's the man, is really supposed to be ingenious. That's what the book says. *El ingenioso hidalgo de Don Quijote de la Mancha.* Judge for yourself. Nut of a knight errant, consumed with screwball mission. Right the world's wrongs. *Tuertos,* he called them. Had to straighten them out, George-of-the-Dragon style. Trouble is he couldn't really straighten them out. Like a one-eyed guy, he was. Other meaning of *tuerto*: one-eyed. That's why he was so quixotic, I suppose.

Don Q. at your service, Señorita Dulcinea. Country wench idealized into a Spanish Cleopatra. Conned by the Don was she. She saw in awe our Don inspired by the English lawyers' *Book of Torts? Tort* and *tuerto* same thing. Latin again.

Moral crusade against the white whirling giants of La Mancha, stretching almost symmetrically south-eastwards from Quintanar de la Orden to Mota del Cuervo. Not on four-legged horses now but on four of a different sort. See those giants whizzing round on the way to the coast? Piled on one after the other. Like pylons.

Down La Mancha we sail. Got to clean the place up. Have to, no doubt about it. The Mancha's a bit of a stain on things. Offensive to our knight's pure and delicate sense of honour and duty. He must have seen *stain* in La Mancha. After all, that's what the word means. *Mancha* = stain. If Shaw had gone to Spanish evening lessons, his Eliza Doolittle would have done more than a little herself. Probably would have sung: 'The rain in Spain falls mainly on the Stain'. Now, that would have been neat, spot on.

Whatever our scrawny madcap did on his nag of a horse, Rocinante, Sancho Panza, a tubby little sidekick, with an overflowing *panza* (paunch) that would have sent the medical community reeling, spent his equally overflowing sense of reason stripping down his master's idealism into some form of realism. A novel novel, the very first of its kind. Mad, adventurous aspirations of a feverish mind brought down to earth by podgy facts. Raving, elongated Quixote, even more elongated with his upward-thrusting lance, versus a portly partner in his donkey-driven simplicity.

Better to escape into our own adventures once again. And the unknown, vast, untamed mountainous region, unvisited even by the *madrileños*, the daunting Maestrazgo of narrow roads and vultured skies. Cantavieja, perched high on a cliff, saw the suspenseful speeches in *El Cid* unfold in its medieval square, town hall in the background.

Spain and epics at the pics. Just the ticket for colour and open spaces. Sid and his girl Ximena, on the high plains of Castilian Spain. Gary Grant and Sofia Loren, already seen them hauling Forester's gun along Ávila's walls. Grave, sorrowful scenes near Soria of Yuri's mum's burial. All very orthodox, this. Jivago, down but not out. Starting up, in fact. Snowy Pyrenean range flaking from sea to sea. Film directors galore, see them all the time. Just up the road from Cantavieja, in Mirambel. Gritty Mike Leigh's *Land of Freedom*. No green, just barren and grit. Want to swagger into a Western? Coastal Carboneras's the place for you. South-eastern corner, near Almería. Ready-made set, saloon bar, tethering rails for horses, and wide, dusty thoroughfares. Primed for Gary Cooper's *High Noon* showdown.

Funny they showed up. Coincidences do occur. Isolated *casa rural*, close to Valderrobres, miles from anywhere, still very much hidden in the Maestrazgo. Ten o'clock in the evening, starry darkness outside. Meal finished for just the two of us. Enter six hearty men, 'hearty''s the word, enjoying a weekend of adventurous walking, all travelling in one people carrier. Food on their table. Left their nearest and dearest at home. Eavesdropping, that's me. Done this before. I'll do it again. Self-invited. Table-crashing. Not routine conversation. R = Ron, G = Guillermo, M = Miguel, *et alii*.

R: Where you from?

G: All from Tortosa, eighty kilometres.

R: What d'ya do?

M: Hospital

R: Yes, but what do you DO? Canteen? Cleaning out bedpans?

G: Medics.

R: That's funny, know a medic. Tortosa hospital. Known him for donkey's years. (*Wouldn't have understood 'donkeys'. Nearly all gone. Same for camels in Algeria. See that later.*)

M: ¿Cómo se llama? (*A bit of local lingo, got to keep up with the local lingo, and make sure you stick in that funny, but convenient upside-down question mark again.*) What's his name?

R: Se llama Iñigo.

G: My mate. Brought pacemakers to the hospital ten years ago. Fitted them to patients. Worked hand in glove with him. Always clean ones, of course. Standard practice now, you know.

R: ¡No es posible! ¡No es posible. ¡No es posible (*Not possible!*). ¡No me lo creo! ¡No me lo creo! ¡No me lo creo! (*I don't believe it!*)

Exhilarating exchange. Interminable, to midnight. Next morning. Breakfast and farewells. Two weeks later, card from Iñigo, blood pressure man. Year later, greets us with his paraphernalia of hospital equipment. Want a bit of auscultation, Ronald?

Cap that! Easy. Coincidences come in twos, like everything else in this book.

Microbiologist turns up, another year. Mirambel, just down the road. What d'you know! Another of Iñigo's colleagues again.

Cap that! Cap that! Fifty kilometres up the road, Morella. Splendidly typical medieval walled town, full of bustle and joyful colour. In an arcade sheltering from the sun, a Spanish-speaking colleague contributor to one of the books of yours truly.

147

Morella. More for our animal lovers. Running of the bulls, communal fun in most Spanish towns and villages. Seen that in Pamplona. No fun, this. Not for me, anyway. **I'm a hotel receptionist** sitting at the bottom of some steps, in the entrance hall. At the end of the narrowest of narrow streets. *¡Dios mío!* Can't get out of the way. Down he comes, smashing through the glass door, overturns the desk. Jammed I am underneath. He's heavier than a bulrush, this guy. Bullshit! There sure was. All over me. Not a bull in a china shop, but a bull signing in for bed and breakfast. Much better an elephant in a china shop. That's what they say. *Elefante en cristalería.* Wouldn't have got through the front door. You wouldn't bet on it. Mind you, the porter could've handled a couple of his travelling cases. The trunk? Another matter.

Want to see this from the other end? The tail end?

Same tale told by the bull

Here I am champing at the bit in a sort of horse stall. Don't stall for long. Out I lurch, hurtling down Blasco de Alagón Street. You see, it's fiesta time. They're acting like wild animals. Having fun at my expense. And gonna charge me up for it, too. Charge me for damage, OK, but I'm gonna charge them! Steer clear, I'm on my way. Pawing away at the cobblestones, with the odd snort, I see arcades on the left, arcades on the right. I'm now racing hell for leather. Want to keep my leather if I can. Don't want a hiding. On the horns of a dilemma. Straight on or turn to the left through that hoarding? Too late. Hell's bulls! Don't take on board the boards. Go right through them. I plough on. My oxen friends showed me how to do that. Fly down a flight of steps towards a glass door. Amazing glazing. See someone just like me plunging towards me. Only time I've ever seen a bull just like me. Feel like the fellow who fell in love with his own image reflected in water, Narcissus. Not the flower, silly. All getting blurred on the glass, everything steamed up, me too. Reception desk. Bull metamorphosed (clever I am at writing up bulletins) into a lovely blonde girl. On reflection, it's a bit like beauty and the beast. Feel just like King Kong for a moment. All I can remember. They must have shot me a tranquillizer. Came round in a spin. Gonna beef up complaints procedure.

Next day. Report in the local *gaceta*. Saturday's market'll have to be bullish to meet the bill. They're not only gonna ring-fence me. Ring-fence some euros as well for next time. Me? I don't care a toss. No horns of a dilemma. Just plain horny with fifty cows on offer. They just put me out to graze in the field. Amazing grazing. Grass and water. Infusion of new life. I just want to recharge the batteries and all those cows.

Name of the hotel? You won't believe this, twice over. Hotel Cardenal Ram. We can ram home *Ram*. Fits in easily enough, but an odd name for a cardinal, all the same. What about *Cardenal*? *Cardinal* OK too. Like Cardinal Newman. But *cardenal* is a 'bruise' as well. All to do with red, like a red rag to a bull.

Fuendetodos next on the return north. As grim as his paintings. Who're you talking about? Goya. Town puts you off. Mark of Goya. Museum closed for the desolate winter. Brushed it off as easily as Napoleon's execution squad aiming dead straight at those terrorized *madrileños*. Desolation of desolation. Not seen the grimacing horror of painted terror? Try *Dos de mayo* (The Second of May), and *Tres de mayo* (The Third of May). May seems to have been a favourite month for Napoleon. Got it wrong in Moscow, though. Set off from France end of May 1812. Hitler caught napping just the same way. All gobbled up like in Goya's series *Saturn Devouring His Offspring*. Nap and Hit should have seen them, writ large they are across the whole sky, abnormal suffering in the murk of darkness.

No relief either through that bare, scrubland countryside, Los Monegros. Makes you think of the South Dakota Badlands. Can't get worse than that. A kind of desolate wasteland, near the valley of the river Ebro. Curious dryness. Grey and dark. *Negros* in Monegros says it all. Montenegro surely can't be as black as this.

Not a blade of grass for a young blade. Sharpen your tool elsewhere, mate.

Once a puzzling feature of road construction in Spain. Sharpest of contrasts on entering a fresh province. Behind, nice and smooth. Suddenly, no warning, uneven, stony top, complete with those fiercely sounding *baches* (potholes). Not quite *bashes* but you certainly feel bashed about. Feel bashful over telling that civil guard over there? No point. You'd be in for a bumpy ride, and he's probably on the wrong side of the line anyway. Went on like this for years and for miles. Mathematically drawn, neat line right across the road, as it were, separating province from province. Potholes with unprotected edges force you down to half the speed, and this at exactly the juncture of the two provinces. Those present in the car saw lack of cash. So no dash, to avoid a crash. Bit like taking pot luck.

Same holes, but prefer the gentle, French, welcoming sound of *nid-de-poules* (hens' nest). But can you imagine a hen laying eggs in the middle of a road? Suppose drivers would proceed with caution with eggs on offer. Like treading on egg shells.

Approaching the Pyrenees. Skirt round Huesca. Touch of fame here. Flame of Republican resistance. Orwell part of the mix, but no quick fix. Injured, so that's your lot, folks. Back to Blighty.

Eastward bound, but one day, please to the west. Must visit Riglos. Something oddly regal about it. Small, largely unrecognized village, OK, but overshadowed by the supremely majestic *mallos*. An impenetrable mystery, this. Confusing, to the Spanish too. Join the club. What's so tricky about *mallos*? To start with, dictionaries leave you up in the air. Go for a real high-flying dictionary, and there you have it. An immense, geological formation resembling huge organ pipes. Gargantua (he's coming up next) would have happily played on, or maybe, with, them. For good measure, there are other *mallos* in the region. Like Vadiello.

Intriguing thing about *mallos de Riglos*. Do you say *mallos de Riglos*, or *riglos de Mallos*. Riglos is so tiny it is not known by anyone. Wriggle as much as you like, but any the wiser? Inescapably clear is one thing: Orwell would have preferred to be London *Mall* bound to *Mallos* bound. Not so sure. Not bound by obedience to the queen, was he?

Aínsa, split in two: the old walled fortress town with a most spacious *plaza*, and enjoying the prestige of a *monumento nacional*, overlooking the new, commercially occupied town well below. Oddly enough, the crossroads for the new town are called *Las carreteras* = roads. After all, they are all *carreteras*. *Glorieta* (crossroads), or even *rotonda* seems a more rounded way of approaching things.

Want to scale a few mountains? Then Escalona, further east, is just the place for you. Want a *casa rural* with fare fit for a pharaoh? And quantities to meet the appetite of our giant friend playing those *mallos* above? Then look no further than Escalona. Food seems to have been hacked out of the *mallos* by the carpinter who owns the place. Casa Carpintera.

Get moving upwards into the Pyrenees before garages end up deep in water. Don't want to negotiate for a new car with the insurance company, do you? You could find yourself in a tight spot. Sudden, prolonged downpours and then, flash floods. They call them *gotas frías*. 'Cold drops', if you want a translation, but you'd still need a meteorologist to clarify things. He'd clear it up for you, no doubt quicker than *gotas frías* clear up. They can last for days. Better drive up to the Túnel de Biescas. Right now.

Still-scorching sun, though. Pyrenean giants all around. A couple of miles of tolerably lit tunnel. And miracle of miracles, you come out to the greenest and most fertile of pastures on the other side. The Pyrenees did two things. 1. Kept Napoleon thinking about invasion tactics. Don't want all that Enlightenment, atheist doctrine marching its way to Madrid. 2. God got it wrong in the workshop. All fertile and lush to the north. All sterile and ash to the south. North: trees. South: unease. North: shade galore. South: sun and more. North: rain and green. South: dry and mean. North: everywhere to picnic. South: not a chance to nitpick. Still, crossing north to south or south to north, food and drink to us.

We run into that modest little town of Foix. Nothing special here. Hold on. Haven't you heard that jolly, bouncy way those French *enfants* trot out their number-one nursery rhyme? Words at the end sound the same but the devil's in the spelling. All spelt differently. Here's the pithy ditty. Bouncy bits lost in translation:

> Il était une **fois** (*There was once*)
> Un marchand de **foie** (*A seller of liver*)
> Qui vendait du **foie** (*Who would sell liver*)
> Dans la ville de **Foix** (*In the town of Foix*)
> Il se dit «Ma **foi**, (*He said to himself 'Heavens above*)
> C'est la dernière **fois** (*That's the last time*)
> Que je vends du **foie** (*That I sell liver*)
> Dans la ville de **Foix**». (*In the town of Foix.'*)

Be bold enough to say it aloud. All the words in bold have the sound 'fwa', and there are four of them. Whether there were ten of them, we Brits could easily get our own back. Just look at all those impossible variations with *bough, although, through, trough*, etc. Ah, but they're not all pronounced the same. And at least the sounds are the same in French. Poor Gallic learners of English pronunciation, dearest creature in creation. Feel a bit of a donkey, can't pronounce monkey?

Animal lovers, bursting with indignation once again. Stuffing of geese and duck for *foie gras* of gastronomic dainties must fill them with rage. And it sure does. I'll duck this one. Get stuffed, we're going north. On a Bacchus-driven palate, from wines of Languedoc-Roussillon, Bergerac, Cognac, over to the Bordelais, and then to the southern Nantais slopes of the Loire. Case of a case or two of *Gros Plant* or the vivid red of Bourgueil just to the west (four hundred miles in all of almost continuous vineyards! – enough to make you paralytic with pleasure). Could do a dry run just to see. That's with *vino*, of course. Or, are we tempted eastwards to the Gorges du Tarn. Les Détroits (The Narrows, like Detroit; that's narrow too), dazzling and dramatic beneath vertical and overhanging cliffs? Better this than a hangover up north. Shooting the rapids, here we come. Second thoughts: sweet-sounding *côtes* and *coteaux*, and *châteaux* by the dozen, all stretching up and over the horizon. But no ten-rated stars of Pouilly-Fuissé. Friends can never pronounce all those *ui*s. The French? Food and drink for them this time. And at the end of it all are awaiting those rolling Champagne hills.

Beyond the Tarn is the Roquefort goat-cheese country. Hundreds of thousands of *brebis* (ewes) graze on the limestone plateaux they call the *causses*. Because all this chewing goes down to the valley for one of the finest and most expensive cheeses in the world. If you can barely afford the euros for the cheese, you can at least save them for that modern marvel of 'arquitecture', Norman (Foster)-designed, a viaduct spanning in breath-taking style one of the Tarn valleys. Three cheers for our Norman, wisdom-led fellow. We don't now spend an eternity queuing at the maddening, bottleneck descent into Millau. Prefer the bottleneck, though, to the battle of those *foie gras* necks.

Drive along the quite recently opened A75 motorway, a spot of carefree motoring. What with no toll? Kilometre after kilometre, cuts up through the most stupendous, most memorable scenery of the high-up *causses*. Width and height provide a marvellous mixture of delight. Nosing its way on up, the car drops us off at the volcanic La Bourboule, high-mountain health resort brimming with spas, and overpopulated by state-aided patients suffering from respiratory ailments and skin disorders. Even the peaky peak ones peak on the peaks. Fits of pique, though. All this *aux frais de la princess* (buckshee) treatment, whoever the princess was. Can't keep it up, not at these heights. Bring the cost down, says the Right. Or someone's for the high jump. Rather like the so-called therapeutic waters taken in the Spanish, western Pyrenean Panticosa periodically invaded by pensioners by their coach load. Profligate spending of the socially oriented ideals of Felipe González of the nineteen-seventies and -eighties had to dry up. State coffers drowned in aqueous extravagance.

On up through the *viticole* areas of Burgundy, then Champagne. Or is it *vinicole*? Don't ask the French. They have no idea, and don't even seem to worry. Too drunk to wonder. Both words, they claim, have their roots in wine-growing, and what's the difference of one letter among drunks? The bottle's handy, that's good enough. They always take the easy way out. By the way, 'wine-growing' seems just as confusing. Have you ever seen anyone growing wine? The French have the last word in wine *dégustatioin* before we start heading back to port, which they are not very partial to. They do adore Ronsard, however. A preferred poet. Penned the joys of wine with 'le vin qui rit dans l'or' (the wine that laughs in the gold [of a goblet]). We'll all enjoy a vinous laugh with our Continental companions. Not too far away is *Gaudeamus Igitur.* Can't be anything more cheering than that. Throw a drop of their language in the wine and we're racked with the stuff. More please. Cheers!

Thus is drawing to a nostalgic close another of those many memorable European odysseys. Even mighty Jason and his Argonauts would have put their oar in. All in the service of a career of magic mix of history, geography, weather. *Carpe diem,* said Horace of Roman times, and we did 'Enjoy the day', and still do. Only the desk is awaiting our arrival home, impatiently calling for the memories of these last days to be fed into the hungry and usually compliant computer. Can be encouraged to comply, with all those funny accents, in any language you care for. It can even stick the *o* and the *e* together. *Nœud* (knot). No knotty problems here, for all the naval knots you do. Have to cross the Channel, you know.

Not before finding the *logis* at Le Wast. Where's that? Inland from Boulogne. Like all self-respecting Parisians worth their pronunciation salt, charged through whole villages asking with mounting frustration: 'Où est Le Wast?' (Where's Le Wast?). Am

154

I in a time warp? No one knew. Don't believe it? It's true. Tried and tried. Thought the accent spot on. Le Wast, easy-peasy. Just like they'd say it in Nantes, Paris, Grenoble or anywhere. Le Vast, with a flat, sharp, north-of-England *a*, as in *fast* (North of England!), with the *W as a V* to boot. But Pierre and his *amis* didn't get it. Trying to find Le Wast was becoming a waste of time. At wits' end, I stride into a bar, spread out the local map, and there it is, plain as a pike staff (flat *a*, please): *Le Vast.* 'Non, Monsieur, eet ees *Le Waa*,' (with the original *W* and two long *a*s, high in the mouth, as it were) and 'eet ees just over that heel.' Half a gallon of petrol lost, not in Wat, but in vat, still gallons in those days, we arrive at the logis. All forgiven, around another of those succulent, wine-enhanced tables.

Cherbourg > Cádiz > Calais, some on the motorway. Fast. Even faster? Could chip away at the time just a bit more. But want to get up real speed? Try the information highway. Microchips'll do it. Cherbourg > Cádiz > Calais, one button. And one key. All Cs. And you're not all at sea. End of the line and now to record it all on line.

Easy enough travelling in Europe. But how do you hop over the Charco (yes, Spanish-speakers do say 'Pond'; they get something right). Argentina, Colombia, Peru, Mexico and the US, if you like, even California, you're not too far away. How come? Same again. The key is, well, in those keys, you know, right in front of you. One ping on a key, and you're off to Buenos Aires, Bogotá, Lima or Mexico City. Whizzing over the Pond is an adventure in itself, and just a second or two away! Jees!

But, have no illusions, my computer does his own computing. I remonstrate. Threaten it with a crash course, cutting-edge technology, laying him out with a change in layout. He ('he', that's getting personal) just goes on in his own cute way. Stay in English, and all is sweetness and light. You just toddle off blithely into another of those lingos, and you could be in big trouble. It's this default, preset programming cavorting Steve Jobs has come up with. Have an ongoing, permanent conflict with this machine. Has he got a chip on his shoulder? Perhaps, he's xenophobic, hasn't said. Maybe he's frightened to. He knows I like all those funny-sounding foreigners with the oddest of words. No big deal there. He even knows I write books with them. With him.

Have to watch him like a hawk. If I quote, inside some English words, the simplest, most innocent of French words like *dont* (of whom/whose), he plays a game on me, and puts in a sly apostrophe: *don't*. Maybe he's been ticked off by Lynn, of apostrophe fame. He must trust her. He knows I'm going to reread the sentence in five minutes' time, but he sticks to his guns, or apostrophe. Back I go, suspecting the worse. Sure enough, the apostrophe's been reinstated. Knock it out, Ron, tell him who's who, move forward a few words, and blow you me, it's back in again. Do you lose your cool? No point. You work out a way of laying him out good and proper. Change the layout, that's the key. Bingo! All is OK. But this is not the end. It's the beginning of the beginning. Stand-off could continue indefinitely, I fear.

A touch of the keys and a touch of frustration. Sometimes, I feel like putting the boot in. But, on reflection, he likes being booted up, you know, starting up, computer lingo. At root, he appreciates the boot.

Sensible wheeze to go into, say, French default mood? A touch puzzling, even for me. Gets rid of the *don't* question. We're safe with *dont* now. You sail blissfully along in French, put in all the cunning little accents even the French themselves don't bother about, the acute (é), the grave (è), the circumflex over the *a*, the *e*, the *i*, the *o*, and the *u*: (â, ê...). This is great. You can even stick in the cedilla, still compliant so no complaints. Of course, the cedilla has to go under the *c*: Les Açores, and we're half way to Argentina. The weird thing here is that the cedilla was really a Spanish trick. Hoping to get on the right side of Napoleon, they let the French have it free, nice of them, and no longer use it themselves. But, you then try to put in that scream of a squiggly

156

thing over the Spanish *n* (ñ), you'd want to get in the swing of things, halfway as you are to Argentina in the Açores, and the machine's not game. Is he playing a game? Raging and ranting does no good at all. You finally outdo that cunning little device by playing around with the *alt* key and numbers. Crunch him with numbers, that's what I'll do. Failing that, as a last resort, pop into Spanish mode, before you go off pop.

Try to write archaeology with the Latin *a* and *e* stuck together. Key in *æ*. Doesn't work? Try again. Go up to *Insert*. Box load of goodies up there. Skiving away is *æ* between *å* and *ç*. You hunt and hunt. Got it: *æ*. OK, Mr Kay? Yanks stick to *e*, and that's fine. Nowhere near as urgent as A&E.

Don't think accents do the same job in French, Spanish and Italian, or Czech and Polish for that matter. The computer does, so more struggles on the way. Try and tell him that the Italian word for coffee is *caffè* with the accent going one way, and then the French *café* with an accent going in the opposite direction. Enough to make you seasick, with all that tossing and turning. Sometimes, don't even know where I am, in Spanish mode or French? Carried away by that most parodic of all war novels, Hašek's *The Good Soldier Švejk*, you saw the need to put a different sort of squiggle over the *s*, the ubiquitous Czech *háček* (hook), you would send your friendly computer into convulsions. You feel you want to do a hatchet job on him. A slice of advice. Sneak round things with a quick dip up above into the symbols, and all done, as you see above. Relief all round.

Torment is not at an end. You continue to use English as your default mode. Want to write within an English quote the Spanish *responsable* with an *a*. Spellings this time, not accents. Your machine frets, corrects and underscores <u>responsible</u>. Scores a point, he does. In some lofty, superior manner, suggests you are in error. Slightly irascible now. Even gets choleric. Hey, this is getting too pedantic. His wayward behaviour takes you back to the English *responsible*. You have to keep an eye on the *i*. I get frantic with his antics. Ants in your pants you start to feel. Back you go to *responsible*.

He still bucks at your bullying. But you get your way in the end. Whoopee! *responsable*. Not finished yet. He goes ballistic when you try it on with the Italian *responsabile*. Just when he's getting used to *responsable*, he has to cope with an *i* between the *b* and the *l*. Keep pressing away with the Spanish *cacao, femenino, éxtasis* and *vainilla*. Same for the French: *adresse, calme, ustensile*. More of the same with Italian: *accidente, esempio, esistenza*. Hundreds of these cunningly similar, but distinct words (even *distinto* in Spanish, damn it!) that he insists on underlining. Even as the words appear on the page. The trouble is these other languages are fun. You sure can play with them. I'm really bitten by the byte bug. Spellbound, and in the land of magic.

A computer splutter. Coughs a bit. Is this a hacker crashing in on me? Almost tries to bite. Not the hacker. He's keener on bytes. I try to key in the symbol CUT, even COPY, but he just gives me a pasting. I look for an error, use the barcode binoculars for FIND in an attempt to justify the manoeuvre. Still no progress. I key in *COUPER* and *COPIER* in French. No avail. In despair, I cut my losses, and put in the Spanish: *CORTAR* and *COPIAR*. Yipee! Wrong language mode all along.

The keys finally relent, and let me have all my own way. Is the computer going soft on the new hardware I've put in? Perhaps conscience-stricken? Alliterative Hamlet, on a misquoting spree: 'The quote's the thing wherein I'll catch the conscience of the keys.'

I don't (he's happy with this apostrophe) torment him with the arabesques of Arabic, and consolation, even elation, comes his way when I tell him that Turkish and Indonesian have changed over to the simplified Latin alphabet. You may not think so, but I do sympathize with the delirium of my lovely little machine, and am finally at a loss to comfort him. Like any well-read person on medicine, you'd suspect delirium sinks into disturbed innards, nausea, and, if I'm not careful, he just plain sulks, when the chips are down. Disturbed innards bring him to the next chapter on the treasure trove of scatology. Easy enough for him to deal with as long as we praise his penchant for English. Oh, no, not again! He's shaking once more. Not keen on 'penchant'. Careful keying. I promise. He chips in with his chips: 'I'll hold you to it.'

5

Scatological Interludes

Eschatology	Branch of theology concerning the end of the world
Scatology	Study of excrement

Surprised? Never heard of one or the other? Don't muddle them up, or you could easily put your foot in it. And you don't want to sink as low as that. The trouble is there's always the risk of mixing up the two in Spain. Cassocks and buttocks really can put you in the mire. Why so? Answer: They see no difference between 'scatological' and 'eschatalogical'. Same word: *escatológico*. Bet you're even more surprised that Spanish speakers are rarely aware of this alarming convergence. At a pinch, they may just know one or the other of the meanings. In all likelihood, neither. No way to alter this at the altar. What do they say, the ecclesiastical hierarchy? Dunno, never fresh in their mind.

Unease here. Both meanings lead back to the ends of things. Look at the etymologies, you know, roots of words. Could send you scatty. 'Eschatology' comes from the Greek *eskhatos*, that is 'the study of life beyond the tomb'. 'Scatology' comes from the Greek *skat* = excrement. What could be clearer than that? Not much. Don't tell the Spaniards we've got two words for their one. They'd raise an eyebrow in disbelief, even dismay.

Let's skate over the **esch**atological meaning of *escatalogía*, i.e. the study of life beyond the tomb. We're into scatology now. Above that, nothing. Run the risk of papal excommunication?

161

That's just a lot of papal bull. We leave **esch**atology to the pope
and his cardinals. The other, down-to-earth meaning, bodily
functions, both back and front, gives us food for thought, especially
when we're on the move, travelling. Keep paper handy and roll
out this second interpretation, and let's flush out the differences.

François Rabelais in sixteenth-century France, you deliver first.
Sure you've settled on the arresting similarities in the French words
scatologie and **eschatologie**. You were a cleric, after all. Dispensed
a spot of wise counsel on the future life, didn't you? And you
shared the lavatorial activities of the human race. Discharged
duties on all fronts. Mind you, Jonathan Swift, also a man of
the cloth in eighteenth-century England and Ireland, could not
have been far behind.

Gallic, Rabelaisian spirit. Infected the young poet Rimbaud.
Privy he was to a stream of anal vulgarities. Let's lay bare the
facts. The alliterative *Vénus, un ulcère à l'anus* (Venus, with an
ulcer in her anus) served as a painful benchmark for future
architects of poetical crudities. Went off gun-running, Rambo-
style, to Ethiopia. Of doubtful sexual orientation, he shot from
the hip, widening the circle of his friends. No love for a bunch
of straight arseholes.

Convenience in matters of urination? Look no further than
over the Channel. How do they channel it over there? Gabriel
Chevalier's the man, master of the bladder. *Clochemerle*, the latest
release in 1948. Novel and film. We tried to separate eschatology
and scatology. Alas, here they are joining forces. How come? Place
a urinal next to a church in the main square of the small village
of Beaujolais, Clochemerle. *Merle* sticks pretty close to *merde*.
Pomposity and prudishness are offended. Puritan America banned
the can, at least the film. Kicked up a stink, they did.

Scene: Two elderly ladies, proprieties-inclined, spying out onto
a newly created, open-air toilet facility. Window of discontent.
To celebrate inauguration, step forward, Monsieur le Maire. Mayor's
hat thrown in air. Cleared the air, he has, and his bladder. Away
with the musty stench of tradition. Prayerful priest, evacuating

his premises, fresh from host and mass, is singling out down below rows of legs, up above tops of hats, peeved by pinging on zinc. Ladies' room next in the square? Knickers!

The first encounter, in 1952, with the ease and sangfroid displayed by the French when relieving their bladder, seemed to me to be *shocking*, as they themselves say. On the side of the road, in full view of his children and wife, with three English lads fast approaching on their bikes, the father just opened his flies and peed. Nonchalance in the public act of peeing assumed the dimensions of an edifying spectacle. The word for flies (*braguette*), together with all the terms for peeing, came pouring in. *Braguette* was learnt in the university library when reading – who else? – Rabelais's *Gargantua*, and innocently enquiring of a female friend what it meant. Uncontrollable blushing accompanied her answer.

Soon, it became of little moment to seek relief anywhere, even on a bike, to save time, an art that had to be, and could be, developed on French roads. No one seemed to mind. And all the Tour de France *coureurs cyclistes* did it, and still do, with the simple difference, and this is a well-known fact, they pee in their shorts, composed of a sponge-like material for absorption sake. Maybe let the sweat do the work. Relief on to the road, easier said than done, if you don't want to splash bike and legs. Such contortionist antics would, of course, be inaccessible to the female anatomy.

Despite, or because of, Waterloo, French speakers have illustrated for many years the art of spending a penny, or should it be a centime? *Waterloo* says it all. Why 'French speakers'? This art even overflows on to the Waterloo of Belgium (and half of them speak French), where that naughty, brazen little Belgian boy, *le Manneken Pis*, pees all day long, in an upwards trajectory, and supposedly all night long, in a Brussels square, near the Grand-Place. Thus far, he has remained immune from prosecution from the Council of Europe. We imagine he is protected by the European Human Rights or 'Droits de l'Homme', as the French say. Why not 'Droits du Garçon' here? As against female inability to pee on a bike, *le Manneken Pis*, alias *le Petit Julien*, does indeed have a female equivalent in Brussels: *Jeannette Pis*.

Yet, these two admirable little demonstrators in the peeing art are as nothing compared to the truly stupendous feats of Rabelais's giant Gargantua in the book of the same name. Water works, just as size matters. In some sort of biblical diluvian parody, to Gargantua it was given to submerge and drown countless Parisians, although mothers with their children were mercifully spared. They usually are. The number to meet this urologic fate are precisely, and here in the original sixteenth-century French: *deux cens soixante mille quatre cens dix et huyt* (260,418). A flood of protest would be of no avail. Try a stopcock, but it'll still come rushing down round the washer. Could help be in the pipeline with a diversionary catheter? Bathometer could measure flow and depth. What about appealing to the *Coq sportif*, you know, the company selling sportswear? But even that *coq* won't be *sportif* enough. All we want is a bit of sporty fair play, as the French say. If, drained of resources and in despair, you could try this diuretic ditty. We do need to arrest this delirious bout of deliverance:

> Bloody bladder, did they cry,
> Gladly, madly, was his reply,
> Piss isn't possible in a pot,
> Joy of giants is to piss a lot.

No wonder the French are so cocksure about their lavatorial humour. So compellingly and fundamentally readable, given their classical instruction in what is, at bottom, part of Gallic wit and ebullient *joie de vivre*.

Peeing anywhere, yes indeed! There was a cinema in the centre of Nantes where queues of males and females for the film would form within a metre or so of a *urinoir* (urinal), or *pissoir*, known more colloquially. The males of our species simply made a second parallel queue. The film showing at the time was, appropriately enough, the Woody Allen *Everything You Wanted to Know about Sex But Were Afraid to Ask*. One wonders if there were anything left for these French queuers to ask, given their lack of bashfulness over penis performances. This certainly explains why a former French colleague would use female cloakrooms for relief rather than walk an extra few paces upstairs for the male toilets. As far as is recalled, this provoked no complaints. It was simply expected of those beyond the Channel. For this sanitary aberration, he was not, as far as is known, condemned to penal servitude.

Urination in Nantes, as in travel generally, posed a particular problem, and in this case, on a recent and very prolonged stay. Accommodation had been located by a French friend who had himself lived at the property. A bedroom on the ground floor offers all the ingredients of comfort requiring little comment. And indeed, comfort left nothing to be desired, save for one feature verging, initially, on despair. Bladder relief was on the first floor. The flight of stairs providing access curled round twice on its upwards journey, what our neighbours call un *escalier en colimaçon*. What's *colimaçon*? The Frogs eat them. Yet, even if I mounted the stairs as slowly as a 'snail', danger still lurked at night-time when bladder conditions spiral out of control.

Now, the lady of the house, tormented with the strangest of idiosyncrasies, would not allow lights on at night-time. Nocturnal use of the upstairs loo? Out of bounds. Stairs sported no carpet, retaining a very high polish. Disaster round the corner. Not possible to banish the liquid polish. Solution for the solution? Unbeknown to Mlle Suzanne now quotable, having shuffled off this mortal coil, an outrageous tactic was resorted to. Mirth it may provide for some, righteous indignation in those Clochemerle ladies. Window of the sash type, up and down. *Fenêtre à guillotine*. No cutting edge of technology this. And no prizes for guessing what it means. Every night, for some three months, the window was secretly, sedulously opened, and held up, since the fastening mechanism functioned badly, and urine poured forth on to the flagstones outside, just below the window. Relieved, I regained my bed and continued to do what beds always invite you to do. Fine, you say? The following morning, and consistently for the remainder of the stay, Mlle Suzanne would enquire: 'Monsieur Ronald, comment se fait-il que les dalles soient mouillées?' (... How is it that the flagstones are wet?), to which the invariable reply was: 'Il doit y avoir une fuite dans la gouttière' (There must be a leak in the guttering). A watertight, if not urine-tight, reply, until that very Christmas. Happily, it rained copiously in Nantes that autumn *comme vache qui pisse* (like a pissing cow), to disperse the acrid smell. Three cheers for the s(l)ash window.

The lady owner's idiosyncrasies affected more than refusal of lights at night-time, and a passing preoccupation with 'water'. She would not allow lodgers to make their bed in the morning. They had to be aired until the evening. *Patins obligent*: they had to be worn at all times when in the room. You may ask what *patins* were. They were, and not *are*, for now outmoded, felt pads used for walking on parquet floors. The furniture and customs of the house, as well as vocabulary and attitudes of the proprietor, seemed so anachronistic, the lodger felt transported to a sort of rickety *Bleak House* of Dickens. Add to these oddities her frequent, unsettling, nocturnal invocations to her long-dead father – 'Mon petit père' – and you had oddball ingredients for hilarity. Ballsache, sorry Balzac, could have poured forth a whole range of eccentric descriptions.

But back to toilets and the needs they cater for. New, unexplored accommodation, even fleeting, often required unusual resources. A weekend in Zamora in central Spain, El Cid territory, began in the most inauspicious of ways. Imagine you are driven from Salamanca, which, as already noted, can flatter itself as among the oldest universities in Europe, to Zamora, and at night-time. Imagine equally that you end up in the briefest of moments in a bed beckoning you before you have had a chance to see where the light switch is. Nature calls at two o'clock in the morning. All that *vino*. Darkness is still total, courtesy of the usual well-fitting interior shutters. ¡*Dios mío!* Where's the light switch? You fumble and fumble, no switch in sight, if you could say that, handle what appears to be a flowerpot, and, relief! Have no illusions, for the trauma is not over. How to empty the pot next morning? Extreme ingenuity of purpose. Reach the bathroom without the friends' knowledge, or to avoid spillage.

The inability to find a switch in the depths of the night syndrome was not limited to Zamora. It provoked disturbance, fear of involuntary discharge, even despair, in youth hostels where dormitories were underground tunnels, as in Reims, or in lofts, as in Perpignan. Camp beds, packed in tight, required immense tactile skill to access any toilet area. The loft situation in Perpignan posed the even more serious problem of climbing down a ladder. Needless to add, the knack adopted in Nantes was converted into a permanent strategy. Wherever windows afforded the possibility of urologic relief, that was the best way out. The defecating art was never researched and refined in these circumstances.

Signore (and I do mean 'ladies'), in Pompei, beware! Female toilets are not in plentiful supply. *Empty your bladder before entry*, should be the sign. Sixty years ago, not a tourist in sight, male or female. Peeing posed no problem. Nowadays, you can walk and walk, talk and talk, queue and queue, fret and fret, in vain. A dilemma confronting would-be female peers (pee-ers). After more than an hour of seeking comfort, the said peer would return painfully full, to empty herself behind a bush, chivalrous husband nonchalantly standing guard. No difficulty for him. He had done his business, possibly more than once, behind the same bush, trained as he was in this skill. Quite evident that loos had not been reinstated after the eruption, for all the eruptions issuing forth.

Bathrooms are tricky places, especially one in San Sebastián, in the Basque country of northern Spain. One bathroom coming to mind offered the most perplexing of challenges. Although consistently instructed otherwise, a massive, white dog of the Samoyed type, soft as Camembert cheese, and lovingly innocent, mounted somnolent guard at the entrance of this bathroom. Cold tiles were among his favourite sleeping spots. Like Cerberus, the canine custodian of Hades, but with only one head, he would obstruct the entrance in the middle of the night, and when you succeeded in passing through the door of Hades, he would impede your need to lighten your load by pressing his furry side against, well, you can guess. Dogged nightly by a ... no prizes for guessing.

As with bathrooms, public toilets abounded in drawbacks, witness this anecdote occurring in reverse, as it were. A Spanish university colleague, tongue-tied in English, but ingenious in short stories in his native tongue, found himself on one occasion in an individual water closet in a New York airport bathroom, as they say over there. José, for that was his name, failed to unfasten a faulty locking device. In true simian fashion, for he lived near Gibraltar, home of numerous Barbary apes, he promptly climbed up, and over, the top of the cubicle. Caught *in flagrante delicto*, and not in fragrant delight for he had not been able to wash his hands, he found himself dragged down, and then dragged up before two members of the Security Service. Poor English. Stuck in the predicament until it became clear that he didn't have terrorism on his mind. Pee-shooting was all he had had in mind.

Approaching certain elements of coarse vocabulary in Romance languages calls for caution. You could so easily comb yourself with a penis, if you said *pene* (penis) instead of *peine* (comb). Here the vertical *i* is all the difference while the need for this extra upward stroke stands out a mile. *Peine* and *pene* are two Spanish terms reaching out to the Italian: *pene* and *pettine*, with similar translations.

How do you deal with the Spanish notice *No pisar el césped*, which is not an injunction to avoid peeing on the lawn, but rather, not to walk on it? A Spanish policeman would spend all day long in Aranjuez, south of Madrid and place of a grandiose *palacio real* (royal palace), whistling to perpetrators of the ultimate English transgression: walking on a fastidiously tended lawn. Most of the arraigned culprits, and, in this case, they were Spanish, continued to transgress. Were hundreds of metres away, unable to understand the gesticulations, I didn't say *testiculations*, of the man of law. Maybe if they had pissed on the lawn they would have remained free from chastisement.

Again, in reverse, a sensitively inclined French speaker would avoid, at all costs, the pronunciation of the county Sussex. If one learnt that the *sus* bit would reproduce in the Gallic tongue the verb *sucer* (to suck), one would understand why. *Sus* + *sex*! Blow you me, that's a blow job. And imagine the torment suffered by an Italian or Spanish speaker in the throes of learning Czech where the ubiquitous *si* (*yes*, although the *i* has a rising accent in Spanish = *í*, just to complicate things still further) comes out in this mid-European language as *anus*, i.e. *ano*. To be more explicit, every time you wanted to say yes in Czech as part of polite international relations, you had to say *anus*! You'd feel a bit of a prick.

Mind you, the student mind relishes this linguistic tweak of fate. Vulgarity in language is the name of their game. Try their toilets, to start with. Just a small payment. They're just to let. Toilet to let. All to do with introducing that erect *i* again.

Language indelicacy? Ultimate test of language competence. You learn a lot. *Merde, merde* and more *merde* or, if you like, *mierda* in Spanish and *merda* in Italian. Now that's education, for you. Easy, they're all feminine!

Which takes us from the urinary tract to anal considerations, from the light to the serious, solid stuff. The first and high-coloured encounter with Continental toilet arrangements occurred in August 1953, and a shock-horror, draining encounter it was. The scene: the youth hostel at Tuttlingen, on the river Danube, that cropped up in Chapter 1. A dribble there. Here, the full works. Job of my companion, Mike, dedicated to German? Intervene on my behalf for one unique, spectacular hour on a balmy evening. Was the splash of his life. All to do with the loss of a wallet. Let the wallet speak for itself.

An Hour in the Life of a Wallet (*taken from a* Diarrhoea Diary)

Ron's wallet I am. Spend their cycling time in Mike's top anorak pocket, nice and cosy there. More room than in the back pocket of Ron's shorts. Safer too in youth hostels. Always fastened down by a popper stud. I look after his passport, return boat ticket, all his meagre dosh. All sweet till that fateful moment.

Ron's shorts are anything but sweet, as you'll see. Nothing short and sweet about what's to follow. He was short-changed in my transfer from shorts to anorak. The narrative runs a downward course:

Mike opens upstairs door. Pong. I suppose it's a bog. But not bog-standard. Has all the conveniences. Hear a catch shutting hard. Mike starts shitting hard. Hell! I'm going down that way. What's happening? I'm falling out of my safe little haven. Down a pipe, all slimy. Stinks to low heaven. Come to a halt, on the edge of a ledge. I see a sea of shit below me, excremental vapour rising up to my nostrils. On bending over the toilet seat to flush away his deposit, and incidentally mine for the return journey, lo(o) and behold, Mike had accidentally shot me shitwards, into a cesspit. Fortunately into a cesspit. Into the main sewer system would have spelt more than disaster. Scenes from Carol Reed's *The Third Man*, set in Vienna, would have come to mind, and we were not far from the Austrian frontier.

Twenty minutes later, they're dousing me with a hose on a clothes line, round the back of the youth hostel, now dark. I get the lowdown from their talk, or could we say, the wind of what had happened. Warden, Mike and Ron with a real drain on his finances. Trying to keep the lid on his feverish agitation. Had taken it off the cesspit, where the fun starts. The tale goes like this:

Mike in dormitory: Ron, something awful's happened. Your wallet's down the shit chute.
Ron: Tell the warden.
Warden: Lock all toilet doors. No more shit and no flush. *Building evacuated. Yet, where could the passing hostellers evacuate themselves? Especially those who were diarrhoea-driven. No laughing matter.*

Ron's thoughts: *They trickled through his mind as the excremental liquid still trickled down the shaft. Flush with discomposure before so much decomposition. Hopes were slipping away, and downwards. Knew he had to get stuck in, and had a nose for practical solutions. There was every solid reason why me (low-level English here, but hell, we're in Germany and we're dealing with crap), the wallet, should be lost forever, in a flurry of slurry. So drained was Ron sinking into the bowels of the earth. Had to pour all resources into retrieving the wallet. Sagging thoughts invaded him thick and fast. Take the plunge, Ron, but don't take the plunge. Care, depends on the plunge.*
Warden: Off with the manhole cover. I'll find a pole, the stick sort, and shovel. Fix them together with a vice.

Back to me, the wallet. Everything to do with 'back', in fact. Here I was, sitting on the edge of a sea of shit. Could I slip more? The plot was sickening and thickening. See a stream of light from a torch, some six feet away, slightly above my head. Shovel nosing towards me. Just as well he hadn't got a nose. See Ron's hand, and beyond that, his dimly lit head. Under me, the shovel nudges and lifts me from the ledge, slowly carrying me towards safety, that bright hole, surrounded by the darkness of the sky. But how could this be done? I heard all the rest from the clothes line.

Ron, straining and straining, probably browned off, stretches out on the ground, sideways to start with. He must be playing it by ear. Not sure at this stage whether I can be retrieved. Mike holds his legs. He pledges his support so Ron can reach the ledge. Pipes up 'Sorry sorry sorry...' Better if the arsehole'd piped down. He's really got up Ron's nose.

Like the stink. Ron's getting sceptical about the septic tank. He's getting even more sceptical about trying to spell *sceptical* and *septic*. The Americans confuse things, for starters. The key to their spelling is k = s*k*eptical. But what about Romance languages? No romance here. My knowledge didn't run that deep then but things have become transparent of late. At a risk of muddying the waters, an Italian tank is *settico*, but if you were uncertain about that, you could be *scettico*. A Spanish tank is *séptico*, but if you were uncertain about that, you'd be *escéptico*. A French tank is *septique* but if you were uncertain about that, you'd be *sceptique*. Seems a bit like Nero fiddling while Rome burned.

Back to my rescue mission. Ron, on the edge of sanity, makes one last-ditch attempt, and I'm free. But that's not the end of the matter, if you see what I mean. The matter has to be removed. I have to be washed down, dried and returned to my original red. Brown stains ingrained in me finally faded. The warden's approach had been spot on.

At stake was the loss of me, a wallet. On the brink of extinction. A wallet lost by a wally. The foulest of meltdowns from those faecal fumes was only narrowly avoided. You would have thought no one could have retrieved me, or had a stomach for it. Fortunately, Ron was as gutsy as they come. Understandable, maybe he had been trying, in some odd atavistic way, to see how some of his own intimate belongings had ended up in the pool.

Back to my owner. A singular hour of triumph celebrated by a glass of wine offered by the warden. Bottoms up! Determined to put it all behind me.

This episode, described faithfully in all its details, ranks high in the lowest form of chronicles in world travel. And, to c(r)ap it all, I got by without a foreign tongue in my head. Never in the annals of anal history has so much effort been wasted in the service of so little. Certainly uncovered their backward sewage system. Miles behind the streamlined scheme we were tapped into in Blighty. Blighted my thoughts towards continental toilet arrangements for years. Still felt obliged to pay lip service to them, however yucky. 'Lip' seems to be the wrong end of the anatomy, somehow. A slip of the tongue, surely.

Back to the western side of the Rhine. WC may indeed be short for Winston Churchill, of some low royal stock. A Gallic

visit to the can is indeed *rendre hommage à **Winston Churchill**.*
But the wedding of real royal stock, **W**illiam and **C**atherine reeked
of **WC**, especially the cake, you understand.

Imagine the privy meanderings of a free-thinking French
journalist. We revolutionary French revel in the royals. Odd, don't
you think? It's playing with opposites, a bitter-sweet game, really.
Laddee Dee (Diana) was our favourite, and philandering Charles
was anything but. Sure enough, the inscription *WC* on the wedding
cake would have been one insulting sultana too far. I mean, how
well would *WC* go down on the *wedding cake*? *WC* on *wc*? Not
too well, you'd suppose. But how well would the wedding cake
itself go down? Of course, it depends on what you put in it. I
bet Buck House would have put a fatwa on a *WC* cake, anyway.
Sure enough, the English media avoided *WC* like the, well, the
stench of *WC*. You don't talk about that sort of thing in polite
circles, and we all have circles, don't we? We need them for WCs.
But, leave WCs to us French.

I would certainly have bet on a royal flush if they had played
their cards right, although they're never in a mood to appease,
even when peeing.

Of course, it could depend on the mix of the cake. The trouble
is that in the middle of the secret mix is Elizabeth: Catherine
Elizabeth Middleton. So what? you'd say. Elizabeth happens to be
the name of the lady running Buck House. Can you imagine the
Queen plumb in the middle of a tainted wedding cake? Heresy
of the most heinous kind. That's really plumbing the depths. You
English always like to wait and see. We Frenchies call it *attentisme*.
But, if they eat the stuff, there'll be convulsions of, say laughter,
or … something more visceral. I'd settle for the cup, *W* on one
side and *C* on the other. That's really my *tasse de thé* (cup of
tea), as the nobby aping French like to say. A rider to this sticky
subject is the delicate, even unheralded avoidance of the WC
syndrome on the improvised toilets along The Mall to cater (oops!
back to cake again) for the thousands of well-wishers on the Big
Day.

Let's not stop at the Kake. There's more on WCs. Stands out on Continental doors as well. WC is quite ubiquitous. No surprises here in France and Spain or Italy? Well, yes, there could be, particularly if you listen to the way the French pronounce it. Rather than the sometimes pronounced *doublevécé*, they go much more for *vc* (*vécé*), tempted to see in *VC* some audacious act rewarded by the English military *VC*. You may think this is all far-fetched. Not so, if you had accompanied me years ago to a tsunami-driven flush in an Alpine hole-in-the-floor sweeping all before it. We refer to Digne, straight below.

The event at Digne, in southern France, also ranks high, prefer stinks high, in the excitement and adventure stakes, even if a little behind the malodorous triumphs of Tuttlingen. *Digne* equals 'worthy', although the experience undergone displayed nothing worthy about it. Arrived at hostel early evening. Had hitched a lift. Beetled down to Digne from Annecy in a German Beetle. Call of nature.

You enter a closet about four feet square. Occupant's nose is almost squashed up against the door resistant to locking. Once inside, you're confronted, for the very first time, with a hole-in-the-floor arrangement, medically recommended, later pointed out, although there is nothing hygienic about what is to follow. The user, accustomed to an undemanding, non-elastic sedentary position, squats over the gaping, fearful cavern in what the French euphemistically call a style *à la turque* (Turkish). Strain on haunches may not be great for the supple legs of youth, but an older, wobbly organism would be sorely tested. How to ease the squeeze?

What is to follow will disturb young as well as old. In the middle of discharge, a frightening, rushing sound, clearly signalling the automatic onset of a flush, gives me a turn turning on a turd. No time to calculate moment of flushing to set the rush in motion, for, of its own accord, or determined by a gleeful, accursed French engineer still irked by the fortuitously, lavatorially named Waterloo, the flood, unannounced, swirls around the feet, conveying with it faecal matter the discharger hoped at least all belongs to him. Up he leaps, shorts dangling around ankles, frantically opening the door. Suddenly finds himself in a corridor, half starkers, stared at by males and females alike. From risky to risqué in one panicky jump. Later pointed out that the flush is malfunctioning, that it needs attention, and is not designed to flood the user with no notice. (How you can flood the user with no notice, I'm not sure.) All this after a covering of pollution has been showered away. A rush of outrage stains the whole evening. Shame, no notice on the door: **OUT OF ORDER**. Out of order, this. They could have put up a more conciliatory notice: Sorry for the *in*convenience. On reflection: Sorry for the *out*convenience. You're out rather than in. Moral: Scan the pan while you can, spare the blushes when it flushes.

More on WC? It's written on the World Cup for football. Points to the need for accuracy in the art of shooting. *W* and *C*. Parallel is there for all to see. Aim well, and time it well. Dollop in the hole equals ball in the net. If you linger, the chance is lost. And you could be sunk.

Which takes us back to Digne. No one had arrived at the inescapable conclusion that timing for entry into, and exit from, the cubicle was of the essence. By this time in my language understanding, things could have been clarified. Any remarks that could have been offered would certainly have included the caveat of constipation. A real log jam here. Several swirlings around feet would have turned this Gents exercise into an authentic drama. The *sel purgatif* of the first cycle trip in '52 would have been useful here.

Mystified by the French description of this method of defecating as Turkish. Much of the Muslim world of North Africa adopted it aeons ago. Travels all over Algeria and Morocco, for instance, reveal, outside so-called European habitation, a widespread application of release into the hole-in-the-floor procedure. Arab hotels in the souk quarters of Fez, inland from Tangiers, provide an excellent illustration of this. Why not call it *à l'arabe*, instead, given the close historical links between France and the Maghreb?

175

A most striking feature: Muslim cleaning of the private parts after evacuation may be seen in the use of water. Toilet paper nowhere to be seen in the Arab hotels in Morocco, for instance. Skill in standing on plinths over the hole followed by washing, often with a jet. Paper even considered unclean, unclean because inefficient, anathema if the Koran recommendations have any meaning. What is certain is that if paper were required, you would have needed to speak Arabic or French to obtain it. So polish up your French, or Arabic, in the interests of *papier hygiénique.*

Suggestions offered by Rabelais's Gargantua for clearing up post-defecation mess would be excoriated in the most vehement of manners in the Muslim world. Strict ritual to be piously observed. In the interests of impish delight, the young giant, by way of spouting advanced intelligence, showed his father Grandgousier veritable piles (hoping you don't have them) of ways to rid himself of the excesses still clinging to him, as all students of *Gargantua* will know only too well. Abundance of objects designed for bottom-cleaning, what Rabelais, together with all his mirthful compatriots, calls *torche-culs* (arse-wipers – careful how you pronounce these two words, arse-swipers?) includes all manner of plants, flowers, animal fur and animals' tails, cockerels, chickens, hares, pigeons, and so on ad infinitum. Pages of it. Search for the perfect tactile sensation runs the whole gamut of rough, silky, prickly, comforting, smooth, ticklish and more. Really scrapes the bottom of the barrel. The current animal rights' movement? Floods of protest. Rejects use of furry friends for excremental purposes. OK for Gargantua, though. The French lap it up.

Western convenience mores stick most firmly to rolls of paper. Yet, even here, there lurk hidden perils. One home in France had placed thirty-six rolls of toilet paper at users' disposal. Said rolls had been sold off cheap. Defective but not advertised as such: supermarket hadn't come clean. Turned out a real stain on their reputation. Individual sheets were stuck together, presumably from exposure to liquid of some kind. Time spent separating sheets from the roll equates hardening of the job in hand. But persist.

An inch into the roll, you could be on a roll. But don't bet on it. The law ought to have had a role in this. Master of the Rolls, please unravel this dilemma. A drum roll call would have brought everyone to attention.

A dilemma only rivalled by the cubicle of a Spanish home where access to paper was well-nigh impossible. Required roll was always squirrelled away behind the *inodoro* (toilet bowl). Any good at contortionism? Study Houdini before entering.

Toilet paper has proved to be an indispensable adjunct in bathroom accessories. The French once thought the same way about the *bidet*, the use of which is entirely ambiguous, if persistent questioning of our cross-Channel neighbours is anything to go by. Failure to enlighten the English traveller deepens the ambiguity when, in response to the question on the function of the *bidet*: 'Is it to wash the baby in?' the answer comes back: 'No, it is to wash the baby out.' Traditionally, the *bidet* was thought to deal with *ablutions intimes*, and all standard monolingual dictionaries are there to support this. But, these days, when use of this bathroom appliance is fading anyway, most French people consider it as a way for washing your feet. Same for the Spanish. It no longer stands as a pressing candidate to supplement bathroom anal devices. So, is the *bidet* no longer fit for purpose and will it soon assume an archaic role? Such a suggestion fills the present author with dismay.

Back in the late 50s, after a Channel crossing, and the train journey from Le Havre to Paris, then on to Salamanca, in central Spain, all on a mission to collect data towards a doctoral thesis, he spent one night at a hotel in the street Gay-Lussac, near the Luxembourg Gardens, although there was nothing redolent of gardens in what follows. The passage from Southampton to the French port must have provoked an abdominal disturbance. A sudden, simultaneous ejection of food from mouth and bottom was only countered by the most convenient proximity of wash basin and *BIDET*! Vomit into the basin accompanied by the fiercest stream of diarrhoea but no floor defiled.

Spelling *diarrhoea* is a pain in the arse. Less pain with American: *diarrhea*. Even less with the comfortable Spanish *diarrea*. This must be a pressing argument for learning Spanish. Have *diarrea* on tap in all schools. Delivery at the point of need. End of argument.

Alas, no *bidet* had been available two years previously in Corsica. Charitably speaking, life was much less sophisticated than in a Parisian hotel. Diarrhoea had conducted there an uncontrollable assault on the lower parts. How come? The evening before, hospitality of the sunniest kind had been on offer. This included bed, and solid and liquid sustenance. Now, wait for it, and he'd been in the dark over this. Not discerning the dainty morsels on the table, for only candles were at hand, given the remoteness of the dwelling, he failed to notice what he was eating. *Erreur!* as they say in French. Spread on bread, with a heavenly taste, the soft cheese was alive with maggots, observation made only the next morning. 'Alive' means 'alive', for in true French parlance, *Ça marchait!* Cheese is on the march, a living organism. Sure was! Cheese occupied less of the plate than maggots, lovely because lively, vigorous, squirming white ones, quite indistinguishable from the colour of the cheese, particularly in the gloom of late evening. He lay on a bedspread after the most succulent of bread spreads. Gloom at night. Gloom the next morning. Down to the coast. He could have passed out as cheese and maggots passed out. Whether these little gems were still alive after a clear-out would not have been clear. The sufferer did get the all clear, though. At the same time, that myriad of tiny squiggling worms had left him pissed off. Colic and choleric go together. Nothing bucolic about this, for all the pastoral scenery. 'Cripes!' he gripes. 'He sure has the gripes.'

Could have been warned? Felt a bit peevish. Attitude soon softened. After all, she was helping me make ends meet. Had to nurse the bottom of my purse. Previous evening's discussion was great. She wormed out of me all my interests, academic, sporting, cultural. And that included the cheese.

A *bidet* would not have been called for in 1955 when assault was of a different kind. The circumstance would have made it inconceivable. Cycling towards Saintes, and after the encounter with the *Française* whose puncture I had repaired successfully, I felt an enormous splodge on both hands and handle bars. Avian, Stuka-style tactics had dropped a large dose of well, *fiente*, a slightly more technical word, but you don't need to be an astrophysicist, or just a little way up there like an airman, to divine its meaning.

Number of Spanish words applied to the euphemistically termed *bathroom*? They're legion. The politest of these is stainless, beyond reproach: *baño* = bathroom. But the spectrum of words, ranging from courteous, or even downright and puritanically absurd questions like 'Do you want to wash your hands?' to the repulsive, as in *cagadero*, leaves a person in any language in gaping disbelief. Many terms are only and inexplicably used in the plural, which is notably the case in French, and again, the reason for this plurality remains unclear. A quoted list would be far too long, as long as a toilet roll. Not a convenient spot to string them out here. Suffice it to hazard that more than one **ppp**urpose is served. Two in fact, peeing and pooing The most baffling feature of all words appended to many Romance doors (some romance!) on the Continent, and this applies not just to Spanish and French but to Italian as well, must not be attributed to our English hero **W**inston **C**hurchill, but to *water closet*, and as explained above, William and Catherine would not want to claim responsibility either.

While we are relating the intricacies of the sundry names for toilet, it has to be stated that Romance languages seem to have stalled and not moved on to accommodate technological progress. The English use the term 'to flush', whether a chain is pulled, a button is pressed or even a bucket comes to the rescue. They can still use 'to flush', which facilitates relating the event. Spaniards and French are landed with the traditional expression 'to pull the chain' (*tirar de la cadena* / *tirer la chaîne*), an action enjoying

179

less viability these days. No chain to be pulled. They still have recourse to the idea of pulling, or something very close to it, as in the French, *tirer la chasse d'eau*. However, the English do not get off lightly. Away from these lower lavatorial preoccupations, the English cannot afford to be cock-a-hoop and crow in this matter.

In relation to telephones, we appear not to be able to avoid 'to dial' when dialling went out with the Ark. To dial, need it be stressed, implies a round object, like a sundial. Now, our Continental neighbours have stolen a march on us. Their established, well-tried terms still apply: *composer* in French and *marcar* in Spanish.

The joys of modern technology. Use of toilet and simultaneous engagement in telephone communications have come into their own with the mobile. Delivery at both ends of the human anatomy at exactly the same moment is a true mark of improvement in living standards.

The thrilling toilet topic cannot be abandoned without detailed reference to French terms, for after all, and in true Rabelaisian but also Classical, vein, two words come to mind. First: *vespasienne*. A most delicate, elegant term, it signifies a urinal for which we are indebted to the Roman emperor Vespasian of Colosseum fame. He launched it as a highly lauded innovation, probably as a site for male relief for the thousands of men attending gladiatorial combat. Heavens knows what the ladies did. Maybe *vespasienne* as a feminine word was good enough. Second, *sanisette*, of much more recent creation, and in England as well now, refers to an individual, paying toilet, on a public thoroughfare, and ladies could use it! Fine so far. But initially, dramas unfolded therein. The entire cubicle would be washed down after use, and, as it was originally planned, after the user had vacated it. On occasions, at the beginning, the timing mechanism quickly became defective. Result? User would be engulfed in a torrent of cleansing water. Whether the person inside suffered the fate of those at the Digne youth hostel remains obscure. What is undeniable is that value for money in the unforeseen *sanisette* dousing was never guaranteed. The lofty Digne *à la turque* procedure, however ill-fated, was free.

As noted above, enter not the hole-in-the-floor business in a state of constipation. Medical assistance may always be available on condition you know how to explain yourself explicitly in the appropriate tongue. Steer clear of the word *constipado* if you wish to extract the right remedy, if nothing else, from your Spanish doctor. It means 'a cold', or 'with a cold'. You could easily leave the consulting room with something just a bit stronger than aspirin, which will solve nothing and will certainly not require paper. What do the Spaniards say, then? Easy enough: *estreñido*. A word deriving from the same Latin root as 'to strain' (*stringere*). Maybe if you put on a strained look in the doctor's surgery, the correct diagnosis, and remedy, would be arrived at.

A member of the medical fraternity, once apprised of the patient's predicament, would regularly prescribe suppositories. Now, there's a word loaded with implications. First things first. The equivalent for this in Italian, French and Spanish is more or less the same, so we will not press this home, although suppositories have to be. Incontrovertible fact: as against English medical practice, Gallic procedures were once in distinct contrast, although they are now in the process of changing. Up to some twenty years ago, suppositories were recommended in France for numerous ailments, from babies' constipation to colds, general feeling off colour and so. Their application – or should one say, insertion? – for they were conical-shaped to facilitate insertion, was so widespread that an abbreviated form of the word came into being: *suppo*. Nothing to do with supper. Commonly put to anal use, suppositories gave rise to a multitude of jokes, and here we arrive again, and inevitably, in the land of Rabelais with all this may suggest by way of possible morbid obsession. One joke would go like this: a cold-afflicted English patient, after consultation with his *généraliste* (GP) was prescribed the all-purpose conical object. A few days later, a review of his condition. In reply to the doctor's enquiry over any progress, the patient blurted out, even accusingly:

'No improvement at all, Doc; I could just as well have stuffed them up my arse!' Clearly, either the doctor had failed in his duty with respect to the initial recommendation of application, or the patient's imperfect knowledge of French did not allow him to read the *mode d'emploi* (instructions for use). Jokes on the common practice of insertion of a thermometer into the anal passage are also bandied about, and even give rise to heated discussion. Some must have found their way into the annals of medical history.

Of course, too much enlightenment on the meaning of words is not necessarily a good thing. The most daunting and emphatic example of this argument may be seen in the name of the Spanish town where the ubiquitous jam *Hero* is confected. Indeed, the factories of this jam of delicious quality and taste hide away (in shame?), down in the south-east corner of the Iberian Peninsula, in the town of Alcantarilla, overshadowed by the city of Murcia, A passing tourist would never know of its existence. Nothing special about that, you may opine. Well, there probably is when you stumble on to the meaning of Alcantarilla. It hits you: SEWER. How the Spanish nation can consume vast quantities of *sewer* jam marketed in all supermarkets, defies belief. A hero to a man eating *Hero* jam they must all be. Perhaps they all know that the name of this town is Arabic, as with most towns beginning with *al* are. But the common noun *alcantarilla* also has an Arabic etymology. One may advance the theory that, in former times, the Arabs in that part of the world located their jam production in sewers.

The foregoing recounting of episodes and the reflections upon them show only too well the differences one comes across in the way in which the English, and English-speaking people generally, have sensed difficulty in adapting to toilet arrangements in France and beyond. 'Have sensed' because habits are evolving and things are changing, largely due to the marked progress in the Continental standard of living, purchasing power, and what is relevant for this chapter, sanitation. Yet, attitudes regarding conversation upon bathroom topics are still coloured by the revelling in the more free-and-easy and frolicsome fun still attaching to Rabelais and his inheritors. Rabelais would most resoundingly have given his blessing to the hotel owner who, confronted by a frustrated foreigner not finding a can after three days' residence, replies: 'Mais, Madame, vous avez toute la France devant vous' (...you 'ave all France before you'). 'appy 'unting for that elusive toilet paper, Madame.

6

En famille

'Consider yourself at home
Consider yourself one of the family'
Lionel Bart

Les puces. Easy enough to nail down this translation: fleas. Not so easy to nail them down, though. An infestation of epic proportions, not quite the flies and lice for the reprobate pharaoh, but there they were, jumping in all directions, thousands of them. I was hopping mad. They really bugged me. Yet, as with Oliver, things took a turn for the better. Soon really alive again.

January 1954, Poitiers, central France. Your university department directed you south and 'Get on your bike' again. Nighttime. You arrive at a house, rue des Petites Vallées. Key at the local café. Owner in Paris. Top floor only is yours. You lug your case up three flights of dimly lit stairs, enter an equally dimly lit attic, undress, lie down. Then it started. Lousy in seconds. Flea bitten, you leap to your feet, and perform one of your few leaps of faith. Kierkegaardian style, you collect all belongings, thrust them into the case, fly downstairs, and wait in the cold until light.

A choice, existentialist style. You are inclined to go down to the river Clin, as an act of disinfection, or purification, not that there was anything religious about this. Baptism, total immersion, this was not. You stay and plunge all your clothes into a water butt. Flea partly unridden, you make for the adjacent town square

185

unaware of a Brit whose sole purpose in life was to speak French, and – damn it! – that's what he was going to do.

Scratch, scratch, let's start from scratch. Life returns to the Sunday morning square, as you remain in excruciatingly itching mode, pleading for a chance to be rescued. Sunday and faith converge. A youth of eighteen, from a side street, rue de la Marne, sees your plight, oozing with water, and *voilà!* You are saved! Purgatory to Paradise in one easy jump. Saved by French Huguenots. No one can ever have been so indebted as that young lad to those Petites Vallées fleas. From the ravages of itching, he leaped into a brave new world where all he itched to do was to be part of the family. *En famille* here he comes.

But he was grateful to these nasty little creatures in more ways than one. They did indeed teach him the art of leaping from a valley into a river (rue de la Marne), but they eventually accomplished infinitely more than that. 'Eventually' is the word. You see, *puce*, oddly enough, came to perform one of the great modern technological jumps. Microchip, you'd never guess that, would you? This tiny, sordid little fellow enables him to soar over the greatest of distances. Buenos Aires, Bogotá. Mexico City, San Francisco, Paris, Madrid, Prague, Melbourne, Mumbai, you name it, he'll jump it. That's why he likes to call it *ma puce*, (*my darling, honey*). Which brings us to the redeeming family.

Funny but the youngest child in the family I soon learnt to call *ma puce*, my little darling. Everyone else did, so I followed suit. Henceforth, I was one of the family, and relished every moment of it, and that includes *la table*. No taste like a French home. Want to go to Châtain, our country house? *Oui, oui, oui!!* Want to visit our friends in Bordeaux? *Oui, oui, oui!!* Want to take the infant for a walk? *Oui, oui, oui!!* What about *le foot* with the older boys? *Où est le ballon?* One round of happiness. An explosion of excitement that never seemed to die down.

But back to *la table*. Exactly the same word in English and French, but pronounced *à la française*, it makes your mouth water. With all nine at table, Maman invites open mouth and eager teeth serving out those crusty, oh so crusty, *baguettes* just brought in comfortingly warm from that gastronomic joy of joys *la boulangerie*. (*Aller chez le boulanger* was a skill I quickly acquired. It was a visit to the lush Elysian Fields, and still is.) Mind you keep your own serviette, and don't forget to put it in a *rond de serviette* (serviette ring), if you can remember after all the fun of the fair. Maman ladles out from the monumentally sized *soupière* (tureen), Papa adjusts serviettes round necks, and away we go. Silence. Any *rab* (extras), Maman? The word is *suppléments, ma puce*. 'Et arrête de faire du bruit en mangeant' (Stop slurping). 'Haven't you got one word like us, in English?' '*Non.*' 'Encore du pain, Maman.' 'Voilà, chéri.' Next on the table: *cassoulet* (meat and haricot bean stew). Tongue loosening by the mouthful. Food feeding greed for knowledge. As food goes pouring in, words come pouring out, from the kiddy stuff to the serious with Papa, from 'On joue au foot après?' (Play footy after?) to 'traduire en justice un fraudeur' (to take a defrauder to court). That *table continentale* lubricates the tongue, fuelling animated, light-hearted banter. A tasty way of eating your own words. Between bites. Sandwich language. Relish that piecemeal talk on foreign tongues.

Probably genders still all over the place, and all over the table. Agreements? Well, just get your argument over and remember it's *le*, not *la* next time. *Fromage* and *dessert* (easy this, same word in English, but make sure you keep two *s*s, or you'll end up lost) to follow. Always plenty of cheese on goodness knows how many boards. Take that on board. As many French cheeses as there are days of the year, that's what they say. And with a drop of *vin rouge*, you're in clover. A chocolaty dessert, and off go *les enfants*. Coffee and then a *pousse-café* (liqueur), and conversation ambled on till mid-afternoon, and you had imbibed a mine of information. You even learnt of wartime France, when Monsieur G. had spent years as a prisoner of war at Pithiviers, just north of Orléans. Glad it wasn't Rancy; that's where all the Jews were held before...

What do you do at a French table? Eat? Yes, but after that. Well, you keep your hands visible, probably wrists looking upwards.

You could be indulging not only in food, but in juicy behaviour of a less savoury nature. And then there's the *cure-dents* (toothpick). No embarrassment here in digging in between the gums for further helpings. And Maman! I've dropped my serviette. Can't reach it. Ask Jean. He can't either. No room. Even less room when Pierre, a sudden, unexpected caller, before squeezing in for a tenth place, feels the imperious need to shake hands with Papa and the boys, and *faire la bise* (give a kiss) to *maman* and *les petites*. Pecks on cheeks, and lots of them, sent both giver and recipient into contortions. No trouble for me here. My turn was to come. No contortion, but a handshake from an iron grip, and the hand as big as a dinner plate, with farmer's fingers as fat as sausages, filled the whole family with fear and trembling. Almost a daily routine, this. But it did get out of hand. We all longed for a limp one, a steady, reassuring hand, even a hand that did not stretch that far. Undaunted, he jams us all up against the wall, mashes all and sundry as he tiptoes round the table, releasing a torrent of *Bonjour*s in full flight, and finally settles on his seat. The joy of animation is there for the taking. The conversation's a bit quick. I can't get a word in edgeways. Don't be fright. You've cooked up a few pre-planned phrases to get you going. Easier, and happier, by the day.

If you have never sat at a family table in France, take the next plane south. Just a wee hop, that's all you need. Eating, talking and gesticulating, it's all part of the fun. Talk about eating and drinking, while you're eating and drinking, on a balmy summer's evening, in the countryside, a pleasure unknown this side of the Channel. *Aimer la bonne chère, avoir une bonne table, avoir une bonne cave* (to like good living, keep a good table, have a range of good wines), it's Epicurean living with *bon(ne)* cropping up everywhere. Where did I enjoy it more than anywhere? In the country house at Châtain. No room for me in the Renault Frégate. Eighty kilometres in a few hours, down to Les Maisons Blanches, turn east, keep pedalling, and they'll be waiting for you. *Ô, les beaux jours!* (Oh, the halcyon days!). Post-prandial moments filled those summer evenings with a golden glow. Joy it was to hear 'Messieurs les Anglais, tirez les premiers!' (... you shoot first). An invitation to the only *Anglais* for miles around to pick up that most charming, most congenial, most humorous of books at that time: *Les Carnets du Major Thompson.* The most passionate and wittiest of Anglophiles, Pierre Daninos, had just brought it to the light of day, a perfect epilogue to a day growing happier by the day. And how I was to milk the occasion dry in this farmyard setting. Page after page of blissfully contrasted homespun truths passed from these *carnets* (notebooks) up to my lips and then sent the expectant French company into paroxysms of merriment. Châtain, over the way, resounded to the uninhibited laughter, the passing of which rings to the lament of nostalgia. The bowler-hatted City man was fun incarnate. How else to see his perplexity as he reflects upon the failure of the French to understand the art of the umbrella? Why, damn it, do they leave their umbrella at home when a sunny day is in the offing? How privileged must they feel to be only twenty-odd miles from the cream, the most lordly and Etonian of nations, a nation whose grandest privilege is to speak no other language but its own. And delight of delights, it was an English lad reading these pearls.

Back to 'Messieurs les Anglais, tirez les premiers!' Endless, light-hearted discussion, assertion and repartee, flowed from the circumstances surrounding this command allegedly heard at the battle of Fontenoy in 1745, and uttered by the commander of the French forces, M. d'Anterroches. But what did he really say? Lynn Truss and her punctuation-stricken panda climbing up a ladder, if not a wall, will sympathize with the uncertainty. Have all French schoolchildren been deceived for over two hundred years by thinking those were the very words of a French commander advancing all alone towards the English lines, not forgetting to take off his hat in deference to English gentlemen? Or should they have paid attention to Lynn Truss' panda and put in some dots or commas somewhere else? We all know this cute creature took out a comma to put the record straight, but punctuation is punctuation, and what's the difference between a comma and a few dots? Our less than courteous French commander may have enjoined his own forces with 'Messieurs ... les Anglais, tirez les premiers!' The three dots are all the difference between shooting first and shooting second, still standing up or now lying prostrate. The command may well not have been addressed to the British but to the French. Take your pick. The result of your choice is of little moment, although Simon Schama would like to hypothesize on other outcomes. The Gallic forces won the day. Could it be because M. d'Anterroches stuck three dots between 'Messieurs' and 'les Anglais'? And if he didn't, would the English officers have understood an order called out in perfect French anyway? But the plot thickens. An equally compelling opposite argument has it that the commander of the English forces, Milord Hay, did not allow his counterpart the privilege of addressing the English, but rather, that he, in his again deferential, noble hat-removing gesture, advanced towards the French lines and, in true Stentorian style, invited the French to shoot first: 'Messieurs les Français, tirez les premiers!'

Unclear all this, particularly in the heat of impending strife. Yet, all English officers, being *personnes de qualité*, would have understood French instructions. That's the argument, anyway. French was the lingua franca at the time; diplomacy was conducted in French, however painful for the English. French still hangs around in car number plates, **CD** = *Corps Diplomatique*, not *compact disk*. But apart from that, it's the reverse these days, however painful for the French. For all the toing and froing, the eternal enemy got in first. But this did not stop a descendant of the vanquished English from deleting the dots for deference's sake. After all, without the deletion of dots at Poitiers and Châtain, he wouldn't have spent those lazy lunches rising to the task of reciting Major Thompson's *Carnets*. And if Milord Hay had invited the French to open fire first, that English student would not have read these *Carnets* from cover to cover, day after day for the whole French family. No fun at table. They loved the 'Messieurs les

Anglais' bit, my cue to read. So I sure did. And had there been no invitation, my French would not have improved on, well, that of Major Thompson.

Is *table* in English and French really the same thing? In one way, it is. Flat top with four legs. But there the similarity ends. *La table* brings us to it with an aroma, a taste, a memory of things past; it carries a different meaning, a different feeling. As the years go by, *la table* comes back to us time and again with succulent reminiscences. The stage is set again and again. Nowhere does this memory catch us more unawares than in that timeless, aromatic sense of the *tartine.* You may rejoin: *tartine*'s just a slice of bread with butter and jam on it. A sort of open sandwich. Well, it is and it isn't. Sure enough, it's a slice of bread but *tartine* has an altogether deeper, tastier, more magnetic appeal. You see, the silvery sound of *tartine* to start with. And sound, taste and smell go together. Freshly cut crusty baguette, cholesterol-defying butter (we were young and had never heard of that sort of thing), home-made blackberry jam and *le five o'clock* put you in dreamland, or could we risk tableland? Add that to hot chocolate, and the friendliest of company, and the play upon the stage is complete.

As a special Sunday treat, we regularly sat down to delicious, home-made ice cream with flecks of chocolate for which I had a really soft spot.

Five children and birthdays galore. Always made their own cards, especially for *Maman.* Scissors, cardboard, string, finding something original to say for the day. Certainly had our work cut out.

Memories of those far-off teatimes recur and recur. Especially during our biannual trips back to the north, Caen and up to Cherbourg. These involuntary memories are jogged by a signpost south-west of Chartres. They point to Illiers Combray, of Proustian fame. Just a few kilometres off to the right of the *route départementale* D921, lies a sleepy village the uniqueness of which is etched in the history of the modern European novel. Marcel Proust, whose narrative masterpiece, *À la recherche du temps perdu* (In Search of

Lost Time), digs involuntarily into his childhood past, eats a sponge cake as an adult and is carried back, by smell and taste, to his great-aunt Leonie's house where, as a child, he ate an identical delicacy. Present and past come together, and on this common experience is constructed, outside time, as it were, the foundation of the modern novel. Passing the Illiers Combray signpost prompts an irresistible surge of memory of the daily Poitiers *tartine*. Dining room, laughing children, *tartine beurrée*, hot *chocolat*, bedroom overlooking the narrow rue de la Marne – it all comes flooding back.

Family life in Poitiers wasn't just Poitiers. I was part of the family. It was *en famille*, with shopping, bringing in the laundry, making beds, shifting furniture, digging in the orchard, all part of the business. Card games – *belote*, for instance – really good fun, and your French, well, it truly skipped along. And part of the growing vocab, too. That's what I was there for. No different at Châtain. Well, yes it was. The orchard at Châtain seethed with venomous snakes, especially *vipères*. Serum was always on hand in case. The summer of '55 was long and hot, too good to expect these slippery creatures not to bask in the sunny grass. As for the orchard: *Défense d'entrer*. Washing in the nearby stream was a hedonistic pleasure.

A grant in those far-off days made it all possible. Grant > study. And study I did. Studying *en famille* invested the activity with that extra spice. If you don't know, just ask, but in French, please. What's that word mean? Does Zola always write about the wretchedness of the human condition? What's another way of saying...? What makes Rabelais peculiarly French? Where's the spot where Charles Martel sent the Moors packing back south? What's the difference between a *barreau* and a *barre*? Do you pronounce the *st* in Marcel Proust? Yes. But, Papa doesn't when he talks about his friend Monsieur Proust across the road. What do you call an inhabitant of Poitiers? Easy, *un poitevin*. But what about Tours? *Un tourangeau*. It's a long way from Tours but I knew that one. Balzac had been born there, and I had read *Eugénie*

Grandet, the one about the miser. Just couldn't explain the Ballsache business we've come across before.

Accompanying Papa on his rounds as inspector of fraud in agriculture, quite far afield, in his posh motor, that was living. Farmers, lawyers, beekeepers, tree surgeons, wine growers, they took us right to the coast, Royan, Sables d'Olonne, La Rochelle. Even went to Bordeaux which saw me again, but on my bike this time. Learnt a lot of the tricky vocab, too, like *myxomatose, phylloxéra, pulvériser* (to spray). A steep learning curve, this. Had hardly heard the first two in English, let alone in French. And I thought that *pulvériser* meant to knock people about. It does, but you also do it to ward off those *bestioles* (wretched insects). Even tried a bit of piety, visiting a monastery at Lugugé. The monks were still enjoying *la bonne chère* as much as Rabelais and co. No wine glasses though, just rough *gobelets,* and no tablecloths. Can't imagine the monks were in the fraud business, though.

Quirks of history. Papa Henri, ten years released from the Pithiviers prisoner-of-war camp, occasionally saw his previous enemy, not on the other side of barbed wire, but sitting opposite him, in the form of a doctoral thesis committed, thirty-year-old student who had asked for the hand of his nineteen-year-old daughter. Permission granted. Handshakes there were, *réconciliation oblige.* Every handshake was accompanied by a severe, sharp, vaguely troubling click of the heels, composition of which was designed to resound and impress. Resonance of Nazism? Our German student must have Herr-brushed all possible Nazi affiliations out of his system. But something lingering somewhere. Could there have been at least a servile complicity with *Mein Kampf,* the Hitlerian call to arms? Subject of his thesis? Nietzsche, Gide and the French Right. A tightrope of xenophobia must have been walked here, with memories of jackboots lurking in the background. Much prefer these days a computer click to a heel click to get to Germany and back.

En famille was one thing. Rue de la Marne was another. My front bedroom looked over onto a non-vehicular road where students filed by in their dozens, on their way for mealtime, at the Cité Universitaire, which doubled up as a hall of residence and the main restaurant which usually fed me. My window was a window on the student world. Greetings galore from *juristes, chimistes, physiciens* (not 'physicians' but 'physicists'), *historiens, géographes, littéraires*, always a constant stream of greetings shooting upwards to the first floor. 'Ça va, Ron, tu descends?' (How're you doing? Coming down?). I sure did, especially on a Sunday afternoon for a splash of rowing on the Clin.

October saw the end of one of the idylls of a life as a learner of languages. Anything but idle. Read and read and read. Talked and talked and talked. Ate and ate and ate. Often wondered if I had been a *persona non grata*, peppering the family at mealtimes with question upon question. *Mais, non*, piped up Maman, as she served up the piping hot soup, words echoed by everyone at the table. That's what you're here for. And before you go, remember to say *vous* to people you don't know, or even people you know but are much older. Better for you to say *vous* to *Papa et moi*, and not *tu*. It's not right. *Tu* for each of *les enfants*, that's OK. And *bonne continuation d'études* (Do well in your studies).

Railway station. About to embrace new, far-afield experiences, but still time for *embrassades* (hugs and kisses all round). *Au revoir, les enfants.* (Sounds like a Louis Malle film, but no harrowing, wartime tragedy, this.) *Madame, Monsieur. Rue de la Marne.* Those happy, happy student days. Will you come back? *Je regrette.* Pastures anew. I have a package, and your dream of a language is only part of it. Over the Pyrenees is the other part, and don't mention those far-off Americas. They're in my sights, but let's get the Iberia bit sorted out first. Linguistic wings were spreading. They had to spread. The dynamics of language. University advice on stays abroad was non-existent. You had your bike. Get on it. My bike accompanied me on the train to Le Havre but it didn't help either. How do you leave a country which allows of a three-month stay, visa-free, but in your case, you had been there for nearly nine months? Not just no advice but no permit either!

You had to tussle at the end with French customs administration, just as you had toughed it out at the beginning with those *puces*. A sort of metaphorical 'Get on your bike'. Officialdom finally relented.

A mind is like a parachute. It only really works when it is open. Mine was starting to open wider and wider and, every time I jumped, I fell on my feet. So it was with Salamanca three years later. Train, no plane. Still no Ryan Air in the early sixties. Paris, San Sebastián in the Basque Country of northern Spain, a freezing night at Medina del Campo on the plains of Castile (much of Spain is three thousand feet up), and no warmer in Salamanca, the destination for data collecting. Doctoral thesis needed some padding. One of the literary giants of modern Spain, Miguel de Unamuno, was going to provide it, or at least his daughter, Felisa, would. He had died on the last day of 1936. House arrest, on top of six years' exile in France. A bit like Victor Hugo in the Channel Isles, or the countless writers who hived off to the Americas before Franco had sealed the place off.

A small hotel, what Cervantes called a *fonda*, and that's what they still call them these days. Had an inner courtyard, a patio, not like our English takeover which has turned it into an area adjoining a house, often accessible by French windows. Very cosmopolitan, this. Around the patio ran a gallery on the first floor, covered in by coloured-glass windows. You could see that man with the sorrowful countenance up there, Spain's very own Quijote, restrained by the podgy realism of Sancho whose second name, Panza, was precisely 'paunch'. The ethereal Don straining upwards, paunchy Panza pulling him down.

The University of Salamanca, the intellectual gem of *Castilla la Vieja*, Old Castile. A university once under the thumb of the ecclesiastical authorities, supported by the terror of the Inquisition, created by Torquemada born in Valladolid and dying in Ávila, just round the corner from Salamanca on both counts. Saint Teresa kept him company fifty years later. Secularized the university had become, Miguel de Unamuno saw to that.

The plague of the Inquisition had already suffered a fatal dose of modern medicine. That goes for the *puces* as well, or their Iberian counterparts, the *pulgas*. No nasty surprises now. I couldn't rely on *pulgas* to find me three months' accommodation. No bike to help out, was getting beyond the pedalling stage. Straight off to the gem of gems, the Plaza Mayor, and a different sort of peddling. I had to sell myself somehow, and a student scholarship could not tolerate a second night in a hotel.

Morning *café* in a *café*. Don't waste your time, Ron, get on with it. Students now buzzing around. Half of them from over the *charco* (pond). They had a funny sort of accent I was only just accommodating. A Cuban medic proved to be just the accommodating person. A *pensión* was a short distance away. I would soon be a *pensionista* or *púpilo*. No, not a pensioner, nor a pupil. Just a boarder. Still learning.

Once settled in, a veritable euphoria of language. Around the table, a mixture of accents, races, skins, but all chiming in on the same wavelength. Casting eyes from left to right, I was introduced by *el cubano* to a sparkling constellation of students from far and wide. We were all given a sort of august title with the definite article – the = *el*: *el venezolano*, *el peruano*, *el argentino* and *el mexicano*, and me *el inglés*. Shades of El Cid and T. E. Lawrence his Arab friends called 'Aurence', thinking the *L* of Laurence was really *El*. No Tower of Babel here. Spanish was the lingua franca. 'Pásame la sal' (Pass me the salt) elicited the desired result in a jiffy. Three Spaniards, surprise surprise, were able to join in the language of high spirits. *El papa, el abogado* and *el marqués*. *El papa*, the high priest of this euphoric setting, was none other than, well, a priest, Don Teófilo. With a name like that, he had to be a priest, lover of God, didn't he? *El abogado*, well, he was destined for the law, and the grandly titled *el marqués*, who had nothing to do with the Marqués de Cáceres wine, always sauntered in last, elegant, smiling, to be greeted by deferential howls of grandee stature. He fitted the part. Tall, in fine sartorial, polished and aristocratic style, he would take his seat to the almost daily acclaim that saw in him the incarnation of Old Castile, an ally of Rodrigo Díaz de Vivar, El Cid Campeador, hero of the *Reconquista*, the Reconquest of Moorish Spain. The treachery of Bellido Dolfos would ring out time and again. 'Treason has done his worst,' I'd call out in English. This was Hispanic grandeur at its most sublime. We were carried off on a wave of laughter. No salvation for me, but Don Teófilo almost converted me with 'Aquí viene el marqués' (Here comes the Marqués). For him, the next best thing to godliness was not cleanliness, but playfulness. The parachute was well and truly opening, and I was landing perfectly in the midst of an exciting new adventure, and language was part of it.

Table again, although *mesa* this time. If you've been to Colorado, you'll have come across Mesa Verde, a high plateau, a tableland. The advantage on the Mesa Verde is you can see four states, set as it is in the south-west corner of Colorado. Our *mesa* took me just as far and wide. It ranged over thousands and thousands of square miles and over acres and acres of food. Tortilla, *chuletas* (lamb chops), *morcilla* (black pudding), *chicharrones* (crackling), *vino tinto* and *gaseosa*, it set the tongue on a savoury trail. How grateful was I to the Aztecs for their hot *chocolatl* that comforted them before battle. My battle was with language and the universe, and *chocolatl* did the trick.

All the Spanish-American students had one aim: qualify and hot-foot it to Yankilandia. Their range of subjects often ended in large technical tomes on the dining room table. All in English, preparation for their own parachute landing in the States. To *el inglés* it was given to read out chunks of medical stuff, right accent and all that. Don't know what 'ingrowing toenail' is? *Uña encarnada.* 'What about knock-kneed?' 'Where's the *k* gone?' Down to the serious bits. 'Blood pressure, what's that?' My Castilian told me this was *tensión arterial.* Not so, those swarthy, beyond-the-Pond aspirants to Yankee millionairedom would call out in unison. We say like you Eengleesh, *presión arterial.* My Spanish was starting to split into two already. More schizophrenic learning, and blood pressure on the rise.

'What about Torricelli's atmospheric pressure, then?' Both sides of the Pond agreed on that. Same as in English: *presión atmosférica*. Tension eased as we wandered through meanings, spellings and those notorious pronunciations, as treacherous as Bellido Dolfos. Then, there's the astrophysics business, Copernicus and his crew: Tycho Brahé, Kepler and Newton's apple. Did the apple really fall for Newton, just like your parachute? We're in a heliocentric universe, now, you know. The geocentric nonsense of Ptolemy went out with the Ark. That's where Teófilo came in.

It didn't stop with the higher reaches of physics. Down-to-earth matters like English terms in bridge building. The Golden Gate Bridge, and his opposite, Brooklyn Bridge, will need repairs one day. What about 'the moment of creep'? '*¡Caramba!* I may be a polyglot, but I'm not a polymath.'

I read and read, pronounced and re-pronounced, sometimes into the small hours. Unamuno, in spirit, and Doña Felisa were waiting for me the same morning. Breakfast was a rush, with *el marqués* late as usual, and almost invariably, that Bellido Dolfos refrain. This performance was enacted so frequently that we suspected it had been orchestrated and choreographed by Don Teófilo from the Middle Ages.

It was not all erudition. The Buenos Aires lad had his own rounded interpretation of the world. It was emphatically not round, if you see what I mean, for all those Newtonian theories and theorems. It was oval. I mean, really oval. No soccer for him, however Maradona would trick the English with his hand of God. Rugby was the name of the game. Trying to convert, not in Teófilo mode, although, God knows, conversions of miscreants did not enter his universe, sending that sphere skywards between the sticks was his form of ecstasy. And he sang as he imagined that oval object adding two points on to the five. 'Land of Our Fathers' rang out true and clear for the try, and 'Men of Harlech' for the conversion. You can't get more Welsh than that, can you? I'm lost. Where's your history, sonny? 1865 saw the Welsh fed up with the English and their rugby, so off they go to that

Southern Cone. A bit nippy and empty, so enough room for a rugby pitch. The Argentinians are among the greats of rugby now, Welsh as they are. Well, not quite. But they're all kicking that oval ball round in Chubut province, and especially in the charming little town of Trevelin, just inland from the eastern coast. The oval infection's got as far as Buenos Aires. Keep that ball going up and through and over. The Venezuelan laughed and laughed, if only to show off all his wealth. It was in his teeth. A top row of glistening, flashing gold. Wealth to health in one easy pull. Just as well those Nazi butchers did not continue their extracting in their safe haven of Argentina, although the Venezuelans had a bit of vegetation between themselves and Argentina, anyway. Goodness knows, Barbie, Eichmann, Mengele knew gold when they saw it.

Perhaps our Venezuelan *amigo* did not spend all his nights laughing in flashing gold. Nashing perhaps. We all sympathized with him, and with each other. Peruvians, Inca extraction, live at great height. Thin air. Voluminous lungs, barrel-like chests. So what? They replace singing by snoring, Ima Sumac excepted. In all the history and tradition of the art of snoring, no one, except another Peruvian coming down from those dizzy heights, could reach the engine-like pounding, the all-invasive rumbling generated from the bowels of the human anatomy. Juan Carlos had refined – is that the word? – the art of snoring to a lusty, scraping, thunderous, stereophonic series of claps. Acute medical condition? Could be, but not cute for fellow sleepers. We discussed tactics to stop it. Before rushing into things, we decided to sleep on it. Would his door well and truly sealed do it? May as well leave it open. More air circulating by leaving his door ajar. That just jarred on our nerves. Sit him upright? Four *almohadas* (pillows)? Nose clip? Operation? A bit late for us. Change rooms? He'd be right at the end of the corridor. Out on the landing? Next-door neighbours... The following morning, from uncontrollable sonority to the gentlest of enquiries: '¿Durmieron bien?' (Did you sleep well?). Needless to announce to you all, this got up everyone's nose, forever dreaming of a quiet night. And all those *n*s... about 20 in the last five lines. Jees, he was bound to go on snoring.

Not just enough merely to look down our nose at him. *Conseil de guerre* at the lunch table. Juan Carlos needed a wake-up call. Couldn't go on playing our cards close to our chest. Put them all flush on the table. Delivered a real snorter, we did. Either you stop waking us up, or you wake up somewhere else.

When we snore, we certainly put the *n* in snore. All to do with *nose*. A lesson in onomatopoeia here. Ready for a nosedive? Take a plunge into all those dictionaries. There's hardly a language in Europe that doesn't stick its *n* into snoring, and even o*n*omatopoeia is in on the act. The Spaniards snort away with *roncar*, and can hear their Portuguese friends over the border with *roncar*. Snoring in unison here. What about back up towards us, with the croaking French? Yes, they do croak but they snore as well. *Ronfler* is there to prove it. Across the Rhine with *schnarchen*. They must snore louder with two *n*s. Any *n*s in the Czech Republic? Sure thing: *chrápánc*. And the Poles? More unison here too: *chrapnąć*. What about those La Scala opera singers? That's where you're wrong. Or is it the exception that proves the rule? They seem to have snuffed out the art of snoring. How could they possibly snore with all those Puccini dulcet tones? If they snore, it must be sweetness itself, if the verb *russare* is anything to judge by. Maybe they whistle a bit? A clue in the *ss*? No snitch sounds here. Double bass everywhere else, but no sneers for out-of-step Corelli's violin. Our Peruvian J. Carlos must surely agree to that.

What about opening up JC's airways on a bike? Offered him a cycle trip. Destination? Alba de Tormes, and on hired bikes. A snorting 'No'. Medic Carlos joined me on an easy, flat, carless, therefore careless, journey. Along the river Tormes we pedalled. Sixty kilometres' round trip. If we couldn't find our way, we'd call up a *lazarillo*, who must have known the area like the palm of his hand. Oops! A lazy, and far too literal, translation of *como la palma de la mano*. Got a better one? Why a *lazarillo*? He's a blind man's guide. And when a Spaniard thinks of Tormes, he instinctively sees that story penned by an unknown hand, the bane of all university students, *Lazarillo de Tormes.* We've seen him before, a couple of chapters back. Remember?

Bits and pieces of Santa Teresa in Alba de Tormes too, as well as in Ávila. Cold, very cold, in March on the Spanish Meseta. Deceptive for the sun-seekers on the coast in August. A keen, cutting wind with a contrary bearing, in both directions. Maybe the saint was ganging up on us with the elements. She knew we were only there for the relics. Nothing else to see in that painfully eroded landscape, dotted with bare boulders, the occasional holm oak, and the timeless shepherd.

San Sebastián, by the sea, was always warmer than Salamanca in winter. The reverse in summer. But the warmth of the SS family was invitingly, cordially, constant. Contrast, too, between the aridity of Salamanca with the desert slowly creeping north, and the fresh greenness of the coast. The effect is striking. But they all speak the same language, and the parachute had opened as far as it could, courtesy of the faculty of modern languages, a sort of c(h)ord release.

San Sebastián has been a kind of staging post between two cultures: the firmer, intellectualized, cerebral Gallic spirit with the sharpest of sounds dictated by an authoritarian, centralizing Paris, and the looser, freer, almost medieval spirit giving an easier rein to the provinces, with wide variations of language to boot. Catalan, Basque, and Galician, all different, but brought together under the umbrella – or shall we say, parachute? – of the language that everyone got along with. Basque it was in San Sebastián, but Castilian it was for me and friends now of more than half a century.

Over the frontier at Hendaye, or back up from the southern Spain, and we call out and hear *¡Hola amigos!* once again, for the *enésima vez* (nth time). Watch out for the tricky bit, you know the Donostia sign instead of what you're used to. You'll end up in Bilbao, not many exits after San Sebastián. Still, if you get it wrong, the lush mountain scenery, dotted about with those solid, white

Basque houses, fronted with arrays of flowers sprouting over balconies, is worth the extra *gasolina*. The extra mile is worth it. It really is worth it. You feel the warmth of the family miles away. Fresh, flourishing countryside is part of the family. The closer you are to Donostia, the more the joy of reunion wells up. The pleasurable sense of expectancy of arrival, the calling up from the *aparcamiento*: 'Hemos llegado' (We've arrived), not *embrassades* this time, but wonderfully welcoming *abrazos* with *besos* from the *señoras*. You feel *en familia*, brothers and sisters just been away for a while.

First, armfuls of presents. Just as well Bergman's Volvo still chugging along. Papa's birthday on *domingo*. Easy on the *coñac*, though; he's trying to cut down. Iñigo, the cardiologist son, knows a thing or two here. And a table cover for Loli all the way from Morella in the Maestrazgo. Very *típico*. We had tried, tried and tried *en vano* (you can guess this) to find peaches in red wine there too, following all the *instrucciones* from Donostia. Peaches and red wine, no *problema*. Peaches in red wine as difficult to deal with as the crossroads just to the north. Barcelona–Madrid, cutting east–west across us, conjured up images of red of a different sort. The sticky stuff. Careful with the steering wheel, hospitals are full end of August. Heavens knows, my translation services made that clear enough. Foreigners + cars > hospitals.

San Sebastián. Windsurfer off the roof of the car, a struggle to put it in the *trastero* (lumber room), squiggling it around four bikes, for the four boys, hanging up on hooks. Four boys there were, all as playful as their university-trained engineer dad, and just as daft. Mum survived this boyish onslaught with the loveliest, the most engaging, of smiles. How else could she have responded to 'What's a mum like you doing in a place like this?'

What's next on the menu? The menu, of course. Either with eight round the *mesa*, or with dwindling numbers down to four. The past few months are trawled through, if the phone hasn't been enough. You have to fill in the gaps, anyway. One, two, three, married, waiting for the fourth. Grandchildren all over the place. Some with Basque names, irremediably unpronounceable.

202

Evening meal on the balcony, lulled with *vino* and the larkish sounds of children in the communal swimming pool. All coming up to the spacious fifth-floor flat, on an avenue down to the sea. Sea and fish go together. *Chipirones* (calamars) in their black ink light me up time and again. Don't worry about that courtesy stuff, soak all the sauce up with the bread. And as for those *cuajadas* with honey...

Fancy a walk along the *Concha*, San Sebastián's famed beach? Don't do it with your Argentinian *amigos*. And if they insist, make sure you keep the *i* in when you pronounce Chillida's architectural conception of a comb, a series of prongs stretching out along the coast: *El peine de los vientos* (The Comb of the Winds). The combination of *concha* and *pene* (penis) would throw up erotic fantasies on a cosmic scale, flooding, gigantic ejaculations. *Concha* may well lead us to the *main beach* in Donostia, but for our South American visitors, it means the most intimate part of the female anatomy. Put *peine* into *concha* without the *i (pene > concha)* and you have a prima facie case for a public disorder offence of the most grotesque and spectacular kind. Recalls Goya's paintings of cosmic disorder.

The view from the *paseo* onto the bay of San Sebastián suggests some sort of higher agent with a compass gouging out the edge of the land to ensure a circular symmetry with the island of Santa Clara bang in the middle. A divine workshop? You'd have to be one of those El Greco spoilsport fanatics from Toledo, the centre of religion, to believe it, but believe it they would. That's as far as they would see a celestial hand. The northern side of the bay, in the form of the *La Parte vieja* (The Old Part), would abound in Babylonian fun. Teeming with happy-go-lucky, self-indulgent *donostiarras* imbued with a permanent festive spirit, they wander from bar to bar, on a *chiquiteo* jaunt through labyrinthine alleyways. By some magic nocturnal formula, we end up meeting the very friends we aimed to meet. We sip a drop of *vino tinto* (red wine) here, a *mosto* (unfermented grape juice) there, another *vino tinto* over there, choose one or more of those appetizing tapas, and just keep on walking and talking. Millions squeezed into a few acres alive with thirst-quenching, libation establishments. If Babylon wants expiation, a church stands right there, confessional box at the ready. Odd for a hard-bitten, frosty Evangelical type, even the local priest is given over to sharing in the friendly fun.

Armando and Loli take their hedonistic jaunts out into the hilly, mountainous, countryside. Restaurants, cafés, *sidrería* (cider bars) with vats of cider that would satisfy, even drown, our gastronomic Gargantua himself, special little eating houses offering, well, something special. *Empanadas* (sort of vegetable Cornish pasties), *besugo asado a la brasa* (grilled bream), same for *chuletas* (chops) and for *sardinas* for that matter. *Tarta con almendras* (almond tart) is a *must*, as our Gallic friends say. No grapes around here, maybe, but Rioja is just up the road. Out early for breakfast? *Chocolate con churros* takes some beating, stirring stuff, if you see what I mean.

Fine wine and fine food, not for the young, just yet. But they grow up fast. They do in Spain as well. Somewhere along the family trail, could I find a cardio-thoracic surgeon for Iñigo to shadow? Easy, the hospital's just across the road. (Fast-forward twenty years. 'How many *marcapasos* [pace-makers] this week, Iñigo?' 'Bastantes [Enough].' 'Can you do take my blood pressure?' 'Claro que sí [Of course].'

A cycle race on the agenda today. Not Indurain, although he was Basque, and cycled off with three Tours de France at least, but the next best thing. The *auto* lifts you up effortlessly to the mountain top, you stand around with hundreds of other *papás* and *mamás*, hoping to see Raúl, the Benjamin of the family, leading the pack, commenting on everything from bypasses (yes, they do say that), to the next Soccer World cup, and then they come, helmets over handlebars, panting, panting up that most sadistic of slopes, the steeper the closer you get to the crest.

All the boys need a bit more English. Waves of them all the way up from the Bay of Biscay, year on year. Waves of ours roll up on the shores of San Sebastián. Exams are just over the horizon.

English one way, Spanish the other.

No boats for parents. Heathrow, Birmingham. 'Hola Armando, Loli, ¿Qué tal el vuelo?' (How was the flight?). 'Bien.' Lake District, Scotland. All in the same boat here. Scottish left us all as confused as anyone else. We needed an interpreter up there as well. Just the same in Cumbria. Commiserations with the descendants of Philip II. Armada cannons retrieved from the sea. At Shieldaig. Said that somewhere else. What Drake couldn't do, the weather finished off.

Teléfono. Ronald, off to Czech Republic? *Sí.* Could you get me a *lima* or two? But we're not going to Peru. It's Prague with our Mexican *amigos.* Silly. You know what I mean. It's more of those class glass nail files you brought back from Kutná Hora last year. And when you get back to *Inglaterra,* a few of those padded neck comforters with the lavender smell.

You probably caught *Ronald* just above. Ronald, not Ron. Being called Ron in Spain is an invitation to permanent tipsiness, sleeping after a dose of Henry Morgan's Caribbean stuff. Not a bad idea for siesta time. We saw a bit of that in Santillana, a couple of chapters back. You don't mind it as a quick one-off in a restaurant, but Ron, Ron, Ron at every turn, becomes a trifle intoxicating. It would give you a turn. The French, you say, avoid this trifle, not that they go in for trifle in any serious way. A bit slushy for them. But they'd like it with a spot of rum, especially if Ron's around to give the ambiance a bit of spirit. Yet, the French are not to be left high and dry in the matter of Ron. They see me purring away as if I had indulged in a drop of the hard stuff. With a bit of savvy, you've rumbled the meaning of *Tu ronronnes, Ron?* It puts me prostrate like a *purring* cat.

Always room for a smattering of culture. Pride and joy of his San Sebastián literary scene, Pío Baroja who was anything but pious, so Mum's baptizing him 'Pious' got it wrong from the beginning, was born there and there's more than a plaque to prove it. Loathing the French and their parading of self-attributed cultural superiority, he must have nursed a paradox inside somewhere. He chose a house as close as possible to those conceited archetypes of culture, right this side of the river Bidasoa dividing the two countries, all the more able to curse them or to ape them? Was he peeved by the propinquity of the plaque (another to prove it) celebrating Victor Hugo's time spent at Pasajes, a small port between him and Spain and the Basque Country. Hugo, the leading exponent and champion of Romanticism, trailed after his general dad until the age of ten as he served up Napoleon's recipe for the rest of Europe. The theatrical result of this incursion was *Hernani*, in praise of freedom from oppressive powers. Where's *Hernani*? A small village inland from San Sebastián.

Memories of San Sebastián are not memories. They are relived time and time again at the home of Armando and Loli. They know that dictionaries, encyclopaedias, maps, telephone directories, Internet, all have to be marshalled, laid out, ready for consultation again. How about *escatología* for starters? What do you call an inhabitant of Cabra? Or closer to home, Azpeitia? Which is the most common surname in Spanish? García or López? A bit like Smith and Jones. How did Copérnico work out his heliocentric theory? Did Simon really stay at the top of a pillar for sixteen years? Much better to take the dog for a walk. Or go to a game of *pelota* round the corner. Better to bash a ball against a *frontón* (high wall) than your head against a brick wall.

A lifetime of learning. A lifetime of friendship. The learning fits so well into the friendship. It supports it, it strengthens it, it gives it life. Keep that Spanish going; it has served you and them for donkey's years, even if all the donkeys have disappeared in a generation. But the donkey is still there as a way of getting from A to B. It's called Internet. And it does all the donkey work, infinitely faster. So here's the next email. Pick you up at Heathrow, and we'll sail through France, all four of us, to the land of *besugo* and *chipirones*, and long, balmy, blissful evenings. ¡*Hasta pronto*! (See you soon!)

Nantes, another pony express staging post, northwards or southwards. Adventure all the way, with expectation high on the menu. The parachute spreads so much these days, just a catch of the wind, and we balloon upwards. Just change that language cassette in time. And Nantes is the place. Jules Verne was born there, ballooning his way to adventure. After all, his very first piece of fiction, *Five Weeks in a Balloon*, saw him fly to the top of the adventure charts, with Phineas Fogg and Passepartout in the slipstream with *Around the World in Eighty Days*, following on in a hot-air *montgolfière* from London to Paris. Escapade piled high on escapade, with Cantinflas, the Mexican fixer we've already encountered in the Arizona desert, saving the day by gaining a day, going the right way across the International Date Line. If ever Cantinflas had an inflated sense of self, this was it.

Feel at home in Nantes. Easy. But a bit disorienting, even so. Anyone think we were back in old *Angleterre*. A quick flashback by a few years. Had brought all those fourteen stained-glass windows. Back in Robin Hood country all of a sudden. Especially when my *RB* name is not my name at all. It's **R**obin des **B**ois! Followed on by 'Robin des Bois, tirez le premier!' (You shoot first, Robin B!)

But that's after a cascade of goodies, books, dresses, and dream of dreams for Monsieur Philippe, the latest in *Astérix* curiosities, a mania holding half the French nation in thrall. Whether paper cuttings, cinema clips, translations to the Chinese or ancient Hindustani, as well as scabrous erotic versions – from the straitlaced Dutch if you please! – of that doughty little defender of the rights of Gaul, all were not only welcome. They were greeted with veritable passion. Astérix, aided and abetted by his right-hand man, Obélix, a sort of Robin Hood's Little John, and even bigger, stands as a paragon of moral virtue, resisting Caesar's cohorts carrying their domains to the edges of Empire. Astérix has learnt a thing or two. He, in turn, has imperial designs, invading and subduing Monsieur Philippe's manor while, helpless, Madame Martine looks on unheeded. The visitor is carried back through thousands of years on a sea of memorabilia flooding the whole of Nantes with exhibitions, speeches, television interviews, grand banquets set in baronial surroundings. All up-to-date, this. The elephantine frame of Obélix, sporting the bulbous paunch of a Breton obelisk, outweighs and outperforms his screen rival, Gérard Depardieu carrying Astérix from *La Petite Bretagne* (Brittany) to *La Grande Bretagne* to Rome, and Cleopatra's Egypt.

One lesson for the snooty English intellectuals. *Astérix* is not for the linguistically faint-of-heart. With all his mates, and for all their skylarking, endless play on words, metaphors, similes, alliteration, twists of all those names into Latin *us* endings, setting a trap for the unwary. A starred first in all this must surely be awarded to his creators, the Pole Goscinny and the Italian Uderzo. You understand: *Astérix* and *astérisque* sound almost the same. Their closeness of sound is perplexity incarnate. Replacing the latter by the former leads even the brightest astray, and even the French aren't always sure about the gender of *astérisque*.

Rich fare all this language stuff, only equalled by that French of French inventions: *la table*, especially when the gastronomic day is heralded, *chez* Philippe and Martine, by the aromas of the *boulangerie* wafting up straight from below, at the earliest of times as you rise out of sleep. Love that smell, *gâteaux au chocolat*, flaky, warm croissants, hot cakes. The *boulangerie* was the permanent toast of the neighbourhood. Removes all the pain, at least the English pain. Keep making that French *pain*, please, *Madame la boulangère*. Never can the introduction to the new day be more welcome, the perfume of *pâtisserie* more pleasant than those waking moments. 'Go to work on an egg' not for me. Croissants and butter more like it. Hot at that. The day unfolds like the layers of croissant. Shades of Proustian memories of the taste of the *madeleine* sponge cake all over again. Pity they moved to house all that *Astérix* memorabilia. Still, selling the house was easy enough, they all sell like hot cakes round there. Number 13 not always unlucky. Ask the baker for his dozen and you'll see what I mean. One over the twelve figures much better than one over the eight.

The baker was a pretty clever fellow. He ran a taxi service on the side over the weekends. How he managed to juggle with two roles beats me. Maybe he could have juggled more easily with two rolls. Would have been much simpler.

Cuisine and conversation. *À table*, everyone. That's what the network of *amis* are longing to hear. An expectant rush for seats. Appetites already primed with the aperitifs of Pastis, kir, and even the kingly *kir royal*. *Amuse-gueules* (nibbles) vie with those trans-Pyrenean tapas. Again *À table!* for the drowsy-induced slow coaches, kir still in hand, sauntering to the table at the end of the garden, kir mingling with banter. Talk at the table about the table, just like in Poitiers. It was *cassoulet* further south; here it's *poisson au beurre blanc* (fish in an [unrivalled] white sauce). Gros Plant, Muscadet, we can stay in Astérix's Brittany territory, and just to the east, Bourgueil, so white to red, and back again for the uninitiated. Ingestion, digestion, that is the question. *Café*, and *pousse-café* as they used to say. Sad about the colourful *pousse-café*, ousted by *digestif*.

Real blow-outs? Just cross the road to Mme G. Epicureanism licking Epicure. Endless gush of courses, on a table prepared to a T, although no tea. A splendidly carved knife lies on a rest, and the knife needed a rest, believe you me. Cutting edge of the culinary art. Nearing the end of a dish? Wise not to. 'Il y en a encore dans la cuisine' (There's still more in the kitchen). As the years roll by, delicacies seem to increase in inverse proportion to the slackening appetite. Need respite for your appetite? Let's try a diversionary tactic. 'Où est Pénélope?' 'Dans le jardin' came the crisp reply. As old and slow as time itself, a tortoise nudges forth from the undergrowth, faithful recipient of lettuce and cucumber. Like her mythological namesake cherishing the memory of her husband Ulysses, twenty years lost, we imagine from year to year her prodding up to our feet. Pénélope back in the undergrowth, washing-up services are offered. Anything but the table again. But that table was as faithful as Pénélope. It remembered *les Anglais* from the mists of time.

Banter, ribbing, all pleasantries, thick and fast. Cross-Channel jesting, public school spirit parodied, old school tie, bobbies on the beat, respect for queues, stiff upper lip, weather talk. Brits' turn now: ribald Froggy behaviour, jumping the queue, overtaking on the left, we do it on the right, priority on the right, all those demos to keep the butter mountains sky high, you get what you want, just tough it out and Sarkozy *et compagnie* will cave in (*bonne cave* or no *bonne cave*). You *British* (yes, they say *British*), all for a bit of order. You Frenchies are seventy million individuals with a number of cheeses to match. Funny, *frenchies* means *condoms*. What's so funny about that? Frenchies say *capote anglaise*, so there. Heard the one about the jar with the label *cornichons* (gherkins) on it? Just tweak the jar a fraction to the left, and you only see *nichons*, a naughty word for ladies' boobs. Done regularly, on arrival. In the right corner, Anglophile Philippe, and in the left corner, Francophile Ron. Entertainment value? Unbeatable. Adventure into jokeland, can't wait to start.

Anglophilia and Francophilia merge in front of the students' blackboard. Double act, students in fits. Aim? Give them the English virus, a dose of Shakespeare, but a bit diluted. I don't know though. Half the Stratford bard's vocab is French, a bit olde-worlde, but still it's from *Guillaume le Conquérant* and his cronies. But explain to me: Why do you French say 'le footing' when we don't? Why do you say 'le préservatif' for a condom when we think less of sex than a pot of jam? And why can you put fifty in a French *car* (coach), and jam in about seven in an English car? And why do you spell *ressusciter* with two *s* and we with one? All these scraps of useless pieces of information are resuscitated time and again. Useless? Not so. Hang on to that extra *s* and you hang on to an extra mark.

What about tricky English for the French? The way you pronounce Bicester, Gloucester, Leicester and Worcester, and the rest. Is that because they come from the Latin *castra*? That's 'fort', isn't it? The soldiers must have done a lot of castrating to cut down all these names. And then, trying to sort out 'Susy' and 'busy' keeps us pretty busy. And it really is tough trying to make 'bough' sound like 'though'. Just as tough for the invalid filling in invalid forms. And there's nothing to entrance us going through that entrance. Back to the *oughs* again! Since we're back to the *oughs*, there's 'though' but 'thorough' is stretching it a bit. Putting a *t* on 'though' and 'bough' doesn't bear thinking about so I'm not buying that. Why can you say 'She won by a hole in one' but not 'She one by a hole in won'? Sounds the same to me.

We're hoist with our own petard. Ask Shakespeare. Suppose he knew *pétard* is a French word. Not sure if he wrote *petard* or *petar*.

So it's not all to do with larder and language, then? Oh no. A trophy is yours if you pass from vertical to supine position with no mishap. No kidding. Tales of woe accompany bedtime. Darwinian survival on square pillows calls for no heroics, any more than that other ubiquitous accessory of the bed: sheets. But, beyond these caressing features of the land of counterpane, beware! This household offers no guarantee of safety in case of abuse or negligence. Take the small matter of a camp bed, a kind of temporary, casual resting place which, deceptively, has no appearance as a camp bed. During moments of peaceful slumber, you turn and edge to the, well, the edge. The entire edifice capsizes, you underneath traumatized, the bed enjoying your softness on top. Health and safety notices, please. Put them up in Aztec homes as well, if our Mexican friends are anything to go by. All sacrificial stuff to them. It's that or futons, couch it in any language you like, it's back-breakers one way or the other. But yield not to outrage. A sense of balance is required of all who enter here.

King Louis XIV required of his courtiers they witness the *lever du roi* (the king's rising from his bed). He did not need to study the art of the *ruelle* (space between the wall and the bed). The Château de Versailles allowed luxury and dignity in getting up. One calculates that the distance between wall and bed would be of some metres, although metres were not around at the time. Still, distances were. Not so, *chez* Madame Martine *et* Monsieur Philippe. Either, in the dead of night, you lie till bursting point, or risk some misfortune as you squeeze all parts of your anatomy between bed and wall, manage to avoid the metal feet of the bed legs, circumvent the railings at the end, and make your way with tottering technique to the place of release. The return journey is equally sprinkled with snags. All this trauma to avoid disturbing your partner's sleep. No reference was made to this nocturnal expedition for many a year. Finally, *le drame de la ruelle* (sounds better untranslated so please try here), met its dénouement. All resolved in that tricky, rickety, camp bed.

Those bedtime dramas sound pretty dreamlike to me. How do I get hold of Philippe *et* Martine? *Simple comme bonjour* (easy as pie). There are Philippes and Martines everywhere. Look out of your car window. Flourishing everywhere, they are. Hundreds of them, all with open arms, *muscadet* and *amuse-gueules* at the ready. Just find one of those comforting, white-towered Breton churches. Go a bit closer, check out if it's a *ville fleurie* (no problem, they're always blossoming), stop at *La Poste*, and off to the right. Say it with flowers. Into a *boutique de fleurs*. Ask the *fleuriste*. Where's their house? Last year, lived in a house right in the middle of a vineyard. Recipe for good cheer. Mobile number? Ah, that's it. Careful, we call it a *portable*. 'Philippe, Martine, on arrive' (We're on our way). Days of bliss, nights of ... well, you can guess. Same again. We relish the joy of it all. That's what the next chapter says. So keep going.

7

Gaudeamus Igitur

What's that mean? Got nothing to do with *gaudy*, has it? Oh, no. Didn't you do a spot of Latin at school? Sat in Latin classes for years, and all enjoyable. Smooth as satin. It's always lying latent up top somewhere. We did enjoy it. There's a clue. We *enjoyed* it. You see, *enjoy* comes from *gaudere*, how about that? Doesn't look like it, though. 'Let us therefore rejoice', that's the idea, but stiff and starchy in English. *Gaudeamus igitur*'s even better when you sing it, like all those students just finishing college with their mortarboards and gowns. A bit like Eton's Boating Song: ... swing swing together ... swing swing together. Do it together, that's the trick. And that's what I've done for all those years.

Our Latin teacher got us going on Virgil and Horace. We loved Aeneas going from Troy to set up shop in Rome but it was Horace with his *carpe diem* business that captivated us. Really couldn't carp at that. Especially in Calpe. Where's that? Down Valencia way. I don't catch on. What's *carpe diem* to do with Calpe? Everything. We're back to *enjoying* things as much as we can. 'Enjoy the day', that's the motto, and what better place to do that than Calpe, give or take a letter or two? You see, *r* and *l* got muddled up in the Middle Ages. French A*l*gie*r*s and Spanish A*r*ge*l* show them jumping around and changing places.

Sun, sea, sand, that's paper talk. Calpe is more than a paper. It's a book, *War and Peace* size. All peace and no war. From across the whole of Europe, from the far-flung corners of Belgium,

Germany, Greece, Poland, to GB, France, Italy and, well, Spain, couldn't miss them out, could we? and the rest, they would come for the joy of celebration: wedding anniversaries, Giorgio's birthdays, Ladies' Days up in the hills, Boys' Days on the seafront, darts, table tennis, stone version of boules, windsurfing, dancing, outings, all packed into the annual thirty days.

Excuse to celebrate? Easy. Three birthdays. Giuseppe, Philippe and Klaus, all rolled into one. How about that? Good festive timing across Europe. Tomorrow, *chez* Pepe. I'll book. Restaurant by the sea. '¿Mesa para veinte?' (Table for twenty?). 'Seguro' (Sure). All safely seated overlooking the waves. Splashes of languages at Babel's table. All exhilarated at the fun time ahead. Fun already in the food. Of consuming interest. Ordering it is a joke. *¿Comprende?* Pepe's lingo's not as hot as his peppers with wave after wave of orders rolling up on the seafront to his counter. After all, he's only Spanish, all the way from Extremadura. Good will and laughter, and aperitifs before us. Pleasantries, wordplay, it all goes down with the kirs and tapas. Back to cracking of cross-border jokes. Did William and Catherine really have *WC* on their wedding cake? Do they really eat bulls' balls after the corrida? What's the opposite of Roma? Amor, *chéri*. I love that one. Are you all right? No, I'm half left. You're all right, then. But if I'm all right, I can't be all right.

Along come dishes of *gambas* (shrimps). Then, the *pièce de résistance*, frying pans of two-feet dimension, brimming with *zarzuela* (multi-fish dish). Fingers from distant places help themselves. No sitting on ceremony here. Just stretch out and mop it up with anything at hand. Bottles of v*ino rosado* (rosé, fun wine, say the experts, sure was), stick up at intervals all along the table. Empty there? Coming up. '¡Pepe! Otra botella, por favor' (Another bottle...). '¿Y postres?' (Desserts?). 'Helado, tarta de limón, fruta.' *Café* to settle things. Ten hands in pockets. They release the visa as the mathematicians among us figure out the *pourboire*, or should it be *propina*? Expressions of thanks, we've 'spent it very well', as they say, kisses for the cook, and *paseo* for digestion, borborygmus a reminder of a good time had by all. Back at the flats with popping of uncorked champs. Tomorrow? No, later today. The day's here already. Giorgio's birthday. Same again. And more.

Not Zorba the Greek, but Giorgio the Greek. Giorgio had learnt from his Olympian masters how to celebrate and be happy. And Anne-Marie, his French wife, was in on the act. Bacchus was on the table, goes without saying. Jumped a bit from Greece to Rome here, but what the heck, we're all having fun. Mid-August, birthday time, for more years than even the gods could remember, we all gathered *chez nos amis* in one long carousel of merrymaking. Thirty of us all packed into Anne-Marie and Giorgio's flat. Champagne on tap. Friends popping in, and soon we were all bubbling over with excitement. But spare a thought for Anne-Marie the cook. Had a lot on her plate. Put even more on ours. Which includes onions, and those she sure did know.

Languages galore, whizzing round the room, like the fan above, a linguist's garden of delights, bouncing and buzzing from balcony to kitchen to a sparky sky. What's he saying, Miguel? More *vino, por favor*. What's Fernande saying, Ron? No difficulty here, Fernande's Belgian, but praise be, she speaks French, like her *mari* Joseph. More *tarta helada, s'il vous plaît. Encore des chaises* (More chairs). Next door. 'Sono arrivati amici inglesi' (English friends have arrived). 'Hai un coltello?' (Have you got a knife?). Giuseppe, all the way from Milano, squeezes in a quick couple of sentences. And so it goes on, fed by food and warmth of feeling. Midnight, a quick stroll along the *paseo* and bed. What's on tomorrow? I mean today.

Giorgio again, and his Anne-Marie. Not mid-August, but mid-June, and not Calpe. All of us descending on a little Breton village, Peillac. Fortieth wedding anniversary. Joy unbounded. But to enjoy it, make sure you find Peillac. There are so many *acs* in France you could be excused ending up in the Dordogne valley. But, let's assume Napoleon's road signs keep you in on the ac(t). You arrive mid-afternoon, kisses and embraces flooding in from all directions. And well-wishers, well, could you cope with Polish, French, Spanish, Italian, German as well as, guess what, a few flecks of English? Almost United Nations, you'd believe. You just plough on in any language that comes your way. And that includes the local farmers. The trick is to look and to feel part of the family.

Safely installed for a night at the most comfortable of comfortable country hotels, you come straight out again. You don't need to know how to find the *Salle des Fêtes*. You follow the whole bunch, driven by expectancy. And you don't need to know what *Fêtes* means. Knock out that funny hat. Fiddle a little with *i*, *a* and an extra *s* and bingo *fiestas*! Cacophony reigns inside. The biblical Tower of Babel is at it again. Still, you figure out where your seat is, or someone else finds the figure for you. You are number 15 and your partner is number 16. Opposite is an array of smiling, infectious faces. With a touch of luck, you can talk to them. Failing this, fear not. Polyglots are just round the corner. And the fun is in the challenge, or the challenge is in the fun.

It's not *vino* this time, it's *vin*. Don't take the edge off that delectable French palate, now. Aperitifs in those golden goblets, the splashes laughing all the way down from palate to paunch, mingling with uncertain words even more uncertain as the *vino* continues its gurgling downwards path. 'Où est l'animateur (compere)?' resounds time and again in the hall. Up pops Philippe, boldly ventures where he has ventured before, and amid the vinous clamours, he hails our Olympian champion, Giorgio, with his bride of forty years, Anne-Marie. *Monsieur l'animateur* jollies the company along, waits for bric-a-bracs of translation, and then on with the memories. Nostalgia. Giorgio and Anne-Marie. One went something like this.

> **On the stage:** *Bernard (B) = Giorgio, Danny (D) = Anne-Marie, Ron (R) = Ron.*
> **Scene:** *Lift in Damara, Calpe.*
> **R:**   Buenos días, Señora, Señor.

B: Bonjour. Mon espagnol n'est pas très bon. [*My Spanish is not very good.*]

D: Bonjour, Monsieur.

R: Vous êtes arrivés à l'instant? [*Have you just arrived?*]

B: Oui. My wife is from Paree. I am from Nottingham.

R: Can't be! I come from Nottingham.

D: Quelle coïncidence! [*What a ...!*]

R: What's your name?

B: Giorgio Antonouris

D: Et moi, Anne-Marie

R: Come to our party this evening.

B/D: Merci!

And that was the beginning of a beautiful friendship, as Claude Rains said to Humphrey Bogart at the end of *Casablanca*, give or take a word or two.

And a beautiful friendship it was. Encapsulated in those few words, or should we say, in that lift, rose a friendship that reached the happiest of heights.

Giorgio and Anne-Marie. We weren't at their wedding. Long before. Didn't know them then.

But we were at Philippe and Martine's. No Nantes wedding without us, you see. No chauffeur, he of the pristine, silver Bergman Volvo, no conveyance to church (oh, yes, I got the *jeunes mariés* [young married couple] to the church on time), to the *Mairie* (Town Hall) (sign in both these establishments, *s'il vous plaît*), to another *salle des fêtes*, no compère, no Engleeshmann battling away on the *entente cordiale* front. Imagine, only imagine, a much-coveted chauffeur of a lord, in a much-coveted foreign automobile, cap-on-head, back erect, serenely unruffled, driving the newly-weds in the streets of Nantes and then on to Le Landreau, proceedings drowned by the traditional car-hooting. You can see the whole Nantes population crossing the Channel in search of the chauffeur's sartorial elegance. The majestic mien of the British they craved for, if only for a day.

217

The *salle des fêtes* was an orgy of colour, a fitting tribute to the merriest of occasions. Nothing more merry than the groom, Monsieur Philippe, Anglophile amongst Anglophiles, rising to stand on the table amid Muscadet and champagne, to divest himself of his trousers, revealing de luxe underpants of another orgy of colour. And what, pray, do the underpants reveal? The Jack of all Jacks, the Union Jack. No starker exposure of the *entente cordiale* than Philippe's most intimate parts, indeed his jacksy, covered, nay, protected by, the British Empire. Underpants and *entente cordiale* were all one for Philippe, the projecting embodiment of Anglophilia. No refined raiment, no knot tied, but they still tied the knot.

Not sartorial elegance this time, but elegant eloquence. A string, or should we say, garlands of panegyric speeches, tripped off the tongue, followed by songs of Rabelaisian humour, interspersed with Italian, English and Belgian quips. The bean feast lasted until late in the evening, topped by the usual post-midnight *soupe à l'oignon* (onion soup). Happiness on a plate. How the newly-weds did what newly-weds get up to on their wedding night was not clear. Their Le Landreau bedroom was assailed vocally from outside, until more than the small hours, by a raucous gathering bent on dampening erotic spirits. But the gastronomic gods were disappointed if they were counting on a three-day celebration. Read a few pages of Flaubert's *Madame Bovary*, where the eponymous heroine is submitted to three days of revelry, driving round the countryside, in high excitement, in a *char-à-banc* (cart fitted with benches) for hours on end. No much-expected frolics for a while. Bacchus before Eros.

Brides-to-be seek out the perfect hairdo before tying the knot. Most brides-to-be, however, would shy away from capillary elegance if the big day were in Calpe. A scrap of French would send them tearing their hair out. The two main hairdressers' in Calpe did not invite custom for one simple reason. Experts in the art of goofing it when it comes to signwriting, they saw grace and refinement in all things French. Show off your French and you'd be well covered. Not by hair, if the following sign is anything to go by: *Dames Laides*. A most infelicitous twist of the pen contrived to convert *Dames Ladies* into *Ugly Ladies*. *Laides* = ugly! A sign presiding over all females aspiring to an exemplary coiffure. Cutting it a bit too fine. A total ignorance of French is thus recommended to all who enter here. Reasoning for the ethos of the present book is turned on to its head. Head for the next town, you have to.

But phone first, just to make sure. You may hesitate at the phone booths round the corner. Why so? Seems a hotbed of seething conspirators gathering there periodically. A touch sinister, all this. Must be a scam going on. Not a bit of it. Entirely innocent and inoffensive, they gang together and speak Spanish, for God's sake! Can't understand them. Can't they speak French, Italian or even English, like everyone else? And they're not from these parts, not even from Spain. Spanish Americans they are, even the proprietor, all as free, easy and merry but entirely incomprehensible for the Poles. And they actually look different. Aztec, Inca, Maya, with their dark, round, chubby faces, and the darkest of eyes, they probably speak Náhuatl or Quechua, for all I care. But the beauty of it is that it's the cheapest on offer in town. Ring the changes if you like, and find another telephone booth, but their disarming demeanour always wins us over.

Back to the Spanish feeding trough, *casa* Miguel. No Pepe this time, and no misplaced orders either. Miguel has it all taped on the table. You can figure out how we're dressed. Up to the nines, but we're not tied to ties. And you can also figure out it hasn't been forty years of matrimonial mourning. Rather, repeat performance of wedding delight at *casa* Pepe. And performance it is, for Pat and Ron. The stage is set, like the meal. As the tapas plus drink meet universal approval, speeches get off to the sweetest of starts, and that's before the sweet. *Entente cordiale, armonía, armonia* for the Italians again but without that accent, easier really, *Harmonie* (Stukas forgotten in the mists of time), an evening full of the fragrance of family feeling, the exhilaration of expectancy. Gaps in the eulogies make way for dishes of high spirits, served with faces flushed with pleasure. No slaves for serving here, just slavering over the fare on hand. It's all part of the show. *Entremeses* despatched with the greatest of gusto, so bring on the *cordero* (lamb) with those appetizing *patatas fritas*. Sounds tastier than *chips*, doesn't it? Miguel, *sal y pimienta, por favor* (salt and pepper...). Speeches are now in full swing. Succulent dishes spice up the stories.

Poles can't follow? Jump across a couple of borders and a couple of languages. Spanish > French > English > Polish. Irena's been in Blighty long enough to do the trick. German? They follow anything. Pretty bright. Like the Dutch. Atmosphere of gentle euphoria. Speeches have gone down as well as the lamb chops, and the Marqués de Cáceres *vino*. Philippe's running the show, he's the animateur, has to be, it's his world. Chops full of chops, he changes from one language to another as smoothly as we change courses. Room left for the *postre* (afters)? It's not post-prandial yet. Miguel's speciality (specia*lty*, to accommodate our American guests): *tarta de chocolate*. No interpreter here. *Postre* complements compliments all the way round. Equals bliss, moments to savour, electric joy of the revelry of language, menu and well-being. Out with your credit card. Klaus the maths maestro whizzes out the figures faster than we can switch them into something meaningful for all, and *propina oblige*. A touch of Spanish + a touch of French, all very user-friendly. No worries, now we're strolling down the *paseo*, midnight past. Don't get caught out this time. See you later this morning. It's fiesta time.

It's always fiesta time. Yes, but it's the village fiesta, this time. All go for a week. And you'll soon know. Rolling crack of fireworks'll wake you up at eight. Not me, I'll be spreading my limbs in that warm, blue liquid stuff with creamy fluff on top, just down the steps. Better hurry for the supermarket, half day on fiestas. So what happens at the fiesta?

There's running of the bulls for starters. Well, not quite bulls.

They're tame little fellows, bovine ladies, in fact, out for a romp. Up in the old part, narrow streets, lined with wooden planks so that the *olés* don't get out of hand. No *toreros* though. Just revellers, Pamplona style, keeping ahead of a charging half-ton of pot roast. Hemingway says it all, more serious up north.

The magic of colour drapes overhead, from side to side, right down the avenue to the sea. Large golden wreaths of stars between the garlands. All lit up in the evening for the Big Parade. Really comes to life now, especially with those bright, sparkling stars high in the sky. Yippee! They're on their way. Who? Can't you hear them? It's the procession with the fiesta queen led by an all-the-colours-of-the-rainbow band, majorettes, trumpets, flutes, drums, childish excitement all drummed up by the sceptre-flinging conductor. Down to the sea they go, following the Pied Piper of Hamlyn, ending up with ooohs and aaahs galore as the fireworks race across the sea and skywards. Bang go my hopes of a restful few days.

More fireworks to come. Not the sort you'd expect, though. The culturally minded set off back up to the square. Too square to stay with the fireworks for long. It's music time, not the yayaya variety. Chaikovsky, Rachmaninov, with readings from Tolstoi. At least, that's how the posters billed it. Spaniards write things differently. Why not? Audience sigh, all the more admiring, it's free, you know, on the house, or preferably on Calpe. Carried away on waves of music and warm air. Fine, all going like a bomb, rapt in silence. Oxymoron? Moronic more likely. Kutusov, the Russian commander hero, sets his guns ablazing in 1812. Or perhaps he hoped to. At high, high point of the *1812 Overture*, Chaikovsky would have felt a sting of recoil. No ignition from the cannon. Finale of the explosive charge? None. Low, low point. No big hit was the cannon. Merely whimpered. A discordant note. Sparky style of these words more alive than the gun. What the blazes is going on? No answer. Gunner keeping his powder too dry? Lit and relit, stuck to his guns. Artillery man really was looking down the barrel. Off his rocket. Nothing but pathetic juddering. Final petering out. But could help be at hand? See next paragraphs for Peter's *Pathétique*.

Laugh? it nearly brought the house down. Triggered ripples of giggles. We almost died. Could have done if he'd got it right. What a performance! Curtains it sure was. Anything but a *pièce de résistance*. An artillery piece that went *phut*. A loose cannon, if ever there was one. Couldn't the gunner have studied the canon governing cannons? Wheel out the *Pathétique* instead? Would have been music to our ears. Never mind. Lean time for the orchestra from the Spanish audience? Lenient would they have been. Kutusov had sent Napoleon off with a flea in his ear, just like Wellington in the Iberian Peninsula, cannon or no cannon. Just as well orchestra didn't try C.S. Forrester's giant of a gun, over near Ávila. All the same, someone under the stage must have stopped a rocket, it clearly was the pits. Whole plan had backfired. Conductor fumed and fumed, never seen anyone so volatile. Incandescent with fury. As explosive as the gun that should have gone off. Latin temperament.

When the discharge petered out, why didn't they call for Peter Tchaikovsky? After all, he'd set the turbulent tone for the whole evening. Or go for Leo Tolstoy? Leo the lion, anything but toothless, would surely have discharged his duties more efficiently. Never a man to bite off more than he could chew. The antidote for petering out must have been Pierre in *War and Peace*. On second thoughts, Tolstoy's Pierre could not have done it any better. His botched pot shot at Napoleon petered out, too. In fact, Pierre's non potshot was to be the most resounding failure in the assassination art in world literature. Not much of a hit man. Shoddy shooting.

Fancy honey, fountain water and mussels and sardines? Not all together, silly. Like yesterday, it'll be fine tomorrow. Mid-afternoon, three carloads of *turistas* climb up into the interior. Direction? Callosa d'Ensarriá. Odd name the last bit. We know where the *tienda de miel* (honey shop) is. Been there a hundred times. Round the policeman standing in the square and off to the right. Phew, need some shade for the autos. Must be near 40 degrees. Shop with barrels overflowing with honey. Want a taste? *Limón, lavanda, mimosa, rosemarie, jazmín, eucalipto.* Can see what they mean, but *azahar*, what's that? The Arabs'll tell you. It's orange blossom. We plump for this one, to begin with. The name is honey itself. Never mind the taste, I'm fixed on the sound. *Azahar.* I could say it all day long. I'd love to be a bee, sitting on, and sucking away at, *azahar. Mil de flores* (thousand flowers), haven't a clue what the bees feed on for this one. All of them, I suppose. *Tomillo.* I can work that one out: thyme. The *señora* scoops it up, ladles it into jars, screws down the top, and honeyed memories for the bitter days of winter.

On higher up, to Polop. Twenty fountains, free, in full flow invite water-carrying containers. Pleasure of pleasures, filling up in the heat of the afternoon. Glad to have the Bergman's Volvo still. Got room? Sure, in they go, *garrafa* after *garrafa* (large plastic bottle).

Steep descent to Altea opening up vistas (no problem with this word) of the Med. Lemon groves on either side of the road, you become green (or should it be yellow?) with envy. Bet the bees come down here. We'll leave the Old Part with its fetching, intimate square till after the mussel/sardine feast. Oh yes, the *habas*, don't forget the beans. Have to walk back up to the square, but there you are. The benches along the seafront see us seated for a couple of hours, conversation flowing along like the *vino*, in languages forgotten because of the *vino*. Could have been French, Spanish, Italian, even English. Philippe would have liked the English. Half the time, I don't know where I am. Polish and German a frontier too far. At least, I could vaguely feel the bucket by my side, rustic receptacle for the mussel shells. All quite mechanical, really. Mussel chewed and shell dropped, repeated and repeated. Now behind the wheel, bend after bend after bend, ambling back to Calpe at midnight and see you, not tomorrow, but later. We learnt to say it like that a long time ago.

Ready for some mental gymnastics? A day in the life of Calpe versus Solzhenitsyn's *A Day in the Life of Ivan Denisovich*. Calpe versus Gulag. You must be joking. It's all about Calpe *sol*, that yellow disc up there for us, but a touch of the author for Ivan, *Sol-*, and that's all the *sol* Ivan's going to get. Calpe: up at nine, sunny daylight. Gulag: Ivan up at five, unremitting darkness. Quick dip in welcoming warm waters, Ivan in Siberian snow and mercilessly icy blasts, coffee and doughnuts, *bonjour/buenos días/buon giorno* to smiling eyes, Ivan silent and sullen, trowel in hand, no doughnuts, under the guard's grim, grisly gaze, jolly daily round of calls, Ivan sunk in solitude. Long treasure trove of a day. Ivan's one aimless, numbing brick on another and another...

Elevenses, sunny banter in anyone's flat, the *amigos* just turn up. Italian *amici* there, too. Poles and a couple of Czechs. Strange sort of bush telegraph with occasional Arabic speaker. Somehow, they just know. Even some scraps of English. Anglophiles there are aplenty. Sure are English lovers around. Jokes galore. Heard the one about the bear who preferred the cinema to the zoo? Ever seen a Zulu? No? Go to a loo in a zoo and you have a zooloo. What's the difference between a Corsican and a tree? The latter moves. Beauty of these, two of them work in any lingo. Not for this one though. What's the difference between a walking Pole and a walking pole? A walking Pole can walk without a walking pole, while a walking pole can't walk without a walking Pole. Any of you foreigners got it right? Let's take a straw poll for a check. And I did say *check*. The Poles were all at sea. It's all to do with the stress on the pole/Pole. Just like blackbird and black bird. No stress, good clean fun.

It wasn't any clearer for the Poles with *polish* and *Polish* either. Or for anyone else, for that matter. What's the difference between 'Is that Polish polish' and 'Is that polish Polish'? Not much really, except you don't pronounce *Polish* like *polish*. The *o* of *polish* is open while the *o* of *Polish* is closed. An open-and-shut case for the English, if you ask me. Stays an open case for the Continentals, though. We're poles apart over the pronunciation business. And don't torment them with *gnat, gnaw, know* and *knot*. Gnash your teeth as much as you like, you'll not knock your pronunciation into shape. And as for the posh way of saying *when, while* and all the others where *w* comes before *h*, and the nobs say *hwen, hwile* and so on, you could knock me down with a feather. The Americans join up with the nobs, not knobs, and say *hwen* as well. How about that? *H* comes before *w* in *who*, and you can hardly hear the *w*. I don't know where I am with these *wh*s. Or with *aitch*. All those telephone secretaries started to say *haitch*, but they'll soon be knocking off the *h* again, what with HD every day on the tele. We've got those foreigners tongue-tied just where we want them.

A v*i*car smoking a cig*a*r really does get them all stressed up in the wrong places. And why do you retain the *ain* bit in retain, but not in Britain? As for reading that Irish fellow's *Ballad of Reading Gaol*, you can't always take *read* as read, can you? But you could read *jail* for *gaol*. However much you hammer away, you won't make wallet sound like mallet.

Prefer French wine to Spanish? Burgundy, Bordeaux or Languedoc-Roussillon to Penedés, Rioja or Duero? High-quality, vintage conversation. Palate for wine just right for the palace. Pity *palate* doesn't quite rhyme with *palace*, however hard we try. The French have it off pat. *Palais* same for both. Refine your *palais* at the *palais*. Better than at the *palais de dance*. Mind you, enjoy a full-bodied, lusty flavour or grab that lusty body, much difference? Lust either way. Soft or hard taste? Prefer hard on.

Reduced we are to clichés. Clicking on to the French again. Red versus white, dry v. sweet, *grand cru* v. *vin de pays*, rough and ready red v. weak and watery white. Ah well, have to take the rough with the smooth. But best of all, fun wine with rosé, especially with Laurie Lee's Rosie.

Male madness, all this. All the men by themselves. The cat's away... You mean the wives? *Wh*at about them? There's that *wh* again. They're out for a spot of *shopping*, as the French say. Light lunch, desultory chatting tailing off into siesta. Siesta to fiesta? Not quite, *le five o'clock* before the beach brigade, towels trailing in the wind. A bit more banter. Then: fiesta time! Whose turn tonight? Who brings what? Piling in they come, bottles in hand, awash with desserts and *bonsoirs / buona sera / buenas tardes*, and kisses all round. Not Ruskie Ivan country this, but just as good a thing with Stanislas and his Poles.

Calpe's all about fiestas, then? Not on your Nelly. Revelry may keep you sane, but you need something to wear off the excess. *Mens sana in corpore sane*: Healthy mind in a healthy body. We've had a good look at the *mens* bit, now for the *corpore*.

You tug a plank of fibreglass down to the beach, not forgetting the pole. I did say 'pole', have to take care with Poles around, especially with a sail wrapped round it. We call it windsurfing or sailboarding. Not sure which. Currently, it seems to be the latter. They both play with wind currents. A Pole is always on hand to help you. In the plank you find the slot for the pole. Not for the Pole, stupid. Mind you, you could be forgiven for this Polish confusion with slot. There is such a thing as a Polish złoty, a currency floating with the current.

Windsurfing? A bit like floating on the stock exchange. Come aboard and you'll stock up on a few practical tips.

Cooperation between East and West was gaining currency. Polarization of friendship. The most upright of Poles were now sailing seawards with the most upright of stalwart English poles. But don't get too carried away with the 'upright' bit. You need to incline the pole forward a few degrees. Or you won't get carried away. But don't let yourself be carried away, if you understand.

You have sail and boom tightly in place. Don't forget the dagger board underneath. Otherwise, prangs will come thick and fast. First lesson: learn how to turn and come back before you go out. But this is nonsense. Like trying to cycle on two wheels before using a tricycle. Or working out how Hamlet ticks before taking a ride on Thomas the Tank. But it's Hamlet's suicide if you don't. Learn to turn, and don't listen to Margaret Thatcher. Not for turning? She'd have to. Otherwise, she'd blow it. Master the skill of lowering the sail a little as you switch sides for the return journey. Otherwise, it's a big let-down, you'd be out on a limb, and all at sea. Losing your grip? Signal to the beach. But don't preach Mrs Thatcher's way.

Tough to begin the art of sail-lifting. Backbreaking for starters, and I do mean 'starters', i.e. those who start. Anything but a breeze, this, but you need a breeze to get going. Ache and no sleep on the first night. But don't be caught off balance. Keep at it. Get involved and don't approach the skill at arm's length. Well, you know what I mean.

It's recommended you pray to the god Aeolus the night before. It's his job to push you. That's what Mount Olympus pays him for. It usually worked for Jason and his Argonaut crew, but don't count on him. Without his puffing a bit, you'll get nowhere and keel over. If invocations to Aeolus leave you breathless, you could enlist a push from another of those Hellenic gods, Zephir, but he's a touch too gentle, always short of puff. If all else fails, try the Aztec divinities. Now you're talking, but you'd need Aeolus to get there. Need a force 10 to break the world record, sixty miles an hour? Try Ehecatl-Quetzalcoatl, and if he's having a day off, give Mexti a buzz. He should do the trick. He'd get you up to hurricane speed. (Buffeted we British are between *hurrik'n* and the American *hurri-cane* which seems to be sweeping *hurrik'n* aside. Another language caning from the States. North-west of Scotland gets another sort of caning, too. Tail end of hurricane, i.e. *cane*).

Still no progress? Appeal to the winsome nature of Huixtocihuatl. She's a goddess and should be a soft touch, although you'd want to go faster than that. Out of breath for trying? Go for a bit of intercession from the really big guy, Huitzilopochtli. Give him a shot, he's the biggest shot of all. Why not just give up and wait? After all, those Aztec divinities don't inspire much confidence, the way you have to pronounce them, so long they are you get out of breath. So the cleverest wheeze is wait and see, or feel. Amazing how the wind comes out to play in the end. One thing's certain, you'll be bo(a)r(e)d stiff without it. The beginner'll be even stiffer with it.

So it's tough starting, even tougher if you've been on your knees the night before. The preliminaries over (see above), wait for a compliant 2 or 3 Beaufort. Ready for a splash of fun? Fine, but don't go overboard with it. Ready to clamber on? Up we go. Board at right angles to Monsieur Beaufort. We'll call him Monsieur, although he was English, and let's keep the *entente cordiale* on a steady course. Important, so let's repeat it. The board must remain in a symmetrical axis to the wind. The wind plays a pivotal role in this manoeuvre.

Good so far. Pull yourself up with both feet on one side of the mast, but not too close to the board's edge. Hands from rope to boom in one quick snatch. Swing the sail round into the wind. And away you sail, tacking as you go. If you've studied politico's zigzagging, you'll tack to perfection. Oh, sorry, you're down there. Don't forget to resurface. So, up you get again. Stay alert, and keep on your toes. No, on balance, don't stay on your toes. Keep your feet flat. You don't want to be caught on the wrong foot, do you? Keep trying until the nth time, arms, legs and back all in melt down. Then, the grand departure seawards. 200 metres and turn round. Just a quick twist of the arms and legs. Balance of feet, switch the sail and boom to the other side of the board, all in one action, and there you are, in the briny deep! Pick yourself up before the wind picks up too much. Return finally victorious to the swell of acclaim, and slide up onto the sandy shore. Gets so easy in the end springing on and off, even your offspring can do it.

Gets even simpler with the harness. Relieves stress on the arms. You clip it to the mast and unfasten it with the deftest of actions. Makes windsurfing so enjoyable. You really become hooked.

Running, or should we say, sailing repairs? Klaus, our German aeronautical engineer friend, always on hand. Really safe pair of hands, especially for kite surfing, next up on water sports. Couldn't tap into his skills, though, he was too high-flying for that. Just couldn't get the hang of the kite stuff in such a short space of time. On and off the sea at breakneck speed. Swell business, especially when there's swell.

Finally settled for windsurfing. Shored up we were by the community spirit. They were all so cheerful. Had to be, buoyed up as they were by the water. Everyone played a part in carting board and tackle down to the beach. They felt so free, what with board and lodgings so cheap. No obstacle to pulling their weight.

A bigger problem: how can you *land* on the sea? You land on land – and you??? –on the sea. Sea on sea? Our Romance friends have landed the right answer. The Italians: *ammarare*. The French: *amerrir*. The Spanish: *amerizar*. And they don't even need the *sea* bit. We're getting submerged in knowledge so let's stay on the surface and keep things superficial.

Merde! And **mer**de again! For all the power of sail and boom, business no longer booming. The once brisk sales of sails drooping like the sails falling from a once brisk wind. Troubled waters ahead. A twist to the windsurfing drama. No more twisting. Things had gone so swimmingly well. But now, a sea change in beach administration. Not much chance of mutiny here. Police have sweeping powers. Could we handle a brush with the law?

'Not to float the boat, *inglés*.' Caught wrong-footed. The wind taken out of our sails. Things have got unstable, wind or no wind. *Ayuntamiento* (Town Hall) + extra revenue = overblown widening of the beach. They've introduced a raft of new measures. Beach safety. Everything's now on hold. Oceans of space with waves of *madrileños* rolling down onto the coast. Case against sailboarding? Unassailable. Wave goodbye to Calpe windsurfing. Disappeared over the horizon. Alas, no point in venting disappointment. Yet, if you're crafty, and there's real craft in all this, and want to nail your colours to the mast, wait for the green light at dusk. Sailboard rules get a bit obscured and irregular then. Things could blow over. No bullyboy beach brigade. Police blustering all gone. A bit of a damp squib, although you could say damp squid.You don't have to take on board all they say.

Weather the storm. Just keep a low profile. Stand on your own two feet, not on your toes, of course. Just seen that. Into calm waters again. So windsurfing not quite dead in the water yet, late evening. You may be on the back foot with the police, bad show. But stay on the back foot on the windsurfer, good show. That's how it's done. Above all, don't play act with the police, even though you're treading the boards. No sailing too close to the wind, and don't lose your grip. Hey, those kite surfers are out before dusk. They'll be for the high jump.

In need of some breathing space? They're all keen to start, Germans, Greeks, English, French, Belgians, Poles; don't exclude the Spanish, it's their beach, after all. Sort of team game of boules, but really with stones, the flatter the better. Flatterers and admirers all round. Stone(s) closest to a line in the sand win(s) the first round. Smooth out the sand with a small rake for the second round. All in the setting of those white limestone hills, the Costa Blanca. Great, chalking up victories. Another momentous milestone in the cementing of international harmony.

First to thirteen. Hope it's not Friday. The French? They're bedevilled by Friday the 13th (*le vendredi treize*). Not forgetting the Belgians. Harrowing it is for them as worries sprout like mushrooms. They love to rake in the victories. Anyone free from Friday the thirteenth? Nope. English, Hungarians, Germans, Poles, Italians, Mexicans, Greeks, Ruskies. No Ruskies around, so how'd you figure that out? Easy. Read some Chekhov. *The Three Sisters.* Thirteen at table torments, or torment? Kulygin. Everything screwed up for him, not just the bottles. Must have a twisted view of the world.

Bad throw again. Damn it! That thirteenth apostle, Judas, a real nuisance. He started this Friday 13th lark, and it's been hovering around us ever since. I'd be hanged if I was going to let him play devil's advocate. Hope it's not Tuesday. *¡Martes y trece!* The Spaniards' turn to fret on the 13th, but Tuesday.

Defeat always on the cards, if not on the stones if you're playing with Joseph, the left-handed Belgian. Imagine partnering Joseph, on Friday 13th. Something really sinister in this treble whammy. Explain yourself, *Señor. Sinister* in Latin = left-handed, and sinister, unfavourable to boot. No chance of winning against those odds. Still, in the line of duty, you play with the weakest partner. All this left-handed stuff gets even more sinister in the next chapter. All to do with hygiene.

Rules suffer from improvisation. Not set in stone, you know. Endless, deep discussion gets bogged down. We delve down into the sand, lodged as stones are upon each other, over the line, by the line, size of stone, percentage of stone over the line, broken stone. Mathematicians are called in, armed with an array of measuring instruments. Klaus, the Munich master of aeronautical engineering, gets us all to toe the line. Bemused passers-by offer their free consultation, and consolation. Wives intervene to calm enthusiasm and smooth the line to reconciliation. Even call in the Stasi, nickname for the beach police. Red Cross student doctors on hand to ease the pain of losing. Greeks and Germans win. English and Belgians, stony-faced, even the score. 'On fait la belle?' (Have a decider?). Things get tight and blurred, underscore the need for a ref. Or maybe more a linesman than a ref. All to keep everyone in line, or onside. And the only person who knew how to draw the line, after victory, or an unexpected wave from the sea, was Klaus again. He drew the line with a twig. Used it like a ruler. The rule of law had to prevail. We all twigged that. Klaus, we knew, would leave no stone unturned to reach the fairest result, always leaving half the contestants stone cold. The other half hard-nosed.

Still, never sure of victory. The decider could drag on. As evening draws in, a draw is almost certain. Can't see the stones. Even in broad daylight, you can't always see the stones. You could be within a stone's throw of victory, and whoosh, an extra big wave covers the lot, and smothers the line. Annoying but we were always as happy as sandboys.

How do you agree on a tie when everyone is in bathers?

Ribald jokes follow as plentiful as grains of sand. Playing with language as well as with stones. One stone lying on another? Making the beast with two backs, Othello style. Shakespeare, sure enough, but he pinched it from the French: *faire la bête à deux dos.* Been around ages before the Stratford bard. Stones always landing vertical? Phallus fever. Stones as onomatopoeically smooth as 'Miss Cuisses Lisses' (Miss Smooth Thighs). Find this a little near the knuckle? You have to take the rough with the smooth.

The game resembles less one of stones than finding the next colourful quip. Any language will do. Translate it somehow. Head like a multilingual dictionary jumping from Spanish to French, to German to Italian. Giuseppe inserts into the proceedings tales of World War II conscription, unwilling invasion of France under Mussolini, up to Grenoble, back to the Riviera, hiding in the mountains from the Nazi usurpers, not knowing if he was defending Italy for *Il Duce* or joining the Allied invaders from the boot. He kept his boots off. Preferred Captain Corelli and his mandolin. Waited to see what happened at Monte Cassino, and that's where the Poles came in, General Anders at the head and that's where he stayed. For ever. In a military cemetery. One of four around Cassino.

Playing with stones is one thing. Playing with the Peñón (rock, crag), Calpe's answer to Gibraltar, is another. A landmark, almost a seamark. Just to the south of Calpe, a mile or two along the beach, the Peñón de Ifach stands and juts starkly out in the morning sun, frequently topped by some affectionate wisps of cloud. A thousand feet high, it offers an invitation to all newcomers to tackle it. Early morning, youthful strides along the *paseo*, an hour's sweat-accompanied ascent, a crawl through a lengthy, slippery tunnel, a survey of the Moscatel vineyards on the plains, with a mountain backdrop blocking off the whole of the western horizon, descent three times as fast, but care! –steep drops lurk everywhere; back at ten for breakfast, with parents vaguely awake. Internet consultation discloses the Arabic origin of the name Ifach. Same as Gibraltar, in fact. Just less phallic, that's all.

Alternative to fiestas. Third-nightly table tennis, on a surface painfully small, third the size of the standard table, a shade bigger than a handkerchief. *Chez* Marc *et* Liliane. First to twenty-one. No superstitions here. There weren't twenty-one apostles, were there? Not even thirteen after Judas topped himself. The art of miniature ping-pong surpasses that of sailboarding. Keeping your feet on the board becomes simple enough but keeping the ball on the table is quite a different matter. Keeping your eye on it was impossible. You can bang the ball, caress it, spin it, chop it, lob it, threaten it, curse it, but the result remains the same. That wretched, little, recalcitrant celluloid sphere insists maddeningly on going beyond the end of the table at every shot. The remarkable feature of this spherical torment is that you actually accumulate points, and can win against all global comers. The brilliant can meet defeat at the hands of the mediocre. Joy of joys: points are counted up in English, the lazy Englishman's ping-pong lingua franca. Which leads us on to the gymnastic exploits of Marc who knew zilch words in English. Just as well, as we shall next see.

Key left in the flat? Door locked by the usual clown. Marc, whose English extends exclusively and uniquely to *Zee End* (with the nasalized *e*, rather like p*ø*nd) you see at the end of English-dialogue films, provides the key to everything. The narrative went something like this. Up to the third floor we all troop. No sweat. The lady in the next flat'll let us climb round. No big deal.

Oh, yes there is! Requests first in low key. But we soon got keyed up. Ready for a cat spat on Saturday evening? No permission for entry, lunacy prevails, or is it just cussedness? Conversation and heartbeats accelerate, still no entry. Verbal hostilities are engaged. Still, still no entry. Our weekend fate hinged on that door. Paws for thought. Lady's cat converted into a catalyst. Exit the cat from the flat, through the flap. Neighbour in a flap. Along the corridor scarpers the cat. Owner of flat and cat races after the cat. No messing with Marc. He's lapping it up. He calls a cat a cat, like all French speakers (*appeler un chat un chat*). Like calling a spade a spade in English. Marc couldn't by now get his head round all this English caterwauling, but he could get it,

233

with the rest of him, round the balcony. Cinema stuntman Evil Knievel was his style. No sooner the cat is out of the flat than Marc is in. Enjoys a lark does Marc. Very quick on the draw as well as on the door, has got the drop on her, flashing past the visitor with a 'Hello, Grandma.' Lady returns along the corridor, cat in arms, but soon up in arms. Agitated she is, like a cat on hot bricks. Marc reappears simultaneously, at our door, at the end of the corridor, not cap in hand but key in hand. In true Latin operatic *La Bohème* fashion, he sings out, exuberant, twirling his arms, flourishing the key: 'Ho trovato la chiave' (I've found the key). The key lies in the cat, notwithstanding Rodolfo. Marc had cut as feline a figure as any cat. Event that closed the door on any further meaningful communication.

Always fleet of foot, in true feline form, and never slow off the mark, Marc saves the day, and the key, once more. Similar scenario days later. Key left in a flat, another flat. No horizontal leaps this time. Rather, vertical movement, in simian mood. Reached top flight in gymnastics, had Marc. Now here he was, climbing to the top flight of the block. Needed no succour from Spider Man. Always raising expectations was Marc from the numerous admirers below. Didn't cut a key, but a caper. No low-key incident was this, and no slipping of standards for the hero of the day.

No obstruction from owners anywhere, so ascent to the top floor is unopposed. Out onto a balcony, up he clambers, only muscular arms necessary as he grips the upright supports, hauls himself up to the next floor, and the next, all done in a jiffy. Stunning for a nifty fifty. No climb-down even when climbing down. Marc was barking mad. Must have been to call his dog Sorbonne, the Parisian centre of intellectual excellence in France.

To come to think of it, all French dog owners are barking mad. At least afflicted with schizophrenic tendencies. They need the psychiatrist's couch at the best of times. The French for 'I follow my dog' must surely fill them with canine torment. 'I *follow* my dog' is the same as 'I *am* my dog'= *je* suis *mon chien*. The only possible way of avoiding this psychological calamity is never to follow your dog, and ensure your dog follows you. But this would place your pet pet on the same couch. He would then be saying 'I *am* my master'= *je* suis *mon maître*. All dog psychiatrists, please call the following number...

Back to Marc's jumping japes which would not have been possible if the balconies had been bedecked with washing. Washing on the balcony wouldn't wash. *Prohibido.* Any transgressor was taken down a peg or two.

Life in Calpe, settling into a kind of carefree abandon, saw keys naturally misplaced, lost, left inside. Misunderstandings galore. Need a new key? Latch on to the locksmith up the road. He must have been the cheeriest fellow in the place. He was the key to all key problems, as useful as Mr Kay, and he wouldn't fob you off with anything that didn't offer a fitting response.

Open up a new phase in your life. How about you young people checking up on your blood pressure? Round up all the friends and you have a full-blooded response, anything but anaemic. Mark my word, in the bright, shining sun, we could soon all be shinning up those balconies with a bit of support. Eleven o'clock is the appointed time. Queue here, *por favor*, in the corridor. Clogged as the oldies' arteries, it was. Thirty to be checked out. So many present they had to line up even in the flat. But no one tempted by flat-lining. Such a crush I felt I'd dropped our student doctor right in it. A sort of drop-in clinic.

Armed with the state of the heart equipment, Antonio, a new injection of student medical blood, will do the lot, and wholeheartedly. Would breathe new life into the community. But peace and quiet, please. In vain he tried against the noise. Was at pains to check on the veins. **SILENCE.** Needs to concentrate on what's going on inside, i.e. in you. Now, he's got his finger on the pulse. Pressure's on to put findings into English, or French, or Italian, or... *Sistólico, diastólico, pulsaciones*, pretty easy really. Don't need to get worked up. Some already worked up. White-coat syndrome. They turn up, leaning on crutches, hand to heavily bandaged head, panting with pain, cheeks oozing with tomato ketchup, a veritable colony of disaster victims, groggy in anticipation. Universal hypochondria. Even asked Antonio to check teeth. What cheek! Still having teething problems with his new apparatus. They didn't have a leg to stand on. All a stroke of luck, this free check-up to duck out of a stroke. Strike while there's time. Everyone's dead chuffed. Photos in support.

Affable Antonio. Everyone appreciated his clean, honest sofa-side manner. Worked flat out in the flat. Not in his vocabulary was hypocrisy, Hippocratic Oath or no Hippocratic Oath. Gallons of Galen good humour, to boot. Who's that? Another Greek. Had to wait three hundred years after Hippocrates for enlightenment, from 500 to 200 BC. No light years here. No greased lightning either.

Not disheartened over your cardiac condition? Maybe you've strained your back or have a bit of torticollis. That's it, stiff or twisted neck. I know just the fellow for you. In the Avenida de Valencia. Haven't got his number but he's Chinese. Look him up in *Páginas Amarillas* (Yellow Pages).

Carpe diem in Calpe, unrestrained merriment. But go inland, south-west, up in the Snowy Range, the Sierra Nevada, for another *carpe diem*, in Cabra. A couple of hundred miles away. A long way, you'd say. Yes and no. You could just about squeeze Cabra into *carpe diem*. Just fiddle with a letter or two. And I'd be happy for us to go to Cabra. I thumbed it there aeons ago for the first time. Have you been paying attention? For starters, it means goat in Latin. Just knock out the *b* and stick in a *p* =*capra*. *Caper* is part of this word. Acting the goat and cutting a caper like Marc above come to the same thing. And intellectual rapture of raptures, Seneca, the Latin philosopher, saw the light of day just round the corner in Córdoba. To round off these various strands of historical relevance, Cabra sees the opening scenes of Mérimée's 'Carmen' ignored by Bizet's operatic staging. Better to launch an opera in a volatile, quarrelsome *tabacalera* (tobacco factory) in Seville than in some backwater of the Sierra Nevada.

Cabra and colour go together. Set in thousands of acres of

neatly tended, symmetrically ordered olive trees, it nestles beneath severely eroded mountains. But the lives of the inhabitants are anything but eroded. Lively, fiesta-minded, they dance to the tune of Pan, half-man half-goat, what else? Come September, they launch into a frenzy of religious animation, climb to the top of an overlooking mountain to a sanctuary where the Virgin Mary presides over her flock (of goats?), and then bring her down on an *andas* (portable platform) in a state of high emotion, lacrimose with joy. She remains queen of all she surveys for a week, and then is conveyed on the return journey by her subjects, again in tears. During her sojourn below, she witnesses a week-long, uninterrupted fiesta where life is turned upside down: day becomes night and night becomes day. Sleep starts at five or six in the morning, so no visits, please, before three or four in the afternoon, just before resumption of festivities again, and again. Awash with banquets, Cabra sees toddlers struggling to stay conscious at unearthly hours, sleeping on benches, grass, in mother's arms. Cabra sees its denizens, its *egabrenses* given up to wine, food and song, an activity running across the whole of Spain, at different times of the year. If you timed it well, and aided by a map, you could fill the whole fifty-two weeks with one continuous burst of rejoicing.

And that goes for Christmas, too. Snake your way up from the coast through a magnificent gorge with gorging in mind. Arrive there on December 24th. *Misa de gallo.* Midnight mass. You think of home, rather than homily, food for the flesh and not for thought. Hurry up you priest fellow, turkey's on the table. A spree till five in the morning. A few hours' kip, and then bring on the musicians.

A morning wonderland scene. Cabra up in the frosty mountains. All around a cheering blaze, in expectancy of that rosy-faced bunch of violinists, mandolins, drummers. We're next in line. A knock on the door heralds a half-hour of blissful, lyrical sounds of the purest poetry, suffused with a warmth of fellow-feeling inspiring a string of tender-hearted thoughts and embraces. Fifteen-year-olds carrying in full-throated chorus the message of 'God is here, all's right with the world'. You yield, in spite of yourself, to the Christmas celebration. Difficult not to. Thank goodness words come easily to cross that divide. '¡Estupendo! ¡Qué bien! ¡Qué alegría!' And chunks more sophisticated than that. And over and above the festivity, the comfort and contentedness that the gift of languages has landed you in a unique milieu: that of sharing the communion of simple, homespun experience. The only homily in all this: keep hammering away with those evening classes, compensation is there somewhere. As the saying goes: 'A Dios rogando con el mazo dando' (God helps those who help themselves). Even if you don't make requests of the fellow upstairs, you can bang away with the *mazo* (mallet). And it'll pay off.

When those fifteen-year-olds play their cards well, they'll go on playing their tunes at university. They'll end up as *tunos* in a *tuna* which has nothing to do with our tuna fish. Now, you could think *tuno* comes from our *tune* or the other way round. And you would be wrong. No, Sir. It just happens to have turned out that way. A rather felicitous coincidence. A touch of Walpole's serendipity. *Tunos* play tunes in a university musical group called a *tuna*. They wander round the streets serenading all and sundry. No tips, please, just the fun of it. Salamanca's Plaza Mayor comes alive to their melodies, both instrumental and vocal, as they parade hither and thither. Zither plucking, frolicking with fiddles and flutes, tambourines, they parade their colourful clothes of striking black costumes, their *bombachas* (baggy breeches), and their *beca*, a yellow ribbon across shoulder and back. The women seem to have got lost in all this. And for a reason. Women serenading women, not on really.

All very gentle and tuneful *tunas*. Not so, further north, end of August, in San Sebastián. We start off really badly, if the eponymous saint is anything to go by. Ever seen Mantegna's (h)arrowing painting of the martyrized Roman soldier? The archers thought they had dispatched him with nine of the best *flechas*.

He lived to die another day, this time with cudgels. If you want to see the point of *flechas*, (*h*)*arrowing*'s a clue enough.

Things didn't improve very much with Napoleon. The trouble started here in the early nineteenth century with Wellington, hot on the heels of *le petit caporal*, as some like to call him. Well, he called us *une nation de boutiquiers* (shopkeepers), so there. A real mix-up, or perhaps, flare-up here. You see, to make sure that Napoleon and company were sent off with more than a flea in their ear, the English ganged up with the Portuguese, burnt and sacked the *Parte Vieja* (Old Part) of the town so as to free it from those dastardly French. No blaze of logic here. Sharp probably had something to do with it. Suppose he abandoned SS with just one street left, now called the *31 de agosto*, demolition day. Just as well these figures weren't the other way round. Could have been worse.

The Ruskies must have learnt a trick or two from the conflagration, getting fired up when Napoleon turned his imperial attention eastwards to Moscow, just a few years later. But no Napoleon in SS for a rehearsal performance.

Really no sense in all this? Oh yes there is. The *donostiarras*, inhabitants of SS get a touch heated. It fuels their fun for fiesta time. Fiesta time, end of August, here we come. Napoleon, Wellington, in all their rich martial regalia, on splendid white chargers, accompanied by their lieutenants in the finest apparel, are heralded down the avenues by drums, drums and more drums. We have to drum it in, for the whole parade is called *la tamborrada*. Want a translation here? Can't strike the right note. Best we can do is 'banging on the drums'. Splashes of colour, red, white, blue, ladies in their Sunday best, every one dressed as part of the act, flushed with the bright azure sky, an effervescence, an ebullience that only Napoleon and his foes could have stoked up.

Do we have to wait another year for another *tamborrada*? Five months, that's all. See you then. Late January. The *Fiestas patronales* (Patron Saint's Festival) go on and on. Like all the other fiestas. As many fiestas as there are *flechas* in San Sebastián. Children's turn for banging in January. And what do you know? Napoleon's soldiers are at it again. Seemed to have survived Wellington and Sharpe last August. Mind you, these'll be back, drums *obligent*. That's just for starters. Numerous flocks of children, too many to count, from all the neighbouring schools, parading as soldiers and sailors, accompanied by squadrons of horsemen, with a carousaling captain at the helm, and finally the Festival Queen, la Bella Easo, as the Basques call her, with ladies in waiting on hand. Nightly fireworks as noisy as Cape Canaveral rockets, brass bands straight out of the film *Brassed Off*, pop music performances, fair grounds, one long merry-go-round.

Fed up with fiestas? How about joining a *sociedad gastronómica*? A bit like *Probus*, they are all-male beacons, beanos included, often daily. Gives the ladies a day off from culinary chores. And the guys a chance to chance their arm at cooking. And singing. All together now. Line up, you fellows, at the oven, roll your sleeves up, put on your *mandil* (apron), fish out of the cupboard the *aceite* (oil), *ajo* (garlic), *cebollas* (onions), *sal* (salt), *especias* (spices), *chipirones en su tinta* (calamars in their ink), and please let's have some *besugo* (bream) while we quaff the cider or sip the Rioja. Don't like the *damas*? Oh yes we do. We even cook for them, twice a year, if you please. Want the dates? 19 *de enero* (January), 14 *de agosto* (August), eve of the Virgin Mary's day, you know when she bounced up, still virginal, to see her offspring. Jees! Some bounce.

SS is really quite a genteel spot, was certainly the most genteel before the Civil War. Elegance was its style, embellished with grand baronial houses of ambassadorial and consular importance. The cauldron of Madrid sent the aristocracy there for a cooler spell. Zarauz, just along the coast, westwards, was equally favoured. Queen Isabel II, and the Habsburg María Cristina summered there. Franco followed suit every summer in his military uniform.

No euros for the five-star María Cristina hotel? Aim for Pasajes, on July 25. You see, it's *El Día del Pescador* (Fisherman's Day). *Sardinas* galore, to spare, and all *¡gratuito!* Down them with red wine, not forgetting ample supplies of bread, and a great time is had by one and all. Don't drop the sardines as the carnaval floats float by, after all they are fishermen, and try to keep the sardines going down in the right direction as you call out streams of 'Hurrahs!' to the tune of the *tamborradas*. All compressed in a jovial, convivial *ambiente* of merry make-believe. Just keep speaking the lingo and eating those *sardinas*, and your memories will stay warm within you.

With all this merrymaking, food, wine and song, in need of a bit of a work out? Change from tubby Sancho Panza to scraggy Quijote? Down to the beach for a quick dip, then enlist for some training in one of those *traineras*, long fishing boats. Maybe you could make up the number to the required thirteen rowers with a cox. That Judas number, thirteen, again. Still, we're all in the same boat, and someone has to lose. I'll give it a whirl, although I didn't pull it off in the Varsity race this year, and those oars really need some tugging. All my energy's up top these days. *Remero* number 13, here I am. But I don't speak Eusquera, that's Basque to you and me, so you'll have to double up on the Castilian stuff.

Straight out for a work out, then, two kilometres there and another two back. So seawards we row. The *patrón* (skipper/cox) keeps us to the east of that Santa Clara island, precisely in the middle of the *bahía* (bay). Can see the *Parte Vieja* on my right and Monte Igueldo high up on the left. America-bound, twenty minutes of muscle-wrenching pulling in choppy waters, with a brown, glossy, sinewy back in front of me. Choppier and choppier the deeper the brine. The Thames a mere drop in the ocean. We turn for the homeward lap. Twice as fast with the tide, we land on the sand in thirty-two minutes. Home and dry. Good rhythm that. Thank goodness we avoid the baneful thirty-one, even though it's the other way round.

Regata time. Pirated that word from Puccini and company = *regatta*. The Frogs and Spaniards did a bit of piracy as well. No tacking for us Brits, we went straight for *regata*, and so did the

Spaniards for that matter. Had to knock off an extra *t* from the Italian, though. The French jump ship as they always do: *régate*. Thank goodness they're all feminine. Easier than the regata that.

Poseidon be praised. Or let's dance to Neptune. Greek or Roman, they're all the same. All those Atlantic-washed villages, Pasajes, Orio, Zumaia, and the other eighteen, have collected their crews ready for a row. Arrow straight they go, without a softy stripling like me. Couldn't have coped with the first Sunday in September, let alone the second. Alas, no trophy to be trotted out for me, no anchor to my expectations.

A hundred thousand of us, bets and watches at the ready, stretched all along the Concha balcony to watch our favourites tough it out to beyond Santa Clara. '¡Mira, están volviendo!' (Look, they're coming back!). No corrupt crookedness here save for tacking in search of calmer waters. No question of the first out and back. Just the fastest time over three *millas náuticas*, and twenty-five *nudos*. No kilometres here, distance or speed. We Brits may have lost an empire but nautical miles and knots still rule the waves. It's the Bilbao team, Urdaibai again, from way west, who are now the current conquerors on the Cantabrian Sea Circuit and bag the Flag of the Concha. Have won three rows in a row. Can't fathom the secret of their success. No greater splash of colour and excitement than this. Keep Barça and Real Madrid. We'll stick to our *barcas* (boats). It's much more real than Real. Got it all recorded on my reel.

You call this tough? You must be joking. See those *troncos* (trunks) over there? No, not swimming trunks, stupid! Tree trunks! About four feet across. Here's an axe, so heave your way through that. Encouraged they are by the stadium's overflowing, heaving crowd. We'll give you half an hour. Balking at the bulk? You're carrying a heavy burden of Basque expectation. Try the *arrastre de piedras* (dragging of stones). No sweat, really. You have a couple of *bueyes* (oxen) to get you going. Four thousand kilos, a snippet. Out for the count? You won't want this rock then. You'll need fingers like sausages, arms like tentacles and a hundred times as strong, a back the size of an elephant's, and legs like football stadium stanchions. Sorry it comes in all shapes and sizes, cube-like, rectangular, spherical, cylindrical. The trouble is the easier to grab the heavier the load. All worked out. Monsters, these Basque lads. How'd they do with the caber up in Scotland? No more than a caper, I suspect. Do you mind if I go back for a few sardines? I'll stick to the cerebral business, thank you. *Adiós*, SS.

Stick to the cerebral business. That's the ticket. Opera at Romeo and Juliet's Verona, now you're singing. The Arena di Verona, all aglow under the clear, starry sky, no star-crossed lovers tonight. Prokofiev's never part of the menu. Nearly all Italian save for the occasional foreign import, *Carmen*, all the way from Seville, courtesy of Paris's Bizet. Fourteen thousand opera buffs ready for July's opening night. Stage the size of a football pitch, enough for a parade of horses, camels, elephants, *Aida* style. Even room for some of those Basque *traineras* going up the Nile. Fair enough, that's where *Aida* was first put on. Trust Verdi to sail calmly through those balmy nights in the 1871 Cairo Opera House.

Physical to the cerebral. Art in all its gory glory, Tosca knifing Scarpia, Don José a repeat performance with Carmen, Butterfly anything but in the pink with Pinkerton, on a high note of hara-kiri, these are the grandest moments of 'Gaudeamus igitur'. Savour, with never a saviour in sight, those closing instants where dying arias really bring us thousands to life. 'Bis!, Bis!' clamour the Italians and the French, 'Encore! Encore!' we pinch from the French. Funny they don't chant it. Another 'On with the motley', Plácido, please, even after *la commedia è finita* (the play is over), for the dead clown Canio. But the last word has to be with the Ethiopian slave Aida and her Egyptian hero lover, Radamès. No gore here. Just entombment. And tombs will be just one of the pictures engraved upon our minds as Algeria and Morocco call us from over the Mediterranean. Islam here we come. So let's stay in the Sahara. Next chapter, s'il vous plaît.

8

Go South Young Man

Sketch map to show places visited in 'Go South Young Man'

'A nomad I will remain for life, in love with distant and uncharted places.'

Isabelle Eberhardt

Lyon airport, Algeria bound. A feral roar, an irresistible thrust, and one leonine leap. What's all this to do with Algeria, and lions, for that matter? Everything. You see, we're going from one lion to another. Explain yourself, young man. Has it ever occurred to you, Sir, that the old English name for Lyon, not too old in fact, was Lyons, and that, in pre-war, and even post-war days, it was not pronounced in that posh way, *à la française*, Lyon, but as in *lions*. So what? you may enquire. Well, that leonine leap takes you all the way, to, well, *Lions*, Oran or, in Arabic, *Wahran*. That means *Two Lions*. I'm still lost. *Oran* means 'two lions'. Clearer now? But where's Oran? On the Algerian coast, the second most important city in Algeria, the second biggest country in Africa, just a few square kilometres behind Sudan, but recently split in two. So you see, lion to lion, or Lyon to Lyon, in one easy jump. Not convinced by my Arabic? You're bound to want to know. Not knowing will just go on gnawing at you.

Two reasons that'll grip you. Algerian friends, many there are, even done books with them. Want a much more forceful reason that'll jump out at you? Easy. Go to Oran's (i.e. Two Lions') *hôtel de ville*, the graceful alternative to *mairie*, and what do you see? A four-times life-size lion each side of the main entrance. Just two, not a pride, although the *Oranais* take great pride in their grand, king-like statues. That's the lions tamed and laid to rest.

Lions, you understand, wandered those sandy lands in North Africa before it got dried up. Climate change not all our fault. Weighty evidence for the prehistoric presence of lions you'll find in Oran's Musée d'histoire naturelle. Want more solid evidence of fauna of all kinds? Elephants, rhinoceros, jackals, hyenas, antelopes, gazelles, leopards and giraffes kept them company. All you see now in the Sahara are those friendly little gerbil fellows. Scorpions, lizards and snakes just sneak away. Some domesticated animals around on breeding farms, and we did come across a zebra crossing in a farmyard. Not a pig or a sow. Maybe that's why they're still in the s(l)ow lane. Don't run away with the idea that camels have always been there. No Sir. Only for a couple of thousand years. Don't see them hardly at all now, even on caravan sites. Jumping forward by a week, however hard we looked for camels, we saw not a single one for hundreds of miles. Could have got the hump with no camel bump. Not so. The silent glory of the desert saw to that. You have to hand it to the sand.

But back to Lyon in France. Can't make that leap yet. You see, there's an Algerian lady in the concertina bit as you board the plane. How did she manage to reach that point with a six-foot floor covering and three bags of aprons? Wanted the lion's share of the baggage space. Not a bundle of fun, this. How on earth, we remarked, did she manage to get that far? A tissue of lies, it could have been, not sure. No red-carpet treatment for her, fair enough. Rather, she ended up on the carpet. The real trouble was she, like most Algerian women, was tied to her husband's apron strings, not that he would ever wear one. She obeyed hubby's orders. So we were held on the airport apron for an hour before reason took hold of her. The hold was the answer. Maybe in the Algerian dialect of classical Arabic she didn't have a word to handle things. Perhaps this was not a deliberate act of deception, but there was no way this could be swept under the carpet. Rejecting all responsibility, she blithely walked into the aircraft and turned her back on the matter. A comedy act if ever there was one.

Soon we were over Marseille. Lost the *s* here in English too, just like Lyon. Conspiracy theory over their theft? We'll leave that one to the etymologists. On over *la Grande Bleue*, that most colourful name for the bluest and brightest of seas, the Mediterranean. The tide was gradually turning, in more ways than one. From the drabber, more obscure tones of the north, we were entering skies as limpid as the waters beneath. With Saharan clarity, prejudices were melting away. A watershed moment, a great divide where Christianity fell away as the plane descended. The Algerian sun soon put all other experiences into the shade. A new society. Lion to lions. One lion to two. That's progress, for you.

Not the stifling heat we'd read about in Albert Camus's *La Peste.* (The Plague). Plague-ridden, claustrophobic Oran was a thing of the Nazi past. Nicknamed in Arabic 'el Bahia', in French 'la radieuse', Oran in winter opened out onto the dream of Algeria, a stream of appetizing, heavenly feelings. No fug here, after all, you could contemplate the crystalline heavens all day and night long. Lawrence of Arabia's *Seven Pillars of Wisdom* says it all. Although how he got to seven pillars when there are only five in the Koran is not too clear, but there you are.

Let's leap on the back of a lion, and see what turns up. Oran hosts sleep on the floor. Don't even need that carpet. Want any money? I've got thousands of dinars under the bed. Don't trust the banks. Don't pin your hopes on credit cards either. You don't need snakes to get stung, just try the bank. How do you borrow cash then? Want to buy a house? Easy. Borrow from the family. No interest either. It's in their interest to loan you cash. They may want some in return one day. House insurance? You must be joking. Put up an iron gate on the outside of your flat door. Pay for a night watchmen, like everyone else. A bit like the Spanish *sereno* chap of a hundred years ago: 'Son las tres de la madrugada, y todo sereno' (Three o'clock in the morning, and all's well). They must have heard this *señor* in Oran many moons ago, like Camus's mum, for she was from Iberia. In the colonial rush, the Spaniards settled in Algeria and Morocco, and still hold out in Ceuta and Melilla. In fact, the culminating feature of the stay in Oran was the climb to the Djebel Murdjadjo on which are built the Spanish fortifications of Santa Cruz overlooking the massive sprawl of the town, as well as the sea to the left. It was a bit of a calvary scaling the heights, for that is what *djebel* means. Had to be a calvary, if the name is anything to go by: Holy Cross. Oran is very much a cosmopolitan city, boasting wide avenues and majestic, colonial-style public buildings. Plenty of room for the odd lion. As well as for Jews putting down roots there after their expulsion from Spain in 1492, and the French settlers, the so-called *pieds noirs* (black feet) who had nothing to do with the Canadian Indians. Why *pieds noirs*? All sorts of fanciful theories, but the only down-to-earth reason seems to be they wore shiny, black shoes. Must have stood out in the capital, *Algers la Blanche*. Ended up as the *bêtes noires* of the locals. Blackened their copybook, they did.

The French squeezed the Spaniards out in 1831, not before the earthquake of 1790 had shattered the town. Repercussions no doubt of the previous year: 1789. The naval port, close by, of Mers el-Kébir allowed some control of entry into the Mediterranean but met no mercy at the hands of the British fleet in 1940, aware of a Nazi takeover. 1,300 sailors met their end, skewered like kebabs.

Archaeology digs down into one hundred thousand years of history. But let's forget the first ninety-five thousand and leave them to the fauna. From the coastal plains of Palestine came Phoenicians, and culture with them. Romans rowed that way too, found it quite heavenly, so they naturally called it 'portus divinus'. Turkish Ottoman Empire stuck its oar in as well, conniving with corsairs ruling the Mediterranean waves, on and off, or should we say, up and down, for a couple of hundred years. Let's hope our contemporary Somali counterparts don't last as long. Don John of Austria, egged on by the pope and our very own Richard the Lionheart (lions everywhere), sorted the Ottomans out in Lepanto in 1571. Poor Cervantes, on his triumphant return, found himself in a pirate goal in Algiers for five years. Returned to Spain, docked at Denia, after his *amigos* were docked a few million as a ransom. Cervantes seen from the other side. We've already seen it from one side. Remember? Red-bearded pirate of all pirates, Barbarossa, must have been in on the deal.

Not a hit with history was Hitler. Had his own hit list. Germany to the Urals was his dream. Caught napping. Napoleon taught him nothing. Could have confused his very own red-bearded, twelfth-century, Germanic empire builder, Barbarossa, with the Mediterranean, Ottoman-inspired lad, aiming his first balls (not his, alleged he only had one), at the Poles. Then at the Russians: *Fall Barbarossa* (Operation Barbarossa). Both Barbarossas, fiercely energetic, almost certainly had more than one ball, with all their mistresses. Odd thing here: the corsair chap was born in Lesbos, traditional home of Sappho, queen of the lesbians. No queen was Barbarossa. Couldn't have been with a red beard.

Now it's Chinese replacing everywhere. They have to go somewhere, damn it! Well over a billion of them, some parading in the streets of Oran on the strength of the yuan. An imperialist yen they clearly have. Whether their pandas will replace the lions remains to be seen. Wouldn't bet against it, though. Whole of Africa seems to be pandering to the yuan. Yellow will be substituting brown when the archaeologists start digging up the imperial warriors in ten thousand years' time, terracotta or no terracotta.

Leaving Oran's disenchanted youth already buried in their forlorn future (is that possible?), with only the Chinese to rescue them, two cars in tandem strike southwards. First the narrow coastal strip running from Morocco eastwards right across to Tunisia. A couple of hours and then the slow ascent into the Tell region, before the higher Atlas Mountains that form the barrier to that grandest of grand deserts, the Sahara, stretching from the Atlantic to the Egyptian Nile, and it's just as long. Keeping the desert at bay has seen the inhabitants pretty busy, from Turkish beys to President Bouteflika. No housing, no greenery, little water, just intense work in tents to create a *barrage* or *mur vert*, a vast reforestation programme that is simply running into the sand. Desire for life-saving vegetation must explain the dominant colour of the Algerian flag: green. Rub of the green against them. Should have invoked the Aztec god of rain, Tlaloc. No watered down prayers, though. Often, just floods of tears.

Sand. You can't mistake it. A vast, dry, empty expanse overflowing with a thirst for the nomadic experience.

Forbidding word, *Sahara*. *Sahara* in Arabic actually means 'desert'. 'Sahara Desert' is really tautological. And if you want to pronounce Sahara properly, row back over to the Iberian side of the Straits of Gibraltar. The Spaniards got it plumb straight. *Sáhara* they say, with the stress on the first *a*, just as in Arabic. And the *h* sounds just like a jota, a sort of guttural Arabic *h*, which is where the Spaniards filched it from in the first place, jowever jard this was to swallow. How the English and French got lost over the pronunciation is unclear. Maybe three million five hundred thousand square kilometres of desert have something to do with it. No Satnap necessary to locate it, though. There it is, a wickedly wide and wild wilderness, but no lions, not even camels, unless you strike two thousand miles or more deep down into the flies-infested Tamanrasset. Not tempted that far. No flies on me.

Precisely in the middle of the Atlas Mountains, stretch out the fertile plains of Tlemcen. A chance for youth there. Yens galore: the biggest university campus in Algeria. If cherries are the fruit for you, go no further than the prosperous plains of Hennaya and Maghnia. But more sumptuous pickings further south where the magnet is stronger. So on you press to Béchar. First taste of Saharan hospitality. You can't speak Arabic while eating? A piece of cake. They pretty well all speak French, which explains why you see names on most modern maps in French.

Hospitality? Seeing is believing. The scales fall from your eyes, if not from those of the most generous of hostesses. In and out she comes, dressed more than up to the nines, up to the tens, up as far as you can go, in fact, all covered up. And that's if you can catch a glimpse of her. You see, ladies eat separately.

What's on the table? Nothing. It's all down below, almost on the floor, on the lowest of trays, like you, cross-legged. What's that bowl for? Washing your hands, silly. Where's the knife and fork? There aren't any. Use your fingers. Which ones? In your right hand. But I'm left-handed. Use your right hand, I said. What's the big deal? Well, it's like this. You know all over Europe,

the left hand, like everything left, has always been seen as a bit
odd, writing with your left hand and so on. All that ecclesiastical
stuff about right being, well, right, and left being not right, wrong,
what the Italians call *sinistro* so that left hand is *la sinistra,* got
that Jesus chap sitting at the right hand of God after getting a
bit cross. Couldn't sit on his left, could he now? All too sinister
for me. What is more, in Muslim, and even Hindu cultures, left
is even funnier, but not funny ha. The other funny. The left
hand you use for, put politely, if you can put your left hand
there politely, ablutions. Water in bowl to hand. All that washing
of the rear makes for a sort of inferior left hand. Dirty business
really. Let's leave the left hand behind for cleaning up, and
concentrate on the right hand, the nice, clean one. Keep your
fingers crossed to make sure you get it straight.

All eight of us on low cushions. Right hand for eating. Got
it? Where's my plate? You serve yourself from that big dish in
the middle. But hold on a minute. *Bismalah* (In the name of
Allah) at the beginning, and *Hamdullah* (Allah be praised) at the
end. Food and religion go together. Thumb, index finger and the
middle finger take some bread which is screwed onto the food,
easy if it's couscous, and down it goes. I know it's a pain if you
can't pick up the 'pain' with your left hand, but that's how it is.
Still hungry? Any leftovers, I suppose it should be 'right-overs',
and they come your way, pushed gently towards you as an act
of friendship. Keep on the right side of things with your French,
and bountiful desserts will be offered to you. If you err to the
left, don't worry, you won't get your just desserts. Mind you, on
the edge of the desert, you could confuse French *dessert* and *désert.*
Easily done in the middle of mouthfuls. Even in English. Clever
lot, the Spaniards, no confusion for them. *Postre* is what you eat,
and *desierto* is that sandy place. Trouble with *postre* is it takes us
back to afters or posterior again. No appetite for that.

But there is for the varieties available. Tomato, aubergine salads
fit the bill and you don't have to pay for all of it with friends.
Add in olive oil and pep it up with peppers, and garlic, but not

so sure about parsley. The Maghreb world was up in arms about that tiny Spanish rock, just off the coast of Morocco a few years ago. You see, its name is *Perejil* = Parsley. A bit like Rockall in the North Atlantic but politically calmer waters up there. Hordes of Moroccans bivouacked on it to claim it as their territory. Spanish warships shot to the scene. The *gaviotas* (seagulls) were soon happy again. They weren't at all dislodged up in Rockall, they only had Tom McClean to deal with, and he cleared off after a month in 1985.

Salads take some beating, sure enough. Same for the *chorba*, vermicelli, vegetable or meat soups. You'll be cooing over couscous, a mixed bag, or should it be a mixed dish, of courgettes, turnips, carrots, potatoes and chickpeas, fleshed out with lamb, beef or chicken, or eggs. And don't put them all in one basket. No pork, nearly all lamb, and no meat not killed according to Muslim law. Wholesome halal meat. All in the interests of hygiene. Keep some room for the *baklawa*, a delight of a tart sweetened with honey and an almond paste.

Drinks? Not too clear about water. Duck away from the tap stuff. Bottled water or from the water crier who wanders the streets, rather like our ice-cream man. No water is watertight, except the bottled variety. And even then, take care further south in In Salah. First, the name itself almost gives you the runs: salt spring. Springing from the Latin *sal*, like the Spanish word *sal* and the French *sel*, not forgetting our Italian friends: *sale*. Ingurgitating this liquid will sour your relations with all and sundry. Trust the Spaniards to muddy the waters with *sal*. Why? it's feminine. All the others are masculine, and that includes the word from Rome. If the salt of In Salah doesn't put you off, and you don't take a rain check (don't need to really), go there with prayer in your heart. The Arabic sounds *In Salah* are comfortingly close to *Inshallah* (Would to Allah), a comfort that could line your stomach. All Arabs and Muslims will sympathize with you. *Inshallah* is on their lips every day, and that includes the UK.

Keen on a drop of *vino*? Best to stay close to Oran, in the

Oranie area, for four of the best seven wine-growing areas are located there, Mascara, for example, but even there its production is strangely masked. But we are already out of the comfort zone, and wine is not on the shopping list of our friends, it's not part of their culture. Odd that they still follow on from the French, export it and even merit a page in Sotheby's *World Wine Encyclopedia*.

But we can always dip into the *thé à la menthe*. Quite a ceremony, quite a palaver, you'd say, where everyone comments on the washing of the mint, several times over in boiling water, and when finally, the mint is in well, mint condition, it is poured artfully from great height, and allowed to stream down into glasses. Still a bit bitter? Lots of sugar needed? Sweet-tempered Touhami finds it by the heapful. Should be simple enough to find, even in the dictionary. English = sugar, French = *sucre*, Italian = *zucchero*, German = *Zucker*, all come from the Arabic *zukkar*. Allah be praised! They're all masculine! Hold on! Not so sweet after all. The Mexicans can't sugar the pill. They bend the gender and make it feminine.

While we've hopped over the pond, *yerba maté* in Argentina brings everyone together like *thé à la menthe*. Same sort of libation, too. With everyone around, it makes us all very matey. Lots of sugar, please. And thankfully, Argentinian *sugar* has gone back to its original gender, too. And you can pour *yerba maté* from those Iguassú heights. Makes quite a splash, so steer clear with your trousers.

Just a short ride from Béchar south to Taghit, ninety kilometres, and the world changes. Oasis country. Spectacular. Miracle country. Get off on the right foot, not left please, and pronounce it *Tarit*. Cleaving your way through the dunes, you suddenly come across Taghit in a hollow. Rather like Laurie Lee's Spanish villages that unexpectedly shoot upwards as you negotiate a bend in the road. A magnificent, immense sand backdrop, straight out of the theatre, there it suddenly is: a palm tree surrounded oasis, with, dotted here and there, low buildings of red earth. Red, red, red, as in Timimoun and In Salah. The first flame-coloured, dazzling encounter with a Sahara lost in time and mystery. Lawrence of Arabia and the Hejaz, *The Seven Pillars of Wisdom*, King Feisal, a real time warp. Lost in time, but also in space. The labyrinthine souk, with dashes of dates, rich in oranges and lemons, a variety of vegetables, all served by the mystery man clothed in a djellaba, a long, full, white, cotton cloak. Overwhelmed? The dazzle goes on and on, down to Timimoun, round to El Goléa, up to Ghardaïa, and then back up to the coast. But, let's savour the sap of life in small sips, if small sips are possible. After all, our cup runneth over.

You are fascinated by the sumptuous, red façades. Contrasts sharply with the limp, bare interiors. Best not to comment on the change. Owners could blush with embarrassment.

Little wonder *desert* has several appellations in Arabic. They slip off the tongue as sand slips through your fingers. Can't get lost with *Sahrâ*, can we? All us Europeans seem to have stuck an extra *a* in somewhere. *Mawmât* and *fayfâ* mean absence of water. Honest, guv, there is no water, unless you know where to look, like Peter O'Toole's guide in *Lawrence of Arabia*. Fat lot of good it did him. One single shot from Omar Sharif and he bit the dust, or better, the sand. Left a gritty taste in Lawrence's mouth. But we know where to look, don't we? Running deep down into the Sahara are all those wells mapped out, clear as water. Undersand? Sure. I understand *undersand*. Forgot the tea? You can make plenty with: *eau abondante, eau bonne, puits* (well) *artésien, eau potable*. Just keep looking on the map, and make sure Omar Sharif is not around. Mind you, Egyptian that he is, he would know these other words like *balkaka*. *Uncultivated, uncultured* it means. Omar fits the bill here, going round shooting people. More? Majhal, place where everything appears the same. No signs. Just sand and pebbles, sandstone, I suppose. Ard Tayhâ, place where you get lost. We are getting more and more lost with these names, so just two more: *baydâ* and *matlaf*, desert of ruins and perdition. But, let's just follow Touhami and Lahouari. Undersand? The water's down there somewhere.

Take care, all the same. Some of the wells are dry or even contaminated. Ne'er-do-wells? Anything but welcome.

Make sure you know where you're going, or, apart from getting lost, you could get into hot water and cross national frontiers unwittingly. Dunes don't stand still. They walk around. *Eau potable* could be on your ten-year-old map in one place, and then, come up in another. It could be a case of *Ard Tayhâ*. Draw a line somewhere, even if you are attracted by *eau douce*. And don't think this is sweet water where all in the garden is rosy. *Douce* here means 'fresh', and there would be little fresh about arrest in Morocco or Mauritania. It would be hotter than you bargain for.

Taghit is magic. Climb up to the top of the surrounding dunes and it's even more magic. They're as old as the hills. We'll play with the dunes, shall we? At least, the French can. There are so many of them, they just keep doubling up. You see, we climb to the top of a dune: *d'une dune*, as they say in French. A dune twice over. That's why it takes so long to reach the top. You have that sinking feeling. Never going to get there. On the crest, the relief is tangible. You can't go higher, casting your eyes over all the other countless dunes that stretch away to the east, rising the one above the other. We sure are building sandcastles in the air. Can only dream of climbing them all. *Somnio ergo sum* = I dream therefore I am. Carted that French fellow Descartes all the way over here for a quick change from *penso* to *somnio*. Don't get it? Soon will. Vast tracks of sandy dunes stretch to the eastern horizon from Taghit: *le Grand Erg occidental*. Erg equals 'dunes' or 'sea of sand'. It doesn't end there. Too much sand for that. Just halfway in fact. Further to the east lies its sister, even more expansive *le Grand Erg oriental*, with Ghardaïa and El Goléa almost buried in the middle. Sandwiched between them, as it were. At least Ghardaïa and El Goléa have water, which the ergs haven't got. They haven't sunk into oblivion yet. Dunes move. Something animate about them. They've cut In Salah in two. Always on the move they are. One minute you're clear, the next you're covered. Hey, where's my house gone? Two generations later, uncovered again. Need to put a house-building programme on a firmer footing.

The Sahara's not all sand. Large areas of pebbles there are. All around Tamanrasset, not much yellow stuff to be seen. A miscellaneous mixture of petrified forest, austere volcanic masses, enormous black stony plains. The romance of undulating dunes leave enduring smiles. The rocks of Tamanrasset leave you stony-faced and hard-nosed.

Sitting astride the top *d'une dune* (got it now?), are you? Funny business, on a winter's morning. Look at those lads skiing down the slopes. No, not quite cold enough for snow. But frost from overnight condensation pouring down from that Bible-black, luminous sky offers a silky ski slope.

Bible-black? The Milky Way's just reached us from biblical times. Sand may be a good second-best to snow but it's a real diversion from Alps to dunes. Alpine travel companies are on a slippery slope here, losing business. Sand putting the skids under them.

Evening now. Fantasy, glowing sun to the west, cold, brisk air from the east. Face to the north, left foot nice and warm, right foot needing a hot-water bottle. Same goes for left cheek, uumm, that feels nice, right cheek chilly, and hands, well put the right one over the other side. Left better than right here. But don't tell the locals you prefer left to right.

Orientation problems. Off we go south from Taghit, still just two cars, lost in space and time. Space, OK, but time? Fifteen kilometres into the desert is rock-solid evidence of man's prehistory presence in the whole of Algeria, as well as their friendly neighbours, lions, elephants, rhinoceros *et alii* who lost out in the Darwinian survival race, sped up by climate change. Fascinating etchings into stone of a whole range of animals, with secrets remaining locked, protected behind iron bars, lest they be damaged by their unfriendly human neighbours who described their hunting skills by etching into rock with metals they used to stamp their authority on the four-footed beasts. Hunting scenes are there to attest it. A most pointed environmental lesson, this. Taghit's stone etchings were just a taster. But, the sands of time were always slipping away. The writing was already on the wall. We had to keep going to fit in with our schedule.

Two thousand miles south-east, more writing on the wall, not that we saw it. Near the Libyan border, at Tassili N'Ajjer, a vast, untamed region, innumerable cave paintings and etchings show an artistically endowed, enlightened society, anything but uncivilized. A visit here and we would have been lost in space, too. A dune too far.

Feeling a touch religious in the wide, open, starry spaces? Gloomy brooding over space seems to have converted Pascal in seventeenth-century France, which must have engulfed Charles de Foucauld in the dune-surrounded, palm-strewn oasis of Béni-Abbès, a mere three hundred-odd kilometres further on. Hermetically sealed off from the outside world, he created his first hermitage there. Someone must have seen him coming. *Abbès* sounds a bit like *abbey*, doesn't it? *S* is very close to *y* in the alphabet, after all. Foucauld became quite a celebrity, and never said 'Get me out of here.' Indeed, he said just the opposite, and stayed on for assassination in 1916. Papal dues came his way with beatification in 2005.

Abbé Foucauld ordered three orders, all to do with *le petit Jésus* (little Jesus) and *le Sacré Cœur* (Sacred Heart). Conversion of the local population was his aim, so touched was he by their simple faith. But he found that the only version of events for Islam was perversion of the one true God: Allah. So he got nowhere, just bogged down. Islam is supported by its five solid pillars, not Lawrence's seven, for all their wisdom. Already seen that. Five pillars rest on: one true God, Allah; prayer five times daily; alms for the poor; Ramadan regressing eleven days every year, and the Hadj, a once-in-a-lifetime visit to Mecca. Only for the rich, perhaps. Our friend Hadj couldn't make it. Almost as many Hadjs as Muhammads, so other Hadjs must have made the trip in his place. Missing Mecca? Marabouts, saints and sanctuaries dotted everywhere. Cemeteries too, all in white, with feet facing east, all ready for the last (s)trumpet. Ecstasy in sex and religion. Saw that with Saint Teresa. Cemeteries kept outside the towns, far from their dead centre, could be banshees on the prowl. That's all Irish.

Talk in French all the way, long days through the sand brought debated comparisons between two of the three monotheistic religions. No Jews around to complete the triangle. Jesus on the cross was about the best we could do for triangles. He was a Jew too, and Jews and Muslims started off as brothers, both Semitic, not that you would have believed it. Abraham's Sarah's offspring was Isaac, and his Hagar's offspring was Ishmael. Nothing clearer than that, is there? No, except that they didn't like each other. Judaism and Islam got off to a bad start. Christianity joined the mix to make up the triangle which became anything but symmetrical. An isosceles triangle, if you ask me, two big bits and a small bit. Which the big bits are is anyone's guess. Mind you, Islam sees Jesus as a prophet, even in heavenly places, taken up in true ascension style. Muhammad did the same. So did the Virgin Mary, to come to think of it. The threesome on His Lordship's right. All this discussed on the trans-Saharan travels, and any heat generated subsiding with the setting sun.

No agreement here. All too ethereal for me. Let's get down to earth, or sand if you prefer. Easier that way. Less sacred substance, more substantial stuff. Food, please. Hang on, where's the oven? No ovens, Aga style here, says Touhami. A hole just dug deep into the ground. Oven it was. Not even oven, though. Sand piled outside. The earth gouged out made for a conical pile above. Ground to mound, as it were. The heat generated infinitely surpassed that of the heavenly debate type. But you had to know the formula. Bury your food in the sand but not your head. Unders(t)and? Catch fire you could if it went to your head. One meal fine, but wouldn't dig more.

Asking questions was a trial. The oven owners knew only some French, *petit nègre*, pidgin French. I had to dig very deep to get our questions across and even then they were only half-baked. Lahouari came to my rescue with his usual concoction of jokes on the rising cost of ingredients. They couldn't go any lower, could they? You have to call a spade a spade, don't you? And they had no money to burn. Lahouari should know, he was an economist of *Le Monde diplomatique* fame. He was always on hand to give us the low down.

Very environmentally friendly, this oven in the sand. Leaves no footprints. Just the occasional one, like Man Friday's. And no over-heads. Ground breaking stuff, this, for most of the group from up north. It sure was filling in a gaping hole, even in their knowledge.

As far south then as Adrar. To continue south towards Tamanrasset or back north towards Ghardaïa? The latter was gaining ground and sand. South was pebble country.

Choice before many on modes of travel. 1. Get on yer bike. Cyclists there were. A trick here somewhere. 2. The *méharée* method, i.e. on a camel, perhaps in a group, and anything for kicks. *Méharée*: a word that has slipped over into France and there it is, as big as, well, a camel, in the dictionary of all dictionaries, *Le Petit Robert*. Environmentally friendly but biblical in pace, and you'd soon get the hump, after hours on end. No unbridled enthusiasm here. Lawrence of Arabia had problems sitting on a camel cross-legged. Could try a caravan? Not behind a car, stupid. Few left, for they are no more than a memory, biblical again. 3. On foot. Yes, W/walkers manage it somehow, but they'd need an awful lot of crisps. And how do you get them from Leicester?

A decision-making, turning point. And we turned. North-east. Two cars further south, not 4x4, with uncertainty of fuel, sand covering the road on occasions, all too risky. And uncertainty of fuel there was. One incident was enough to fire our imagination. Petrol, petrol everywhere, but not even a tot for the tank. Fill up with fuel whenever you can, and carry plenty of extra fuel cans. Failure and you could be left stranded. Happened, at a service station, in the middle of nowhere. Had to wait for hours for a fresh delivery. Straw that broke the camel's back. No point in burying your head in the sand. But that's where the oil was. Lots of it down there, none up top. Modern technology had run into the sand. But no parking ticket.

So, Timimoun next stop. State hotel where pillows were as rare as water in the desert. Want an extra one? None, Sir. Understood my French but still no *oreillers*. Hadj hurried to the scene. Lots of pillows, Sir, but they are on the first floor. Only use the ground floor in winter. Persuasive Arabic brought two pillows from above. Not a private hotel. Get paid if you satisfy the customer or not.

Salt lake, dunes, brightest of moons, magical, fairy-like panoramas offering more rest than the pillows. A painter's paradise. So starkly striking, a most loony lunar landscape. Timimoun, the vivid cutting edge of colour, sand yellow, oasis green, sky blue, building red, people black, all the curving colours of the rainbow, not merging, but chisel-clean each one. Sharper than Van Gogh in Arles with his sunflowers and ears of corn. All colours flower here, even the colour of silence. Van G.'d appreciate that, with half an ear.

Oasis water, how do you share it out? From a two-metre-wide river, seven narrow channels divide it into a number of directions. These channels flow outwards like an opening fan to feed vegetables, fruit and animals. Following my drift? A neatly conceived system modified over in Spain and that we call *acequias*. No guesses as to where the word comes from. One drawback. Some channels were placed slightly higher than others. Less water for them. Seemed an arrangement that didn't hold water. Volume of protests had grown over unequal distribution of the waters. But help at hand. A leaked document disclosed a correction to the system. To calm the waters, less volume less dinars.

Currently, everyone pays the same quota with rebate for some. So there's no undercurrent of ill feeling. The water may well be split into several directions, but the scheme is conversely non-divisive. Efficient and streamlined. The provenance of the water? It's conveyed underground from hundreds of miles away, and is a testimony to the once fertile lands of the entire Sahara, formerly under many metres of water. An inland freshwater sea, in fact. Absence of surface water was caused by climate change, so attraction to Saharan life dried up. Only waterholes now and oases.

Surprised to see camels at the oases. Lucky to see any these days, anywhere. Bit like disappearance of Spain's donkeys. Sterile observation or sign of the times? Desert ships replaced by fuel-driven transport. All we saw in the desert were camels' bones, smooth from wind-driven erosion. Change from camel to car was a real bone of contention.

No threat of a fully blown sandstorm. But the next best thing. A very strong southerly wind. Protection please, Touhami, against the merciless, gritty grains of sand. A voluminous white turban. Is that all? No siree or *shereef*, if you wish. You put it on like this. There follows the most convoluted of procedures on how to cover the face with the Touareg-inspired *taguelmoust*. His eyes? Easy with Western-style sun glasses. There he stands in my photo, proudly, majestically, inscrutable, by his Audi 80, like El Awrence, not by an Audi, but by his Bedu friend of the desert, Auda Abd Tay, again in a full-faced photo from *The Seven Pillars*. Me put on the *taguelmoust*? I'm blowed if I would. But Touhami, Auda style, was more than an adventure. Foreign, unexpected, out-of-the-blue, sky-coloured, almost took us up there.

Next up, that is to the north, the promised land for the friends of fruit. There suddenly appears the most extensive of oases, El Goléa. Can't miss it, it's the only way. And yes, the plural of oasis is *oases*, for all the romance of Continental *is*, all stuck with the singular, however many. Trust the Italians to be different, though. They go their own way with *oasi* and no change for the plural. A word they love when *fiscale* comes after it: *oasi fiscale* (tax haven). Maybe that's why they invaded Libya in 1934.

Heavily, richly laden palm groves. Produce all vying for space, apricots, cherries, dates, figs, oranges, peaches, plums, all shooting upwards in luscious disarray, not respecting the alphabetical order we linguists like to observe. Ignorant we may be over Déglet dates, but we know where the storks come from. Migration is the key. Winter sees them in the welcoming expanse of El Goléa water, not forgetting the more austral Tamanrasset, spring calls them to cooler climes, so over they fly to France, among many other countries. Can't miss them. Black or white. Go to Marseille at Easter time, or anywhere along the Mediterranean coast, and there they are in full flight, on their almost legendary travels to Alsace's lakes, the Lac de Gérardmer, for starters. Maybe they have always seen water at Gérard*mer*. *Mer* is the end of the word as it is the end of their world. Piles of storks fly in from stock piles in the Sahara. A stroke of good fortune

Troublesome they can be, though. That's if they don't stick to what they're best at, parading in water. Other summer habitats include the towers and spires of Spain's Valladolid and Salamanca. Free, untaxed tourism lets down dollops galore, and no avian respect for religious niceties. Masonry is falling away as quickly as piety in Old Castile. Storing up trouble they sure are. The Church is in a real scrape, and all the scraping up there is not doing the trick, however many euros they scrape together. Anyone for loft conversions? The difficulty is that they store pride in their storks, and not just in storks. Valladolid boasts a whole district with avian appellations, a bit like an aviary: Calle de la Cigüeña (Stork Street)/ de la Tórtola (Turtledove) / del Pato (Duck), del Pelicano / del *Águila* (Eagle) / del Pingüino / de la Urraca (Magpie). They love their birds, and never ruffle any feathers. There is even a Calle de la Esquila (Shearing Street). What is more, they give storks a ride in automobiles if garage names are anything to go by: Automóviles Cigüeña. And even feed them nuts: *Frutos secos la Cigüeña.* Hitchcock's *The Birds* must be hovering up there somewhere. Or above Gérardmer, for that matter, diving on to pickings from the Restaurant Cigogne. Wines from Alsace are flown everywhere with a stork as a label. Advantages there were for one and all. Feather your nest, that's the formula. Another stroke of good fortune.

Mind you, storks are useful for restocking the population. Humans, I mean. Algeria's independence in 1962 was witnessed by nine million Muslims. Now, there are thirty million to ruminate on it. Nine to thirty million? How d'you do it? Call in the stork brigade. Stands to reason. Depends on the season, though. Reason and season go together, like male and female. Rhymes in French, too: *raison* and *saison*. How about that? Babies don't have mums. At the bottom of the garden you find them. Is this a fairy tail? And the storks, thousands of them, do the restocking. But they keep the nappy, hanging on the end of their beak. Environmentally friendly, you see. The beauty of it is there is no bill to pay.

No gardens in El Goléa or Tamanrasset? No worries, pop down to the oasis, clear away the reeds and there it is, a Moses basket, name on ticket n' all. But there are gardens in France. You find babies at the bottom there, stork style, but most of them are taken straight to Alsace from Algeria on a delivery service. Elsewhere in France, you find them in *choux* (cabbages), if they're boys, and near *rosiers* (rose bushes), if they're girls. Pink for girls, has to be. A bed of roses for them. Anything dull and rough for the boys.

Could flamingos and herons nose their way into the delivery market? I'm not sure about herons, or flamingos. Don't think they are in the baby-boom business, but flamingos could at least do a bit of cooing or singing. You see, in Spanish our *flamingo* and *flamenco* are the same word. You're larking about. Listen to me, birdbrain. Whether you're standing or singing in Spain, it's *flamenco*. So ¡*Olé!* And don't forget that upside-down leg at the beginning of ¡*Olé!* And they do say storks surprise us on one leg. What about the French then? Well, *flamingo* in French is *flamand* and *flamenco* is *flamenco*. Simple, that. Gypsy-style *flamenco* has migrated everywhere, even to Flanders, which is where the word *flamenco* comes from in the first place! All this sounds a touch highfalutin to me.

Storks have long legs. They can stand on their own two feet, don't need a helping take-off to wing their way as far as Ireland. Catholic country, like France and Spain. So conversion from Islam and back again must be in their diary, whether they yield dairy produce or not.

Desert discounts must be had in Ghardaïa, the next oasis northwards.

Carpets are to be haggled over in the most famous of markets. Try to beat them, not the carpets. They'll try all ploys to make a clean sale (a contradiction in terms if you catch on to the French *sale* = dirty), even give you the red carpet treatment. More cunning than car salesmen, they start off at some ludicrous price, ready for the unwary tourist. Extend generosity as far as their carpets will stretch. They weave in and out of prices like Mohammed Ali in a boxing ring. A long way to go for the starting price was at the top of those palm trees, and there's a big drop to suit you. The ground price can't go lower, so that's it folks. Take it or leave it. We took it. Ghardaïa bedecks our bedroom wall, too expensive for the floor! Clever fellows, those carpet merchants. They're always ready with the knockout punch. Ali must have learnt a trick or two from them, knock down prices and all that. You grin and bear it and take the price on the chin. You know you're going to be floored so wade in and enjoy it, especially if the haggling falls on the *Fête du tapis*, in March and April. If you can duck the carpet blow, watch out for another on the chin for a wicker fruit basket.

The only privately owned hotel was in Ghardaïa. New Year's Eve it was. Fortunately not Ramadan, a regressive festival, coming forward eleven days every year, already seen. Could fall on New Year's Eve. Even blow-out day, Christmas Day. Allah not be praised. Pillows were as plentiful as the dates, even during Ramadan. So was the fare. And the haunting, up-and-down music, played on flute-like instruments by locals in their burnous or djellaba, turban to top it all. Concession to the absent Scots as they rolled out that most nostalgic of nostalgic tunes 'Auld Lang Syne'.

When buying dates, make sure you are buying dates. Sounds nutty. Not so. They still speak French here, remember? All right for a date or two, but side-step for a bunch, and do the usual politico spinning, or a punch could come your way. Oddly and inexplicably enough, a French bunch of dates gets a bit political.

You see, a bunch of dates is *un régime*. A dictator may not take kindly to *un régime pourri* (rotten...). Surely no punches will find their trajectory to your nose if you buy a bunch at Ghardaïa in November. That's the *Fête de la datte*. Put that date in your diary and you'll be wallop proof in the whole Ghardaïa *wilaya* (= *département*). No mistake over your intentions, surrounded by over a million date palms. A juicy prospect.

Priority for dates most certainly. None for the ladies. Nearly all doors are closed to them, and that includes entrance to their own house. You see, Ghardaïa decrees one door for the male and one door for the female. All mail for the male. Rings a bell, doesn't it? Amazing the Ghardaïa ladies can find any door at all, walking as they do like Cyclops, although at least he had his eye in the middle of his head.

A few words from your hubby, Madam, and you're off for good, out on the street. Instant divorce. No appeal. Try to do that to me, lady, and a long, legal procedure lies in front of you. Dad, brother and cousin'll be against you. You need them on board if you want to marry in the first place. Little justice for the fair sex.

You can get away with a bit more, if you get away. Education, and you're in clover with three languages: Arabic, Spanish and French. The young tutored elite of the female species jump from one language to another as easily as they jump squares in hopscotch.

Time was running out, and tracks had to be made, not that we could always see them. Algiers is in our sights. Hey, you said we'd be using all French names. So, why not *Alger*? Of course, I could be a little pretentious, switch the *l* and the *r* around, and end up with the Spanish *Argel*. Saw that before. We posh linguists call these letter switches '*metathesis*'. Jees, that's some deal. The metathesis of Algiers/Argel was no big deal to Cervantes, though. All he wanted to do was get out of the place, after five years in clink. Back to Barbarossa again. He was the fellow who did a sort of Turkish Henry Morgan. Didn't just play ducks and drakes, you know.

Nelson was not to be outgunned by that filibuster Barbarossa. He bombarded Algiers in 1804. All on his colonizing mission which really backfired. Pretexting help for the Brits to clear the Med of piracy, the French captured Algiers in 1830 and, no *entente cordiale* this time, outlived their welcome for one hundred and thirty years. But, no delaying tactics for the French. Hadn't heard yet of the politicos' filibustering in the States. They set about building their own palatial district below the labyrinthine Casbah, above which stood, and still stands, an impregnable citadel. The Casbah: lair for the FLN (Front de la libération nationale) leading to the 1965 cult film *La Bataille d'Alger*.

Westwards we went, with the rich, prosperous hinterland on our left. Sorry, you have to use *left* sometimes. But here we go again: Algiers was soon left behind. Destination? That permanent challenge to the passing of time. Tipaza, fifty miles. Worth it every inch of the way. Survived a severe earthquake some ten years again, most pillars still standing. The Romans built for glory, for eternity, as they did for Cherchell, further west, and Djemila, further east. Tipaza almost the size of Pompei. And Camus did them all poetical justice, no, real poetical justice, especially Tipaza and Djemila. Doubtless inspired by the ancient breath of the Romans, he speaks of the wedding of the elements, sun, sand and sea. Mind you, you've got to be sharp to catch those highly charged kisses, erotic metaphors and all that: the sensual sound of the sea sucked in and out of the sandy rocks.

Taken round Tipaza by a French-speaking Algerian guide. Unhappy sort of fellow he was. Seemed permanently down in the dumps. Maybe because his life was in ruins. Rather like that weary, g(l)um dentist who always looked down in the mouth. Occupational hazard.

Back along the coast to Oran. Time ran out. Luck had been with us all the way. Even the United States president would have been thrilled. He knows what luck is all about, doesn't he, with a name like Barak. Fits quite nicely into Algeria, does Barak, even if he was born in Hawaii. You see, *la baraka* in Arabic and in

French means precisely 'luck'. And Barak had already been with us in spirit, if not in the flesh, when we visited Morocco.

Exchange is no robbery, as the French say: *Échange n'est pas vol.* Understand? No? What about 'quid pro quo' = reciprocal exchange? Can't do it in Arabic, but French more than gets me by. Could do it in Spanish, too. Lahouari's wife, Rachida, teaches the stuff. If you can't do it one way, try another. They'll soon be on their way to Sherwood Forest, Robin Hood country. Permanent invitation to visit they'll take up one day. And did.

Not Spanish but French in Morocco. Ready for it I was, going back to university days at Besançon. No meals at the Cité Universitaire, closed on Sundays, so *le mess des officiers* (officers' mess) cleared things up quite nicely, and made life very palatable. Nothing turned out amiss. You could turn the tables on Oliver Hardy. Hardly could I say to the university authorities: 'That's a fine mess you've gotten me in to'. It was indeed 'fine' but nice 'fine'.

Didn't need to hurry from *la messe* (mass) to *le mess.* Besides, the Moroccan soldiers who served us were always happy for us to give *la messe* a miss. They were Muslims, after all. And me? I was nothing at all. All too messy for me. Business was conducted in French, goes without saying, but paying all the same. The price without wine: *cent vingt sans vin.* Light francs it was in those far-off days, before de Gaulle's heavy franc, and it was no weighty affair to convert, not me, but the francs into pounds. *Cent vingt* = one pound, twenty pence. You could always sort out all those identical sounds if you had the meal *sans vin* (without wine), with a clear head, of course. Our Muslim friends were doubly happy not to serve wine. No messing with the *messe,* and no time for fine wine.

We had come across Moroccans in Spain too, not soldiers, silly. Caravans of them, not on camels, but in old, clapped-out estates, returning to their homeland for the yearly summer *vacances.* Loaded up to the gunnels, roof-racks overloaded even with domestic appliances, for the family back in Casablanca, they would trundle along, one eye on the road, one on massive hoarding signs cautioning against conmen and crooks.

Met them again in Gibraltar, before the Algeciras ferry. A decision to camp on The Rock was a not too soft an option. You get what you pay for, and The Rock does exactly what it says on the tin, and it was as hard as tin. Camping on The Rock turned out to be a choice between a rock and a hard place. Try driving pegs into rock. No real enjoyment here. Nowhere to go, nothing to do. Always clouds clinging to the top of the rock. Holiday really on the rocks. May have been the bedrock of British Mediterranean policy but no good for sleeping.

And no monkey business, please. No sleep that night. Sticky, salty water too, and I haven't shaved since. Safekeeping for the car, so let's rely on Barak again, and see if the camels can cart us all the way to Fès and Meknès. Didn't need the camels. Barak, bless him, had a Moroccan engineer student all geared up to lay things right on the line. Nothing askew with him, or out-of-true; he was straight up. That's what you'd expect of an engineer, isn't it? Barak was working hard for us. Failing him, of course, we could have called on *Dame Fortune*. But Barak was a better bet, bits of Muslim there were in him. Hadn't he been in Indonesia for a bout of unbiased education with his mum?

You've got a tongue in your head, remember that? No sooner on the ferry boat than Ahmed, dolphin gazing, catches my eye and my tongue. Invites us to Fès. Not a shallow offer. He's studying engineering at Grenoble, making for Fès to see Mum and Dad. Had one of those Bergman Volvos again. Must be reliable, we're always involved with, well, you can guess the car. All now plain sailing. Easy to get Pat on board. Geographers'll travel anywhere. Has given us the seal of approval, even the dolphin, if you could say that. Pat would have been the last person to rock the boat. So, rock on, Ron.

Tanger la Blanche, just like *Alger*. Not *pieds noirs* here, but would have stood out all the same. Bet they would have done the same in Casablanca with all those white houses, if *casa blanca* has any meaning at all. Whether it was the white of Tangiers that made Matisse Morocco bound is not clear. Checked in his morocco-bound books but still not clear. Yet clarity of colour was clear to him. The sea blue of Tangiers drained through into many of his paintings. Tangiers blue = Matisse marine.

But we needed dosh, *dirham* dosh. Gone were the money boys of Tangiers' International City status. Tangiers had been an open city. Bring your dollars, ladies, gentlemen, Russian princesses, Scottish lords, no questions asked in this most fabulous of ports. A tax haven. Has to be a haven. It's a port, isn't it? Why 'had'? 1962 saw Moroccan independence from the French. Rabat the capital, not Humphrey Bogart's Casablanca, snapped up Tangiers who immediately felt the pinch. No longer plain sailing for a free port. It had run out of financial steam. A golden opportunity lost for ever. Harbouring of regrets there must be.

Off the boat, and off I went to the bank. Morocco's currency, like Algeria's, was a floating one. Never sure of the rate. But, transactions easier than in Algeria. Gone an hour or more, and Pat, my wife, felt uneasy in the middle of the medina.

Two hundred miles lay before us, Fès first stop. Ahmed behind the wheel. And that's what I enjoyed. The wheel, or put more roundly, the *noria*, an extremely high water wheel, straight out of the Arab world. And that includes the word too: *nâ'oûra*. As large as a fairground wheel, or the London Eye. Useful for feeding dates. Now was a chance to see them fed. Irrigation channels again, as in Algeria. This was one date I could not miss. Can't translate this ambiguity over into French, Spanish or Italian for that matter. Simplest of lessons: tricks of a language are just that: tricks of *a* language. *Datte* in French, *dátil* in Spanish and *dattero* in Italian. These are the only dates you can make. No rendezvous here. Browned off with this data? You'd brighten up with the distilled spirit it makes, arrack. Are you listening, Barak?

Right the way through the rugged Rif mountain chain we travel. Not just rugged. Rebellious as well are the inhabitants, never submitting to the Spanish occupiers, accused by their 1922 leader, Abd-el-Krim, of the usual colonial crimes. No difficulty in plotting our path. French, as well as Arabic, appears on road signs.

Arrival in Fès, once the Moroccan capital, the oldest of imperial cities, Delphic in its combination of pious tradition and openness, splendidly cultured but decrepit, or could we risk *decrapit*? Try some of the toilets. Even if you knocked the *i* out of to(i)let to let them, you'd be hard pushed. Stench of mismanagement. Staying in there turned out as an heroic act. Crouching style, *à la turque*, was anything but Turkish delight. Mind you, always plenty of water on tap. If you had a hole in your budget, there was no choice but the hole in the floor.

The architectural riches more than amply compensated for our being cut short, of money, I mean. The sumptuous ninth-century mosque Karaouiyne, symbolizing its spiritual influence and prestige, is there to prove it. And the muezzin from the minaret makes sure you know. No mumbo jumbo, this. Five times a day. As we all know, entry is forbidden to Muslim non-believers – are there any? Or non-Muslim believers – got that right, haven't I? And even they have to be in spanking-clean condition. I was never that sort of spanking clean. Mists of religion had somehow dissipated and I was demystified. Cosmopolitan travel had cleaned me out. Even a wash and brush-up does not suffice for the mosque. No shoes either, Algerian *pieds noirs* or not.

Hospitality? Out of this European world. Ahmed's family is the gentlest, the most considerate, the least prejudiced, the most open-minded, hold on, I'm running out of superlatives. Take your shoes off, Ronnie. And that goes for you too, Patsy. Easiest strip-off ever for a mutton stew, beans, prunes and honey. I wouldn't exchange those prunes for all the tea in, well, Morocco. Especially if it were *thé à la menthe*, but steady on the sugar. They understood me here, *sugar* being an Arabic word. And I see you've done a good job on your hands before you come to table, or the floor. Ahmed's mum sees to that with a bowl and flannel. No knife and fork. Just hands, as in Algeria, but anything but a hand-to-mouth existence. Desserts were in plentiful supply. I plumped for melon, not plums, but plumb splendid, whatever it was.

Meandered round the two medinas of the city, Fès el-Bali (Old Town), and Fès el-Jédid. Soon would get lost, save for Ahmed. The town of Medina del Campo in Spain's Old Castile was easier to negotiate. Didn't need a mediator either. The *medina* was one thing, but have you ever tried a souk? As in Toledo, you would have needed Theseus again, but this time, tied to Ariadne's string, to find your way around. Want to locate the tanning business? Open up your nostrils, breathe in hard, and you can smell that corrosive, toxic reek miles away. Legs and arms naked, the tanner tans the leather standing in a vat, after a three-week soaking in a lime solution. Dangerous work, tanning his own hide, as well. Innumerable, huge vats over a wide area, the leather steeped in magical splashes of myriad colours, blue, brown, cream, red, yellow, the whole scene invaded by the hypnotic beat, beat, beat of local music streaming out of cafés and loudspeakers. No bill of health here in the vats. Not one either at Marrakech for the dyers. Hope the dyers don't know any English. Could be too close for comfort. They could be dying from dyeing. But, I bet they don't pay VAT on their vat

Want magic in a medina? The souk is the place for you. Early in the morning with the rising sun, semi-darkness is the order of the day. But just linger around for a while. Midday sees the sun driving down its rays through the lacy openwork onto the black burqas and white djellabas below. Is that all? Far from it. Arabesque designs flash at random, in all directions. Pat had suggested a walk from end to end. Hints of sunshine combined with dots of darkness on moving bodies. A cinematic feast, a sea of movement. An entrance into an entrancing world.

In the souk food calls. Now you're talking. Open up those nostrils again but in a different direction. Just follow your nose. The odour here is as paradisiacal as it was infernal back there *chez le tanneur.* Can you pronounce that *para-* word in the last sentence? *Infernal* is a damned sight easier.

Already alerted over spices. Marseille, Grenoble, Lyon and Paris, all in the market for them. Algeria and Morocco, leaders in spices, make you feel heady a mile off. The fragrance of aromatic spices, their most enticing pungency invades you as you near those tempting stalls. Taste the virtues of saffron, cinnamon, ginger, pepper, curry, or rose petals for tea, coriander for fish. If these don't send you, try musk to perfume your clothes, and heaven is just round the corner. Don't bank on the ladies, though. Forbidden fruit, that's if you can see them.

Maybe the spice is just too spicy. Need to sweat it off somewhat? The hammam's the place for you. Failing Morocco, you can try them in France. Bubbles up like a Turkish bath, but it's Moroccan, or even Algerian. Recalls the Roman baths, yes and no. Men in the morning, males first, females later. Don't get steamed up. Never the twain shall meet. Not even on the massage table. Would no doubt rub our American friend Mark T. up the wrong way. Mind you, Mark could fudge his identity with a fez.

Sands of time again. Couldn't even make it to Meknès. Train straight back to Tangiers. Homage had to be paid to Tarik Ibn Ziad, the converted Berber chief who found 711 a golden time to cross the Gib Straits and send those vulgar Visigoths back up north. Clever lad was Tarik. Still around really with Jbel Tarik (mountain Tarik), leaving his name as Gibraltar. So are the monkeys. Call them Barbary apes. The Muslims only stuck it out in Granada till 1492, not without doing a Tarik, though. Arabic names all over Spain, even Al Andalus > Andalousia. Gib went through three sets of hands, but is in the safest set now, after the Treaty of Utrecht in 1713. Wouldn't you Brits agree? Ceuta and Melilla are the British insurance policy. No Ceuta and Melilla for the Moroccans so no Gib for the Spanish. No monkeys, either.

> Lament you may the loss of your donkeys
> We still do not give a single monkey's.

Homage also to Hercules. Had to be. He dug out the Straits of

Gibraltar, Mount Hacho to the south and Gib to the north. Probably needed more than a hatchet and a jib to get to the other side. There you are, all done and dusted: the Two Pillars of Hercules. Not as many as Islam's five but it's asking a lot after his twelve labours. Did us a favour. Found our car easily enough.

Thank you very much, Hercules. You even called in further up the coast and did a job on the Peñón de Ifach (Calpe Rock). *Gaudeamus igitur* once again. You probably started in the construction business with the *Chenoua*, at Tipaza. Easier to get orders from your dad, Zeus, closer to home. No Internet in those days, but he may have had an Olympia machine.

9

Go West Young Man

Sketch map to show places visited in 'Go West Young Man'

1492. Landfall. We are about to witness the birth of a new nation. Let us therefore not give these western approaches a wide berth, mused Columbus. As revolutionary an event as Faraday's invention of electricity. Flow of current worked efficiently for both of them. Thus:

Fourteen hundred and ninety-two. Columbus sailed the ocean blue. With a name like Cristopher, he had to. Cris(t)s-crossed it four times, in fact. Fond of the Pond, was he. Genius he was, born in Genoa, so destined to do it. Had it in his genes, if Genoa

275

is anything to go by. Genoan name? Cristofero Colombo. All in the name. Hey, don't forget that Saint Christopher chap. You know, the patron saint of travellers. Must have kept an eye on the traveller of all travellers. What about the second eye? Spain's King Ferdinand's. Oversees things overseas.

Colombo ended up as *Colón* in Spain: *Cristóbal Colón*. His boat? *Santa María*. Holy Mary, mother of God! And who came after? Drake in his *Golden Hind*. Behind by fifty years. Colon, no accent here, please, had a lot to do with it. He needed one, like everyone else.

Godliness versus the devil. God versus gold. The devil may have taken the hindmost. Drake among the coarsest of corsairs. Our Good Queen Bess, could call her Isabel, versus *Isabel la Católica*. Same name, although dates not the same. OK, but what's fifty years among enemies?

Repeat 1492, you *niños* (children). You could say that again, three times over. You see, it's the Spanish 1066, and all that. Saw that before, but now seen from the other end, or rather the other side. So here are all three. 1. Jews and Arabs ousted or else... Sephardi started to wander. They must have wondered why. The crux was in the cross. It all hangs together. The Jews did him in and none of the popes have really forgiven them for it. 2. Fall of Granada. Isabel and Ferdinand saw to that. 3. Columbus sailed...

You'd think they'd have called America *Columbus*, or *Colón*, wouldn't you? After all, he 'discovered' it, although he thought he was in the Indies. The East Indies, I mean. Perplexed, perhaps, he sent his men high up in the trees, not just to pick coconuts, but to see further afield, or further a-sea. But they were all shinning up the wrong tree.

The privilege of naming that western landmass fell, not to Columbus, but to Amerigo Vespucci, an Italian who arrived there in 1501. A German, and they are usually at the top of the efficiency list, printer by trade and by name Waldseemüller, floated the idea of Amerigo's name. Pretty shallow thinking. Called the place *Amerigo*, ignored *Columbus*, and there the matter rested. Took the wind out of Columbus's sails, it certainly did. But don't confuse that German Herr Waldseemüller with Johnny Weissmuller. Could do, our Johnny spent a lot of time in the water. And in the US at that.

Along comes Drake. He knew what he was about. Didn't need computer piracy to hack through all that red tape. Waived claims of Spanish jurisdiction, having learnt a thing or two from that most pacific of pirates, Barbarossa. Beards were all the rage in those days. Let's let our hair down, Drake must have thought, and singe the King of Spain's beard, not in Cádiz this time. He needed a shave, so we gave him a close one. Coasting around Barbados, what did Drake see? Long, stringy strands hanging from the local fig trees. Looked like hairs on a beard. There you are: *barba* in Spanish for 'beard'. How about that? Stretch out *barba* and you get *barbudo*. Making all these connections just grows on you.

And barbs there were aplenty, flying all over the place. Must have been pretty hairy. Lesson in all this for little Billy eleven-year-old learning Spanish. *Barbado* means 'bearded'. Fine, but by far the most common word is *barbudo*, but the Mexicans drag it out, splitting hairs with *barbado*. Just about the same meaning and maybe more common beyond the Pond. Not easy tying up all those loose ends dangling around.

We're not yet beyond San Salvador. Bahamas, you know, not to confuse with bananas, although, in the M/main, they hung down as plentifully as those Barbados hairs. Not that Columbus knew when he arrived. San Salvador, the saviour of mankind, wasn't helping him very much. Still, he stuck to his guns, met some Arawaks, nice people they were, but the anthropophagus lot, you know those cannibal types, were a difficult bunch to swallow. The word 'anthropophagus' is even more difficult to swallow. Better learn a thing or two before they swallow you. Columbus caught on in the nick of time. He mixed up *cannibal* and *Caribbean* but was never in a stew. He just took pot luck.

We fluttered about from island to island, all treasure islands.

Airline tarifs anything but sky-high. The Caribbean airline Liat worked on a reduced budget with very low running costs. Their efficient turn-around schedules whizzed as fast as their planes' propellers. No jets here for the jet set. We tried a pilot scheme to start with: St Kitts and St Lucia. Choice was wide. Hovered between decisions over numerous islands, Things really took off when we booked for Antigua, Nevis and St Maarten. Dropped into English, French, Creole and Dutch, with Spanish never very far away. Landed bargains everywhere. Even free language lessons. They just came out of people's mouths straight into our ears. Listened and listened lest words were lost. Flew like pigeons from pidgin French to pidgin English, to pidgin Spanish and even pidgin Dutch.

Rica Martinica (really French Martinique but rhymes better like that. Thank goodness the Spaniards are helping us out with the rhyme). Martinique made imperious demands on our time. That little Corsican fellow's spouse Joséphine was born there, after all. We wanted to visit La Désirade (island so desired by Columbus and company after months of travel), perform *un acte de piété* on Les Saintes, and a touch of gallantry did no harm on Marie Galante. Flitted around we did, and finally settled, like all domesticated butterflies, on Columbus-'discovered' Guadeloupe, in honour of the Virgen de Guadalupe, in eastern Spain. 1493 it was. Bust in (don't mean 'break into') the village of Sainte Marie to prove it. Butterflies do feel at home there, you know. *Hogar, dulce hogar* (Home sweet home), as all reputable insurance companies advertise in Spain. They see it so from above, butterfly-shaped, Basse-Terre and Grande-Terre. Two big wings joined by a bridge. All rather funny, this. Topsy-turvy. Basse-Terre is high and Grande-Terre is low. That's what you'd expect, isn't it? The fellow keeping it that way is a bit of a clown. What d'you mean? Look at the capital, stupid! Pointe-à-Pitre. All double Dutch to me. Bound to be. *Pitre* is Dutch for Peter. A bit of acrobatics and you end up with 'clown' in French. The *pitre* plays around keeping the butterflies in order, seems to me. *L'administration française* + *Guadaloupéens* = clown + butterflies. Nothing simpler than that, is there?

If you don't catch all this lepidopteran stuff, don't get too hot under the collar. We're off hot foot to the volcano with Élizabeth and children. Suggestion of the climb sent my spirits soaring. Even so, quite a tall order. Halfway up and feelings were running really high. Right to the steaming lip. Fumes squirming their way out of the vents, those side cracks, had already heightened our sense of vulnerability. Puffing all the way, so few words. With rarefied air, wasn't at the peak of my powers. Don't breathe in all that smelly sulphur. You've been warned. La Soufrière, it's called. The whole of the Caribbean is sitting on a cauldron. Don't know which one suits best; Caribs or craters. Both swallow you up. Maybe Macbeth's witches would know. They cook with cauldrons, don't they? Very proud we felt scaling those conical, anything but comical, heights of nearly five thousand feet. A rugged sense of triumph stayed with us for days afterwards when we really walked tall. All had enjoyed it in a peaceful sort of way. However tired, no one erupted in volcanic fury.

On the way down you see them everywhere. Sitting on all the cattle. Gentle souls they are, these feathered friends, feeding off the fat of the land. And doing a good turn. Food for the *pique-bœufs*, and cattle comfort. Really piqued I can't translate *pique-bœuf*. Any offers? What about oxpecker? While you're working out the translation, and looking over the vast and most stunning banana plantations covering the whole volcanic area, careful over those skins. You may not be able to slip me the English I've asked for.

Back *chez* Élizabeth *et* Jacques. A drink, anyone? Punch, please. Love the stuff. Pineapple and our very own pirate Henry's rum. Hope no Spanish-speakers around. Invitation, not to a dance, but to a punch. Put *rum* into Spanish and bingo! *Ron.* Too much of that and it could knock you out.

Going for a walk? No complications. I'll put you straight. The allée Dumanoir, a mile long and elegant of design, right out of a country manor. A sumptuous double line of palm trees, a splendid tourist site, really provided a sustained avenue of interest. An impressive sight of trees. Just as impressive as the boys climbing them down on the beach. Look, Mom (we're near the States, remember?), no ropes. Nothing, just hands and feet. Right to the top. Go on, Ron, have a go. Certainly not. Shiver me timbers. You must be barking mad. Not going to start branching out, simian style, at my age. Lack of commitment and courage has always been my downfall. I wasn't going to compete with those lads. They'd always have the upper hand.

A happy time was spent on the beach. But no Élizabeth for safe conduct. Accidents could happen. Why are all the locals sitting out in the blazing sun? No tans needed for them. Perhaps one on us, though. The answer is stunningly obvious. All those coconuts waiting to fall on your, well...

Hire a car? Advice. Don't do it on the spot. You're left with what is left. And what is left didn't turn out all right. Hardly ever does. Electrical faults here, there and everywhere. Especially up in the Basse-Terre. The car certainly had its ups and downs. Bumps galore. Rumbled onto that. Locals again. Not rocket science, that was just up the way, Cape Cañaveral. But they put two and two together, and we were all square again. Smiles, thanks, a tip into the bargain, and away again, for fifty miles... The saving grace: no pidgin French here. The real McCoy. You needed a mack with those sudden downpours. Don't be coy, ask for one. No deluge? There will be one if you slip on one of those banana skins and end up under a hundred-metre-plus waterfall cascading down the volcano's sides. No shortfall in expectations here. Even less under the *Cataratas do Iguaçú* racing towards us. Rafts of projects before then, though.

How about flitting off to Dominica? A sweet-sounding name. Has to be with all those sugar plantations, and bananas, to come to that. I mean, even when you land you almost walk through the stuff. You'd expect that at the airport, *Canefield*, wouldn't you? A nice touch at the customs: fruit juice, and it has to be pineapple. And no hanging around, longing for it.

Standard of living in Dominica, compared to that of the French islands, Martinique and Guadeloupe? Difference between the latters' welfare state regime flying in from metropolitan France on which they are still dependent, and independent Dominica. France sells Martinique's and Guadeloupe's bananas on the European market, now closed to Dominica. Dominica's bananas have nowhere to go, only downwards. Economy on a very slippery slope. Hence, in some parts, grinding poverty, although they seem to have no axe to grind. Their axe is useful, though, if you look at their fabulously forested mountains. But how they ground out a living was never clear. They just sat aimlessly thinking and figuring, like Tom Joad and co. in Steinbeck's *The Grapes of Wrath*.

Butterfly style, you flit (too far to swim) from French to English, Guadeloupe to Dominica. Not so sure, though. Half the names are in French, and all the visitors speak, well, French, squeezed as the island is between Guadeloupe and Josephine's island. Why Dominica? Cristofero Colombo had a hand in it. He landed there on a Sunday, 1493 again. But Dominica's neither here nor there. *Dimanche* in French, *Domingo* in Spanish. No sense, this. Ah, but you're forgetting. The lad saw the light of day in Genoa, got it? They speak a sort of Italian there, so Domenica. Fiddle with that *e* and there you are. Mind you, he could have called it Domingo, having to navigate turbulent waters to get the cash for the voyage from Isabel and Ferdinand. Needed it for the caravels. Took a long time. Months in fact. The French, cunning lot, with their Caravelle, cut the time down to a few hours. Don't believe you. True. Their flagship of the 1960s, the Caravelle, wasn't a ship at all. It sprouted wings and flew, like Ron, that rum fellow.

Had hired a car well in advance. All in order. No broken reed was this car. You could have thought it, though, provenance being the capital *Roseau* = reed. But remember: drive on the left. That's about the only injunction. Injunctions at junctions? Proceed with caution. Especially on the first night, no road lighting, sheer drops on the left, Layou Hotel miles up the coast. Bridge. Room for one car only. In one direction. Locals apprised, visitors not. Latter had to back. Couldn't see to back. Driver in the car facing us jumps out, takes the wheel, and reverses with all the skill in Dominica. I'd got out and sat on the barrier. No language barrier here. So no need to sit on the fence. The driver was a ton of muscle, like all the Dominicans, muscular specimens they were, of prehistoric proportions. No steroids and no gym, either. Took some photos. Want a peek at these pics of their pecs?

This time, the car was a dream. Would have suited even Walter Mitty. Even more of a dream with a naturally French-speaking *Martiniquais* couple in tow. Worth their weight in gold. Up in the mountains, came across a village in fiesta mood. Streets crowded out with mask-faced, gruesome-looking, painted individuals. Collecting they were for some disguised purpose. Moment of uncertainty bordering on nightmare, a sort of Macbeth witches situation. Henri Cheviot handled the situation with aplomb. Easy enough for two reasons. 1. The French word *aplomb* came to him with ease. 2. Centuries back, an ancestor had had links with the Cheviots, a French word we suppose. The Cheviots knew how to deal with those barbaric Picts and Scots. So, on we passed.

Best to rely on the locals. Especially climbing to the Boiling Lake. Town Hall administration strongly advised against doing it solo. Any mishaps and you could be in very hot water. Finding a guide was in itself a mountain to climb. Agency after agency, again Town Hall. Finally, four hours of toil on unspoiled soil to see some of the bubbly borborygmus stuff. Borborygmus: a word as indigestible as the stuff that produces it. Not in Reims, champagne country, no siree. Four hours for the return, and stiffness for ten times four hours. Pat and getting into the car were two incompatible concepts. She almost needed a hoist. Ascent was one mountain of mud, through dense rain forest. More slippery than banana skins. Two skins up, one back. Reaching the Boiling Lake drives you to the brink.

Ever been attracted by frogs' legs? Well, here's your chance. All looks a bit misleading, however. It is. They're not really frogs' legs at all. *Cuisses de grenouilles,* frogs' thighs, they are. Sounds a touch sexy? And our Dominican friends dress them up as mountain chicken. What did it taste like? Mountain chicken, of course. Standard fare it was, skinny, unappetizing, sliding down as easily as we slid down from the Boiling Lake. Felt queasy. Almost leapt from my chair, like a, well, a frog. All very appropriate, really, surrounded by froggies croaking French. Almost lost my voice, as if I had a frog in my throat. Stuck to the fish dish after that. Perhaps chickening out.

Caravel westwards, Columbus style? Why not north? Cowboy and Injun country? Bin there many times, had read all about dem Injuns and Black Feet in Twain's Huck Finn and that fellow Sawyer. Mark my words. Seminal, or Seminole, texts they are, but they didn't give them Seminole Injuns much hope, not partial to fighting. Not a bellicose patch on those tomahawk Apache dudes further south and west. Plain this? No? Well it will be, when you realize that the Las Vegas tribe in Nevada come from, well, Las Vegas, 'The Plains' in Spanish. All very straightforward, not for the First Nation Inhabitants, though. They had the shoddiest of immigration laws.

All the American colonies, north, centre or south, provided the fruit from which the maximum of juice should be extracted. The natives seemed all the more stupid as the European was less intelligent. It was never anything but the organization of racist domination. Dressed up as a civilizing mission in its most noble apparel, colonization made pariahs of people in their own country.

Instead of westwards, why not try the Inuit, like Eric the Red centuries before? Did, up in Alaska, but when they talked we hadn't a clue what they were in to. Goes without saying I was polarized towards Mexico, and all those other Injun types south of the Río Grande. In any case, Butch Cassidy and the Sundance Kid were my heroes, Laramie jailbirds or not, so Mexico here we come, on their plundering trail, not forgetting all that silver in Argentina.

West we went. In nineteen hundred and ninety-two, PatRon flew over the ocean blue, but not bossing everyone around, in patron mode, in the wake of Columbus. We would have preferred 1991, or even 2002. Of course, Columbus hadn't figured out palindromes in those days. Neither had Cortés. He was still in the crusade business, picking up after the thirteen crusades that proselytizing papal Europe had unleashed in the other direction on the Arabs two hundred years before. Not keen on the game of Aztec fanaticism, although he wasn't deprived of this particular talent.

Cortés came to see and conquer. But did his crew concur? Didn't matter very much if the apocryphal story of boat-burning has any truth. Gone the chance of walking the plank. Hopes of home all but sank. Plank or no plank, Cortés saw them off.

Half a millennium later than Cortés, here we are in coastal Veracruz ('True Cross' in English). And a real cross the Mexicans had to bear. In 1847. The time General Winfield Scott handed it to them when he landed here and set off in conquering style for Mexico City. Winfield Scott's arrival in the port of Veracruz was almost as much a watershed in the history of Mexico as Cortés's landfall in 1519. That's where Mexican colonization started. Veracruz created in the interests of truth and the cross.

Poor Mexicans. Just like the Aztecs in 1519, they'd got wind of the enemy's fleet days before, but any opportunity to defend themselves slipped through their fingers. Could never have reversed the tide, real tsunami it was, poorly equipped and ill prepared were they. Nothing true from Veracruz rubbed off on the American military sweeping into the Mexican capital. Put the cadets of the military academy to the sword in the fortress of Chapultepec. Striking feature: youthfulness of the defending combatants. All under twenty-one. Cadet resistance proudly attested to by a memorial. Result? A sorry page of history rewritten and reread many times. They finally lost over half their territory to the marauding northerners, courtesy of the American–Mexican War. A Mexico freed from the Spanish imperial yoke bows once again, this time to the imperial designs from the other side of the Rio Grande. Texas, California, New Mexico, Nevada, Florida and

Arizona ended up as just a number of arid zones of memory in the minds of Mexicans. But they did cling to Veracruz. Needed it to proclaim the Mexican constitutions following the revolutions of 1857 and 1917.

Plane, not train for there are hardly any, into Mexico City. Airport? Benito Juárez's the name. He's everywhere. Has to be. Great liberal reformer, given to peace. Blessed is his name, if his first name is anything to go by. Touch of the pope about him. Same name: Benedicto. On this southern side of the Río Bravo, there he is, Ciudad Juárez. On the Yankee side with Davy Crocket's El Álamo in support, flows the Río Grande, Yankee style. Same river, two names. As confusing as the turbulent waters.

Our Mexican *amigos* don't get confused. There they are, at the Benito Juárez airport, Jorge and Adriana, Guillermo and María Teresa, Alejandro, two Chihuahuas, the whole shooting match, and not a shot fired. Usual warm, effusive *abrazos* (embraces). Whisked away through seething masses, twenty-five million of them, to a gated community. Things not too safe at night. Food? The fruit was as effusive as the reception. Mexican mango left us drooling. It only takes one to mango, and it's just as delicious as two to tango.

Very hot? Not really. Seven thousand feet up see to that. But they also see to slight bouts of vertigo. The more you go up the more blood pressure goes down. Not a chance then with the *puna* (mountain sickness) of Peru. Neither with Bogotá. More *amigos*. It weighs on me not to see them but downloading does the trick. A touch of a button and up we go.

Going up is one thing. Going down another. For two shaky reasons. You see, Mexico City is built on a vast, now dried-up lake. Aztecs settled on islands within the lake. Splendid protection with access via causeways. A sort of American Venice. Once Moctezuma II, the god king, was finally dispatched, Cortés and his discourteous crew, drained the lake. Mexico City has had that sinking feeling ever since. And no coming back up. If the Aztecs had spent more time getting to know you, rather than reinvigorating the gods with your bits and pieces, they would have taken a trip to Silicon Valley for some Hitec know how. The Mixtecs, Toltecs and Zapotecs could have been in on the act. But, weep, Moctezuma, your world is no more.

Collapsed from the western invasion and from underneath. For that's where earthquakes come in. Aztec's low buildings coped with uncertain foundations. They took a risk with the pyramids, however. Still, fun for latter-day diggers. They are still digging down to bring things up. Excavation of the Aztec's capital city, Tenochtitlán, is proving as difficult as it is pronouncing it. Not only are the archaeologists finding *one* temple, but temple built upon temple.

Why not do your god-appeasing elsewhere? No, *Señor.* We had a prophecy, you see. Some of us early settlers, come from the north, filled with god-fearing gusto, were looking for a sign. Happened in Jerusalem, Abraham, Jesus and Muhammad and all that. So the first temple, a template for all the others, went skywards on the very spot where an eagle was seen devouring a snake, perched on a cactus. If you can swallow that, you can swallow anything. Not a nice god was the top dog. A bit like Mars, he was, and anything but fetching. Take a bite of Huitzilopochtli, a sort of Jewish Javeh, and you'd soon be seeing some of the arterial red stuff. Keen they were on sacrifices, you know, the human variety. Back to Abraham again. He had a go at Isaac, didn't he? And, if you can pronounce the rain god's name, you deserve salvation. You ought to by now, he dropped in on us two chapters ago.

Cortés and company's construction plans were even more ill-founded. It just didn't sink in, did it? Take a walk around the Zócalo, one of the most enormous squares ever built. Could square up to Tiananmen Square and not be knocked down. Half a dozen Trafalgar Squares in there, too. Maybe Nelson's not on his way down. The Catedral Metropolitana is. Enormous blocks of stone at the base are slowly being nibbled away.

Cortés was a touch shaky on the Náhuatl lingo, too. Couldn't get his tongue round the ends of words. Needed his local wife and translator La Malinche for that. *Tl* for *Náhuatl* for starters, or maybe enders. I mean, how do you pronounce *chocolatl* and *tomatl*? Cortés slowly inched forward with *chocolate* and *tomate*. Huitzilopochtli wasn't helpful with his *tli*. As for Mictlantecuhtli, wouldn't have mixed with him at any price: the god of death. Tonacatecuhtli did the stork bit, sending down kids, but that was all. Quetzalcoatl, the plumed serpent, could not be trusted either. How could you rely on a combination of the still prized quetzal bird and a rattlesnake? D.H. Lawrence relied on it for a bob or two. And he didn't need flyers to advertise *The Plumed Serpent*.

Volcanic region the whole area. Popocatépetl, boiling like a kettle; Itzaccíhuatl, it's as unsafe as wattle, and the youngest, Paricutín, anything but cute, exploding as it did in a farmer's field in 1943. Zero to 500 metres in one quick burst. We all erupt in awe, breathless as the plane circles upwards from Mexico City.

If you can't pronounce Tenochtitlán, chances are you can do no better with Teotihuacán. Can you? Easier to say 'place where men become gods'. The most astounding of ancient cities, built before Christian times, it exudes divinity. At least, that's what the Aztecs thought. They came upon it in early fourteenth century, travelling from the north. Temple of Quetzalcoatl, Pyramid of the Moon, Pyramid of the Sun, left for them by some unfathomable, mysterious force, the plumed serpent, perhaps. D.H. Lawrence gave this theory some flesh and blood in his novel. Places of sacrifice. Only the warriors would do, only the best cuts, thank you very much. Blood of the conquered ran down the sides of the pyramids after hearts were gouged out from bodies stretched backwards over a sacrificial stone. Nothing sharper than some pointed obsidian. You can still buy chunks of it now. Can be mined in the area. Wonder if Abraham had refined it like this? 'Can we have a drop more of the red stuff please?' they cried from the bottom of the slope. Insatiable business, placating the thirsty gods. The high priest knew this only too well, especially at the top of the pyramid. Proper high tech was the Aztec. Does the Aztec really tick like this? Sure thing. He had to keep the sun alive. And Tláloc, the rain god, needed comfort, too. Without him, they were sunk. Would do a daily bow before him. A sort of rainbow. Better if they'd been up north in Canada on the Bow River. No need to bow up there to scrape a living. A constant, raging torrent. Bow in full flow.

We must feel indebted to the Aztecs. After all, inflamed by burning desire, they assumed the grim, savage burden of keeping the sun coming up every morning. Would He turn up the next day? We all need warmth as well as water, don't we? Does us more good than a fellow nailed up for three days.

But surely, all this is pure speculation. More high-spec than high-tech. No Copernicus over there. He was around (round the other side of the world), but too much of a jump. Not much of a jump here though. Just a little hop for Cop. He's in the next chapter.

History is not congealed. It runs on. Aztecs and co. were soon deleted from the chronicles.by the next set of zealots. Sacrifice again. One barbaric and unreasonable. The new one civilized and reasonable. But not that reasonable. Mexico, and the whole of Spanish America, the *Nueva España*, were exclusively ruled from Spain. Spain's privileges were the order of the day, to be safeguarded. All nice and cosy? For a while, until the whiff of independence blew across the *charco* (Pond) from the land of the guillotine. Not forgetting a clean break for Washington and Jefferson. They washed their hands of the British in 1776, celebrating with a tea party. Step forward, Father Miguel Hidalgo, to take your place among the new martyrs. We know you didn't last long, three years, in truth. But not before you uttered the rallying *cry* to independence: *¡El grito! de Dolores* in 1811. In the village of Dolores. Pain all the way, it was. More than one. *Dolores* = 'pains'. His Via Dolorosa was execution in 1811. The *grito* is remembered, year after year, and what do they do on September 15–16, *El Día de la Independencia*? Shout, of course, all day. And you're soon hoarse. Only Miguel Hidalgo? Are there more? Morelos, can't forget him. But not the same fate as his tutor priest, Miguel. Firing squad for José Morelos. For Miguel Hidalgo the guillotine. Ten years later, and there you are, Mexican independence, together with the rest of the continent.

Plenty of heroes still to come. *El Señor Presidente Juárez?* A Mexican Mandela, but he blotted his copybook allowing the execution of the French-imposed Emperor Maximilian. Days of maximum alert. Colonial intervention, this time French, all over again. Poor Maximilian. He was there to cause the minimum of trouble. Was a softy, really.

Which is more than you can say for Emiliano Zapata and Pancho Villa. Their dates overlap in more ways than one. Over each other, pretty closely, and over the nineteenth century and into the twentieth. Both stirred by revolutionary fervour, in the service of downtrodden peasantry. Zapata was destined for insurgency. I mean, look at his dates. Born 1879. May not have got his lines crossed, never passed to the other enemy side, but probably got his figures crossed, as well as his fingers. Saw 1789 instead of 1879? Revolutionaries rely on luck, you know. Figures crossed, he would have, wouldn't he? Dates got muddled in the middle. Easier to read seventeen eighty-nine than eighteen seventy-nine. Have I got that right? Ought to. I taught Voltaire and Rousseau. At least, Zapata kept his head in execution. 1919 that was. A nice, symmetrical number, not palindromic but there you are. His *compadre* (*amigo*) Pancho Villa kept his head, too, didn't live in his shade, so lived a shade longer. Four years. A quiet type? Not really, although with first name Pancho we could be excused to think he was. *Pancho* = quiet, unruffled. No execution this time. Assassination. Bullets were the name of the game. Cartridge belt slung across their shoulders.

Which brings me back up to date to the alcohol shop in Mexico City. Guard at the tequila place. Outside, he stood, short, stout, squat, moustache drooping like his sub-machine gun resting in the crook of his arm, hardly visible for the bands of bullets. An insurgency pose, I suppose. All he needed to complete the picture was an Emiliano Zapata *caballo*. And there I would be, in John Ford's next film. Monument Valley? No, in the cactus-covered Sonora Desert, still up north, though. Soon up there, not on man's best friend but by plane. In a hurry. All revolutionaries are in a hurry. Destination would be Chihuahua. But careful. Miguel Hidalgo and Pancho Villa saw their end there. And it wasn't due to rabies. Up to a point, could have been. Steer clear from Spanish *rabia, rabies* and *rage* all in one.

Revolution in cannons is one thing. Revolution in canons, artistic ones, is another. They knock out everything, including cannons. The pen, or the painting, is mightier than the sword. Just don't forget to knock out an *n* from *cannon*. Cannons are pretty good at that, too. Unsaddle the Establishment, that's the lesson Diego Rivera learnt from his forerunners on horses. He almost did a *Torres Gemelas* job. You mean that fifty-million-pound Chelsea footballer fellow? No silly, the Twin Towers. You see, Rivera was most famous for his enormous, riveting *murales* (murals). Demure they were not, explosive if anything. He painted on walls, too, didn't he? Don't you mean *morales*? That's 'mulberry' bushes, and I am not spending all my time going round them explaining it all to you.

Now, here's the bombshell. Diego was commissioned to paint a mural for the Rockefeller Center. Trouble here. Anti-gringo he was to the tips of his paintbrushes. Everyone agreed on the title. Fine so far: *Man at the Crossroads Looking with Hope and High Vision to the Choosing of a New and Better Future.* Phew! Takes as long to read it as he took to paint it. But wait for it. Lenin ended up right in the middle of the wall. Scandalous. Explosive. Brought the house down, rather like the Twin Towers. A tale of two cities, New York and the one in Mexico. But that's not all, for the sting was in the tail. It brought the mural down, too. New Yorkers destroyed it. Rivera almost knocked down the Rock. And that's where he went to cash his pesos. Rockefeller Bank. All a doleful tale, although they did dole out his dollars. No laughing matter, this. He must have cried all the way to the bank.

Of course, famous he was for his devotion, non-devotion, devotion, non-devotion, keep going on this for a while, to his companion painter Frida Kahlo. A Sartre–Simone de Beauvoir yes/no, yes/no set-up. About the same time, too. Off on one of his amorous jaunts? No fear. She in turn had it off with Lenin's buddy, Trotsky. Another sorry tale, with more than a sting in the tail this time, more in the head. A psycho Stalinist agent, Ramón Mercader, found a path to Trotsky's abode in Mexico City, and improved his parting with an ice pick. Another commission job. Stalin doled out the roubles this time. Clear it must have been that the psycho'd learnt his hairdressing skills from Dostoievsky's Raskolnikov. Scissors would not have done a clean enough job. Maybe he nurtured Chichikov's neurotic passion for skulls, inspired by Gogol's *Dead Souls*. Gogol simply bought up skulls and souls from farmers as a form of investment. Same vested interest with Ramón Mercader in this particular type of skulduggery, or should we say *skuldiggering*?

Never any cock-ups with all the fiestas. Public holidays in Mexico? No such thing. The whole year is a public holiday. Kicks off with *Año Nuevo* on New Year's Day. Easy translation that. *Día de la Constitución* in February. Getting easier. Along comes *Natalicio de Benito Juárez* in March. You can guess that – natal clinics, nativity and so on. Lots around Easter. Three cheers for religion. A cheer for each day off. May 1 = *Día del Trabajo* (Workers' Day). We go for it here. The European Union started that one. Let's jump a bit till September. The summer months are holidays anyway. September 16 = *Día de la Independencia.* You translate this yourself. No help needed. October 12. Now you're serious. *Descubrimiento de América.* You've *discovered* the meaning? 20 November = *Día de la Revolución.* Doesn't need a Trotsky to clue you up on that one. *Navidad;* lots of hols here.

But they all vanish before the most joyful of times with *El Día de los Muertos* (Day of the Dead). Most joyful? You're joking! No, I'm dead serious. Morbidity this is not. Come down, you dead souls, we need a bit of company for a couple of days.

Kiddies' souls first in the queue, October 31. Anxious for the sweeties, you know, the hand-outs. Adults' souls next, please. You dead souls, mooch around the cemeteries till we wake up. Give us time at the *Mercado* (market) for sugar candies, flowers and skeleton toys. Got to keep you safe and happy. Don't want you wandering off. Never sure whether we should wear those skull masks. They must frighten you dead souls stiff. Goodness knows, there are enough stiffs around as it is. We've livened up our altar at home for you, pictures n' all, candlesticks for a bit of light, and incense to keep that awful decomposition whiff away. Diego Rivera's in on the act, sure enough. Dedicated to skulls, he was. Not lugubrious at all. Take a look at his *Dream on a Sunday Afternoon in the Alameda Central.* The *Calavera Catrina* (Catrina Skull) won't disappear. It's dead in the middle.

It's fiesta time, down Mexico way, over the border, say the Yankees. A leaky border, sure enough. Has to be, river nearly all the way, 2,000 miles of it. Flows out into the Gulf of Mexico at Matamoros. Odd name for a town distant from the Moors, and why anyone would want to kill the lot is unclear to me (Matamoros = Kill Moors). There's not only a gulf here, but another separating a third from a first world country.

A day off? Jorge floats the suggestion for a punt on the only sizeable lake left in the whole area, Xochimilco, once connected to the main city of Tenochtitlán by one of those causeways. Semi-submerged *chinampas*, flower beds with a scattering of vegetable gardens, you see them as you glide by on a gondola, propelled by a *chilango*, inhabitant of the city. A most agreeable, weekend diversion. Could stay there for a couple of days, on a brightly coloured punt, roof-covered and table in the middle. The whole scene bedecked with flowers, splashes of colour, and lawns at the edge. Couple of days are too long, really not on, on the gondola I mean. They try it on with *Bienvenidos* (Welcome) written up everywhere. By now, you know you're welcome.

Take one of those crazily overfilled *peseros*, buses once costing a *peso*, but the price as uncertain as the *pesero*. Cheap all the same, but don't get on on a Sunday afternoon. You'll find one hundred thousand on your bus going to a soccer game at the Estadio Azteca, paving the way for a football rave-up. They'll all be standing up, swinging their arms up and down, to the *ola mexicana* (Mexican wave). So don't waver. A hundred and ten thousand for *el clásico* between the teams América and Guadalajara. Bit like Barça and Real Madrid, and they're not reciting *Hamlet*. Hold on tight, or you'll do yourself a Frida Kahlo. The most serious of bus accidents left her extremely incapacitated. Painted thereafter horizontally for much of the time but her pictorial achievements gave her lift-off. Also grounded by polio.

Just as well you're not the driver. Look high skywards to see advertisement hoardings that are not called *espectaculares* for no reason. Never in the experience of man has so much sky space been devoted to encouraging you to lighten your pockets of *pesos*. *Pesos* are designed to weigh them down, if *peso* has any meaning at all: weight. Eroticism stretched across the firmament. Amazing the driver hasn't lost his licence, beguiled by so much overt carnality hanging from the sky.

Our driver hasn't lost his licence. He delivers hordes of us, enough for a football stadium, to the open space outside the Museo de Antropología Nacional. Ana María: 'Want to see the *voladores* [fliers]? It's the highlight of the square.' 'OK, let's give it a whirl.' *Whirl*'s the word, you'll see. We see those fliers climbing up to the top of a hundred-foot pole, standing out against the brightest of blues, almost in orbit. Dressed in white like Morris dancers, ready for the maypole. On a platform less than the size of a dinner plate, one man plays a drum and a reed flute while the remaining four whiz round and down, spreading outwards like a quetzal. You really have to know the ropes to use them as you swing dizzily round and round, twister style, upside down. Down they come, from the top, collection pot at the bottom. They string you along, keep you watching and looking up to their skills. Before you can say Moctezuma, more flyers have landed, collection pot again at the ready. There they are again, in pole position, in high profile against the sky, ready this time to circle down in the advancing twilight. A real star turn. Sure is, late at night. Must have landed all the circus prizes. With the generosity of the numerous admirers, always enthusiastic with their lavish applause, it's a roaring success. The *voladores* cannot but fall on their feet in the most acrobatic of feats. And they don't fall for a straw poll to be the last one up again. When the flying is in full swing, spectators gaze down, then up, in their hundreds. You see, then you saw. Rather like a seesaw.

Level of interest soars as we contemplate this crazy act of bungee jumping. Much more than a circus act, the feat seems to relate to some logical cosmic force. As they circle the pole thirteen times (not a fatal number for them), they twist their body four times, hence fifty-two revolutions from top to the ground. Fifty-two corresponding to the weeks of the year – i.e. the time it takes for the Earth to revolve round the sun. Add to this calculation the invoking of the four corners of the universe before the *voladores* jump into space, attracting to the ground the warmth of the sun and the fertility-bearing rain. A breath-taking ambition with the mind in orbit. Risks were always there for the flyers, so the stakes were pretty high. Easy to understand when you see how high the stakes were.

Funny this. Came across no flyers advertising it. Not necessary. You could see them from afar. Not enough? Above Mexico City's cathedral rises the statue of a pipe-playing *volador* with inscriptions giving the lowdown of the ritual.

Fiesta time without mariachis is no fiesta, especially when marriages and birthdays are to be celebrated, if mariachi is anything to go by. You see, *mariage* in French. Eight round a table, the best of Mexican fare, and that includes those wandering minstrels. Decibels of siren intensity overwhelm the ears as they approach. Numbed you become to the point that audition protection overtakes food consumption. You keep your mouth more and more firmly shut the more they open theirs. Volume of voice rivals the vision of advertising, overwhelming the senses. Swept along we were by those powerful, deep-throated voices. Then, a vote of thanks, please, Ron, not with *ron*, but with *tequila*. And don't blow it! Get in a bit of the Mexican stuff, none of that colonial Iberian accent, *s* instead of *th*s, you know. Gra*s*ias, not Gra*th*ias. And, *compadre*, we serenade, until we're paid.

Too boisterous? Want some peace and quiet? A two-hour drive south to Cuernavaca for a short vacation. Up early for a generous, elegant breakfast at one of those *haciendas*, country estates. *Servicio impecable.* All right on the Spanish, are we? Grace, polish, sumptuousness personified. Straight from the prosperous nineteenth century. Good job the 1910 *Revolución* didn't destroy them all in the interests of equality and social justice. Loss of poetry for the gain of prose? Fortunately, some of the poetry has found its genteel expression once again. Porfirio Díaz, elected and re-elected on many occasions, while yet responsible for the *Revolución*, succeeded in restoring and remodelling *haciendas*, after the style of English stately homes or even European castles, *châteaux de la Loire*. Breakfast was spot on. Spotless, if you like, *impecable* again. Could have had breakfast in the *baño* (bathroom).

Lunch with academia in Cuernavaca. Soothing climate at nearly five thousand feet. Summer residence, even for foreigners, enjoying the welcome breeze from the surrounding sierras. Cortés got this right. He built his palace there. What's it called? Palacio de Cortés. Obvious, isn't it? Diego's massive earthy murals again, illustrating Mexico's history of torment, concluding with the *Revolución* and starting with the Conquest. Understood all the Spanish so far? If not, go no further. Countless doors are open for language courses, so latch on to one for next year. Too far? Salamanca in Spain's OK for you, then. Hurry up, though. Americans are making the reverse journey, in droves.

It's about time we flew up to Chihuahua, and have a front-seat dekko at that volcano Popocatépetl, snow-capped all times of the year. Fabulous sight from the air. Pilot takes us round a couple of times. Hope he's keeping his eye on the fuel tank for Chihuahua. You know, that dog place.

You need to jump through a few hoops now, quite a lot, in fact. Surprised? Mexicans would be surprised with their *¡Ah Chihuahua!* And they'll be more surprised with what's coming up. Food for thought for all those football-hungry Mexicans. Thousands more *¡Ah Chihuahua*s! You think I'm barking mad? Not so. Follow me, doggy. Scratch below the surface and what do you find? Allow me to trot out a 100 per cent credit-worthy theory that will keep even the sharpest of etymologists at bay, assuming they are always ready to pounce on any weakness.

First, if you're French, you'll queue up for surprises. They have the same word for *queue* and *tail*. Awfully confusing, which is why Parisians are hopeless at queuing. Hold on. We're a long way from Chihuahua, aren't we? No, not really. Can't you hear them barking? *Woof! Woof!* They don't say *Woof! Woof!* over in Mexico, or in any Spanish-speaking kennel, for that matter. You've guessed it. They say: *¡Gua! ¡Gua!* The *g* is swallowed, so we end up with *¡Wa! ¡Wa!*, wagging tail and all. Which brings us all the way to Chi*huahua*.

But did the Chihuahua dog give the name to the town of Chihuahua or Chihuahua give the Chihuahua? Chicken and egg. Ongoing research. Any theories? What is certain is that Cervantes' dogs lying around in Chapter 3 would be proud of me. They're smart, you know. Can sniff anything out.

This is not a wag's tale, not even a shaggy dog story. But it is the story of a wagging tail. This woof-woof business started in the Canary Islands, almost a hundred years before Columbus rode the ocean waves. When the Spaniards colonized these islands, in 1402, they came across two features: inhabitants – why not? – and peculiar-looking dogs. The islanders they called 'guanches'. Why? Is it because they tripped over numerous canine creatures that were *guaguaing* = woof-woofing? Is this why they called the inhabitants 'guanches'? All this is very unclear, even for present-day Spanish-speakers. But surely they came across more canaries than woof-woofs? That's where you're wrong. Those small doggies are *cane/canis* in Latin. Hence *Canary*

Islands. Trouble is they're no longer lying around. Dead as a dodu.

But the buses on the island are not dead, anything but. They're still moving. You see, their name conveys the idea of well, *guagua*s = woof-woofs, and they run faster than *guaguas*. You're not going to swallow this either, but jump onto any dictionary and what do you know? Still in the barking business. *Canarios*, the inhabitants, don't use wings. They ride around in *guaguas* = buses. All together, now. They even join Cubans and Porto Ricans, all barking in unison in *guaguas*.

Chihuahua breeds more than Chihuahuas. It still breeds discontent, revolutionary fervour. Wherever you go, you're haunted by the spectre of Pancho Villa. Old house now converted into a museum, an imposing statue dedicated to him. A folk hero, he had his headquarters at Chihuahua, more comfortable with a horse than with a Chihuahua. A complicated character who succeeded in combining murderous behaviour with help for widows and orphans in his northern territory. The talk of the town.

Not much more, though, than the baggy, denim-overalled Mennonites.

Persecuted from pillar to post in Europe, they were given land by tolerant, post-revolutionary Mexico. Women in Gothic dress, and you are on course to speak German. Just the spot to practise it during Hitler's monster years. Nowhere else, – was there? –unless you could have nailed Namibians in Southern Africa. Mexican Mennonites, where do they live then? Look for the villages around Cuauhtémoc, just south-west of that woof-woofing city. Handy really, if you're on the way to Creel. And that's on a train straight out of Victorian Britain. Odd, time-warp travel. Interest really getting up a head of steam.

Creel. Genuine Wild West country. Not the sanitized stuff of present-day Tombstone City, Laramie and Sundance. Mind you, I have a soft spot for Deadwood with Calamity Jane and Wild Bill Hickok. They cosy up to each other in a tiny cemetery. But Creel? You have the feel of outlaw country. Go into the only grocer's in town, but leave your six-shooter at the door. Owner's name? Dalton. 'You're not one of the Dalton gang, you know, the OK Corral shoot-out?' 'No, that was the Clanton's. 1881 in Tombstone City, Arizona, up north. Amazing they didn't shoot their very own selves, everything back to front, with that funny palindromic date, 1881. Marshall Wyatt Earp heroics it was.' 'What about you and the Dalton gang?' 'I'm part of them. One of my ancestors was an in-law to an outlaw.' How an English-speaking Mexican came to be selling tequila in a one-horse town was beyond me. Maybe came down with Butch and the Kid. Border country, you know.

Tarahumara country, too. Hid themselves in the Sierra Madre Occidental to avoid perversion, oops! conversion, by missionaries. By the way, don't fall foul of the way Mexicans slander objectionable creatures with the son-of-a-bitch *madre* (mother). Odd the way your nearest and dearest can shoot down the most despicable of dudes. Why not go straight for the jugular with the *sierra*? After all, it is a saw.

And watch out, too, Tom Courtney, in *The Loneliness of the Long-distance Runner*. These Tarahumaras can run for days on end. Attract all the attention, do all the running. Clearly too speedy for the Olympic marathon. Kenyans and Ethiopians beware. Up and down the Barranca del Cobre (Copper Canyon) they race, sandle-shod. Us? In a 4x4, four hours down and four hours up, on the roughest of rugged tracks. Narrowest of stony paths, scary views to the left on the way down, and to the right on the way up. But no hurry to return up. A filmed banana shoot-out at the bottom. Unfinished business at the OK Copper Canyon. A showdown deep down in the canyon. Keen to try your hand at a duel? Don't worry, even if you are a spot yellow with all those bananas. All for cine camera's sake. Heliodoro (dazzling Greek novelist, has to be dazzling with a name like that = Golden Sun) Jorge slips out his Colt 45 *à la* Jesse James, Ron *à la* Emiliano Zapata. Roles inverted. Under a blazing sun, thousands of feet deep. Banana bullets bend like the banana. Both survive. Same as in the Californian duel. Dick Johnson versus the bandits at the end of the Golden Age of Opera. Which one? Puccini's *La fanciulla del West* (The Girl from the Golden West). Surviving hero and heroine Minnie go off into a sunset as golden as that yellow metal mined in the 1850s fever. No gold for Jorge and co., just bananas. But still golden.

Back up in the Sonora Desert and polar temperatures. Mean temperatures in March were, well, mean, and so was the hotel with heating. Sharpest of Sahara Spring contrasts again. Usually, it's sun, sand and sea. Here, it's sun below and snow above. No blanket of cloud to keep you warm. And hardly any blankets at the hotel. Freezing in the bedroom but no freezing of prices. Explosions of protestations at *Recepción*. In the mood we were for another shoot-out, and no slip-ups this time. *Madre* would come in handy here: *¡Chinga a tu madre!* (Fuck off!).

Barranca del Cobre. Funny really. There's not just one canyon. There's an abundance. They can be viewed from the *divisadero*. That's where all the softies stand. A sort of *belvédère*. Sorry, that's French. Let's try *mirador* then. None the wiser? Spot with panoramic view all right? See things more clearly now? Spaniards will. They would view from a *mirador*, but a Mexican from, well, a *divisadero*. But they'd all seem the same canyons. As difficult to take them all in as it is to digest their pronunciations: Areponapuchi, Basaseachi, Carocauhí, Maguarichi, Memelichi, Tomochi. Easier to pronounce the ends of the words, the *chi*s. The Mennonites would be pleased with this, cheese being their best-known product. Taste it at their cheese factory. Ask for *queso menonito*. Not on Sunday though. All the blue-eyed, blond believers shut up shop, and head for the temple. Can't miss them with that blue and blond. Tall, too. At least they don't go round perverting, there I go again, people.

Like warmer nights? Chiapas's the place for you. Where's that? Right the other end, to the south, a thousand and a half miles away. Can't plane all the way in one go. That'd leave me just plain flat. Stopover in Mexico City. What's wrong with that? *Toda la bola* is there. Sorry, I should be speaking nice round English.

The whole gang. But they don't play bowls. We're not in France, you know. Or Spain, to come to that.

Waterless in Chihuahua? Waterfalls of the stuff here in Chiapas. Vegetation so thick you'd need a *sierra* to get through it. It wasn't far away either. Sierra Madre del Sur just to the south. Still, don't let it dampen your spirits. Credit card at airport. Better at figures than in the Sahara, they are. So happy to pay up like that I joked all the way. Became quite a card. But keep the son-of-a-bitch *madre* jokes to yourself, although we weren't in polite society. Off we went from the airport at Tuxtla Gutiérrez. Only one regret. Can't get my tongue round *xtl.* The Aztec pronunciation syndrome all over again, but coming into Mayan territory. Had a conspiracy theory. Aztecs and Mayans hated foreigners just that bit more than they hated each other. Make us suffer bunching up all those consonants. Must have studied Polish at some time. There it is in the next chapter, so be forewarned.

Jorge at the wheel, spiriting us away, snaking through the one road deep in the Chiapas jungle. No faster than a snake, mind you. And the car rattled along. All those *topes*. What on earth is that? For starters, they're on the earth, mountains of them, and you soon came across them. We call them speed retarders, you know, they're instead of Mexican policemen. They'd be asleep anyway, like our sleeping policemen. The calculation, Jorge mathematician style, figured a couple of hundred to San Cristóbal de las Casas, eastwards. And between San Cristóbal and Palenque, even more. But I'm racing ahead of myself. Hardly, with all those *topes*. Should have smelt a rat, perhaps a snake, in Mexico City, hundreds there too.

The Chiapas administration must have been in cahoots with the locals. Something top priority here. Why so? *Topes* meant five kilometres per hour which meant all those friendly, smiling farmers' faces, with children to boot but no boots, not even shoes, appeared through your window. *Topes* = sale of goods, and not just mangos. Mathematics again. Flowers, leather goods, pottery, a colourful range of *artesanías* = crafted goods. *¡Flores para la señora, señor?*

Muy barato (Flowers for ... Very cheap). Bet you can translate *señora* and *señor* now. You've been here long enough. But make sure you get the *a* on the right word. Artful like that in Italian, too.

See all those birds? Not many eagles, hawks and buzzards. They're up north. Macaws (squeak rather than caw), toucans (can often be seen in twos but one of its huge, multi-coloured bills is enough for two), parrots (never got sick of seeing them), parakeets (small parrots, never got sick of seeing them either) circle over the road, if 'road' is the word. Prefer them to those predatory types just above, on line one of this paragraph. Wouldn't want them to come down, would you? Even see the occasional colourful quetzal, not forgetting the flamingos. More of those in Yucatán. Could see them at Chichén (not Chicken) Itzá, if we don't stay on and get too paly with the guide in Palenque.

Nearly at San Cristóbal. But let's shoot up north for a couple of hours. The Cañón del Sumidero (English *canyon* not *cannon*, why a *y* in one and two *n*s in the other takes some explaining. The same word in Spanish, make things easy, don't they?) is worth a shot. It's a fabulous circling fissure, half a mile deep, and nine miles long. Launch out in a power boat and stay without breath for an hour or so, if you can last that long. Panorama from above cannot equal the view from the water. *¡Estupendo!*, *¡Maravilloso!*, *¡Fantástico!* bounce off the sheer walls of the canyon. All right for these superlatives? How about *¡Asombroso!* and *¡Apabullante!*? Same really, just showing off. Could find a list as long as the canyon.

The hotel in San Cristóbal de las Casas. Full name again this time. Was getting lazy with the vacation rhythm of things. Nineteenth century it was, with a gallery running round the dining area below. Service delightful as in Old *México*. First stop next day, the *mercadillo*, you know the market, but one they pack up overnight. Bought a leather case there. Just a few *pesos*. Would have bought half a dozen, but plane and all that. Only had three. But where? I'll be brief in case you're in a hurry. From a small-time vendor at the end. Real, raw hide. That's what he said.

Straight from the horse's mouth, and, I suppose, from its side. Took out my *cartera* to buy the *cartera*. Don't get it. Why buy another? There's the Spanish catch. Two catches, in fact. 1. *Cartera* = wallet. 2. *Cartera* = briefcase. Clever that. Mind you, we cut down on words, too. Useful 'cos I was feeling lazy. But, if you want one, don't stall at the stall.

Meal that evening along the street. No distance. Just as well. Excellent three course all washed down with a violent thunderstorm. The street turned into a river. How do you deal with a deluge? You wait and don't wonder why the pavements are over a foot high. Curbs your ambition to venture anywhere. Hardly safe there, though. Couldn't have paid the fare for a taxi, even if we wanted one. Still, the restaurant fare was more than good enough.

Walked round the town with Jorge the following day. Casts a dozy, colonial spell over you. Founded in 1528 by the 'discoverers' and proselytizing missionaries, isolated for centuries, high at seven thousand feet, it enjoys a peaceful and refreshingly cool air. With a name attached to *San*, it has to display numerous religious buildings: cathedral with elaborate interior, the Templo de Santo Domingo, the Iglesia de San Cristóbal and the Iglesia de Guadalupe. The Virgin's everywhere: Spain, the Caribbean...

The Zapatistas, of largely Indian extraction, just won't stay in their place, will they? We offer them heavenly salvation, a few social security hand-outs, and all they do is complain. San Cristóbal is a hotbed of malcontents. They even remonstrate with the central government in the capital.

Palenque, a medieval Mexican miracle, is next on the list, Jorge still in the driving seat, even when I'm driving. Countless *topes* with wares-waving vendors barred the way. Same wildlife, same speed. Almost stop at all the *topes*. That's what they're there for. Must stop, too, at the Cascadas de Agua Azul. Understand? All right with the first word? Even dummies fall in line here. The meaning just flows out. *Agua is* easy enough. It's that colourless liquid stuff in your tap. You swallow it like the pronunciation of *gua*. Remember *Chihuahua?* And what about *Azul?* Knock off the *l* and stick on an *r* and you have a strip of the French Riviera. You know, the Côte d'Azur. Got it? One more go, then. Try lapis lazuli. I'm a bit colour blind but they say it's a deep-blue colour. And that's just it. Stunning, most beautiful. You can use all those other superlative adjectives five paragraphs up. It would have revolutionized intense colour-mad Van Gogh. A painting Rubicon he would have crossed here. Could even have the warmest of swims. Could have done his ear some good too.

Palenque in a couple of hours' time. Pyramids steaming out of the jungle. Get engulfed again. Not all the rain fell on the waterfall. Out with the machetes, lads. Or it'll disappear again, and again. Didn't know it was there till the eighteenth century. A Mayan civilization reaching its peak, and the pyramid peaks, when King Arthur and his knights were supposed to be holding court at Tintagel, Cornwall. All they have left is a table at Winchester. What the Mayans bequeathed the human race was a phenomenal, extra-dimensional sense of identity, an architectural perfection of form defying the invasive sylvan elements. King Pakal created an illustrious, majestic Templo de las Inscripciones, completed by his son Chan Balhum II, among numerous other consummate gems like the Templo del Sol and the Templo del Jaguar. Just as well Cortés and Co., with his missionary acolytes, didn't know of its existence, or the axe would have fallen, and all doors to a glorious culture would doubtless be forever closed. A sense of past glories pervaded the central areas as we climbed about with our guide, of Mayan descent. Language took us into another, distant, unsuspected realm. These buildings are a milestone in man's creative genius.

Choose between Chichén Itzá in the state of Campeche in the Yucatán peninsula or Bonampak on the Guatemala border. North or south. Danger of wandering into Guatemalan territory was real, as real as wandering into Morocco from Algeria. Jungle or sand boundaries come to the same thing. Bonampak required an army escort. I stuck to my guns. I had always craved after Chichén Itzá, if only to see how the locals pronounced that *tz* business.

So north-east we went. Still more *topes*, and thousands for the return to Oaxaca. Meanwhile, sit in the modest Palenque hotel and follow the monkeys' antics. Teeming like ants and like five-year-olds chattering. We get into the swing of things just watching them. So Chichen Itzá, it is.

A city built on ceremony and sacrifice. Abraham and Isaac all over again. High, elaborate platforms set on temples, de los *Guerreros* (Warriors), del *Jaguar*, del *Águila* (Eagle), dominated by the *Castillo* (Castle), all an archaeological wonder. Mathematically perfect in design. But got stuck, they did. Star-struck. No spin-off in the geo-helio polemic. Too polarized for that. Should have had a chit-chat with Copernicus. He was around at the same time. Not copper-coloured, though. But he could have coped with all those *ch*s. Have you given Polish a whirl? Czech's enough for me.

Have a climb up that pyramid? Watch that two-serpents' head thing. Not just a gaping mouth. He'll haunt you at the equinoxes. Moves up and down the staircase, at least its shadow does. Mouth'll gobble you up, it's big enough. Likes a bit of sacrifice now and then. Always in a quest for the odd victim. The Mayan Quetzalcoatl, that's what he is.

Out with your calculator. All the way west to Oaxaca. But make sure you know where you're going. Please not to upset the locals, so don't pronounce that *x* like an *x*. One of those *x* factor things. Sounds like the *jota*. It is the *jota*, silly, not just sounds like it. I'm not so bothered about the *x*. I am about the *topes*, though. How many from A to B? Let's see. Roughly a thousand miles. Rough is the word. One *tope* per two miles. Five hundred *topes*. The height of madness, if *tope* means anything to you. Good for trade, even so.

Oaxaca airport. Plane over Monte Albán. We see the lot with the pilot. Seeing all those ruins was plain flying. Circled three times, we did. There on a mountain top, no *topes* here, and flattened out by a spectacular engineering feat below, rose up the most astounding of Zapotec cities. (Not Zatopek, the Czech runner. As bad as Astérix and asterisk.) Began with the Olmecs, 500 BC. Sacrificial-style pyramids, high, elaborate platforms for ease of ceremony and more cardio-thoracic surgery, a gigantic *Gran Plaza*, and a most conspicuous, hundred-yard-long ball court, a real pre-Columbian gem. *El juego de la pelota* (the Game of Pelota). Not the Basque sort. The competitors come out of it alive in Spain's San Sebastián. The oddest of games for the oddest of oddballs. Two teams. A large rubber ball. Put it through a stone ring high up on a wall. Goal? Maybe try and lose. A fate worse than death to win. Honourable thing to lose. So what? Public school spirit. Nothing wrong with that, is there? Well, there is. Everything right with it. The losers shoot straight up to an Olmec or Aztec Valhalla. Keep your eye *off* the ball, up you go to Paradise Hall. Goal for the winners? Not gaol, but better luck next time. Make sure you lose. Don't keep your eye on the ball. Can't imagine they had a ball.

Rang a bell, although not very appealing. All over *Mesoamérica*. Could pop back to Chichen Itzá. Another ball court there of fabulous size. The two biggest in their world.

Now back up to the 'beautiful game' of football, at the Estadio Azteca in Mexico City, to kick-start a trip to the land of silver: Argentina. Land of Silver, the French called it. Little wonder Conrad's adventurers in *Nostromo* salivated over its steely brilliance.

We did cry for you, Oh Argentina, wreathed in silver. We loved you so much. As soon as we stepped off the plane. That's after we'd flown over the Canary *guaguas*, Madrid > *B*uenos *A*ires. All silvery smiles, Mariano, topped by a four-year-old boy, Santi(ago), sitting astride his shoulders. *Auto* right through the middle of BA. Not used to *auto*, was I. Iberian *coche* was my way of conveying the thing. All excited, although we were both old enough to have BAs. Do you want to see the widest avenue anywhere? Yes, please. Up we whiz, jousting our way through, almost that fateful number again, thirteen, but this time we stop short, eleven lanes of traffic. Twenty-two, counting both sides. Needs an expeditionary force to help you from one side to the other.

Opposite ends of the Spanish-speaking world in Latin America, some 2,000 miles further than London to Beijing

I've heard you many times before, Mariano. Accent different from the one up north, you know, Mexico. Well, it's all that Italian input. Half the names are Italian, for starters. Take that

306

hand-of-God footballer, Maradona. Handling the ball into the English net was as close as he got to the Vatican. Mind you, if you squeeze his name a bit = Madonna (Our Lady), he's almost there. Maradona cottoned on to that. Clever girl, Madonna, she hedged her bets for sanctity straight from the start. Wouldn't have got much backing from those southerners, though. Not too keen on her Evita. Proud lot, the Argentinians.

Still, the proof of the pudding's in the eating. Let's go to Tortoni's, a delightfully gracious, old-style Italian *caffè*, fronted by an equally gracious *portero* whose supreme joy in life seems to be to open doors. Maybe the more doors he opens, the more commission comes to his door. Inside, walls graced with pictures of old Buenos Aires, portraits of the great and famous, Borges, with all the other glittering literati. Leather chairs and art nouveau cherished by poets and intellectuals. You walk straight into another era. A *salón de té* unrivalled no doubt in all the Americas.

Just like the Ateneo where the same glittering literati draw their inspiration. As richly adorned in the interior as it is unprepossessing on the exterior. An apparently banal bookshop in la calle Florida (Floral Street). Just like all the others. Step inside, Señor Borges. Unfortunately, your poor sight no longer allows you to enjoy the sumptuous, gilded fittings, the three-tiered galleries, the exquisite lighting, the ornate stage. Stage, you say? Oh yes. Once, it performed the role of a fabulous movie theatre cum opera house. You almost feel you need a hundred-dollar ticket for entry. All you want is a book. Can't come out without one. Really taken in, outside and in? On reflection, no. The flowery name of the Calle Florida puts you in the picture or on the stage from the outset.

Culture you want? Culture you'll have. Grandest of venues for opera in the Teatro Colón. Grandest of avenues, too, the Avenida 9 de Julio. Opulence exquisite and perfect acoustics. Has to be. Workshops, costumes department, and rehearsal spaces lie underneath some of the twenty-two lanes of traffic. On last count, 22,000 pairs of shoes! (1,000 pairs a lane). Must keep the cobblers busy. Three orchestras, the city's ballet, and three opera companies.

If Maradona hasn't yet booked his place upstairs, or even two at the time of writing (obesity *oblige*), there could be room for you, so hurry up to the *Paraíso* (the Gods). Only temporary audition with the angel authorities but what do you want for a few pesos?

And if you're thinking of driving to the Avenida 9 de Julio for a spot of shopping, you must be parking mad.

You really feel in the pink after a quick homage to the Casa Rosada. What's *rosada* about it? Just look at it. Pink it was and pink it still is, all over. Heard Casa Rosada and *Buenos ERES* every day twenty-odd years ago. *Malvinas* they said. *Falklands* we said. The French, they said *Malouines*. First ones there were the *Malouins*, all the way from St-Malo. *Îles Malouines*. The conquering French triggered off claim after claim, naval invasion after naval invasion. The Brits waived everyone's rights. I'm all right, Jacques, and *Air* your feelings as much as you like, you, just over there, but nothing *Good*'ll come of it. Or should we say *Buenos*? You've got all the silver you want, haven't you. I mean, *plata* is cash, shoals of it in the Río de la Plata, and Argentina, well, the French saw cash in *argent* straight away.

'Pink' sounds nice and clean, doesn't it? But there's something dirty about it. The Casa Rosada stands in the Plaza de Mayo square. Take a walk down the Avenida de Mayo, on the way to the Avenida 9 de Julio. Nothing grubby about this either? Wander back and wait around in the *plaza* and you'll soon see. It's all about the *la guerra sucia* (dirty war). Since 1970, the *Madres de los Desaparecidos* (Mothers of the Disappeared) have demonstrated over the loss of their loved ones. No real answers or retribution up till now. General Galtieri and Co. have lived in the pink. Same for the hundreds of Nazi war criminals. President Juan Perón saw to that. Pink was stained with black with the harbouring of Eichmann, Mengele, Priebke and Barbie. Paradise for them? Probably not, except in the Teatro Colón, and they would have plenty of room up there. Maradona not (a)round yet.

Plenty of saints around to help them out. What about San Martín in his *plaza*? They could have done a bit of praying ten blocks north of the Plaza de Mayo. Or, even along the port in the San Telmo district? They could have enjoyed a delightful stroll among artists' studios, antiques shops, cafés and small museums. Nice reward for some anti-Semitic antics in Auschwitz. San Nicolas district close by for a welcoming wander, too, And all those *San* churches, San Ignacio de Loyola, San Francisco, San Telmo. Go in any of the *Sans*, and you come out with a clean bill of health. Our public schools will vouch for that. They all say san for sanatorium, don't they? Try Eton to begin with. Eichmann and fellow monsters wouldn't have wanted to wait for palindromic President Menem at the turn of the century. Like Laval in chapter four, unreliable he was, not knowing whether to turn to the left or the right.

Fancy a dance down Caminito Street, in La Boca district? Name's a bit of a pleonasm, really. *Camino* = street, way. All that erotic tango swaying down there. Do some dodging yourself, too, just to keep out of harm's way. Risky spot. Still, worth a visit with an army of bodyguards. See the local football giants, *Boca Juniors*, the South American Barcelona. They'll give you some tips on selling dummies. You can even see the dummies, the handmade dolls on a house in La Boca. Admire the riotous colour of the sheet-metal structures further on. Even more riotous when Boca Juniors lose.

Takes two to tango, one to mango. Heard that in Mexico, didn't we? Fits most succulently into La Boca = Mouth. Too clever, by half, or by two? La Boca for tangoing and La Boca for mangoing. Go for them, both, if you wish. After the tango, a mango. You could be a bit sweaty with the first and cool down with the second. All very juicy.

Juicy too is the *asado*, a sort of roast. How's your digestion? The whole family bunch on a Sunday, *casa de la familia de Mariano*. Large chunks of *bistecs*, bee*fst*eaks, but they can't get their mouths round the *fst*. Cooked over an open grill, with wood as fuel. Conversation whizzes on for hours. What's it like in the *Reino Unido* (UK)? When are you coming back? You come over to our place, for a change etc. Grilled you feel at the end, and at the funny verb endings. Examples, Madrid style: you eat = *tú comes*. Argentina style: *vos comés*. Madrid style: *tú tomas*. Argentina style: *vos tomás*. Try to follow the stress on the *e*, or the *a*, and you have, well, stress. Jumping backwards and forwards from *tú* to *vos* and you're soon hopping mad. Bet the Italians are in there somewhere, but can't make it why or how.

Stress or no stress. Loved it. Plane to Bariloche. Plains for a lot of it, towards Bariloche. A several-hundred-mile arc around Buenos Aires. Can't be plainer than that, can I? All this is very straightforward. The locals with their Quechua language smoothed it all out for us. *Pampas* = plains. A vast savannah. Look at all these seven *a*s. It's got to be even and flat, hasn't it? Oops, more *a*s. But the most comforting run of *a*s has to be La Pachamama, a motherly flow of four *a*s. Motherly? La Pachamama is a sort of Andean earth goddess, keeps everyone happy, abundant source of life and food. Regular rituals sustained throughout the Andean and Inca calendar but, thank Pachamama, no sacrificial lambs. Plenty of meat, though.

Pampas, the breadbasket, or meat basket, of Argentina. Thousands of cattle down below, as we fly by, tended by those *bolas*-swinging cowboys. Gauchos, really, for it would be gauche to call them cowboys, wouldn't it? They sent the meat in for Mariano's *asado*. Too far down for a thanking 'Gracias'. And grass but no airstrip. They'd not understand the *gracias/grass* trick. *C* here sounds like *s*. I suppose *gracias* ends up as *grassy ass*, and plenty of *ass* for Mariano's *asado*.

Ernesto 'Che' Guevara would have loved it there: 'Perhaps, one day, tired of circling the world, I'll return to Argentina and settle in the Andean lakes' (*The Motor Cycle Diaries*). Butch Cassidy and the Wyoming Kid, all the way from Sundance, did settle there, in Cholila, photos to prove it. Stayed for a while, but the US Pinkerton detectives tracked them down. Always knew there was something peculiar about pink, especially after the way that sailor fellow Pinkerton treated Puccini's Butterfly.

Bariloche. No more than an airstrip to get there. If you don't feel like climbing to the top of Aconcagua at 22,000 feet, the highest in the Americas, just look into the lake's *agua*, its water. You're right there, walking on air, at least on the top of the world. Reflected upside down in the lake: Lago Nahuel Huapi. Same in Lake Kluane in the Alaskan Rockies. Same upside down feeling. You could wobble and fall in. Watch out for the Narcissus syndrome, though.

Want some practice in the local lingo? So used to the Castilian stuff. Formula's easy. Hire an *auto*, as they say in these parts, and set off along the lake. Stop fifty miles up the road. Do that narcissistic stunt of self-admiration. Miles and miles you can do that for. There they are. I told you so. In need of fresh air, out they come. Four Argentinians. Sort of. One Latvian, one Hungarian, one Pole and one Italian. Two couples. Three blondes, blue eyes. One a shade darker. And they all speak Spanish like natives! Wow! Like that Dutch fellow with his wife in the Buenos Aires Galerías Pacífico. Fair as fair can be. Aryan as Aryan can be. Hitler would have been proud of him. Had a white shade over one eye. Just out of the hospital. His wife just a shade darker, with no shade. Effect unnerving, so used to Spanish speakers being, well, darker. As odd as speaking French to French Canadians. Straight out of eighteenth-century France.

Back into the lake. Fifteen hundred feet deep in places, and thousands of square miles. No self-indulgence to be risked. But there is, at the side of the lake. Spanish with Spanish speakers who look anything but Spanish Mediterranean speakers. Gets odder and odder. And all the more thrilling because odder. Keep this chit-chat up for ever. Chilly, perhaps, but splendidly clear. Nice, warm conversation brewing, fed by the *yerba mate*, a sort of tea with a touch of bitterness.

Plenty of ice around but it's broken easily enough. The *mate* ritual of the mountain lake reflects the *thé à la menthe* ritual of the Saharan sands. Groups share *mate*, often standing around. It's the matey thing to do. Sure was with us too. A bit too sharp, despite *Aconcagua* amounts of sugar. Home-made cake, and that odd Spanish language galore made it all so palatable. Emails exchanged, as everywhere. Back home, one button and *Acongagua*, there you are again.

Another fifty miles up to Villa la Angostura. Undreamt-of vistas all the way, up and down, north south, sky and mountain lake, if you see what I mean. A small quiet town with a comfortable, village feel to it, it opens the door to the *Ruta de los Siete Lagos* (Route of the Seven Lakes), the most famous route in the whole of the Argentinian Lake District, taking in seven lakes. Lakes, lakes and more lakes. Aches it would give to describe them all, and Nahuel Huapi and a few of its northern friends suffice. Can't describe them in all their richness and splendour any more than try to translate the *arrayán* forest near to the Villa la Angostura. A perennial tree, the *arrayán*, almost uniquely grows here to its full, regal height. Bark-less tree, cold to the touch and cinnamon-coloured, with whitish flowers they produce in early summer, and later in March, a blue–black fruit. Do anything to follow their colour changes, even turn over a new leaf.

The following day, strategically placed benches gave us the soaking up we revelled in: contemplate the giant Andean chain, in and over the lake that gives Bariloche its enticing charm. Light relief enhanced by high relief. The eye ran from the crystal-clear, limpid lake, up through beautiful beech forests to the lofty, snow-capped peak of the Tronador, a sort of Valhalla *Thor.* Thunder it did not, to break the calm. But nothing peaky about this Tronador. It must thunder at times, if the name is anything to go by. Would move heaven and earth to return there. Compliments by the thousand to complement such a stirring scene.

El Calafate. Another thousand, and not kilometres. Twice as far as that. Name of the hotel? Mirador del Lago (Panorama of the Lake). Nothing to do with getting mired in the lake. Well, on reflection, there is. You are transfixed by it, caught in its silvery surface, the greatest watery expanse in Argentina. Topsy-turvy views of the Andes, Bariloche style. One guess for its name? Lago

Argentino. Easy, hole in one. You'd lose your golf ball for good here. Depths almost like the heights that bounce off them.

Not here for the abundant fauna and flora. Nor even for those extraordinary berries, the *Berberis buxifolia*. Latin term, am struggling to put it into a modern language. Description'll have to do. Spiny, hard shrub, tough to stick the harsh steppe conditions, it sends out a bright yellow or orange flower dotted along its branches in spring. Wood gives a red dye.

Been in Patagonia long enough, though, to wonder what Patagonia means. They speak about the Himalayan Yeti and the Rockies Big Foot. Well, they have their own oversized policemen feet here, too. The only truly indigenous group in this sparsely inhabited area, from Bariloche south were, not are, the Tehuelches. Don't need to comment on the *were*. We've got that straight already with the Aztecs. They had outsize feet, so outsize in fact that the predatory Spaniards exclaimed *¡Qué patagón!* (What whopping feet!). Their numbers dwindled, until finally they were all kicked out by the late nineteenth by the smaller feet of the Spaniards and Italians. Pity. They would have made excellent footballers.

Really here for those rivers of ice in *El Parque Nacional de los Glaciares*. The latest craze, it's really cool to be here. 'Discovered' and explored by that intrepid, number one Argentinian voyager Francisco Pascasio Moreno. Clever lad he was, if his nickname is anything to judge by. That clever, in fact, he gave his name to the world-famous glacier: Perito Moreno – 'Skilled Brown'. He may not have been *moreno*, he certainly was *perito*. As capable as Capability Brown he certainly was. And probably browner, too.

They call it calving. We all herd around, cameras at the ready for another block of ice tumbling from frighteningly high blue walls. One of the few glaciers still advancing. Still on the up is the Upsala Glacier. While yet going down. Disproving global warming? Mont Blanc's Mer de Glace's disappearance's at the other end of the argument. Withdrawing more and more is the Mer de Glace. Mont Blanc starting to draw a blank. Not so with the Upsala Glacier.

Upsala? Oops! Shouldn't it be *Uppsala*? Original Swedish, anyway, and that's what we write in English. But the Argentinians aren't keen on two *pp*s, any more than the Spaniards. Never use them together. Still, northern hemisphere again. Uppsala's in Sweden, isn't it? Yes, that's the place that Bergman's *Wild Strawberries* professor started from to collect his honorary degree. On through Stockholm to Lund, near Malmö, in the south. Must be some glaciers near Uppsala, too, although Uppsala's not much further north than Stockholm, you know. Ice-cool knowledge needed here.

We launched out into the Lago Argentino, after an hour's bus ride. Multiply that by two for the boat to reach within viewing distance of the Swedish-named glacier. Yes, but why Upsala? I've just asked that. Uppsala University commissioned a survey of the glacier in 1908. By glaciologists, I suppose. They came across a glacier of striking, unsurpassed natural beauty, white perfection even. The Perito Moreno was a tiddler in comparison. Covers three times its area. Chunks of ice keep falling off, leaving the pilot driving forward, slalom style. Scattered about the lake, they number hundreds of ice floes, rising higher than the boat, and uncalculatingly deep down into the lake. Blazing white colour, ice-blue of the lake, intense blue of the sky, adventure this was. The deepest of experiences.

Not the only deepest experience. We are in the land, or lake, of Spanish speakers. Adventure in language, too. Want to have a chat with a Bolivian, a Peruvian a Venezuelan? There they are sitting next to you. Just turn to one side, please. Not only are their origins from up north, but also from much further afield. Further than the ice fields. Lithuania, Latvia, Ukraine. All speaking Spanish, and Yiddish! Warning. Keep off the Nazis and the Jews. Could be skating on thin ice. Conversation raced ahead like the launch. Kept us nice and warm, too.

So don't miss the boat, the Spanish-speaking boat. Take the plunge and don't just dip your toe in. Try your tongue at Spanish and you break the ice with all and sundry. Warm to the task and go with the floe/flow.

Coleridge kept me as warm as all those South American speakers of Spanish. How? With 'Hymn before Sunrise, in the Vale of Chamouni'. Simpler to remember the quote than the title: 'Ye ice-falls ... and stopped at once amid their [the torrents'] maddest plunge! Motionless torrents! Silent cataracts!' And that's where we're going. Las Cataratas do Iguaçú. Would have liked the *Ruta 3* drive up along the Atlantic coast, to the Península Valdés, to work out why so many penguins survive from all those predators. Clearly, the predators couldn't get the wrappers off. Wrapped up are all the penguins in all that blubber. Could have stopped off a little before to play rugby with those Welsh pioneers in Trelew and Rawson. Practised a bit of Welsh, too. Fifth columnists they are, the Welsh, teaching those Argentinian rugby players to put one over on us, over the bar, I mean.

Las Cataratas do Iguaçú. Anyone offer a Coleridge for them? Not in a hurry. We have to see friends in *Good Airs* again. Acclimatize a bit. Two thousand five hundred miles from El Calafate to Brazil. Come out in a sweat to think about it. Pretty hot up there. And they're hot at Portuguese, into the bargain.

Falling between two stools, I am. Or even three, countries that is. Uruguay, Argentina and Brazil. Falling between three languages as well. In Portuguese, *Cataratas do Iguaçú*. In Spanish, *Cataratas del Iguazú*. In English, Iguassu Falls. And I get wet on top of it, or rather underneath it. Like the rest of the jovial Spanish-speaking band, didn't catch on to what the Argentinian guide was saying. 'Y mañana, la ducha' (And tomorrow, the shower). It's what those posh literary gents call 'litotes', understatement. A slight watering down of the wet experience. Fell for it, we all did, hook, line and sinker. But we didn't sink under the Falls. Motor boat dealt with that. It sure was an understatement under the Falls.

Three times under. Once, just a dry run to see how we'd cope, we circle, twice, we circle, and once more. Follow the instructions we all do. Divest ourselves of everything save vest and underpants. All belongings in a hermetically sealed rubber bag. Going under, but a roaring success. Thousands of tons of warm water cascade upon us, thrice. From hundreds of feet up. No jokes, please. Keep your mouth closed, as tightly as your bag. The widest falls in the world, if not the deepest. Stretches over kilometres. Twelve sets of falls there are. From the Brazilian side Salto Santa María (sure enough, it was Holy Mother of God Falls!), right round to the Argentinian side Salto dos Hermanas (Two Sisters). Back up on the walkway, hundred yards long, soaked as much by the spray as by the falls themselves. A real cliff-hanger. Don't want to do it again? Come on, don't rock the boat. Anyway, we're all in the same one. Cheap day, this was. The guide sailed on a high tide of pride in his country. 'Ninguna propina, gracias' (No tip, thank you). '¿No me entiende?' (Don't get it?). 'Ninguna propina, gracias, he dicho' (I said 'No tip, thank you'). Left the hotel under cascades of applause.

You won't believe this. Perhaps he was a residue of Nazi escapees from Nuremburg. A German speaker accompanied by his dog. Under they went, too. Needless to add, the creature got vet. Vet he didn't need, although he howled and howled. Why can't they pronounce *wet* like everyone else?

Back to the departure point through the steaming jungle, on an open-air bus, hair swept back by the breeze. So exhilarating, we talked and talked, never dried up. Not even when we returned to the UK. Still at it, now. Drawing, I am, on a reservoir of memories. They resurface time and again, adding to the joys of Eastern promise. For that's where we're off to now.

10

East But Not Least

Sketch map to show places visited in 'East But Not Least'

Yeast and language, they go together. Language is the oven of friendship. Long preparation, ingredients aplenty and to spare, and getting on with each other grows and grows. Talk and talk, it's so tasty. And travel is the icing on the cake.

Oft-times visited Greece in the East. Walked all over Crete, too. Gorged with the spectacular scenery, especially the Sumariá Gorge. Greek wasn't a walkover, though. Even declining Mr Kay's Latin declensions didn't help. Greek declensions went even further down the line. A line too far. Still the symmetry and harmony of the Acropolis I always admired. Greece invented those two words, didn't she? But, my mission was going to take me further north. Had no Greek, but a fleck of Czech.

Held in Greece which is where we're staying for a moment. Oil and Greece, that's the drama. Ay, there's the rub. Hold on. We're in Greece, not in Hamlet's Denmark. We'll not make a crisis out of a drachma, will we? Not at all. Once again, they're both Greek words. We owe them a lot. Œdipus should know that as well. Anyway, it's blindingly obvious. Of course, Œdipus couldn't see straight, had it off with his mum, Jocasta, blind about that too. Freud was anything but blind about it. That's a *joke. **Hasta** la vista, **Jocasta**. You see, we're not coming your way, Mum. We're off more to the north, and no self-immolation, please. Don't shuffle off this mortal coil just yet. I may need you, Jocasta, in the cast.

As for Œdipus' dad, Laius, he killed him at some mythological crossroads. Didn't know he was his dad any more than he knew Jocasta was his mum. Crossroads for me too, metaphorical one this time, but I decided to go well north. No complexes for me.

No Greece, but check on the rest, and that includes Poland, as well as the Czechs. So, let's do a trial run with Prague. The castle would do very nicely for starters. Would Kafka agree? Not so sure, his *The Castle* is a bit of a *Trial,* even for him. He couldn't find it to start with, but we stuck to the Kafka trail.

We finally found the castle, if not *The Castle*. In Prague, capital of Czech Republic. *Czech Republic's* a bit of a mouthful. Not any shorter than *Czechoslovakia*. Our continental friends thought that too. Off they go to shorten things. Easier for all. Spanish: *Chequia*. French: *Tchéquie*. Feeling a bit lazy in the sun, the Italians avoided checkmate so followed suit: *Cechia*. The Czechs put it on the map with *Cesko*. Set the ball rolling. No checking it after that.

Antonín, Antonín, Antonín. Not started Czech crash course yet. But Antonín in Čimice, north of Prague, speaks French. And so do his offspring. That gave me a lift. And spring's quite a leitmotif round here. Just wait a few lines.

French? Whoopee! Architect had Antonín been in French West

Africa. Three Antoníns, what's all this about? My phone signal for his wife, Věra. She speaks Russian, but surely she ought to speak English like everyone else! Antonín *on* the phone. Say *on* in all those Romance languages, and it becomes a painful matter. But Antonín gets the tone just right. Prague this spring? Forty years after their Spring, Jan Palach self-immolating in Wenceslas Square. Cottoned on to Václav (Czech for *Wenceslas*) Havel. Soon to be the 'Good King Wenceslas'. They certainly sang for him in the late eighties. Where? Wenceslas Square, and it wasn't just carols. The present president's in on the act, too. With a name like Václav Klaus, he had to be. Gone for ever is Václav Havel. Have a good vacation Václav, you deserve it.

But don't forget the Prague Spring of 1968. The flame of freedom from Soviet occupation all began there. Jan Palach's act of self-burning was the first spark. A remembrance plaque. Where? Wencelas Square, where else?

Crash course first in Czech. Began on a real high. Could even say *Dobrý den* (Hello), *Děkuji* (Thank you), *Ma schlenadou* (Goodbye). Tensed up with tenses, but didn't get too tensed up with *Kolik?* (How much?), though. But, declensions or no declensions, things soon declined. No help for the pronunciation. Did a hopeless hatchet job on the 'hook', the *háček*. Capital *Ř* and his little brother *ř* left me reeling, then floored. *Ř*s are easier in English, aren't they? But *Musique oblige*. Ought to feel comfortable with Bedřich Smetana and his symphonic poem *Má Vlast* (My Home). No more than with Dvořák and his *New World*. At least the easily pronounced Antonín bit left me on a high again. After all, it's my friend's name.

Accents all over the place, up, down, on vowels, on consonants. You'll soon get in a knot over that inoffensive little town Kroměříž, in Southern Moravia. Easy? Well, you'll get into a fluster over a cluster. Vlčnov. Four consonants in a row. It's not reasonable. It ought to be. I mean, one of the most enlightened men of the Renaissance, who set the humanistic trend in education, Jan Ámos Komenský, his name's OK. Born in Nivnice, he was. Launched the birth of education as we know it. Is that why we have at home five painted egg shells, all from, you've guessed, Nivnice?

Komenský travelled from persecution, all those fanatical religious devotees, you know. Not Jewish, but all over Europe he wandered. Knew more than a little German, Swedish, Polish, English and Dutch. Almost forgot. Spoke Czech, too. Took refuge in languages. Wrote *The Gate of Languages Unlocked*. I could say 'unhooked' with all those *háčeks*, I suppose. Hey, Jan, unlock all those knotty consonants for me, please. It's a bit trying but I am trying. Jamming all those letters together. Could you release the squeeze before we arrive?

For the Czech encounter, initial rendezvous at the *logis* with French Algerian colleagues, in a small village on the Rhine, south of Strasbourg. Where exactly? You won't believe this. *SAND*. But no sand. Crossing of the Rhine on a *bac*, a ferry offering free conveyance. Recalled the more dramatic Dawson City crossing of the Yukon River. Free as well. A feel-good factor, because free. Have I got my point across?

Southern Germany, via Nuremburg, scenes of former Hitlerian hysteria. Small hotel near the Czech border. Now, you would expect a contingent armed with four languages, French, Spanish, English and Arabic, would be able to order a pork-less meal. Not on your nelly. Or should I say pork belly. And no porky this. Along came belly of pork. Muslims can't eat that any more than I could horse meat. Lesson number 1: Learn *pork* in German. *Schweinefleisch*. Sounds positively barbaric. Were I Algerian, I couldn't stomach it either, even with wine.

German/Czech border. Chaos one way. Our way. Domestic appliances piled high on passing cars, at least on what passed as cars, constant checks on their contents, in and out of customs offices. Phew, that's got that out of the way. What next? Recommendation to take out a year's pass for the national motorway. Can't take it without. Out come *koruny* (crown) galore, Kč for short. I'd love to chop off that *háčeks*, make life simpler. Not caught out on the plural of koruna, though. Year's toll paid for, so all the way motorway to Prague. No, *Pane Havel* (Mr Havel). Motorway runs out thirty miles before Prague. No more motorways anywhere. Contribution to Pane Havel's coffers. Gladly.

Lack of motorways and their accessories is all to do with the Soviet occupation which ended in 1989. Sounds like revolutionary France in 1789. Just change one digit. Flimsy building projects were left in the air. So flimsy they were almost floating. Bridges were in a parlous state. Communist red tape had been holding up one bridge in particular (imagine that!), the one leading on to Prague. So back on ordinary roads.

Past Plzen. Easier to drink it than pronounce it. Then the gentle Arcadian landscapes of Bohemia, Elysian fields if ever there were any, so musically embraced by Dvořák and Smetana's symphonic poems. These gently undulating dreamlands carried a dark stain. Miles of forest, pine and fir. Yes, but a nation denied its sylvan joys. They had lost their silver lining. Even the silver birch trees stand in industrialized and polluted ruin. Promises of root and branch review. They could be so much dead wood. Could take some time. Always a back log to deal with. And no deal, wood I mean, for building at the end of the day. Come on, Czech government. You just haven't twigged, have you? Stump up more euros. Start digging deep. After all, stumps are all that's left. Several visits later and still not out of the woods.

Through Prague to the northern side. Čimice somewhere here. Try all those languages, and Arabic gets us nowhere. Just out of Sand, it should not slip through our fingers as easily as that. Hey, let's try a spot of Czech. 'Promiñte. Znate Praha?' (Excuse me. Do you know Prague?). 'Ano' (Yes). 'Muvlíte anglický? (Do you speak English?). Hole in one. Five minutes later: Vehlovická Street. Splendid reception. Food as generous too. Has been ever since.

Next day, down from Čimice, through the district of Libeñ, and on to *Karlův most* (Charles Bridge). Hold on, too fast. You've got to slow down, anyway. See that bend on our left? Just a pause before we get there. Why?

Sudetenland first, then the whole of Czechoslovakia. Three

million German speakers up in the north, a good reason for invasion in 1938. Nice little number for that culturally minded, gentle soul, the Reichsprotektor Reinhard Heydrich. Settled down in imperial style in the *Pražský hrad* (Prague Castle), after a blessing in person from the Reichsführer himself. Conquering visit, Paris mode. Back to the wide, sweeping bend. Just the job to slow down the Reichsprotektor's car. It didn't just slow down. It halted. British-trained Czech parachutists made sure of that. Halted the car, his life as well. Retaliation: most of the Czech underground were eliminated. Betrayed by double agents. Not enough for the boys from Berlin. The village of Lidice was totally martyrized. Saw that in Oradour-sur-Glane, didn't we?

Try again. Held up by Nazi horrors. Down to the Charles Bridge. Walk across, if you can, crowded out by people like the four of us. Still a lovely saunter over the history-laden Vltava river, the inspiration for the second movement of *Má Vlast*. Rills of water rise with the trills of music. Emotion runs real deep here. As deep as the river *Vltava*, often called by the German *Moldau* by Westerners, probably easier to say, what with those three consonants again.

Music, music, music. It surges from the Prague Spring Festival. Inauguration piece every year? No prizes for getting it right. A thrilling blast from the past. Smetana's *Má Vlast*. There he was presiding, above us, Pane Havel with an English conductor leading proceedings. The emotion runs just as deep here. Music the following day, every day. Mozart, he spent time there, Beethoven, and Dvořák and his furious Slavonic Dances. More live than that even. Just keep sauntering. Tickets on the spot for student performances ten minutes later in the local church. Enjoy that? Cast piety aside and hear some more divine vocal streams of Schubert's *Ave Maria*, Gounod's *Messe de Sainte Cécile*. Patron saint of music, she is, no discord here. She made sure all Czech primary teachers knew a musical instrument. You couldn't pull any strings either.

We're not over the *Karlův most* yet. *Pražský hrad* up ahead.

Prague Castle. A city all in itself. Inside, as fast as you fall through, or are thrown through, the window. Asked Pani Haýek. Pani with one of the few words in Czech I knew at that time. Clear enough. 'Kde je defenestrace'. (Where is defenestration?). 'What?' 'Defenestration, you know. But where's the *the*?' 'We don't have it in Czech. Don't have *a/an* either. Same as in Latin.' Soon got the lowdown on *fenestra* = window, too. Same word all over Europe. Famous for that, if for nothing else. Don't try it yourself at home. It could trigger a thirty-year-long war. That's what it did in 1618. Contestants: inside the window, a number of Protestant Bohemian noblemen. On their way out, two royal governors. Believe what you will, religion was at the bottom of it. Always is. Contrary to popular belief, blow cushioned by cartloads of cabbage and cauliflower. Not just window dressing. Saved, not by the bell, but by two veg, yet no roast. Did get a roasting, though. Survived they did to teach the world *defenestrace*. Caught on, it did. Window on European history. Window rage became the rage. Waves of waltzing through windows. Even finally came down to Jan Masaryk, plying the political trade for Czech Republic. Third *defenestrace* of Prague, he was. Spent wartime in London, too. No practice there. But he sure ended up down there, bottom of the line. Communists at the bottom of all this.

A massive, majestic castle is Prague Castle. As records go, it's impregnable. Just records, of course. Nazis saw to that. Six football pitches long, well over one wide. Acres and acres to make you ache. You'll end up shaking, so go and have a rest in the Katedrála Sv Vita (St Vitus Cathedral). May not help you, given its name. If piety is not your passion, music will appeal to you. An evening at one end of the castle, in the crystallinely bright Španélský Sál (Spanish Hall). A stunning hall bedecked with a shower of chandeliers, only rivalled by Mozart and Beethoven down below.

Kafka, a seminal writer of the modern era, was born and lived most of his life in Prague, but, racked by tuberculosis, he ended his days in Vienna, Mozart territory. The nightmarish horrors of uncertainty, the endless corridors of searching, the overriding fear of his father. Guilt and damnation say it all in *The Metamorphosis*. Not so for Jaroslav Hašek. No Kafka German language for him. Too dour and weighty. He preferred lighter Czech stuff. Parodically serious. The irony of life, filled with comic intervals. Read (pronounced like RED, not REED, there's a question mark at the end of this sentence) Joseph Heller's *Catch-22*? Next on your list: Jaroslav Hašek's *Good Soldier Švejk*. Learn how to traipse across Europe, fighting on two fronts, almost simultaneously. The Austro-Hungarians, a bunch of blockheads. Versus the Russian imperial army, equally so. Learn how to salute your superiors with all the satirical caricature you can muster. And learn another word: anabasis. A long, tedious journey. Greek again. Could have been useful to catch up with Œdipus. Can't find *Good Soldier Švejk* on the bookshelf? Hostinec U Kalicha's the place for you. A café/pub. The book's sold there. Our Jaroslav spent his indolent days there too.

Good Soldier Švejk. A sort of underground novel. Just like the restaurants in the Staroměstskě Námesti (Old Town Square). A step change in the art of dining. Quite a few steps down, very useful for hiding from the enemy. Come up just before the hour sounds. Opposite is the astronomical clock set high in Staroměstská Radnice (Old Town Hall). In a circular movement, a parade of the twelve apostles knocks out the hour. If you're confused on how this fits in with the celestial beings, just knock up the Renaissance astronomers, the German Kepler and his Danish friend, Tycho Brahé. Neither was Czech but they had plenty of Czech mates. Although not easy to know who was Czech in those days, all under the Austro-Hungarian umbrella. Prague was the rage. Was the meeting point of arts and sciences. Could have given Kepler and Brahé some clues on Copernicus and his heliocentric theory. You know, we go round the sun. See you later Copernicus, in Cracow.

Prague and Cracow bring the crowd together on sunny days. Want to go for the big time? Stand beneath the Astronomical Clock in the Old Town Hall Tower. Where's that? You should know. In the huge Staroměstské Náměstí (Old Town Square), the main marketplace and heart of Prague since the tenth century. Wait for the spectacle of the Apostles' parade going round the intricate, constellation-covered clock face. Appointment with Death on every hour. He rings his bell, setting the next hour in motion by inverting his hourglass. For whom the bell tolls, again, shades of John Steele in Sainte-Mère-Église.

An architectural luxury is Prague. Jewels in the crown are Lesser Town (Malá Strana), the Roofs of the Palaces of the Lesser Town, the Old Town Bridge Tower overlooking the Vtlava, the Powder Bridge, the Golden Lane, the Tower of the Jewish Town Hall, the Old-New Synagogue. What's all this about Jews?

Ghetto there had been in Middle Ages Prague. May have started off in Venice, after all it's an Italian word, but it soon became a pet passion for those needing to dish out retribution for deicide. The Jews stuck him up there, didn't they, and the pope's not been keen on them ever since. Walled in, in Staré Mesto, Prague's Jewish community finally settled outside in the Josefov. Until they died. The Old Jewish Cemetery gave them their last resting place. Would have liked them to end up somewhere else, a more distressingly sad place you could not come across. Hundreds and hundreds of graves, all jumbled into each other. Grey graves they were. And the claustrophobic synagogue was just as grey. The narrow, spiral, slightly crumbly staircase did not hold out hope for an encounter with Abraham. Hope there's more room in their Elysian Fields. Mind you, the Nazis left them with a chance. They left it 'intact', if 'intact' is the word. An ironic emblem of an extinguished race, for Hitler and co. at least.

A gloomy, dispiriting place. Need a pick-me-up? How about some out-of-this-world panoramas of Prague? *Karlův most z Kampy*'ll take you up a long way. Not up to heaven, but as a start. You can view the bridge from down the river. While you're still there, look up to the heavens and there rises up in all its majesty, the *hrad*, Prague Castle. Want to have another view? From the *Strahovské zahrady* (Strahov gardens). What about Hitler's favourite? From the castle ramparts down onto the city. All mine, well for four years.

One or two trips around Prague? Sure. Kutná Hora. A pearl it was and still is. South-east of the capital, built on the silver exploitations there, it rivalled Prague. Wencelas IV even moved his royal residence there, leaving palaces and fabulous churches as a legacy. Declined after the Thirty Years' War. It's clear defenestration has a lot to answer for. Transparent enough. Want some Bohemian glass? They've just smashed the previous lot. You know, that big window. Keep going to Poděbrady, south of Kutná Hora, for some prized Bohemian crystal. Elegant avenues to boot. A leisurely stroll, and a leisurely meal, all so easy on the pocket.

Mělník, once in German-claimed Sudetenland, to the north of Prague, a simple day's excursion. A lovely loll in the sun, after a gentle drive of fifty miles. Graced by a tranquil square and a sumptuous château, fit for a queen, more than one in fact, for the Bohemian queens from the thirteenth century. Demolished by Swedish troops in the Thirty Years' War, it was resuscitated to its modern splendour.

Clear it is that this defenestration business is smashing all records on the glass front. Stay clear with that Bohemian crystal. Stay clear as well of that Eagle in Hitler's SS Waffen standard circling overhead. Memories of the encircling Nazis, Sudetenland annexation in 1938, as a start. Chamberlain's negotiation skills were as fragile as Bohemian glass. More protection he needed. And more French. If he had known the olde-worlde French for 'umbrella', *un chamberlain* to be truthful, he could have stayed out of range, at least, of the Eagle's dollops.

If the Czechs don't catch on with Malliga's Arabic, let's try Mexican Spanish, three visits later. They show no savvy with my Iberian Spanish, even when I tell them that 'savvy' comes from *sabe*, you know. That's what it means: you know.

Who wants to go to Mexico to speak Spanish? Too far. Take the Mexicans to Czech Republic. Much simpler, and cheaper. So here we all are, in Luhačovice, in the eastern province of Moravia, a most hospitable, leafy spa town. Promenades and white-painted colonnades providing an endless supply of mineral water. For drinking, if your palate can take it. As bitter and harsh as ten concentrated lemon zests, a tang on the tongue, with almost a pang of pain, a sulphurous smell that would put bad eggs in the shade, a Brno medical man (Can you pronounce that name? Easier to say Bren – of the gun, that is) saw it as the peerless panacea. Cure or... A jaw-dropping, bitter-sweet experience. Where's the sweet bit? Jests on the zests.

To celebrate our Mexican friend Jorge's birthday, all twenty present, and that includes Adriana, his wife who offered the party. Jorge: had a banana duel with him in Mexican cowboy land. Remember? Language + birthday + travel = icing on two cakes. But Mexican Spanish didn't work, Iberian neither. French with Antonín would. He passed from Czech to the Gallic tongue and back again, with food always on it, me from French to Spanish, Jorge from Mexican to Iberian, throw in some English, a language pot-pourri. Oh yes, a square meal with Czech wine to round it off. Vlčnov it came from. Easier on the palate than pronouncing those four consonants again. Where did you say the wine came from? Vlčnov, a few miles away. Go there tomorrow. See the wine cellars before the annual, two-day, last weekend in May festival of the entirely unique folk festival *Jízda Králů* (Ride of the Kings). The ladies, so bonny with their many-coloured bonnets and lace dresses, danced to the gentlest of pastoral music. Spring time, alas! Spring of 1939. The Kings were crushed under the hooves of those other less pastoral riders, Hitler's Valkyries. An unequal race. In both senses of the word, at least for the Führer.

Privileged we were for the Ride of the Kings, the only outsiders to witness a celebration of the spring's new crops, and the rites of passage from youth to manhood. Parades, songs and dancing. Nowhere to stay here. Back to Luhačovice for another evening's entertainment. Fiddlers, five of them, and dressed in their typical colourful sparkling waistcoats. Over a ridge, trees, spas and fountains. Couldn't contain ourselves for enjoyment. Requests for more, repartees, laughing, all fun. They may not have been on the roof, but they brought the house down.

Close to the Slovak border, so over we go. Broke away, the Slovaks did, in a sort of velvet divorce in 1993. No break-up, balkanization mode, here. No lawsuit. Not even kid gloves. In and out of love with the Czech Republic for centuries were the Slovaks. More or less the same language. Understood Antonín and Věra to a T in Trenčíaské Teplice, an enchanting spa town, after passing through the dull Trenčín, dominated by one of Slovakia's most impressive castles, seen towering above from the road below. A slower-paced life, soaking up the atmosphere as well as the lavish hammam, a sort of Turkish bath. France is now awash with them as well. Trenčíaské Teplice also sports a large complex of sanatoria. You'd need one of them after a dose of Luhačovice mineral water. Next stop, Poland.

Poland, knocked about from pillar to post by Austria, Russia and Hitler's mob. Sovereignty lost, regained, lost, regained... Poland was heaven itself. Fortunately, the Czars were no longer on the radar. They'd spent too much time navel-gazing, Czar-gazing. Ignored the more earthy needs of the Poles. Hitler didn't ignore these earthly needs, he just burnt them with a scorched earth policy.

There lay Poland for us on the other side of Slovakia, up in the Tatras Mountains. A mere fifty miles away. Not too high, but pole-vaulting was out of the question. All that could be done was star-gaze under the vault of heaven, Copernicus mode. He did a better job at star-gazing than the Czars or anyone else at the time. Ploughed a path right through the geocentric theory of the universe. Geocentric? Hop down three paragraphs for a flash of solar enlightenment.

Meteoric rise to universal prominence with his *Revolutions of the Heavenly Spheres.* 1548. Unacknowledged brilliance shone on deathbed. Lazarus-like, in death he came to life. Stellar astrophysicist if ever there were one. On another planet, he was. Astronomer versus a Ptolemy-led constellation of astrologers, all as blurred as the Milky Way. Settled on a copper-bottomed theory. Hammered home the truth like Mars. Real food for thought here. Science v. no(n)sense/non-science. Scientific facts v. inquisitorial hacks tightening the racks. Unlimited universe v. limited chapter and verse. Open v. shut case.

No time to polish up my Polish. No crash course. Just a flash of lightning. *Dzieńdobry* (Good morning), *Dzieńkuję* (Thank you), *Do widzenia* (Goodbye). Just as well didn't need the doctor, dentist... Still, Irena was always on hand to reciprocate. Her Polish in Poland was worth my Spanish in Spain.

Bound for Cracow we were. Like Copernicus, a thorn in the papal side. Had to be, born as he was in Toruń (Thorn), two hundred kilometres to the west of Cracow, where he studied and taught. Could have been fatally attracted to the skies in Rome. Inquisition and all that. Bologna, Padua, Ferrara, astronomical efforts he made there to get round to the heliocentric theory of the universe. Kept it under his hat, or skull cap, even until the end of his life. What's *heliocentric*, pray? You know, we go round the sun. Popes and cronies still saw the sun going round us. They still gravitated towards the geocentric theory set going by the Greek-cum-Egyptian Ptolemy. Diametrically opposed, Pole Copernicus settled for the less sunny skies of Poland and for a bit of peace and quiet. Knew what was at stake. Clever lad. Must have foreseen Michael Servetus going up in flames in Calvin's Geneva, and Giordano Bruno following in hot pursuit in Rome. So much for fiery convictions.

Never saw Marie Curie in Poland. Couldn't have. Spent most of her life in France, from age of twenty-three, and a bit before our time. Who's she, anyway? The nucleus of the explosive new industry. Research radiated out to the whole world, starting with her bones. But not before she put research Poland on the map with polonium.

What about Chopin? Wouldn't have seen him in Poland. Spent all his adult life in France, like Marie above. Didn't do his French much good, you would never have guessed. A bit like Conrad.

He started in Marseille, sailed the seven seas and ended up writing an odd sort of English. Even so, a breath of fresh air for the European novel.

Funny, there's a *c* in all these names. Copernicus, Chopin, Curie, Conrad. Gets curiouser and curiouser, Alice would agree. Her English's as odd as Conrad's. All names contrived, save Copernicus, and he has two *c*s. Chopin owes the *c* to his French dad, Marie married Pierre Curie, and Conrad, well his names for Western ears were beyond the pale, not pole: Józef Teodor Natlecz Korzeniowski. Konrad seems to be in there somewhere, but this is far from clear. All very complicated. Even Marie Curie started off as Kłodowska, with a funny sort of *l* for good measure.

This *c*-sounding business just won't go away. Why? 'Cos the Poles see *k* most of the time when we see *c*. Even Copernicus is not Copernicus. It's Kopernikus, so there, say the Poles. I've even got it on my sweatshirt. Want more *k*s? First stop: Kraków. See what I mean? All us Westerners aren't keen on *k*s. Italians are happy with *c*s like the Spanish: *Cracovia*. The French are not far away: *Cracovie*. Whether you see it or not, that's where we're going. Landing in an airport, you come across it, almost unexpectedly, straight out of a wood, and straight into a fetchingly small hangar sort of building. Planes seem to arrive and take off by the coffee shop. Very handy for the thirsty pilot and crew. Same in Gdańsk, cradle of contemporary Poland.

Polish pilots were top notch. Mad but top notch. Ask Bomber and Fighter Command. How did they get here in UK? No romantic flying over enemy skies westwards in the flimsiest of plywood planes to reach British airfields. Not a chance over Germany with the Valkyries patrolling the skies. Corridor through ambivalent Romania from bleak Poland saw them leak out to the Black Sea. Round to Gib, and Stanislas's your uncle. Hitler must have rued the day he didn't close all those loo*pholes*. Don't close Poles' loos. Hitler's, go ahead, if you like.

Cracow remained inviolate. Lovely, like walking through a field of violets. How come? Nazi culture vultures – or shall we say *eagles?* – saw to that. Change from vulture to eagle was easy enough. Hitler had an eagle on his standard. Spread its cultural wings all over Cracow.

Not suspicious about Oświęcim (Auschwitz), just off to the west, Nazi (not German these days, PC and all that) self-styled Governor General of all Poland Hans Frank surveyed the jewel of Cracow from his magnificent Wzgórze Wawelski (Wawel Castle). *Gdzie jest Wawel?* What's that mean? 'Where's Wawel Castle?' Of course. Where's the 'the' again? Like the Czechs. And the Ruskies. No word for the 'the'.

A Hitler henchman, Hans Frank drew no blank when it came to *Kultur*. But to be frank, I'd never be Frank, even though he had a keen, appreciating eye for civilizing polish, not for Polish. Blessed with immaculate good taste. Highly educated and literate, in the enlightened and compassionate mould of the culturally delicate Dr Joseph Goebbels, he swanned around the architectural gems of Cracow. Keep it white, spotless and untainted, please. All nice, pure and tidy. And clean. Clean? How d'you do that? Easy. Empty it of Jews. Clean out the Kazimierz district just down the road. Those Jews are just not blond and Aryan enough. The Reich's long arm, at the end of which was Hans, stretched to all corners of Cracow. Hans had a nasty (oops! Nazi) finger in every pie. No chance of knuckling down and doing your own thing. Every chance of an unwelcome knock on your door. No messing, even at mass. Gerries had a papal blessing from Pius XII. Concordat with Hitler. Mass got muddled up with mess, genocide. You know, mass extermination. Pope happy with extermination after mass.

Plain frank was Dr Hans. Showed his hand no sooner arriving in the cultural pearl of Cracow. Made it the capital of Nazi-occupied Poland.

60,000 Jews in 1940, 2,000 left in 1945. Can't argue with him. Had the law on his side. Was, after all, a doctor of law. Knew all his rights.

Find *wawel?* (no 'the' in Polish, remember?). You'll soon get used to it. Can't go wrong. On top of Wawel Hill. Hans, with handbook, would have relished those leisurely walks through the truly enormous, fabulous Rynek Główny (Main Market Square), with its astonishing, lavishly decorated Cloth Hall bequeathed by Flemish artists to the town's denizens. Don't poison all those hundreds of pigeons, but you're free to have a go at Hans. Main Market flowers are on hand to keep things attractively fragrant. Flagrant disregard for all this though, thinks Hans.

Hold on, and here a pun for the Hun. Hands off Hans. Our Nazi lad probably did some expiation work in the cathedral, inside the castle walls. Maybe a tear for the national hero of that splendidly resounding name Tadeusz Kościuszko, rising up as an equestrian figure dominating the main gate? No chance. No chance either of doing a defenestration job on him. Bet the Cracovians chanted *defenestracja* in Polish around the castle. If they'd chorused it out in German, Herr Hans might have seen through it. Either way, it wouldn't have suited him down to the ground.

Mind you, failing defenestration, they could have salted him off to the *Wieliczka Kopalnie soli*, to the west of Cracow. What's that? Give him a taste of the salt mines, for that's what they are. Cheaper than sending him to Siberia. Pretty close to Auschwitz-Birkenau, too. Just thirty miles away. Nice and convenient. Railway takes him straight through the gates. Herr Frank must have sensed the camp was the end of the line for him, too. Still, don't want to insist and rub it in but he'd love the salt mines. Massive vault of a mine, plenty of room for him there. Deep down. And warmer than Siberia too, but not quite as warm as Auschwitz. To sugar the pill, they could have taken him for a stroll round the Jewish cemetery. Saved him the trouble of going down the road to Auschwitz. Jews piled in the cemetery, quite a jumble, almost like in those lime pits. Would have felt quite pure with all that white stuff. Another dose of Prague, and that includes the exiguous synagogue. Squeeze and squeeze to get inside.

Undercome by remorse, our Hans could have spent time on the far side of the Vistula, to take in the stupendous view of his castle residence. He could have admired it all the more as he had nothing to do with its construction. Just like Joseph Heller's Yossarian in *Catch-22*. Forgiveness just round the corner, though. Cracov's Bishop Karol Wojtyła, conclave bound, announced by smoke, Injun style, ended up as John Paul II. Could he have done an absolution job on our Hans? Could he have been inspired by concordat-waving Pius XII? You have to hand it to him. Much less wily than impious Pius. But still a safe pair of hands. Could he have pardoned Hans Frank, even when his hands were covered in blood? After all, Hans was passionate about cultural gentility and good breeding, so had no dirty hands. Let others do the mucky work. No hands on was general Hans. Not even a Panzer for Hans.

Not enough protection in *wawel*? (Getting used to no 'the', aren't we?) Run for cover, Hans, to the barbican, you know, the extra bit that sticks out of the fortifications. Friendly fire could fix you. A gigantic, most impressive, partly rounded bastion for the city's defences. Shoot all the barbs you like from there. Wouldn't give you a cat in hell's chance against the Luftwaffe, though. The cat didn't stand a chance in London's totally demolished Barbican either, whether they played Wagner or not. In any event, you knew what was going up in flames, wherever you were in Cracow. A fireman trumpeter is seen and heard blaring out from the tower of St Mary's Church on the hour, several times a day. Not sure about *seen* but definitely *heard*, high up. Only ever plays half the tune, for tradition's sake. Should have avoided being seen hundreds of years ago. Those tartar of Tartars must have seen him from his peek hole. An arrow they sent, straight and true, *à la* Robin Hood. Too tardy to stop the Tartars? Townsfolk alerted and resisted.

Culturally inclined, our Hans would have most genteel tastes. That he would most certainly have trumpeted. Handy Herr for Hitler, he was. Extermination and enlightening polish go Hans in Hans, don't they? No Nazi opera companies around? Let's listen in on the composer Stanislas Moniuszko's *Straszny Dwór*. All Polish to me but we knew it was all about a haunted manor house. Can't imagine that Herr Frank was ever haunted by anything.

Yet, he had to face the music in the end. Nuremburg and execution. Best to stay in the Main Market Square if that's what he wanted. Could have seen the Lajkonik performing his dance, crown and all. Stay there, Hans, for the pageant of the Fraternity Parade. Not so sure, though. Could trigger a riot. Who's parading, then? The Marksmen. Wild game may be their aim, but Herr Frank, you are fair game. Dunno about the fair bit.

No tight spot up in the Tatras, down south. No Tartars there. Zakopane's the place. Winter resort, skiing, and a colossal ski jump. The biggest in Poland. Facing the other way, to Slovakia, straight over them hills you'd sail. Fiddlers' music could send you on your way. Proud they are in their national costume. Like the devotees swarming out of church, with splashes of white and blue, and such happy faces. Religion and the Message of Fatima reach deep down into their soul, carry them blithely away as on the ski slope.

Meeting of old and new. Ride in a medieval carriage with driver's mobile running with the horse. Sudden burst of yellow. Pass fields and fields rampant with dandelions. Where on earth – or should we say, in the earth? – does this word come from? *Dent de lion* (lion's tooth), says my Collins, but it's *pissenlit* (piss-in-the-bed) in Gallic mode. With all my pole position French stuff, surely I can cut through this chaos. Nope. How we get *dent de lion* from *pissenlit* leaves me, well, pissed off. Working it that way round, though, it's like the Polish postilion's cart before the horse.

Back at the hotel. Lost in translation, I am. No pole position in Polish. But help is at hand. Italians around? Sounds like it, from the kitchen. Larger than life, singing their way through the evening meal. Back in the land of Verdi. Polish hosts, really, ten years in Italy, learning the trade. Want tomatoes? Irena, take a back seat. *Pomodori, per favore.* Apples? Golden delicious and a golden opportunity. Lots of melody. 'Apple' in Italian = *mela*, plural *mele*.

All those Czech and Polish consonants got me in a knot. At

home again with Verdi, unwound, relaxed. Taken a ride through sixty years of language, from two wheels to four, from boats to trains to planes. Across the plains of Europe, the sandy plains of Africa, not all dunes you know, not forgetting the pampas plains, and here are taking the plane back to UK. A journey on language, and the language of a journey of a lifetime.

Life had gone full circle. From the Nazi smoking gun, from the early playground of bombed buildings of the blitz to the later discovery of Oradour-sur-Glane, Lidice and Auschwitz. Yet the nightmare of Nazism converted into a beautiful dream. Totalitarianism, religious or political, had more than met its match, even in the leanest of times, in the tolerance mastered through the genius of modern living languages. One moral lesson learnt in the generous language-driven, harmonious intercourse between nations. Let Albert Camus, labelled by numerous admirers as the conscience of Europe in the wake of the terror of World War II, have his word: 'There are more things to admire in mankind than to despise.'

So, what's it like, drinking from the rich pastures of foreign languages? A cup of joy. Like Beethoven's An die Freude (*Ode to Joy*). That's from his Ninth? Sure thing. Like the music of languages. Rhapsody on cloud nine.